THE ULTIMATE GUIDE TO SINGING

GIGS, SOUND, MONEY & HEALTH

CONTRIBUTIONS FROM OVER 100 SINGING STARS, PRODUCERS, ENGINEERS, COACHES, DOCTORS, AGENTS, MANAGERS AND SOCIAL MEDIA GURUS

Gregory A. Barker & Kathy Alexander

SINGDAPTIVE

SINGDAPTIVE

aims to be the most trusted source for singers who want to be better than they were yesterday. Our courses and intelligent singer profi le come from leading industry professionals and experts in music education. You can take our courses, read articles, listen to podcasts and learn our values at **singdaptive.com**

ISBN: 978-1-7752940-8-5

SINGDAPTIVE

Victoria, British Columbia, Canada support@singdaptive.com

Permission requests can be submitted to support@singdaptive.com

Special discounts are available for quantity purchases of this book. For more information, email support@singdaptive.com

Cover design by Jamie Drouin
Illustrations by Stuart Meredith
Chapter icons by Peter James Field
Interior Image of Divinity Roxx by Christoph Huber
Print book design by Joel Friedlander

94 The number of Grammy Awards and Grammy nominations received...

193 The number of books...

1,772 The number of albums...

280,000,000 The number of YouTube views...

...by the contributors to this book.

Contents

What We Discovered

We bought—*and read*—most of the major books available for singers today. In fact, my shelves are sagging under their weight. Two factors quickly jumped out at us:

- Some of these books are excellent (so we asked those authors to contribute to this book!).
- All of these books face huge limitations. (Can you expect a voice researcher to offer guidance on using a sound system?)

We thought: wouldn't it be great to have a book where an ear, nose & throat specialist reveals how a singer can best cope with the flu—and a microphone manufacturer gives guidance on choosing a mic? What about Grammy award winning sound engineer discussing how to get the best vocal recordings at home, a social media guru on how to grow a Facebook page and a voice scientist on healthy vocal technique? Thus, this book was conceived.

Full stop. Who's the "we" that conceived this approach? Kathy Alexander, Kevin Alexander and Gregory Barker through their work with TC-Helicon, a leader in audio equipment for singers. Since then, the gang of us have formed Singdaptive, a holistic learning platform for any singer.

Just to make sure we were on the right track, we polled one thousand rock, heavy metal, R & B, pop and jazz singers from all over the world. What they revealed to us about their struggles and dreams are pivotal to what we decided to address—and you can see the actual results of this survey in every chapter.

Two features we all love in "how-to" books are concrete actions and "frequently asked questions" (especially when these are real). So, we organized our entire work around Actions and FAQs—and ensured that each one was brief, relevant and to the point.

You'll see that the "author" of some pieces is "The Ultimate Team"; these are a group of TC-Helicon employees working in fields as diverse as technological development and artist relations who are in close contact with each other. You can read more about this group in the Acknowledgements.

Nearly every piece we gathered was written FRESH for this book (an exception being the quote in FAQ 4 of Chapter 1—and you'll soon see why we did that). We were blown away by the eminence, professionalism and quality of each contributor—and think you will be too.

How to Read This

You can read this book straight through or choose a chapter that interests you.

We've laid it out so that the content follows a singer's life from getting gigs (Section 1) to working with gear at those gigs and at home (Section 2), to improving technique, health and relationships (section 3) and, finally, by looking at money matters and markets for one's voice (section 4). After each section you'll find an essay that summarizes all of the wisdom shared, relating it to a single, powerful word.

Or, just choose a topic you want to work on: vocal health, looping or how to handle money at live gigs—there are 18 focus areas, covering all of the challenges facing today's singers.

Now, I'm looking over at that huge stack of books for singers on my sagging shelf and feeling just a little jealous of you. After all, you now hold a world of insights from singers, doctors, media consultants, coaches, producers and sound engineers—and it fits in your hand.

—Gregory A. Barker Editor, with Kathy Alexander,
The Ultimate Guide for Singing: Gigs, Sound, Money and Health

Note on Editions

In this new edition the publisher has changed from TC-Helicon to Singdaptive. All of the changes in the second edition remain: insights from singers on working with a band in the all-new Bonus Chapter at the end of the book.

We've also updated some of our social media insights, as the digital landscape is rapidly changing. We thank Charles Chemery for his contributions in chapter 3.

The new image at the beginning of the book perfectly captures the joy of singing and the attitude that runs through this Guide—many thanks to both Divinity Roxx (pictured—www.divinityroxx.com) and Christoph Huber (the photographer—www.christophhuber.at).

Our army of contributors have updated their bios and we have attempted to address minor issues from the last edition. We thank the host of singers who have given such encouraging feedback on book as well as our contributors for such engaging, down-to-earth content. Any remaining errors or inconsistencies are purely the responsibility of the editors.

Acknowledgements

At the heart of this book are the insights of 135 of big-hearted industry professionals and specialists who care deeply about the challenges facing vocalists. The best way to thank them is to point you to their Bios in the final pages of this book. You'll see how their insights emerge from years of valuable experience.

But I'd like to take you behind the scenes. This book is the result of three and a half years of glorious arguments. Anyone can have a fight, bruise some egos and walk away. What made these arguments special were that a team of gifted people haggled, fought, laughed, tweaked, fought some more, had another coffee—and didn't get up from the table until something incredible had emerged.

This could have never happened without the vision (and patience) of TC-Helicon and their generosity in sharing industry contacts built over many years. In particular, Kevin Alexander, CEO, championed this project, offering the rare kind of wit and grace that put "glorious" into all of the fights.

This project was also made possible by a team whose knowledge spans from singing in pubs and stadiums to designing the latest technology for singers. Tom Lang is a phenomenally gifted singer-songwriter who is also the consummate communicator of leading edge technology. We simply couldn't have addressed vocal effects and looping without him. But we had so many areas to address, even after consulting 135 experts, that we needed a team to check details, fill in blanks and tweak text: a heartfelt thanks to TC-Helicon staff David Hilderman, Laura Clapp Davidson and Craig Fraser. Joey Elkins offered important advice when we first outlined the project and Jes Vang and Tobias Weltzer made invaluable connections to accomplished contributors with something to say. Thanks too to Carri-Lynne Eldergill for making connections to artists. We appreciate the careful work of Christoper Ashton and Aled Thomas in looking over (and over!) the manuscript before publication.

There is one person who fought beyond all others for this book to be rooted in relevance and depth: my co-editor, Kathy Alexander. Kathy spoke with leading professionals all over the world, transformed complicated ideas into compelling text, and tirelessly presented strategies to make this book even better—even after we *thought* we were done. She also spent hours pouring over one thousand survey responses, ensuring that each chapter stayed on track with addressing what singers most want to know. This book is at the heart of her vision for singers and her personal stamp on its contents is a major reason why it turned out so well.

—G.A.B.

Getting Gigs

CHAPTER 1

Getting Gigs 101

Out of the house and onto the stage.

"Whatever you can do or dream you can, begin it.
Boldness has genius, power, and magic in it."

—Goethe

"I still keep asking myself—why am I doing this music? And the answer still comes loud and clear: 'because I want to hear it!' That's a way better answer for me than 'because I want a contract with Sony.'"

—Judge Smith, founder member of Van Der Graaf Generator

Getting Gigs 101

Out of the house and onto the stage.

Actions:

1. Pursue What You Love
2. Prepare Your Product
3. Rehearse the Smart Way
4. Make Performance Connections
5. Take Almost Any Chance to Sing
6. Prepare Promo Materials
7. Practice Good Gigging Etiquette
8. Have a Plan for Your First Fan

Frequently Asked Questions:

» *How can I get money out of this and how much should I charge?*

» *How do I know if a song is right for me?*

» *How can I stop listening to that inner voice of doubt?*

» *Can you tell me the most important secret to a successful singing career?*

» *My rehearsal time seems frustrating, a waste of time. Help.*

» *There's a venue I want to sing at, but I'm not getting responses to my emails and phone calls, should I just give up?*

» *Is it OK to perform with karaoke tracks?*

» *What songs should I sing?*

» *Can too much rehearsal kill the passion?*

» *How do I find musicians to back me?*

» *What's the most important stuff to bring with me to my first gig?*

» *People aren't responding to my singing—what do I do?*

» *Crisis: I can't make a cold call ... help!*

» *My gig flopped. I want to die.*

» *Can I improve my musical abilities without going to college or university?*

» *A band that needs a singer just asked me to audition—what do I do?*

» *I just don't know where to look when I sing! Nothing feels comfortable!*

Action 1: Pursue What You Love

Look in your life for the passions that are already there—and we aren't only talking about music.

When the day comes that you need an arena to hold all your fans, you'll be standing on that stage because of one reason only: you were courageous enough to remain true to yourself during those years that nobody knew your name. Flash back to today. Your goal as a performer isn't to please everyone (that's impossible), but to present yourself in a crystal clear way so those who are like you can recognize the connection.

A gig is a one-way conversation; it's like posting a Facebook status—you have to put it out there and see if there are any "likes." Hopefully, you will be making a unique statement that allows people to give you a thumbs-up or a thumbs-down. In a live setting, that response is known as applause. When people who have similar values see you pursuing your passion they will "like" you—and even help you go viral. Why? Because they think you're like them. We love people who have similar values to us. Don't worry if it seems there are just a few new fans at each gig. Believers have more energy than non-believers.

If you were a new client of mine I would ask, "What music do you really like?" If you gave me some bland answer such as, "Well, I like all kinds of music … " I would say that's bullshit because you don't pay for much of what you download—so there's no emotional connection. I want to know the music you actually pull your wallet out for. This is the music you should be singing. You'll be asking your fans to put down their own cash for your music—so make sure it's stuff you'd pay for yourself.

Making sure you clearly represent yourself applies to other things too. Your clothes, your hairstyle and your general appearance are a billboard for your values. Think back to your early teen years when your parents would want you to wear certain clothes and not wear other clothes. I bet you had a line that they couldn't cross—a line that you'd fight back on. That line is YOU, your statement. So, make sure that your songs (whether they are originals or covers), your clothes, your appearance and your style represents what you're truly passionate about.

—Mark Baxter: acclaimed vocal coach with Aerosmith, Journey, Goo Goo Dolls and many others

Action 2: Prepare Your Product

Every singer needs a song to sing.
We'll show you how to choose the right tunes for you.

Work out where your true passion lies and your unique selling point.

What is it you do better than other singers/performers? My advice is to lengthen your long rope—make the most of those talents you have in abundance rather than trying to be good at absolutely everything. If you have an extraordinary vocal ability, show it. Sing songs in which you can show off your vocal athleticism. If you have a talent to connect to text and engage your listeners emotionally, sing repertoire that allows for this. If you have charisma and energy and are fit and good-looking, the more commercial market might suit you.

Your choice of songs is vital. If you choose to sing covers rather than write your own material, work out which songs you really care about. Look at the text and establish whether you can relate to the song emotionally and in terms of your own experience. There are so many thousands of songs, there is no point in singing something you do not resonate with.

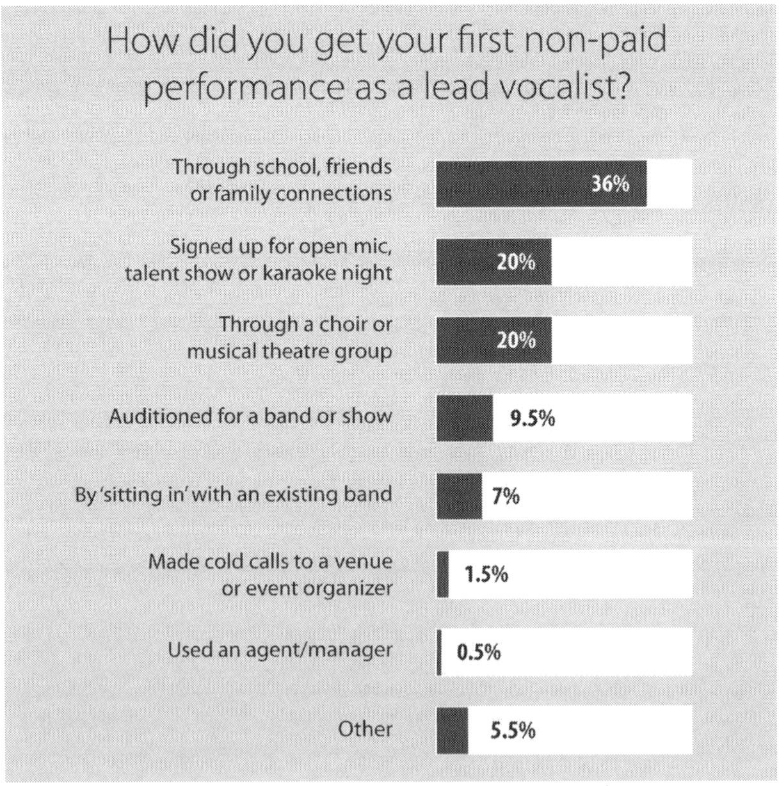

—from the 2012-2013 TC-Helicon survey of 1,000 singers

A great song does not necessarily have to be technically difficult. It is important to choose songs that you can sing successfully given your vocal ability at any given time. This means your songs should be in the right key for your voice and the rhythmic and harmonic complexity should be manageable.

It is a good idea to think carefully about your program/sets. You may want to start the evening with some up-tempo songs to get the audience going then sing some ballads that allow the audience to connect to you as a person. Use YouTube to explore songs and other artists and, if you write your own material, play this to your friends and ask them which songs are their favorites. Time will tell you which of your songs will last, and which ones seemed like a good idea at the time but are not really that interesting. Your songwriting craftsmanship will take years to develop, practice and perfect.

> *You go to two performances. The first features a singer who is technically exquisite, but demonstrates little emotion. The second has a singer who doesn't demonstrate great control, but makes something move inside you. Which would you go back to see?*
>
> ***—Simone Niles:** leading vocal performance coach, author and singer*

Here are a few warnings: your audience will not want to see a victim on stage. Vulnerability and honesty, yes, but not endless negativity. They want to see a person who faces challenges and makes an emotional journey. Emotional repetition is boring. Beware of using songs as a cathartic experience only for yourself. You are singing for your audience. It may feel good to wallow in your own negative experiences but once you lose the audience, it is difficult to win them back.

Many famous artists present their concert to a small circle of friends and invited guests before embarking on a major tour. This is an excellent idea and one that I highly recommend. Accept constructive criticism and know what you stand for.

—Leontine Hass: Artistic Director and founder of London's Associated Studios

Action 3: Rehearse the Smart Way

A "bits and pieces" approach to practicing will strengthen your memory and improve your recall.

We have been learning so much recently in the field of voice science about effective practice. In fact, several time-honored ideas have now been turned on their heads.

The first thing we have learned is that it is better to distribute your practice time throughout the day rather than do it all in one chunk. In the old days you might have spent two hours working on a chromatic scale without a break. Now, we know it is better to practice 15 minutes here and 30 minutes there and then to put it aside for a few hours before taking it up again. This distribution of practice time has two benefits: first, your voice does not get fatigued and, second, it creates more recall of the motor patterns—this means your "music memory" will improve.

So, if I am going to give a performance at night, I'll begin in the morning with a light, 15-minute warm-up. Then I will do something completely different—have breakfast, read, work on a paper, etc. I will have another warm up around noon and one later on before my performance.

> *As for all rhythmic training the metronome is your best friend (and sometimes, your worst enemy!)*
> ***—Daniel Zangger Borch, PhD:** one of Sweden's most established vocal coaches, Head of the Voice Centre*

The next thing we've learned is that it is far better to practice songs, parts of songs, and exercises in random order than in the same order. So, instead of running though each song from beginning to end, you start at the end of the song—and just forget the intro. Then, you may work on a passage from the middle of a song and then on the intro. Short vocal exercises in between the songs are also helpful. This "bits and pieces" approach to practicing is yet another way to strengthen your memory and improve your recall.

Finally, we have learned that it is great to practice with interference. In the standard model you ran though things several times in a row until your singing teacher said "well done." Then you might step on stage and blow it! The problem with the stage is you don't get to try your song five times. Why might singers blow it after so much practice? Because of interference: the curtain, strange equipment, noise from the audience—all kinds of sights, sounds and interruptions that

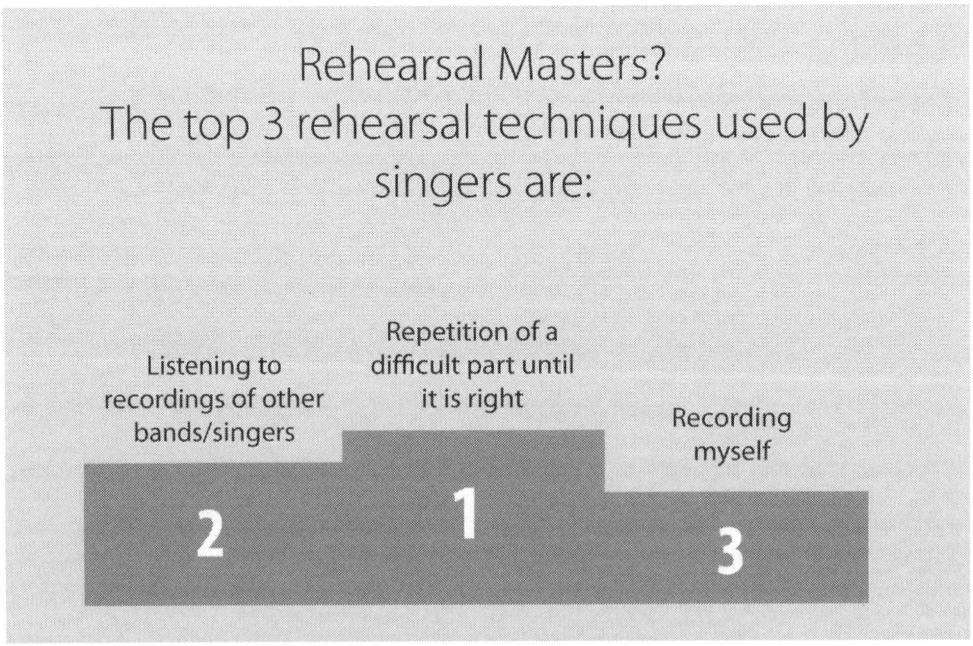

—from the 2012-2013 TC-Helicon survey of 1,000 singers

weren't present in the rehearsal room. You need to bring this interference into your practice. If you are rehearsing and the phone rings, keep singing. If you are in the middle of a song and someone knocks on the door, resist your temptation to stop and keep singing as you open the door. Keep going and don't let the interference stop you. This is excellent preparation for live performance.

–Ingo R. Titze, PhD: one of the world's leading voice scientists and Executive Director of the National Center for Voice and Speech

Action 4: Make Performance Connections

From bulletin boards in guitar shops to your vocal coach—find performance opportunities you may have never considered.

Recently, one of my students sang at an open mic night at a club in Hollywood. She was asked back several times by the venue and, after the fourth time, they asked her to do her own show–cover charge and all. You can find open mic nights at clubs, coffee houses and even guitar shops in many cities. All you have to do is sign up. Singing at an open mic is a great way to get experience, get heard and get to know a venue owner.

If I had to do my career over, the one thing I would do differently is to wake up every day that I didn't have a gig, and make it my job, 10 hours a day, to find my next contact. You ask someone, "Where can I find opportunities to sing?" If one person doesn't know, they will connect you to someone else–and it goes from there. Even once you've got your website, demo, headshots and resume ready, you must still be willing to put in 100 percent to finding performance opportunities.

I tell my students to look for every possible opportunity to sing. Sports events need someone to sing the anthem. Workplaces need music at their staff parties. Singers are needed for weddings and funerals, and the pay is usually good for these. Singing at a religious ceremony introduces you as a singer to a whole community of people, and one of them may connect you to your next performance opportunity.

Don't forget that taking a class or joining a choir are great ways to make connections. Here in LA, singers can make valuable connections to agents and contractors who come as guests to vocal workshops and sight-singing classes. By joining a choir, you'll make valuable connections with singers and music supporters in your community.

By getting involved in your local music scene not only will you gain experience through "paying your dues," but you will also be getting your personality out there, so people know what you are like to work with. Most people I know who are looking for a singer would be more likely to book you once they have asked around and discovered that you are easy to work with and are doing well in the local music scene.

—Gerald White: prolific singer-songwriter who has worked on over 100 TV and commercial productions

Action 5: Take Almost Any Chance to Sing

Often the right opportunity only comes along because you took the unpaid wedding gig for your brother's friend.

Connecting with your audience is crucial to your art and your career, and doesn't require a prestigious venue. I did it in a bunch of bookstores.

I arrived in LA with some gigging experience and a plan to build a singing career. When I asked one venue manager about performing at his club, he actually laughed in my face and told me if I didn't bring at least thirty paying fans, it was never gonna happen. The only person in the city who knew me was my band-mate, Nick.

Refusing to accept defeat, I began going to the concerts of other artists as a way of meeting people and getting to know my new surroundings. At one concert, I met a man who offered me a chance to do weekend gigs at Borders bookstores. There would be no pay and no guarantee that anyone would be interested in my music. Plus, Nick and I would have to lug our own heavy gear—sometimes through the whole store (I often wished I played the kazoo, not the piano!). Still, I knew my answer had to be, "Yes." This was my chance to develop a fan base. I did 125 performances at Borders stores over two years.

These gigs were an opportunity for me to develop one of the most important performance skills: the ability to connect with people. If I wasn't connecting with people, they could simply leave the store! After all, they had come for books, not music. I made it my mission to keep their attention.

I told stories to lead people into my world. I experimented with my repertoire. I set up a table with CDs and a jar on it so that that people could put money in and buy a CD while I was playing.

It wasn't too long before I noticed that certain people came back to hear me—with their friends. I had found my first fans. I now have a busy career doing what I love: writing and sharing my music. This career happened because I took opportunities that were neither glamorous nor lucrative but gave me a chance to hone my skills and find fans.

And yes, I went back to that venue—and the booker didn't laugh in my face. I had more than enough fans.

—Marina V: award-winning Russian-American singer, pianist and songwriter

Action 6: Prepare Promo Materials

Make it easy for people to find where you are, who you are and what you're about.

Your Bio

A brief (100 words or less) and compelling personal story can be one of your most effective tools to make and nurture fans. This will go on your site, your Facebook page and cards you hand out at gigs. Here's what one gigging singer, Marina V put in her bio: "This red-headed, piano-playing songstress grew up in Moscow, blessed with an angelic voice and long last name (Verenikina). Raised during the collapse of the Soviet Union in an educated but not wealthy family … ." What do you think other people would find quirky and meaningful about your journey?

—Marina V, award-winning Russian-American singer, pianist and songwriter

Your Brand

Establishing your brand and creating a logo is a hurdle for singers that can kill a lot of time. People end up getting worried about the choices and delay the process because they think they have to determine the perfect, final look. You're right to think brand is important—but it is more important to move ahead on this and tweak things along the way. Get a simple business card with your/your group's name on it and some kind of simple and clear graphic that somehow represents your style. Take that to someone who can make it digital and then get it out there to your fans—in print and online.

—Evan Lagace, marketing and physique specialist

Your Pics

Avoid posting pictures of yourself that don't represent the way you want to appear. After all, social media is just an extension of how you want to express yourself in person. It's about how you want to carry yourself, speak, and appear when you meet someone. On many occasions I've contacted friends to ask them to take down a picture they've posted of me that's just unnecessary to be sharing. I monitor my online identity according to the way I like to conduct myself in person.

—Dot Bustelo, internationally recognized music producer and music technology strategist

Your Vids

We see thousands of singer vids; a handful of these go viral and/or lead to contest and performance opportunities. You need three things:

1. A good performance that shows that you are totally into your song, communicating its magic to the audience. Singing "to the camera" is usually essential for a home vid.
2. Decent image and audio: the camera is on a tripod and you are using a good external mic and/or have experimented with room placement for the best sound.

3. No distractions: no picking, scratching, combing, people walking in and out of the frame and NO endless talking before the song. Remove any crap vids from your YouTube page. One or two quality vids is better than dozens of experimental posts.

—The Ultimate Team

Your Outreach to Fans

What you really want to do is invite people to join you on your musical journey. Don't just think in terms of only offering a finished album. You can offer "treats" to your fan base such as a photo of the first lyric sheet from a song on your album, or a bit of video footage from your backstage warm up. These things contribute to the story of your music, inviting people to be a part of your journey. Take care of the quality of what you share online about your music—it can't hurt to contact people to ask them to take down material you don't think represents you well. The more you put yourself out there the better; people feel that they are joining you on your journey.

—Laura Vane, singer-songwriter of Laura Vane & The Vipertones

Your Recorded Music

Once you are confident that you have a few great songs, you've performed them a lot and people have responded well, take some time to work on a recording—see our recording chapter for help. In the "old days" singers would do a rough demo on a tape to give people an idea of their gifts. Demo days are over. Everyone now wants to hear a finished product—so spending some money on getting your songs professionally mixed is essential. With a great recording and the other materials in this action, you will be ready to charge ahead with new gigs, new venues and new audiences.

—The Ultimate Team

Action 7: Practice Good Gigging Etiquette

Organization, presentation and ethics go a long way to building the kinds of bridges that see you getting invited back.

> *People get the same chemical hit at a concert as they do watching sports—but there's no loser at a musical performance. It's guaranteed that your team's gonna win.*
>
> ***—Mark Baxter:** acclaimed vocal coach with Aerosmith, Journey, Goo Goo Dolls and many others*

Early in my career, my band lost out on getting a regular gig, three times a week, because of bad gigging etiquette.

You see, we weren't organized: too many band members asked too many questions about the deal, the free beer, the time, and so on. The venue manager got really annoyed and said that he didn't have the time or energy to answer the same questions over and over again from different band members. In addition to this, we came across as being more interested in the benefits than in our music. Learn from our mistake.

So, let's talk about the key elements of good gigging etiquette.

Timing is the most important way you can make a positive impression: know the venue's time schedule, their preferred time for the sound check and their expectations about the length of sets, breaks, etc. You'll want to show up on time, end your sets on time and also leave on time. Sometimes a band starts packing up when people are still partying and this can be precisely the wrong move; other times you need to pack things up straight away to make room for a DJ—just be sure you know the deal from gig to gig.

If you are in a group, you will find it really efficient and professional to let ONE person in the crew or band become the spokesperson with the people at the venue; you don't want to ask the same questions about free beers over and over again just because you don't communicate within the band.

The more you know about what is expected of you (i.e. how many sets, volume, genre of music, etc.), the more prepared you'll be to match your art to the venue. It will be more likely that you'll be invited back.

Finally, here is a checklist of things to keep in mind when you are contacting venue owners, managers, promoters or events organizers:

- Don't be afraid to call people you don't know.
- When contacting someone for the first time, rehearse what you want to say and where you want the conversation to lead.
- Don't call at inappropriate times like Friday afternoon or lunchtime. This simply creates an irritation.
- Never arrive late to a meeting, audition or job.
- Keep a list of people who need to be reminded of your existence. Call them from time to time.
- Try to be seen where the action is. It is important that people are aware that you are in the game.
- Try to remember the names of the people you meet. This instils confidence.
- Be positive, open and believe in yourself. You are unique! There is no one just like YOU!
- In the bigger picture it's not only about gigging; it's the way you present yourself as an artist ALL the time.

—Daniel Zangger Borch, PhD, one of Sweden's most established vocal coaches, Head of the Voice Centre

Action 8: Have a Plan for Your First Fan

Your very first fans will help you achieve your goals—all you need is some strategies that they enjoy.

A database of your fans is worth its weight in gold–and your first fans can be involved and active in helping you grow and develop it.

Social media is not a place to make "sales." It's a place to attract new, potential fans through offering an experience and providing value. Have you heard of the artist Pretty Lights? Look him up–he made a radical decision to view his music as the "giveaway" and his database as his "income." What he does is to give away his music in return for an email address (and donation if you wish) and the chance to send you updates in the form of email marketing. He now has a worldwide database of fans that own his entire collection, attend his concerts, spread the word, purchase his products and help him to make an impact with publishers.

At this stage you don't even need to know exactly how you'll use your database–the key thing is to start building it–don't delay this any longer! When it comes to your business, you are as strong as your database is large (and active).

Here is what I want you to do: come up with some ways this week to give away your music to fans in return for an email address, a Facebook "Like," or a Twitter "Follow." (If I were in your shoes, I would carry a notepad and collect the email addresses of everyone I speak to …)

Then, watch your fans' comments and identify who is especially effective at online communication. Reach out to some of these fans with further opportunities to hear your music, encouraging them to share their thoughts online. You might even start a VIP program that could involve making some video clips of rehearsals, or back stage antics and give these away to your VIPs in return for their sharing your status updates with their communities and replying on comments, mentioning your music.

Finally, don't forget to build your database at your performances: "If you give your email address to that guy with the clipboard over there–I will send you a song tonight!" or "The first person to post a picture of their ticket stub on Facebook will get … ." Create games, surveys and contests live and online to increase your influence through fan engagement.

To get started you only need one fan.

–Evan Lagace, marketing and physique specialist

Frequently Asked Questions

> How can I get money out of this and how much should I charge?

Answered by Jennifer Truesdale, singer, songwriter, coach and author of "Get Paid to Sing"

While there are many different types of gigs out there, a lot of singers start out performing at open mics and then move into small clubs. These gigs provide the perfect "classroom" for developing your skills, growing musically and at the same time helping you to get some name recognition. While club gigs don't tend to be the highest paying gigs it is possible to make some money if you take a few simple steps.

- **Build Your Fan Mailing List.** When it comes to club gigs the #1 key to making money will be your mailing list. For club gigs, you will generally be paid a percentage of whatever the club charges people at the door. For that reason, the more people you are able to get to your gigs, the more money you will make. Encourage people to sign up for your mailing list and then promote your gigs to this list! Additionally, the larger your fan base, the better your chance of scoring the more high profile, higher paying gigs!
- **Sell CDs and Merchandise.** Regardless of where you are performing you should have CDs for sale. These can be full length CDs, EPs, or even CD singles/digital download cards. Additionally, if someone buys your CD, digital download card or T-shirt they are also much more likely to remember your name.

When it comes to how much to charge, as I mentioned, most clubs pay performers a percentage of the door cover charge. How much the club charges at the door and what percentage they pay the performers will vary from club to club, but in general the performers should get at least 50% of the door. Be sure to ask the club management ahead of time what their policy is for paying performers. Have fun!

> How do I know if a song is right for me?

Answered by Neil Sedaka, legendary American singer, songwriter, composer and pianist

Don't go out of the style that appeals to you; don't screech things out that are too high or too low. You want to please yourself with your songs so that your audience will feel your pleasure. So, you need to sing songs that mean something to you, that you can transform into your own feelings. Emotion is the key factor: you need to bring your emotion to the listener—if you feel it, they will definitely feel it. Start with the songs that you know deeply, that you have an affinity for. I am a product of the music I have heard all my life—Patti Page, Mel Tormé, Stevie Wonder ... and so many others. Focus on the kind of songs and styles that you feel are believable to the audience.

> How can I stop listening to that inner voice of doubt?

Answered by W. Timothy Gallwey, million selling author of "The Inner Game of Tennis, co-author of "The Inner Game of Music"

I've long been impressed by how some of the solutions to performance pressures crossover between the field of sports and the arts.

So, let me tell you about a strange golf tournament in California called the BOO Tournament. The rule of this tournament was that anyone could say anything during the swing of the player who was hitting—which is usually forbidden in a normal game of golf.

So, the crowd and other players would shout out anything they could think of that would disturb the player in order to introduce fear or doubt. Some people were very clever: "The last time you hit that ball into the woods! You don't want to do that again!" Of course the crowd was very good at this because of their own inner voices! It was so interesting to see how the players did. Most players performed terribly at the beginning of the game, became better as the game progressed and, by the end of the tournament, were playing better than they usually play. They knew that the only good solution was not to pay any attention to that voice of doubt and fear.

My guess is that singing is even harder than golf because the quality of your voice is closer to the part of you that is sensitive to being judged. But the answer is still the same: don't listen to the voice of doubt; become fascinated by some aspect of your singing.

> Can you tell me the most important secret to a successful singing career?

Answered by Malcolm Gladwell, bestselling author (with Kathy Alexander)

We think that bestselling author Malcolm Gladwell answers this question perfectly when he points to the importance of time in his book, *Outliers*:

> The Beatles ended up traveling to Hamburg five times between 1960 and the end of 1962. One the first trip, they played 106 nights, five or more hours a night. On their second trip, they played 92 times. On their third trip, they played 48 times, for a total of 172 hours on stage. The last two Hamburg gigs, in November and December of 1962, involved another 90 hours of performing. All told, they performed for 270 nights in just over a year and a half. By the time they had their first burst of success in 1964, in fact, they had performed live an estimated twelve hundred times. Do you know how extraordinary that is? Most bands today don't perform twelve hundred times in their entire careers. The Hamburg crucible is one of the things that set the Beatles apart.

In other words, even though Lennon and McCartney were exceptionally gifted, their inherent musical ability, alone, doesn't fully explain their success. Important aspects of their situation are just as crucial, including the chance to accumulate thousands of hours of performance experience very early on in their career.

Gladwell refers to many studies that prove the 10,000-hour rule. The neurologist, Daniel Levitin observed the same factor in studies of composers, basketball players and even master criminals: 10,000 hours of practice is required to achieve the level of expertise that comes with being a world-class expert—at anything.

Do you want to be a truly great performer who stands out above the rest? Talent and intelligence are essential, but won't get you there alone. Ten thousand hours of performing—that's 2.7 hours a day for ten years—will.

> My rehearsal time seems frustrating, a waste of time. Help.

Answered by Gerald Klickstein, veteran guitarist, educator and author of "The Musician's Way"

To get the most out of our individual practice, we musicians need to set meaningful goals and know how to attain them. Here are six keys to productive practice:

1. Choose Fresh, Accessible Material. To ignite your motivation to practice, pick fresh songs that inspire you, yet that fall easily within your abilities and range.
2. Pinpoint Goals. Pick several smaller objectives for each practice session. For instance, instead of aiming to learn an entire multi-verse song in one sitting, after warming up, master the first verse and the chorus, take a break, and then work on different achievable goals. The next day, review the first verse and learn the second one.
3. Use Targeted Strategies. As opposed to repeating a difficult passage over and over, zero in on problem spots, and experiment with possible solutions. If you encounter an intonation problem, let's say, you might sing a troublesome passage on neutral syllables and then reintroduce the words.
4. Repeat with Wonder. Practice entails repetition, but we can repeat in ways that expand rather than constrict our creativity. As an illustration, after one clean statement of a phrase, for a second pass, you might aim for a clearer tone and looser shoulders; the third time, you could reinforce those objectives while also adding crispness to your articulation. In my book *The Musician's Way*, I wrote: "Whatever the material, your repetitions should lead somewhere meaningful—to greater ease, higher beauty, and deeper feeling."
5. Keep to a Schedule. Regular, concise practice sessions are more productive than inconsistent lengthy ones. If you haven't been practicing steadily, you might plan daily 30-minute practice sessions for one week, and then see how you feel.
6. Be Flexible. As you explore practice strategies and scheduling routines, stay open to the unexpected. Sometimes an interruption will cut a session short; other times you'll want to do extra work on a particular piece. Aim to be organized but also open to possibilities because creativity and flexibility go hand in hand.

> There's a venue I want to sing at, but I'm not getting responses to my emails and phone calls, should I just give up?

Answered by Laura Vane, singer-songwriter of Laura Vane & The Vipertones

Never give up—especially if you really want to play in that venue, and you are convinced that playing there will make a difference for you. There is nothing better for you to do than actually sticking yourself in front of somebody. I have done this many times. You want to make sure that people see your face—this can be more effective than phone and email. I am a bit impatient so sometimes I will call a venue and simply ask them when they are going to be there—then I will drop by for a chat. Venue managers often appreciate this.

> Is it OK to perform with karaoke tracks?

Answered by Jennifer Truesdale, singer, songwriter, coach and author of "Get Paid to Sing"

Whether or not it's appropriate to do a live show with tracks depends on the venue and on the musical style. Some genres, including hip-hop and electronic music, actually benefit from the use of pre-recorded tracks and many artists perform with tracks or a combination of live instruments and tracks to re-create the recorded sound live. Other genres such as rock, folk, blues or jazz really sound best with live musicians.

If you're considering performing to a karaoke track, I would ask a couple of questions. Are you thinking of using a track instead of live musicians because you don't know many musicians? Is it financial (the venue isn't paying enough to split between 3–4 other people)? Or is the venue too small to accommodate a larger band? If any of these are part of your reasoning you may want to consider finding one other musician to play with, ideally a guitar or keyboard player, and perform "unplugged" versions of the songs.

If on the other hand you are thinking of singing to tracks because the songs demand sampled, sequenced sounds that are difficult to duplicate live, then be sure to get REALLY high quality karaoke tracks. Commercial karaoke tracks can range widely in quality from good to decidedly NOT good. Spend some time and extra money if necessary and get yourself some really good tracks!

Finally, as I mentioned earlier, it also depends on the venue. If you're going to perform with karaoke tracks then be sure to find clubs/pubs where the owners and customers are agreeable to it, then give them your all out best performance!

> What songs should I sing?

Answered by Jeannie Deva, celebrity voice and performance coach

Whether singing your own material or covers, use the following as a guide when choosing songs to perform. All or most of these should be true for every song you sing. This list is especially important in the case of cover songs, so that you can give them your own signature.

1. You believe in the message strongly enough to pour your heart and soul into it.
2. The style of the music allows you to do things with your voice that bring out the best in your tone and showcase your unique vocal attributes.
3. It is a song or interpretation that will not automatically compare you with the original artist.
4. The song permits you to take chances both emotionally and vocally.
5. The song inspires you to make certain melodic and phrasing changes (from the original recording) while still keeping it true to the basic song.

> Can too much rehearsal kill the passion?

Answered by Mary Hammond, leading educator and vocal coach for Coldplay and many other star acts

Your question is making good point. An inspiring process actually makes your vocal mechanism work more easily and naturally. The important question is, "How do you keep the kind of spontaneity and energy alive which produces good singing"? No singer can be inspired 100% of the time. The reality is that you will always come to barriers and need to come out the other side. Your task is not to expect that you will be constantly inspired, but to learn how to rekindle your passion when things have become stale. This is why I encourage singers to just sit down and look at the words of the songs they are singing and ask themselves, "Why did I want to sing this in the first place?" When you have an answer to this question you can sing again with passion.

> How do I find musicians to back me?

Answered by Lisa Popeil, celebrity vocal coach and creator of the Voiceworks® Method

Before you can begin your quest for the perfect back-up musicians, you have three choices: pay professional musicians, pay amateur musicians, or look for band members (free but fraught with problems).

The benefits of paying professionals to back you include (i) musical skill, (ii) performing and recording experience, (iii) easy to hire, easy to fire, (iv) minimal ego, (v) low drama. The down-sides might be (i) too pricey, especially if they're union members, (ii) too "old-looking" for your band and (iii) they may not have a fire in their belly for your musical vision.

Here are some ideas on hiring pros who'll get the job done:

- In the US, check out Musicians' Union aka American Federation of Musicians for recommendations afmentertainment.org and try musicianaudition.com
- In the UK, contact the Musicians' Union at musiciansunion.org.uk
- Ask music producers for recommendations

The second option is to find and pay amateur musicians.

Pros:

i. Cheaper than full-time professionals. Pay is negotiable unlike working with union members who must charge union rates. For non-union musicians, make offers for a rehearsal fee, recording fee and performance fee and see if they bite.

ii. Your band might be a dream come true for the talented amateur, resulting in s/he becoming a devoted asset to your band.

Cons:

i. These are people who may play music as a hobby and have other lives/families which might make touring unfeasible. Ask up-front if they're free to tour and for how long!

ii. Might take them a bit longer to come up with satisfactory original parts. However, if they're just performing parts from a pre-existing recording, that's easy.

Here are some ideas on hiring semi-pros:

- Check out online musician contact services such as bandmix.com and musicianscontact.com in the US. In the UK, try gumtree.com/other-musicians-wanted.
- Ask music producers for recommendations.
- Go to other gigs and chat up players to see if they're available and interested in working with you for pay.
- Search for a local pop/rock music school and put up a notice with what you need, who your influences are and your contact info. Say "for pay." Ask them to email you samples of their playing before you set up a personal meeting.

Working with non-pros can be a mine-field, but if you want to go that route:

- Put notices up at college music departments, pop/rock schools, coffee-houses.
- Ask around—tell everyone you know what you're looking for (bass, drums, keys?).
- Hang out where musicians hang-out and make friends.
- Use online musician contact services such as joinmyband.co.uk, Musicians Classifieds in the UK or musicianaudition.com

> What's the most important stuff to bring with me to my first gig?

Answered by Jaime Babbitt, renowned jingle singer and backing vocalist, former Disney Records coach

Designate one large bag for all things singing-related. Please take a look into my gig bag; I think when you do, you'll realize that, YES, you need one:

- A large bottle of room temperature water: we singers don't drink cold OR hot drinks when singing; extreme cold and/or heat cause contraction/swelling (respectively) of blood vessels and tissue ... like the kind around your vocal cords.
- Throat lozenges, like slippery elm. Yucky, but effective.
- A snack, like an energy bar.
- Makeup, of course.
- Advil or Tylenol (Nothing worse than trying to sing when your head is exploding).
- Hand sanitizer (I'm not a germaphobe, but if it's flu season, I'm carrying Purell).
- iPad, tablet, lyric notebook (if needed).
- SmartPhone: yes, it's become an extension of your ear, but if you're playing a gig, you'll be tweeting and posting a bit until you go on. Get those last-minute fans!
- Microphone: most venues have mics but I bring my trusty Shure SM-58 (labeled, of course). It makes me happy to spit all over the mic I call my own.
- Earplugs (the cheapo kind, or the made-to-order ones that reduce frequencies in a balanced way): at my advanced age (joking), I try to preserve my hearing; you should, too, however old you are. You never know how loud it'll be onstage, or how loud the band will be before YOU. I hate having my ears blown out before my own show.

Bring whatever else you desire ... and pack the night before so you have one less thing to think about on gig day. That "Being Prepared" philosophy has been around so long for a reason: it makes sense!

> People aren't responding to my singing—what do I do?

Answered by Rachel Bennett, lead singer-songwriter of RAIE, London-based lecturer and vocal coach

I want to applaud your courage to ask this question—you're at a turning point and want to become more aware of what is really going on. It is now absolutely vital that you seek some good input before you come to any conclusions. There are three ways to get that input:

1. Ask an experienced musician whom you trust to attend a rehearsal or a gig and take some notes for you as a "punter."
2. Ask your voice coach or teacher to attend a band rehearsal and work with you as an outfit. He or she may have a lot to say about your body language or timing; perhaps even your technique.

3. Ask a friend who believes in you and your voice to give you some constructive feedback. If they are shy about criticism, tell them to give you two stars and a wish—two things you are getting right and one thing you could do to reach the audience more effectively.

Here are some common reasons vocalists don't reach their audience—with solutions:

- Your band may be playing too loud. They may be playing in opposition to your feel/sound as a singer or you may be insensitive to their feel; either way the outfit isn't complementing each member. Record your rehearsal/performance, assess and discuss.
- You aren't having fun on stage. Sometimes it's important to have a bit of fun on stage with your band; it can help you to "gel" your sound because you are a little more relaxed.
- You are hiding from your audience. Talk to the audience in as natural a way as you can when you introduce songs or band members; it's like making new friends every time you play!
- A lack of musical preparation and tightness is causing you anxiety on stage—you may need to work harder in rehearsals so you feel more comfortable with the tunes.
- Poor sound on stage may be making it difficult to hear the nuances of the band (and vice versa). Attend to monitoring issues.

Remember, you are in the front line on stage so the emphasis should be on you!

> Crisis: I can't make a cold call … help!

Answered by Jaime Babbitt, renowned jingle singer and backing vocalist, former Disney Records coach

Ah, I know the feeling, that rollercoaster in your belly; your heart beats faster, you sweat …

"Forget it!" you say. "I'm not calling!"

Oh, no you don't. Not on my watch. Listen up:

First, UNDERSTAND THAT THIS PERSON IS NOT A KNOWN ENEMY, just someone you haven't met. Maybe they're a really nice person who'd be happy to help you, right?

Second, PRACTICE THE CALL. Practice makes perfect. Boom. Write a script —verbatim—especially those first sentences. True, the other person is going to respond; however, run with me here. Memorize your "script" like you memorize lyrics. This way you might feel more like the captain of your ship and less like a seasick passenger.

Third, IMAGINE THE WORST CASE SCENARIO. What is the most horrifying thing that could happen? The person screams at you and says they hate you: probably won't happen. The person laughs and hangs up: not likely to happen. You get their voicemail, which happens about 89.5% of the time. So you'll leave the message that you also PRACTICED. My point: nothing is ever as bad as you think it's going to be.

I saved my favorite for last:

ALLOW THE CALL TO NOT BE PERFECT

Scenario #1: The call went perfectly? Congratulations!

Scenario #2: You stammered? Laughed nervously? Congratulations!! Why? Because you made the call! If you'd never called, you'd never have messed up and you'd never be able to correct yourself and do better next time ... and we all know that we learn more from our mistakes than our perceived "perfection."

And look. The world didn't stop spinning. No one hates you. More importantly, you made your first cold call. It gets easier. All is well. Go have some cookies. Learn some new songs. Don't stop believing, hold on to that feeeeeling ...

> My gig flopped. I want to die.

Answered by Mark De-Lisser, vocal coach with The Voice UK and the ACM Gospel Choir; has worked with Jessie J, Olly Murs and more

There are many things I want to say to you, but the first is this: give yourself credit for getting out there and performing.

Look, there are pressures on the stage and you've faced them. There is a massive difference between the safe environment of the teaching studio and being on stage. This is why I will no longer teach any singer who doesn't have a gig lined up at least every 6–7 weeks. You just can't really solidify what you've been learning in rehearsals without trying things out in front of people. You've been on stage, so you've faced the pressure. Check.

Now, the next thing I want to say to you is: you are not alone. Even for the top singers I coach in TV reality shows, all but one of them "flops" in the sense that they do not win. Even the winners find themselves down in the dumps when they realize that once the show is over they are quickly forgotten and have to struggle to move their career forward. I find myself working with very talented singers each week who feel exactly as you do.

OK, now let's get down to business and talk about turning this around.

The ultimate goal is to come away from a gig feeling great. That's what I want for you. I want it because when you are enjoying your own performance, we will too.

So, how do you get from where you are now (feeling devastated) to a much more positive stage experience?

The key is to focus on just one or two things that didn't work in your performance. Do what it takes to identify these things. It might be anything from a technique issue like breath control to what you say in between songs. But only choose one or two issues. Take these things to a coach and work on them. Then, perform again with the goal of showing improvement. Celebrate that you made some progress and then move on to the next challenge. That's it.

Did you catch the process?

1. Choose one or two things that are areas for improvement.
2. Work on these.
3. Get back on stage to test your work.
4. Celebrate your gains.
5. Repeat.

Yes, repeat it all again. As you repeat this you will learn to enjoy the "process" of performing. I just heard that Beyoncé, who must be the top performer of our generation, is now learning music theory and how to play guitar. She is doing this because she has the attitude of wanting to improve, test out what she's learned in performances and keep trying.

> Can I improve my musical abilities without going to college or university?

Answered by Mary Hammond, leading educator and vocal coach for Coldplay and many other star acts

Yes—by listening carefully to the music around you and opening up your ears to develop your own music sense. This is possible without formal training. In fact, it's possible for formal education to stultify your musicality and kill your instincts. Is there anything that can be said for school? Well, if you want to look more deeply at the structure of music, understanding chord structure and theory, then school can be a very good place to develop as a musician (though this is possible through self study and private instruction). The other reason is eminently practical: college or university is a great place to find inspiration as well as other musicians with whom you may want to work. Amy Winehouse and Adele found a great deal of support at The BRIT School and I've worked with Coldplay; they met each other at University—though they weren't undertaking degrees in music (supporting the original point!).

> A band that needs a singer just asked me to audition—what do I do?

Answered by Daniel Bowling, Music Supervisor and Director in London and New York City, author of "Auditions Undressed"

Just like applying for any job, preparation is key. Knowing who you're auditioning for and what they want is central to whether or not you stand a chance of winning that audition. Of course, talent and charisma will play their parts, but you're likely not to get past first base without proper preparation.

First of all, ask yourself these critical questions: what kind of band are you auditioning for and where do they work or hope to work? Do they cover Pop Standards at weddings or do they play original Garage Rock at local clubs? Are they looking for an R&B type singer or a Heavy Rock vocalist? Are they interested in a singer/songwriter or solely someone who can front the band? What is the image of band? Are they Glam Punk or Indie Rock? The more information you have about their needs and wants, the better you'll be able to fulfill them in an audition by knowing what songs to prepare, what to wear and how to present yourself.

If you're asked to sing a song a cappella, make sure you use a pitch pipe, piano or smart-phone to consistently acquire your starting note. Practice starting and finishing your song in the right keys. Pitching should always be a priority and never a moveable feast. Just as important, always be prepared for the possibility of singing your song to either a backing tape or accompaniment—it's important that you demonstrate that you can sing effectively with others!

Perhaps the band will want you to sing one of their songs or a song that you've written yourself. Regardless of whether or not the song is original, make sure your focus remains totally on telling a story through the song. By doing this alone, you will ensure that your delivery is authentic and affectation free—the last thing they'll want to see is how many vocal acrobatics you can perform on a given melody.

> *Getting comfortable in your own skin comes with repetition. I find it easier to connect with myself—and others—on stage when I am letting go of the formal mindset and having fun. For me this means being somewhat vulnerable and letting the audience share in that vulnerability.*
>
> ***—Peter Hollens:*** *Pop Singer & Producer/ Youtuber with over 175 million views*

It's unlikely that any band will want a carbon copy of their previous singer and it's important that you show your individuality in an audition. Be confident in who you are, but do not ignore your research! Try and find a way to fuse your knowledge of what they are looking for with your own talents and capabilities.

The vibe or atmosphere of each audition will inevitably vary and it's important to remain receptive and malleable to what is asked of you on the day. There are no black and white answers in how to handle any given audition predicament, but the more you know about who you're auditioning for and what they want, the more you'll be able to intuitively and confidently respond to how the audition unfolds.

> I just don't know where to look when I sing! Nothing feels comfortable!

Answered by Juliet Russell: singer, composer, choir director and a vocal coach on BBC 1's The Voice

One of the biggest realizations that helped me overcome being shy on stage was that it's not about me. It's about the music, the emotion and the audience. Once I understood this, I was more free to use eye contact as a part of my performances. You'll feel freer to use your eyes as a part of your performance as you think about singing and performing as an act of generosity, something that you want to share.

Singers are often told to look over the heads of their audience, straight ahead and to the back wall. Personally I don't agree with this approach for most pop music singers. This can sometimes make a performer seem aloof and remote, disconnected from the very people that they want to engage.

You already know how to use effective eye contact. You use it naturally all the time in daily life and the basic principles when singing are similar, but magnified. Here are some specifics to keep in mind:

1. Open your eyes. Sometimes inexperienced singers get so nervous that they keep their eyes closed for the majority of the song. While this may help you to focus, your interaction with your audience suffers. Closing one's eyes can be effective for a line or so, but only when it serves to express a specific emotion in the song
2. Try to make sure everyone in the room is included in your performance so think about eye contact in terms of proximity and distance, width (look to the sides as well as straight ahead), depth and height especially if the stage is elevated or if there is a balcony or tiered seating etc.
3. Keep eye contact steady and focused. Too many quick changes can make you seem nervous and erratic.
4. Don't fix your gaze on only one or two people or for too long. You might make them feel uncomfortable and you will exclude other members of your audience.
5. Don't be freaked out that everyone's looking at you. You're a performer. They are supposed to be looking at you.

CHAPTER 2

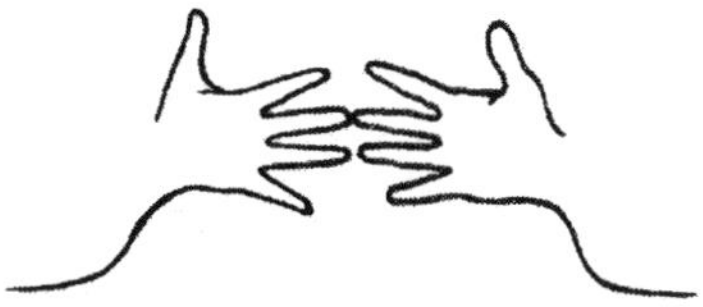

Getting Gigs 201

More people, more recognition and—maybe—more money.

"Ironically, your chances of making it are far better if you don't sound like what's popular today. Successful artists make music that moves them and then set out to make it popular."

—Mark Baxter: acclaimed vocal coach with Aerosmith, Journey, Goo Goo Dolls and many others

"You are on a journey through a wasteland littered with the bones of mediocre singer/songwriters and average voices. To survive, you must find a way to stand out while staying true to what makes you who you are."

—Mister Tim, viral video star, voice artist, composer and sponsored kazoo player

Getting Gigs 201

More people, more recognition and—maybe—more money.

Actions:

1. Get in Touch with Your Goals, Again and Again
2. Improve Your Product
3. Evolve Your Identity
4. Understand and Target Your Venue
5. Pick Your Battles
6. Commit to the "Hustle"
7. Build Your Fanbase
8. Harness the Power of Your Fans
9. Use Social Media to Make Your Gigs Succeed
10. Don't Ignore Local Power

Frequently Asked Questions:

» *When do I say no to a gig?*

» *Should I stick it out with this band or branch out?*

» *At what point should I record an "album"?*

» *Do I need an agent?*

» *Why didn't the venue ask me back?*

» *How do I find more cool songs?*

» *Should I concentrate on originals or covers?*

» *How can we make our rehearsals more effective?*

» *I don't have an interesting story for my bio.*

» *Should I go on a tour?*

Action 1: Get in Touch with Your Goals, Again and Again.

Fame, money and adoration are great, but what is the essence of what you love?

Most musicians I know never made it big—yet they still love making music. Most office workers I know make a pretty good living—yet they still hate going to work. If your focus is only on income you're missing the value of living with passion. Singing music that's "popular" will backfire if it's not something that excites you. So, when planning your musical future, ask yourself this all-important question: are you willing to starve to sing your songs?

When someone's voice is in bad shape, I often discover that it's not their technique—but their situation that needs adjusting. It's simple: when you represent yourself in an untruthful way, your voice will fatigue. It's kind of like me in a suit. My wife appreciates my attempt to dress up—but after an hour I'm feeling tight around the collar. If you sing music that is not 1000% authentic

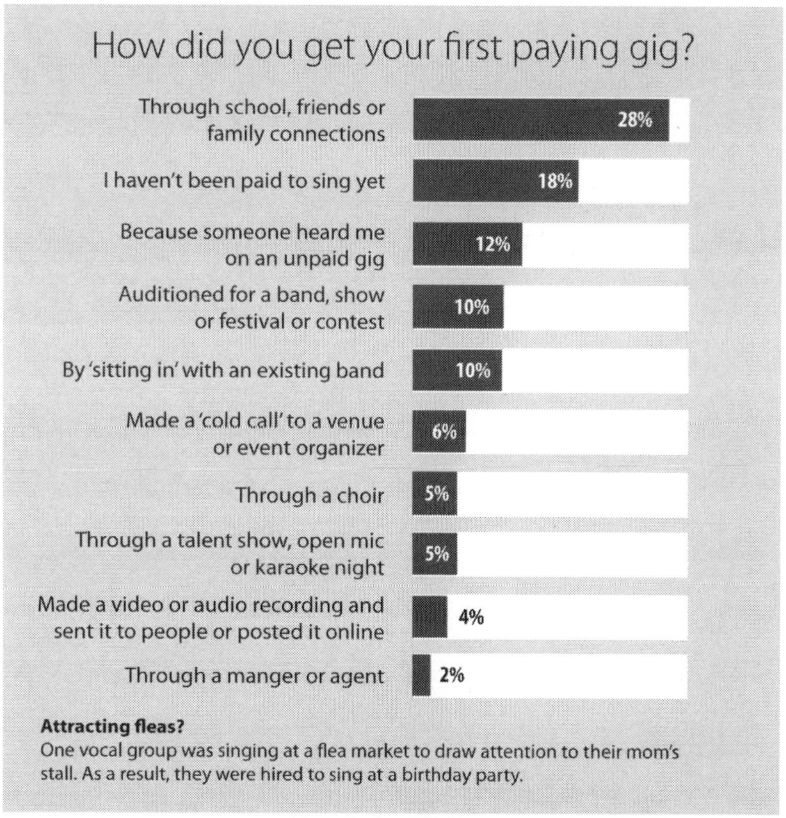

—from the 2012-2013 TC-Helicon survey of 1,000 singers

you'll experience tension and swelling. Of course there are exercises to alleviate that, but then you start a cycle of distress and recover. It's the singer's version of a hamster in a wheel.

To my way of thinking, there are two kinds of successful singers: technical and emotional. The technical ones have incredible skills and draw an audience who enjoy vocal prowess. These singers can cross genres and their fans follow them because it's all about the voice—not the songs. Then, there are singers who make it because of their LOVE of the music. Ozzy is a perfect example of this. He'd be the first to say that he's not a singer's singer, but every time he performs he's the biggest fan of Metal in the arena!

Some artists know exactly who they are but most of us have to do a little soul searching. Use your voice as a gauge. Can you handle singing your music every night? Use your fan base as a gauge. Do you think of them as friends? It's vital that you constantly assess your heart as a singer. I once suggested to a Heavy Metal client of mine that he try Country Music. He had a great voice but something was missing. Turns out he was only singing Metal because his brother's band needed a vocalist. Now that he's switched to Country, his voice sounds like it's found a home. That's the difference between singing for a living and living to sing.

—Mark Baxter: acclaimed vocal coach with Aerosmith, Journey, Goo Goo Dolls and many others

Action 2: Improve Your Product

Some simple experiments can put you on the road to being a great musician.

Authentic emotion is key to great singing. Yet, if you want your listener to truly experience the emotion you've expressed, you have to sing in tune and in time. Poor intonation and poor timing can distract your audience and make them miss your message. If you want to be an excellent singer, always challenge yourself as a musician, starting with these two skills. Here are two deliberately tricky training exercises you can use to find out just how slick —or sloppy—you are with pitch and time.

> *Every singer should have a set up to record themselves at home. As a singer or songwriter, your home studio is your musical kitchen.*
>
> ***—Darrell Smith***

First, get out your metronome app. Make sure you can fade the volume right down to nothing while the beat still continues. Start clapping to the beat—be perfectly precise. Now have a friend fade out the volume for about a minute, while you keep clapping. Then have your friend fade the volume back up to see if you are still clapping precisely on the beat. Make sure a ticking clock isn't throwing you off. Choose a relaxed tempo, such as 63 BPM. You can make this more challenging with slower tempos and for longer stretches.

Here is a similar exercise to challenge your sense of pitch. Choose a song for which you know the starting and ending notes. Play your starting note on a piano or even a keyboard app, then sing your song a cappella (with no instrument but your voice). When you get to the end, play your final note to see if the note you are singing matches it. If you are off pitch, start at the beginning again, this time checking your sung pitch against the actual pitch at the end of each phrase. As soon as you find a phrase where you are not perfectly in tune, try to find the exact spot where you went off. Try to hear that starting note as a constant reference in your mind, against which every note you sing can be compared. Make sure you are singing free of tension, and with healthy technique (see chapter 10). Even singers with a great ear can sometimes go off-key because of poor technique. You may need to take an extra breath in certain spots. Make sure your room is silent. Even a slight buzz or hum from a fridge can interfere. Work on each wavering phrase until you can sing whole sections—even the whole song—in tune with no pitch reference.

—Kathy Alexander: singer, vocal coach and staff writer at VoiceCouncil Magazine

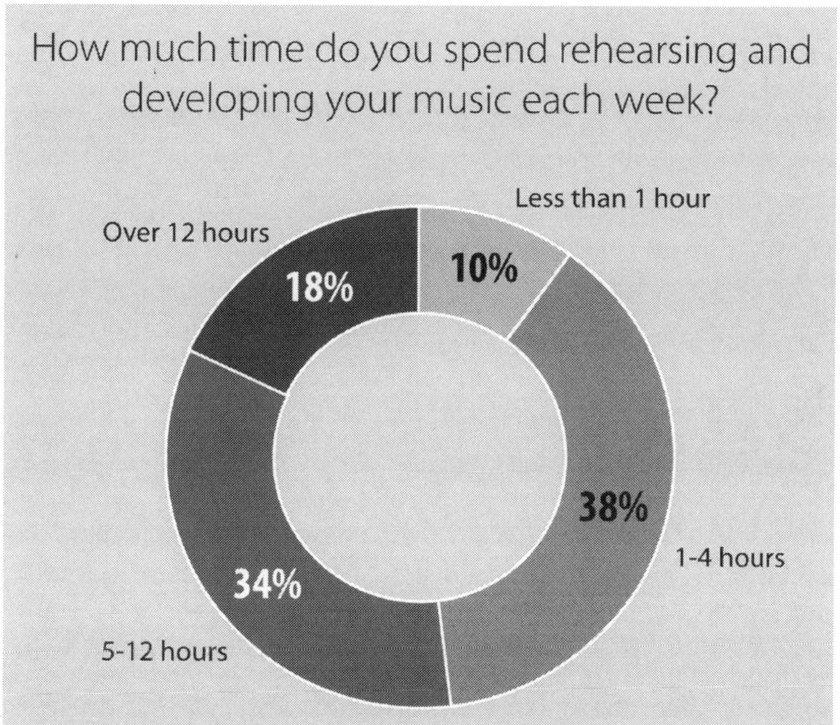

Teacher's pet?
Those who spend over 12 hours per week rehearsing their music report connecting more with their audience (14% higher than the group as a whole).

—from the 2012-2013 TC-Helicon survey of 1,000 singers

Action 3: Evolve Your Identity

There's no mystery about how to get people "hooked" on you, your music and your style.

There is a deeper question behind the issue of finding one's unique musical tastes: how do you become more of an individual? In fact, by addressing this larger question, your music may evolve more easily.

After all, your unique musical sound is just one aspect of your self-expression; fashion, thinking and lifestyle are others. So, it's absolutely critical that you take steps toward who you really are. One of the ways you can do this is to make sure that you surround yourself with people who feed your individuality and creativity—whether that means going out to night clubs, hanging around music stores or being in nature, looking at the stars, sunsets, or taking a walk in the park.

Be alert to all of the ideas and styles around you. When you are walking down the street, take note of the fashions you see and what you are drawn to. It's the same with music—expose yourself to as much music as you can and then take a step back and ask "what really works for me?"

On your path to uniqueness get comfortable with being uncomfortable. In other words, allow yourself to be drawn to places a part of you wants to be, but part of you feels uncomfortable with, whether an underground night club, vibey coffee shop, dance class or expensive clothing store. Then, embrace that awkward feeling—notice it and don't run away from it. Be comfortable with being uncomfortable. In time you'll find the awkwardness subsides from the familiarity of it, until you allow yourself to enter the next unfamiliar situation and begin again the cycle of expanding your world.

I remember entering music clubs where I felt completely out of place. I really thought that everyone was cooler than me, danced better than me, and looked better than me. Then, I simply acknowledged this feeling and told myself, "I will stay here and expect to feel uncomfortable." Over time, of course, I became more comfortable.

On a deeper level, if you are truly working toward individuality, you will always feel a little uncomfortable. But once you embrace the idea of being different you'll start to realize that there are so many other amazing people who are also different. You begin to gravitate to these truly inspiring and visionary individuals, who feed these qualities in yourself. You come to a place where you understand that being different is what you share.

At the same time, you'll discover that your music will have developed its own unique sound and path.

—Dot Bustelo: internationally recognized music producer and music technology strategist

Action 4: Understand and Target Your Venue

It's time to find a venue with a good stylistic fit. Know who's in charge of your booking and what they need to make their venue work.

In the past, many venues were often willing to join your efforts in promoting your show. That can still be the case, but often you really have to convince them that you are absolutely willing to promote the ass off your show!

My advice is to be crystal clear with the venue about what you are going to do to get people to the show—how you will use Facebook, Twitter, other forms of social media and advertising, traditional flyers, etc. Let them know about what you have achieved in doing this elsewhere and how many "friends"/connections you have. Show the venue that you have something special to offer: talk up what you are doing, who you are connected to and what a great night it will be.

Be aware that promoters in venues do not usually want to part with upfront fees for booking you and your band. What they often offer are door splits. This means that you will reach an agreement on a percentage of the door charge that you will receive. For instance, if the door charge is five dollars, you might agree that they get 2.50 and you get 2.50 for each entry. You might arrange a more favorable door fee—perhaps a 80%—20% split in your favor in return for something extra that you might provide. For instance, you might cover the price of their security or sound engineer. Don't pussyfoot around the money issues. After all, everyone would be happy to have you turn up and sing for free.

> *Do some research by attending lots of shows. Make sure your music and your "brand" are a good fit for the new venue you are pursuing. You want an opportunity that will challenge you but also let you show off what you do best. Then you have to find out who books the bands, and how to get your demo and resume in their hands.*
>
> ***—Gerald White:*** *prolific singer-songwriter who has worked on over 100 TV and commercial productions*

Venues want to feel that by having you perform they have something that is special in comparison to other venues. This is why I will often mention to venues that I will not be performing anywhere locally on that day—or that week. In fact, I will often do just one event in that area so that the venue can feel more confident about filling the space.

You are making a commitment to the venue, but don't forget that they need to make a commitment to you—so be clear about what you need. You want to see all of your details on their website and social media channels with links through to your band. Establish your flat fee or door fee and let them know of any other requirements you may have. If you are coming from out of town, you may need a hot meal and a dressing room. Of course, all of this depends on what level of venue you are in—some may only give you water. But perhaps you can negotiate some free drinks? You'll want to know about the procedure for loading your gear, the power available on stage—don't be afraid to ask these questions.

—Laura Vane, singer-songwriter of Laura Vane & The Vipertones

Action 5: Pick Your Battles

There are some times when the singer just can't bend—be certain to know when those times are.

It doesn't matter if you are Madonna or someone in a band just starting out: there is a way to talk to people—with respect. There's no need to act like a diva. Your band is like a family and, if there's a situation in a family, you try to sit down and talk it through.

As a singer my monitor is my lifesaver—I just have to hear it fully. I set up my monitor just off center from my drummer, slightly to the right or left so that his drums are bypassing my monitor. I also ask the bass player to turn his amp out a little more to the audience, so it isn't coming over into my space—and the same with the guitarist. If you have a really tiny stage you don't need anything more than your voice in that monitor. If you are on a big stage you might choose to have a little bit of the mix in the monitor. At the end of the day your vocal is what you need.

***—Nikki Lamborn:** singer-songwriter of the English band "Never the Bride"*

There is usually someone who is better than others at instigating this discussion: "I think we all need to sit down and talk." It has to be done thoughtfully and diplomatically so that no one person feels they are being pointed at. You don't want to say "Let's all sit down and talk about Johnny's drumming." Diplomatically bring things to the table, ask people how they feel and ask, "How can we fix it?" Give people the opportunity to generate answers.

Still, there are several areas where I will not hesitate to put my foot down.

The first is playing too loudly. If things are too loud, you begin to over-sing and mess up your voice. I tell the boys, "Look, we have to stop a minute and sort this out. If we can't hear each other, then we can't be a team. It is about throwing the ball so that someone can catch it and shine. It is not about getting up there and turning the volume up."

"Look, you have an amp and you can turn it up ... and up. You have a guitar that plugs into it and you can turn it up ... and up. You can break a string and you can just put a new one on. Or, if you whack the drums and break a skin, you can get a new one. But I can't do that with my voice. If you guys don't bring your volume down, I will be in surgery and out of commission for a year."

If you go and watch some great bands (Eagles, Fleetwood Mac, the Stones) you will see them working together, eyeballing each other all the time. You get a sense that they are enjoying working together with their music. Just watch any of your musical idols, and you will see this team experience at work.

There's another area where I'll put my foot down. It's just not cool to come onto stage with a can of lager and a cigarette; it isn't cool to come on pissed. Even Axl Rose can't get away with it. I had to fire a bass player—we had a 42-date tour and, with only three dates to go, he came onto the stage drunk. When you're drunk the first sense that goes is your hearing and you start to push louder and harder in order to compensate. This throws the entire performance off. Not only that, it's disrespectful to the rest of the band.

Also be firm on showing up on time for gigs and sound checks; make sure you have someone whose job it is to ensure that you all get to places on time. Never miss a sound check or be late for setting up for a gig. If someone is continually late for rehearsals or sound check it comes to the point that someone has to name this as disrespectful behaviour—we actually fined someone in the band 10 dollars for every 30 minutes they were late.

—Nikki Lamborn: singer-songwriter of the English band "Never the Bride"

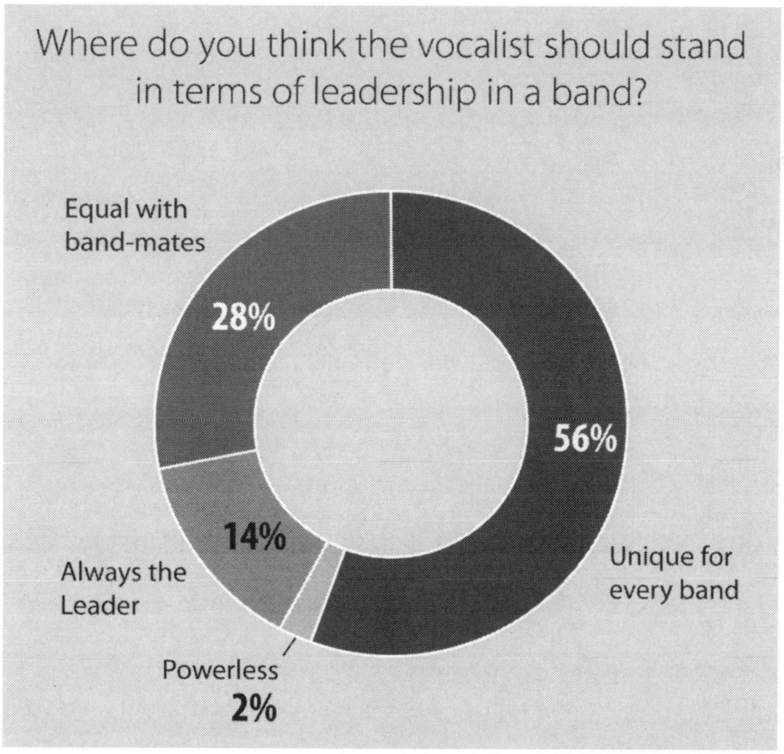

—from the 2012-2013 TC-Helicon survey of 1,000 singers

Action 6: Commit to the "Hustle"

It's time to go back to all of that stuff in Gigs 101—but this time you're "upping your game."

I've been gigging in New York City for three years—putting in a lot of hustle—and it all paid off recently. An artist who was booked for the "Late Night Groove" series at The Blue Note (my dream venue!) had to cancel and asked me to fill in. How did that artist know me? Through a $50 gig I've been doing every week at a lesser-known venue. The show went well, but that's just the beginning. My next step is to go back with my own show. I left my CD with the guy at the door. He said he'd talk to the bookings guy. I'll send email after email. I'll show up. I'll remind them that I've been there as a special guest. I'll make phone calls. This is how I will make it happen.

> *Send links instead of files in an email to someone in the music business. Write a concise paragraph saying the most significant things you have done in the last three months, and/or major career highlights.*
>
> ***—Emily Braden:*** *award winning New York City jazz singer*

Whether it's a new venue, an agent or any new contact you want to work with, you have to be persistent. Don't overdo it, just keep showing up on their radar. This is part of the "hustle" of being an independent artist—whatever your music, whatever your city.

Follow up from all angles: email, phone and show up. Top venues like The Blue Note in NYC often have showcases specifically for up-and-coming artists, but they are totally overwhelmed with emails. You have to actually show up, give them your CD and talk to them.

I started in NYC with small gigs (often paying me nothing or only $50). Through those gigs, I met some great musicians and was heard by people who then recommended me to others. It took a year or two longer than I expected, but that's how I've built it up.

Another part of the hustle is keeping my promo materials up-to-date. I always try to have a video on YouTube. After any significant gig or musical achievement, I update my bio, send out an email to my mailing list and post photos from the event online. Always gotta keep it current!

I'm prepared to hustle as much as it takes, but there is one enemy I have to be aware of: burn-out. I want to have this career when I'm 50 years old, which is why, at some point, I need to hire a team, starting with a booking agent, with the right skills and knowledge to do more for my business than I could do on my own.

—Emily Braden: award winning New York City Jazz Singer

Action 7: Build Your Fanbase

Employing different strategies for each type of fan will see your fan base grow more rapidly.

The real work of building your fan base begins even before the live gig happens—it doesn't have to cost a penny to promote yourself online. Don't just post the dates of your gig on your website; no one is hanging out there. Go to where they are: on the social networks; tell them on Facebook and Twitter where you are going to be—and when.

Perhaps you are opening for another band—or are a part of five acts on a larger bill—that's four other databases you can tap into! Simply post: "I can't wait to play with Band X on Saturday at X venue at X time." Tag Band X so that it shows up on their Twitter feed and their fans can see it. There's a good shot that some of these fans will come and check you out since they will already be at the venue.

> *Don't forget that there are people who are willing to pay for what you play—you may not be able to demand the price that you want, but don't assume you always have to play for free.*
>
> ***—Danielle Ate the Sandwich:** nationally recognized independent folk musician*

At the gig, especially if it is a smaller venue, make sure that everyone leaves with something that is free: a leaflet, a download card—or some other form of online promotional access.

I've just returned from The Rock Boat, a cruise in the Bahamas with 35 bands. We printed up "Do Not Disturb" door hangers, making these kind of "jokey": "Do not disturb because A) we are hung over, B) we're busy giving the band a massage, C) ... "—you get the point. On the backside of the hanger we put the band's website, release dates and an address to go to for a free download. You always want people leaving with a reason to come back later.

When you are onstage, interact in ways that will create an effect after the show is over. I have one artist who, just before his last song, brings the house lights up so that he can take a picture of the crowd. People love this! Then he says, "I will be posting this picture on Facebook—make sure you find it and tag yourself." The fans want to see themselves on his page and when they tag themselves it comes up on the newsfeeds of all of their friends!

You can come up with your own ways to be interactive—but don't forget: at the end of the day your fans are the greatest promotional team you'll ever have.

—Chris Maltese, artist manager, formerly a senior producer for MTV

Action 8: Harness the Power of Your Fans

Some of your fans will want to help you reach your goals—so, involve them.

"Is there anything I can do to help?" This question came from one of my first fans in LA at a time when I had very few fans and very little help. My answer was a resounding "yes"! I needed my bio-cards handed out, help with setting up equipment and help spreading the word about my next gigs.

Working with fans has become the centerpiece of all that I do. Now, my work with fans goes far beyond helping me out at gigs and includes social media, websites, moderating my forums, making important connections, sponsoring recording sessions and even hosting concerts. I have something I call my "V-Team." It is made up of fans who want to give their time in specific ways to help my business and my art.

The key to maintaining healthy relationships with fans is to offer different levels of involvement. People should be able to "plug in" to your musical journey in ways that they feel are most appropriate, and with commitment levels that suit their lives. Some people merely want to feel a part of a musical community. Some people want to do much more.

It is also important to line up your fans' passions and interests with what you are doing. Think through the different areas of your singing life and where you want to go. Think through how you could put your fans to work to help you to reach those goals. Remember: always be clear about what the commitment is and when it ends.

Don't be caught off guard by the fact that certain fans will actually want to help you. There will always be people who are drawn to you and your music. Many of them will want to get involved with what you are doing. You just have to recognize these supporters and be proactive.

–Marina V, award-winning Russian-American singer/pianist/songwriter.

Action 9: Use Social Media to Make Your Gigs Succeed

Whether it's Facebook or Twitter, harness your potential to reach and keep your fans.

Many people you want to come to your gig also have 500 friends on Facebook.

This means that if a single individual is personally engaged and excited about your music then 500 more people could know about it–without you having to contact those 500 people.

This fact underscores the value of one meaningful personal contact. Here's an example of an email or Facebook message that a singer might write to a friend about their gig (not a status update): "Hey, I know it's been a little while since we've talked but I wanted to let you know that

I have this new band and we're going to be playing a gig at ... it's a cool place and I really think you'll like it. I'd love to see you there and if you know anyone who is into this kind of music, I'd really appreciate you letting them know."

This is a one-by-one way of reaching out that can easily translate into you reaching the critical mass that you need at your gig. Your venue may have space for 100–200 people and if every member of your band takes this personal approach, you could see the room packed.

If your music is good, people will want to come, but you may need to offer some incentives because it's early in the game. This may involve announcing a contest or a draw. When I started off with my band, Soulvation, we would talk to the bar owner and work out a drinks special—bar owners are usually able to play ball with this because they want to get people into the venue as well. The drinks special you've worked out (or the giveaway, quiz, contest ...) then becomes a focus in your communication with fans and friends.

Combine your personal approach with a general approach by following up all of those personal messages with general announcements—reminders of your gig all the way up to the date. There's nothing wrong with general messages as long as you have the personal approach with it.

Some people have success with tweeting. Here it is the same: a personal message followed by general announcements. People are likely to re-tweet a piece of interesting news if you've already reached them with a personal message. Social media is always about being social.

I know one singer who has built up a huge following. It's not because he's signed to a big label and has a platinum album, but because he always takes the time to reach out and write. Of course he has talent, but the reason for his success is that he is a super friendly guy with talent; he gives a damn about reaching out to people in a positive and personal way.

—Clifford Schwartz, President and Co-Founder of NuMuBu, the global music industry network

Action 10: Don't Ignore Local Power

You may not need to skip town in order to make the "big time." Local opportunities such as radio time, festivals and house concerts can make a huge difference.

You must gain a following in your own town before you can hope to build a following elsewhere. This requires being a part of your local music scene both as an audience member and as a performer. For me this process didn't involve getting paid for quite a long time. I sang at open mics which eventually led to gigs at local hip hop clubs, which eventually led to opening for bigger hip hop artists (many of whom were my idols!). On one occasion, I drew a bigger crowd than the headlining artist, many of whom left after my set. This is when people actually started to call ME (it used to be the other way around) about gigs, and of course this is when I started getting paid as well.

Tapping into the power of your local community goes beyond just the music venues, however. Live music is often required for charity events, corporate events and other community happenings, such as the opening of a hospital, or a summer fair. Singing at these events not only introduces you to potential fans who might not come out to clubs, but they often pay much more than the clubs. You might be surprised that even charity gigs often have a sizable budget for entertainment.

Giving back to the people who have supported me is very important to me. I recently raised money to fund a music program in my old hometown where all of the music programs were being cut. I offered to do concerts, plus I used connections in the tourism industry to garner valuable donations for a silent auction. I raised $22,000 in under two weeks. This allowed me to hire my former kindergarten teacher to direct a community children's choir that has recently performed their first concert! Now I know that those children have an opportunity to learn about music like I did when I was young.

For me, connecting to people in my immediate community is about more than building a career—it is the whole point of being a singer. I'm always hungry to learn about people and find a way to connect with them through music. The power of human connection is strongest with the people who are right in front of me. I can give something to them through my singing, and what I get in return is much more—it's beautiful.

—Georgia Murray, singer-songwriter, nominated for Urban Recording of the Year

Frequently Asked Questions

> When do I say no to a gig?

Answered by Tim Howar, of "Mike and the Mechanics," currently starring in "Rock of Ages"

I have a friend who says that as soon as he can answer "yes" to two out of these three questions, he will do the gig:

1. Are you getting paid?
2. Are you learning something new by doing this?
3. Are you sharing something that is unique to you?

You can interpret "pay" flexibly—I once received rights to a musical arrangement as "payment" for singing at a wedding. I've had a long-lasting relationship with the arranger and it is a killer arrangement that I have used since. In terms of learning something new: I may sometimes accept a gig for no pay if it gets me working with gifted people I want to have a connection with. Of course, as singers, we always want to give something of ourselves to a performance—and have it mean something to the audience. Go for two out of three. In other words, if you are not sharing, learning or getting paid, forget the gig.

Now let's go to a deeper level: you also have to trust your gut reaction. When you trust your gut instinct, you are coming from a place that is real—not manufactured or fake. If, deep inside yourself, you feel that this is the wrong gig, then you have to say "no." Remember: life doesn't stop when you say "no."

Let's say you said "no" and then realized later that it should have been a "yes." It happens. Don't be afraid of mistakes. In our hyper-concerned-to-be-right state we actually miss the deeper insights and realizations that come to us when we've made a "wrong" turn. A mistake is simply the soil in which you plant a seed. Move on and create new opportunities. If one bridge is burnt—find other bridges.

Think of when your first romantic relationship went bad. Let's see: how many people are there on the planet? Seven billion. There are a lot of men or women you could have a relationship with—so pick yourself up and start meeting them. It's the same with gigs.

> Should I stick it out with this band or branch out?

Answered by Ron "Bumblefoot" Thal, Lead guitarist, Guns N' Roses, solo artist and producer

If a certain band doesn't give you something, then another group on the side will. You need to have a way to get everything out of yourself musically that needs to get out. This is why having more than one project on the go is helpful. Fulltime musicians would consider this normal.

No one band can be everything for everyone. With Guns 'N' Roses, I get to headline festivals with audiences of 100,000. I love it, but I don't get to sing very much. I get to sing lead in my solo shows where I can also play all the melodic guitar lines I want and enjoy the most musical freedom. Tony Harnell's acoustic shows give me a chance to sing harmony, be spontaneous (we often play unrehearsed songs that the audience calls out) and show up with no gear other than my acoustic guitar. I get something different out of each situation.

Let's say your band is not quite as metal as you want; you can have a group on the side that is hard-core metal. This will allow you to feel more complete, unless of course you are involved in an all-encompassing project that demands your devotion 24 hours a day, in which case a side project wouldn't work.

With commitments to more than one band, there can be insecurities and hurt feelings. The guys from one band might say, "You put more time into that other band than this one!" Everyone views a situation differently; for some, you can tell them until you are blue in the face that they are your main band and it won't be enough. We all have baggage, and we can't try to change other people. They feel how they feel. As long as you have a way of juggling both commitments and are honest with each group, you've done all you can.

> At what point should I record an album?

Answered by Jay Frank, leading author (Hack Your Hit and Futurehit.DNA) and Owner/CEO of DigSin

I always tell emerging artists that thinking in terms of recording an "album" as an initial activity is absolutely the wrong thing to do. I could spend hours detailing all of the promotional and financial reasons for this, but in the interest of time, let me go right to the main reason. People are consuming music these days song by song—not album by album. This means that you have the opportunity to get valuable feedback as to what songs work best for you. If you rush ahead and make ten songs and put them into an album, then you've missed out on the golden opportunity of making one song and then getting feedback that could help you improve your efforts and increase your chances of success.

> Do I need an agent?

Answered by Lori Maier, Founder and Executive Director of Chick Singer Night

My answer is, "yes," if the work of promoting and booking yourself becomes unmanageable or takes too much energy away from your creative process. But here's the catch: when someone else represents you, you are no longer in control of how you present yourself in the music industry. Your agent must have a clear idea of who you are as an artist, the kinds of opportunities you want to pursue and how to present you in the best light.

I never hired an agent because I like to be in control of the tone and style of my communications with a venue manager or producer. I found that I had the skills and training to manage my own bookings without jeopardising my creative energy.

The reality for many singers, however, is that this work can become too much to manage on one's own. Agents go after bookings on your behalf. They choose where you play and who you might share the stage with. This can be an enormous help, as long as they know how to choose situations that compliment you and that move your career in the direction you want.

Whether you choose an agent who is an industry veteran with hundreds of contacts, or a trusted friend, he or she must understand you as an artist. They must understand what your ideal gig looks like, and what kind of compromises you are willing to tolerate along the way. A single-minded agent may ignore your artistic goals in favor of filling up your week. If you are a folk artist and your agent books you at a dance club, the experience could be disheartening and disappointing for everyone.

I could talk about many more important skills your agent should possess, but one tip I will leave you with is this: above all else, choose an agent who believes in you 100%.

> Why didn't the venue ask me back?

Answered by Lori Maier, Founder and Executive Director of Chick Singer Night

It is generally the artist's job to pursue the next gig with a venue. Do this by contacting the same person you dealt with when you made the booking, using the same form of communication you used prior to the gig (email, phone, in person).

Make sure you do this follow up on the day after your gig or shortly thereafter. Your job is to show the venue manager how thrilled you were to perform there and that you are eager to do it again. You must keep reminding them that you exist and that you are available. Maybe another act will cancel three months from now. If you have been in touch a few times since your gig, they just might call you to fill in.

If the person who booked you was at your gig (which is not always the case), consider asking for feedback as part of your follow-up. "Do you have any advice on how we can improve for next time?"

Getting your next gig will certainly be easier if you do a great job on the first one. This means making an impact with your music and your infectious energy. It also means treating the staff with respect and showing that you care about those who support the event. There will be times when the staff are not as accommodating as you'd like—this is not necessarily a reflection on you—so stay the course and be appreciative and gracious.

Once you have a critical mass of people buying your music, a buzz that has really taken off, and a fan base that is so locked-in that they will drive distances to see you, you may find that some venues will start to call you back. That will be a great moment, but until then, be prepared to do whatever it takes to be remembered and land that next gig.

> How do I find more cool songs?

Answered by Jaime Vendera, vocal coach renowned for his wineglass-shattering voice

It all begins with your favorite songs/singers. Right now, grab a pen and paper and write down your top five bands. Now, for each band, write your #1 favorite song on the list. Now, pick a different song from each band, one that you feel you can easily sing, (sometimes we pick great songs that we may not yet be able to tackle). Personally, I would pick Led Zeppelin. I love the song "Friends," but I just don't do it justice like "Babe I'm Gonna Leave You" or "Immigrant Song." So, I would probably pick "Friends" and "Babe" for my two songs for one of my bands. When you have your ten songs, review the list. Are these five bands in the style you would want to write? If not, ask yourself the following question:

"If I was booked to tour five different times, opening up for five different bands, what five bands would my style fit?"

This could reveal that you'll need to swap out one or two of the bands to fit the style you're going for. After you have the final five (two songs from each band) add the ten songs to a playlist on your smart phone or MP3 player. Begin listening and singing along to these ten songs every day. Eventually, you'll discover how your voice differs vocally, having its own unique tone and style. I guarantee that this will begin to help you unlock your own voice. But there's more: doing this will help you begin writing your own music!

> Should I concentrate on originals or covers?

Answered by Tim Howar, of "Mike and the Mechanics," currently starring in "Rock of Ages."

Don't drop doing covers. Your creative edge is not only forged in writing original music, but in interpreting existing music. So, stretch yourself vocally by exposing yourself to some of the great interpreters of music: Tony Bennett, Rod Stewart, Ella Fitzgerald, Amy Winehouse ... Each of these developed their own sound through their unique take on the songs that came their way. You could hear a million people sing "Tell It Like It Is," but there is only one Aaron Neville. That's it.

So, stick with those covers, but pick ones that are really suited to you, your soul, your voice and your range. Allow yourself to interpret these songs in your own way—and evaluate your interpretations by recording yourself and listening to what you are doing. This is tough to do! How you sound in your head is always so different than what people are hearing outside of your body. You may have an "Oh my God" moment of not sounding as you'd like, but keep at it, listen to your interpretations, take note of what you are doing that is unique and cool and grow into a great interpreter of music.

AND slip your original music into your show. You need to have faith in your own songs. If you believe in your music and its message, then others will too. Just remember to not expect every original to be a hit. Even the great artists have their "B" songs. But your hits grow out of the foundation of all of your originals.

Let's bring this full circle: don't separate your writing from the covers you love. Sometimes you need a muse, someone to inspire you—those great, big melodies that you love will inspire you to write. In fact, one path to writing great originals is to write them for your favorite singer: Adele, James Morrison, Amy Winehouse, Steven Tyler—whomever it is.

> How can we make our rehearsals more effective?

Answered by Gerald Klickstein, veteran guitarist, educator and author of The Musician's Way

When we practice in groups, our success hinges on more than our musical abilities. Our ensemble culture, interpersonal skills, and rehearsal strategies also determine whether we accomplish much or little in any practice session. Here are 10 tips for better group rehearsals.

1. Commit to Professionalism. Agree to be punctual, prepared for, and courteous at rehearsals.
2. Get Organized. Smart organizing helps minimize conflict and frees us to focus on art-making. For those reasons, collectively agree to a rehearsal schedule and specify your objectives in advance.
3. Set Reachable Goals. Our rehearsals crackle with intensity when we target them toward motivating, near-term goals. So, choose manageable music, and then conclude each rehearsal with plans for the next one.
4. Begin Rehearsals with Communal Material. Instead of starting with unfamiliar music, run through a favorite tune or excerpt that renews your musical bonds.
5. Rehearse Strategically. Use varying techniques to tighten up your execution and bring your music to life.
6. Communicate. During rehearsals, try out collaborators' ideas before commenting on them. Listen attentively, critique tactfully, and admit when you mess up. Still, limit verbal exchanges. Aim to reach consensus through musical more than verbal interaction. When thorny non-musical issues surface, set up separate meetings.
7. Balance Leading with Listening. Inspire each other by listening and responding to your spontaneous musical gestures.
8. Transmit Positive Energy. Personal energy is contagious, especially in the close-knit setting of an ensemble. We uplift our colleagues when we keep up senses of humor and broadcast enthusiasm.
9. Help Each Other Succeed. Let your co-performers know that you value their talents, and strive to be easy to work with. Respect personal differences, and, when conflicts emerge, treat them as opportunities for your group to attain greater synergy.

10. Keep Art at the Core. All ensembles face difficulties. Personalities can chafe, opinions diverge, and priorities shift. But you can surmount troubles by steadfastly applying these and other ideas in service to your art. Most of all, in rehearsals and on stage, reinforce your bonds through wholehearted musical expression.

> I don't have an interesting story for my bio.

Answered by Marina V, award-winning Russian-American singer, pianist and songwriter

It is all too easy to think that others' stories are more important than our own. Lay this kind of thinking aside—it's defeatist! It may be that you have grown complacent about your own story, or have forgotten how your challenges and successes are relevant to others. To turn this around, you have to think of what you've accomplished, what you are most grateful for, and find those little quirks or details in your journey that are of interest to others.

In my case, I came from Russia to America—so that journey is always in my bio. I also include the fact that I have a long last name and red hair. What is unique about your own journey? Perhaps you are a twin, or you were bullied as a child, or maybe something quirky—like you never saw *Star Wars*! There are many people who will find these details interesting.

To find out which parts of your story are most interesting to others, you have to do a little experimenting at your gigs. Whether it's a short sentence or a whole story, try talking about your journey in between your songs and take note of what interests people the most. You will see that by sharing aspects of your story and your struggles, you help people to understand you—this will help them connect to you and your music.

Don't forget your musical story. As a gigging vocalist, you are a part of a musical movement: your own. That's pretty interesting in a hum-drum world of bureaucracy and bill paying. Share your current musical goals—these are part of your story too. Even if you have only one gig lined up in the next six months, get the word out. Share what you are planning to do at the concert. If you are recording a CD, that needs to be shared too. At your gigs, with your friends and through the web, tell people about your journey—musical and personal.

> Should I go on a tour?

Answered by Chris Henderson, singer-songwriter-guitarist of Bronze Radio Return

If you handle things right on the local level, you can open some great doors to touring. First, though, you have to know about the catch-22 around playing local shows. On the one hand you could argue that you should do as many local shows as possible. After all, you want to be out there performing and showing that you are active. This also has the advantage of tightening up your band through playing more. On the other hand, you could be over-saturating your market; your frequent shows could be less well attended and have less energy.

What we've decided to do is to play in our home market once a month rather than eight times a month. This has the advantage of turning our show into more of an event for our fans instead of having eight watered down, low-energy crowds. In terms of marketing, you have to work the angle that if people miss this show it will be a long time before the next one. You kick in your social media outreach and other promotional tools and you make your local show as big as possible.

Once you have one bigger show, you have a piece of the pie that is attractive to other bands. Let's say that you want to play in the next biggest city to you, one that is an hour away (that keeps your traveling costs down). You could reach out to a band and say, "We'd love to come and share your show and then, in return, you can play to our crowd." Now you have just expanded your market—this is way more sustainable than picking eight cities at random and trying to make a tour work. Doing this also honors the idea of music as an inclusive team sport—everyone is benefitting.

If the band is much bigger than you, but doesn't have a fan base in your town, they may be very interested in coming to your town and having you open for them. It's another line on your resume and another chance to make more connections.

How do you find these other bands? The internet is a wonderful resource. You can look at any town, find the active venues and learn about the bands playing there. You can simply find lists of bands on a club's website—then open another browser window and look at the Facebook and Twitter activity of those bands in order to judge how popular they are. Out of 100 bands, you might find 10 that you feel have potential to be a good fit to share a show with you—shoot out a message to them.

When you are promoting these shows, make your social networking creative and engaging. We did one video with us all in a bathtub wearing shower caps talking about our upcoming show—people re-posted this. Get away from generic messages such as "come to our show." The posts that go the longest way are always cool and unique.

CHAPTER 3

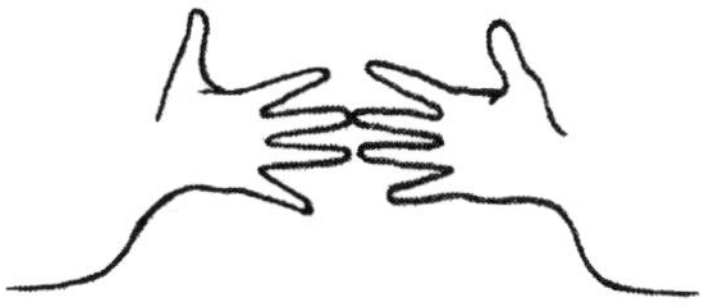

Promo and Web Tools

Use them, own them and unleash the power of your fans.

"I celebrate the fall of the traditional gatekeepers (the major labels) because they were doing a lousy job of making the cream rise to the top."

—Brian Felsen, President of CDBaby, BookBaby and HostBaby

"Think of social networks as a place where your future fans are already hanging out."

—Bryan Kim, Director of Business Development at Tracksby / Hipset

Promo and Web Tools

Use them, own them and unleash the power of your fans.

Actions:

1. Unleash Your #1 Asset
2. Interact or Die
3. Harness the Power of Your Website
4. Make an Impact with Your Videos
5. Get More "Friends" on Your Social Networks
6. Make Your Online Music Take Off
7. Bring the Stage to Your Page
8. Don't Forget the Old Fashioned Stuff
9. Steer Clear of These Promo FAILS

Frequently Asked Questions:

- » *Why do some people get 30,000 hits on their YouTube vids when I get 300?*
- » *How do you deal with a bad comment at a concert or on a website?*
- » *I tweet, post pics on Facebook and update my status, but it seems that no one is watching ...*
- » *So many websites out there look dead—how can I keep mine alive?*
- » *Is social media just a fancy distraction for my career?*
- » *People seem to like my songs, so why don't I have more fans?*
- » *What is the secret to getting my BIO statement read?*
- » *Should I invest in an MTV-quality music vid?*
- » *OK I get it that social media is important. So, how do I get going with a successful strategy?*
- » *How can I make a good YouTube video when I'm not a technical person?*
- » *Should I pay for my promotion? What should I pay for?*

Action 1: Unleash Your #1 Asset

Everyone starts with one fan—not everyone unleashes him or her to find more ...

You are driving down the road and you see this huge billboard that says, "We have the best burgers in town! You've got to taste these!" If you're like most people, this probably won't mean anything to you. Now compare that experience to this: your best friend calls you and says, "You're not going to believe this; I just tasted the best burger in my life–you've got to come and try this with me."

Why is word of mouth the most effective advertising? Because we respond to people we trust. It's not about someone on the radio or TV telling us to do something–it is about our friends. Here is the main point: singers and bands create word-of-mouth advertising by creating an atmosphere for fans to want to talk about them.

> *My greatest publicity is people telling their friends—word of mouth. That kind of process feels genuine and true, though it can be a slow ladder to climb.*
>
> ***–Danielle Ate the Sandwich:*** *nationally recognized independent folk musician*

There are three main areas where you can create this atmosphere–through your own discussions with fans (live and online), through a product that connects to them (like your music) or through great live shows. You want all three working for you. At the end of the day you need to give your fans a reason to talk about you to all of their other friends.

We all know artists who have had ONE big song but then they soon fade from view. What this means is that people fell in love with the song, but not the artist. Your job is to make sure that your fans fall in love with YOU. Once you have a fan base who loves you at least as much as your songs, then you have a career. You will also notice that there are some artists who can put out any song and it will sell because they have fans who love them.

Your job is to create artist-fans not just song-fans. This will take connecting with your fans on more levels than just the song–this idea is key to your growth–and this chapter will help you figure this out.

–Chris Maltese, artist manager, formerly a senior producer for MTV

Action 2: Interact or Die

Even one fan needs something to see, hear, watch, read and respond to.

I know a musician who makes a classic error. He spends a lot of time sending generic messages and status updates that are little more than links: "please post this, I'm going to be doing a gig—check out the info at www.etc." I get these kinds of notifications regularly and delete all of them without looking at the link.

However, this kind of message is appreciated: "Hi Cliff, really enjoyed the new video you posted. Hey, for your next evening out, consider coming to my gig. I am actually going to have a contest where we will be giving away a CD, poster and t-shirt! We are going to be playing at … let me know if you're coming and I'll make sure that …" This is interaction—you are showing that you care enough about people to say something to them individually. This takes work; you cannot do it en-masse. But consider this: you can send out 500 generic posts/updates/emails and have no-one come to your gig and you can send out 50 personal messages and have 30 people come. Do the math.

> *I don't share with people what I had for breakfast or that I'm heading to the gym—too many of these silly meaningless "window into your life" tweets will turn people off—you'll be ignored by your potential followers. Remember the old story about "the boy who cried wolf." Just share the important stuff!*
>
> **—Elliott Randall:** *legendary guitarist, formerly a musical consultant for Saturday Night Live*

Without personal interaction you can forget about marketing on social media. I always say social media is about being social, not anti social. Banner ads don't cut it; people don't trust them. And simply announcing things doesn't cut it either. However, if someone is your friend, they will be more interested in what you have to say—or announce.

In social media marketing, the concept of "what you give, you get back" really works beautifully. One has to give in order to receive in society, and nowhere is this more true than with social media.

Of course it's critical that you start by building up your database of email addresses, "friends" and "likes." You need to make a concerted effort to gather this information at every gig—this can happen by literally standing at the door and asking people to share their address with you so that they can get some interesting news and updates on your performances. Or, you can pass around a pen and paper during the gig. These traditional ways of signing people up really work. Or, you can walk around with a smart phone and ask people to like your page on the spot.

Here is something that has really worked for a number of musicians I know: announce a contest during your gig in which people like your Facebook page in return for a great prize. The contest giveaway could be that you will bring your live musical performance to their house for a house concert. Contests are big motivators. The result of the contest also makes for great news for you to share on your social media; it shows that you follow through on your promises and care about your fans.

> *I heard about a web designer who lived under a flight path of an airport, and painted his website address on his roof!*
>
> ***—Laura Vane:*** *singer-songwriter of Laura Vane & The Vipertones*

Finally, stay positive in all of your interaction. It is never a good idea to trash anyone—even if it's justified. You attract more flies with honey than vinegar. Even if you are a thrash metal punk band that makes a living by hating the world, keep that hate on stage and out of your social media. When you are both personal and positive, everyone wins.

—Clifford Schwartz, President and Co-Founder of NuMuBu, the global music industry network

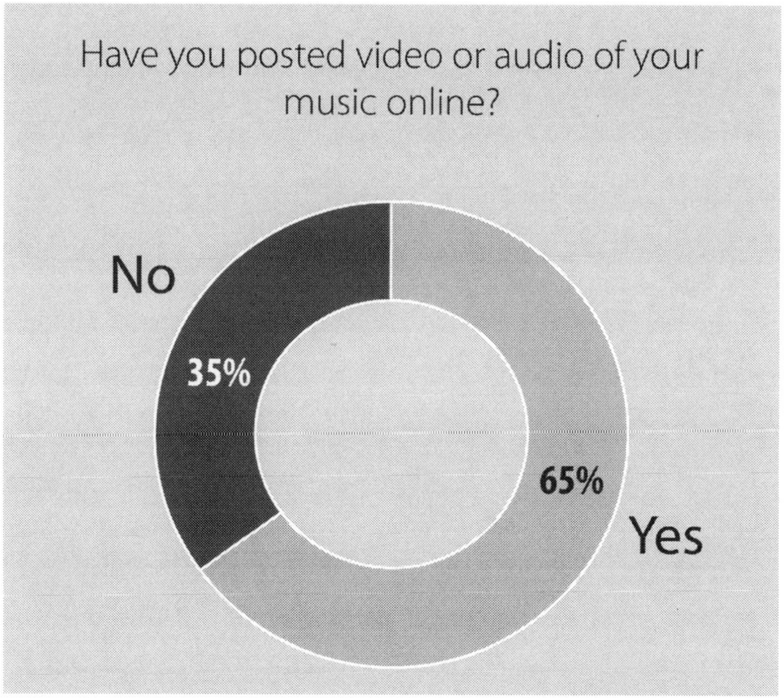

—from the 2012-2013 TC-Helicon survey of 1,000 singers

Action 3: Harness the Power of Your Website

Don't simply be "present" online; increase your traffic.

The game has entirely changed with websites.

A website is no longer the only way to have a presence on the web. In fact, successful vocalists sometimes forgo a website altogether, focusing on Facebook, YouTube, Twitter or other platforms. Still, a website can be a great part of your online "portfolio"—but simply "having one" is not no longer a central achievement.

Elliott Randall's Top Website Tips:

1. *You'll need an attractive website with clear navigation.*
2. *Add value for visitors with information, humor, gifts/giveaways*
3. *Don't have a site that only screams "me-me-me"*
4. *Make sure that people can get where they want to go within 1 or 2 clicks.*
5. *Clarity is everything—make sure none of your points are muddled.*
6. *Remember that white space makes things easy on the eyes*
7. *Take time with design—study the competition; decide on your own "look and feel" and hire a good designer.*

—Elliott Randall: *legendary guitarist, formerly a musical consultant for Saturday Night Live*

You don't even need to be concerned about how to build and design your site. There are many popular tools that have rules in place to ensure a good level of graphic design and layout. For example, just go to wordpress.com and choose from a database of hundreds of templates. Of course you'll want to choose a template that you can customize to reflect your "brand" and you may use a designer to customize your site. But having a great looking website is not the all-consuming concern it once was.

What you really want to focus on is getting traffic to your site.

A website is useless if no one is finding you and interacting with you. You don't need to pay someone to do SEO (Search Engine Optimization); just using an SEO plug-in on your website will take you a long way to improving your visibility. In addition to this, here are three ways to increase your chances of getting found:

1. How might people come to you and your music outside of your name? Make a list. If you are a rock singer in Springfield Arkansas, then you will want to have your site come up when people Google "Rock in Springfield AR." Also think about the venues you want to play at—what are their names? Any popular artists of the same genre active in your area? Add all of these possible associations to you and your music to your list.
2. Now, put links on your website to the names you identified above: places you've gigged at, places you want to gig at, artists whose music is similar to yours and other sites that

are associated with your style of music and location. Some experts believe that Google will notice who you link to on your site and tie this into their search algorithms. Even if Google isn't monitoring these links for SEO, adding some sites will give you credibility for the third step (below). So, write a post about gigging at Venue X, put up some pictures and include a link to venue X. If you want to do wedding gigs, then put links to popular wedding venues on your site—you might even have a page on weddings with links to popular locations.

3. The final step is to complete the circle: see if you can get some of the sites you've linked with to link back to you. If you can get venue X to put a link to your site somewhere on their pages, then you're really rocking. Similarly, you may be able to encourage a fellow artist to link to you in return for a post or link about them. The key here is to be reciprocal in your web work: show that you are going to promote others in return for their mention of you.

When you start moving on these three steps, you will find that you are moving up the search results. Why? No one knows exactly how Google calculates its search results (this is a very carefully guarded secret). But you can be sure that they are noticing shared links between sites and calculating this into their results.

Finally, when you are thinking about naming your act, band or site, do a Google search to see what comes up. This is exactly what we do when we are brainstorming about the name of a product at our company. If you have a huge "wall" of results coming up with exactly the same name you've chosen, then you will want to think of a different name. If, for instance, you thought you might call your band or your site "Raspberry," you may want to think again—as it will be difficult for people to find you underneath the farms, products and places which make use of that term. "Raspberry Rock Band" may be much better.

—Kevin Alexander, CEO of TC-Helicon & VP of Business Management at TC Group

Action 4: Make an Impact with Your Videos

Strut your stuff with killer vids.

Think about it: you often don't get to share your music with large numbers of people when you perform live. Many performers are lucky to get a couple hundred people listening at a time. But on YouTube you can post something online and someone 6,000 miles away can watch. You can develop a really huge fan base this way.

The YouTube thing is amazing. You share it with the world with the click of a button. You hear what people think; you get reactions. It's completely different to other ways of sharing music.

In order to use YouTube effectively, first and foremost you have to find your connection with the person who originally wrote the song you are performing. Put yourself in their place—otherwise you won't be able to move your audience.

Then, you have to make a connection with those who are watching your video. It's important to look at the camera; you have to think that, through the camera, you are singing directly to the person who is watching. Unless they feel connected to you, they will "switch channels"—you don't want to lose the person who's tuned in. Also, you don't want your songs to be too long—most of my YouTube clips are 2–4 minutes in length.

One of the most important things to remember is that no matter what song you are singing, you have to find a way to have fun with it yourself. If you do this, the person who is watching will have fun too. Also, let people know about yourself. I do some "bloopers" at the end of my videos; they're always popular.

Remember that you can use YouTube for more than performing. One way that I've connected with my fan base is to have fan video contests. The way this works is that someone makes a fan video and posts it. People vote and the winner receives a hundred dollars. I had 68 entries. Hundreds of fans voted and over 30,000 people have watched the video that announced the winners: This has been a fantastic way for me to interact with my fans and to say "thanks" for all the awesome support they've given me.

—*Tiffany Jo Allen, singer-songwriter and YouTube star with over 30 million hits*

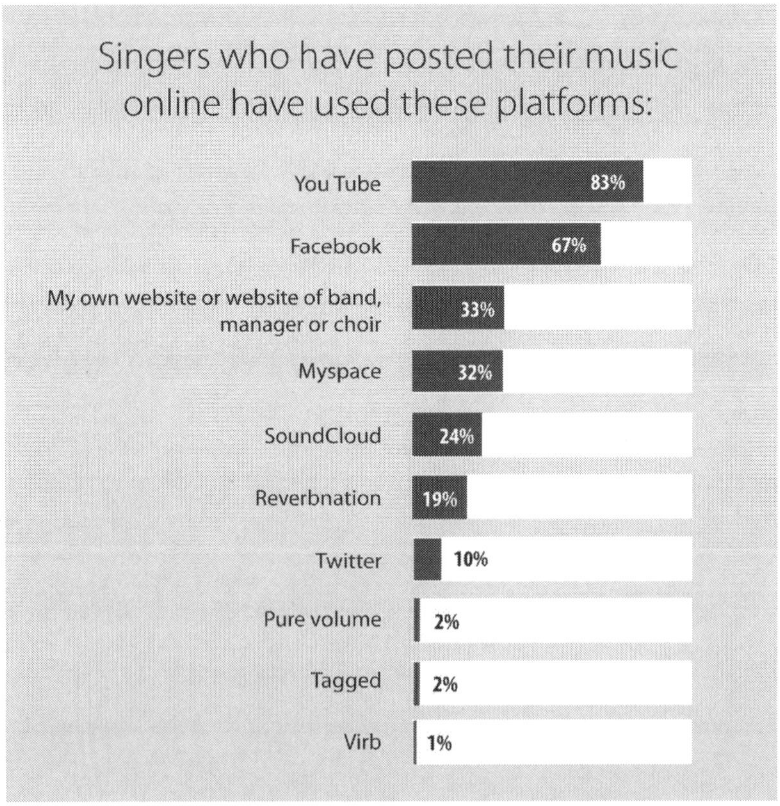

—from the 2012-2013 TC-Helicon survey of 1,000 singers

Other popular places that people posted their music include:

Bandcamp
Tumblr
Soundclick
Vimeo
Jango
Buzznet
Starnow
Bandmix
Singsnap

–from the 2012-2013 TC-Helicon survey of 1,000 singers

Action 5: Get More "Friends" On Your Social Networks

Growth is the name of the game ... and isn't as difficult as you think.

They say half of succeeding at poker is picking the right table. Similarly, a successful social media strategy starts with choosing the right platforms to play at. As of this writing, the obvious networks are Facebook, Twitter, and YouTube, with Instagram, Pinterest and Tumblr nipping at their heels. The primary metric for determining where to spend your time is simple: # of active users.

Once you pick the networks you want to play at, it's important to be observant of best practices of the community itself. Different platforms have different rules of behavior and distribution. For example, Facebook has an algorithm for determining which of your followers see which post on their news feeds, whereas Twitter publishes everything. Or, YouTube leans heavily on the ratio of likes to dislikes in determining which video they recommend. Get to know these basic rules of distribution on your network of choice.

> *If you find an early, fast-growing social or media network, you may experience early mover advantage, when network effects of a few early friends can compound over time as the platform itself grows. A lot of hip hop artists like Diddy and Questlove are big on twitter beyond the proportions of their general fame because they were early adopters.*
>
> ***–Bryan Kim:** Director of Business Development at Tracksby / Hipset*

Beyond algorithms, get to know the "culture of sharing" per respective network. For example, you can get away with a higher frequency of posts on Twitter than Facebook before followers start to get annoyed and un-follow.

As for the content itself, remember that these networks aren't purely broadcast mediums for self-promotion, so go beyond the press release. Remember that the greatest advantage of social networks is the direct connection to fans. Talk as a real person on these social networks, and remember to interact with individuals as well as your entire follower base. Most networks these days publish the friend-to-friend interactions, so potential fans are more likely to follow or stay engaged with your account if they see you actually talk to your fans. Also, the direct one-to-one is a shortcut to being more personal on the network, which is generally good practice.

> *One needs to be deliberate about getting a conversation going. Getting something to go viral is very tricky but not impossible. I generally don't like to tweet about tragic events, but when Alvin Lee passed away I tweeted something nice to show respect. It got re-tweeted a lot.*
>
> ***—Elliott Randall:*** *legendary guitarist, formerly a musical consultant for Saturday Night Live*

If all else fails, stick to the monkey-see, monkey-do rule. Find the leaders of each network, see what they're doing right, and incorporate it into your own routine.

A word of caution: avoid third party services or bots that accumulate fake account follows. Long-term, you're really only fooling yourself. There are better bots that auto-generate the kind of activities that might lead to follows from real people, which can be genuinely beneficial. These are better, but, as always, use with discretion.

Lastly, don't forget about metrics and analytics. Facebook has a full suite of analytics on their pages that provide great feedback. As of this writing, Twitter's analytics are pretty bare bones, but you can plug in third party analytics services like Crowdbooster to get more meaningful analytics. As in anything in life worth doing well, it's hard to succeed without regular feedback. And with networks, you can get very quantifiable feedback, so take advantage of it.

Now go out and make friends!

—Bryan Kim, Director of Business Development at Tracksby / Hipset

Action 6: Make Your Online Music Take Off

Increase your chances for your music making an impact.

There's no magic bullet or formula to getting your online music to take off. If there were, everyone would be doing it—including me. I would quit my day job. Musicians who become very successful are either outliers in talent, so absurdly overqualified or over-talented that they cannot be ignored; or, they are musicians who are very lucky to have their particular talent reach the "felt need" of a certain genre. They may also have produced something clever or timely that has fit in well with the currents of social media.

When Regina Spektor started here at CD Baby, she was a talented but not yet exceptional singer-songwriter. She did fine, but her song writing improved, her lyrics became more weird and edgy, and she became a star. She was a tireless performer and networked well, but there was no predicting her success. There are no guarantees; these things are hard to predict.

Still, there are a number of smart things to do to increase your chances of your music making an impact:

- Make sure your recordings are solid with an easily comprehensible song that is well-produced with good vocals.
- You'll want to have a catchy chorus that you get to quickly.
- A clever video never hurt anyone.
- Distribute your song everywhere you can online.
- Spread your work through live shows and online.

Live performances are never going away; and tours can be strategically designed to help you build an audience organically. Martin Atkins, for example, recommends choosing a secondary market such as Cleveland rather than a primary market (such as NYC or LA). You then flood a number of suburbs with live shows around that market before promoting a larger show downtown.

In terms of social media presence, having a website is crucial. Being active on Facebook and Twitter is really helpful but you need a hub from which to pull and push content to the social media sites. It's easy to get your own customizable site up and running. And when it comes to releasing your music online, don't think in terms of the old model of going into a shed, fighting with your muse and producing and promoting an entire album at one time every few years. Release small EPs and watch the number plays and interactions before releasing more.

—Brian Felsen, President of CDBaby, BookBaby and HostBaby

Action 7: Bring the Stage to Your Page

Grow your online network every time you step on stage.

I absolutely love packing up the car and driving around the country playing music. However, it's the relationships that you create on these tours and how you interact with those people a few days, months, and years later that can really have an impact on your career.

So, don't forget your EMAIL LIST! Don't just grab an old torn notebook out of the backseat of your car and throw your name on the top of it; make it look presentable. Whether you print something out with your logo or picture on it or paint something up with watercolors, make it a part of your brand. Then, find a visible spot for your email list and provide a pen. I often place mine at my merch table, close to the stage, but not so close that people feel awkward coming up to sign it.

During the show I mention that if people would like to know when I'll be back in the area to make sure and sign up. In addition to asking for their email address, ask their name, the city they live in (they could be visiting from somewhere else and might just bring a crew of people when you pass through their town), Twitter details—any info that you can use to stay connected.

People love free stuff. There's something about the word FREE that makes people come running. Try giving away free download cards, lollipops, stickers, anything in exchange for an email address. A great tool that I learned from my publisher is to hold little competitions during your show for a free CD or T-shirt. It can be done for Twitter, email sign ups, or Facebook likes. During the show, say something like, "If you like the music, follow me on Twitter and tag me in a tweet about the show. I'll select one of the tweets at the end of the show and that person will get a free CD!" If there are 100 people at your gig and 20 people actually participate, you have 20 more followers for the $1.50 it cost you to print the CD.

There's a great way to help people who have been at your shows to find you afterwards: Facebook and Twitter tagging. Find the venue on Facebook or Twitter and tag them in your posts. That way, when someone who may have had too many drinks during your show remembers your band but can't remember your name, they might stumble to the venue's Facebook page, and see your post of "Great night last night @xvenue! Thanks to all who came out!"

Oh, and don't forget that Facebook has an amazing geo-targeting feature that allows you to post a status to a specific state or city so that when you're blasting posts about your show in Florida your fans in California aren't getting spammed for shows that are nowhere near them.

—Jenn Bostic: award winning US singer-songwriter with a #1 album in the UK

Action 8: Don't Forget the Old Fashioned Stuff

These the time-honored promo tools aren't going away.

Social media will help you manage the interest that's already there—and it can even help you spread that interest. However, when you need to get those local and regional gigs filled up, don't forget to use the tried and the true. Here are the most effective strategies we've seen singers employ:

Talk it Up—with your friends and family members face to face (or phone them). Leave no stone unturned: are you a part of a church group? A bowling club? Invite your associates! Book a table so that they can sit together.

Have a Clipboard—with a pen and a paper to write down people's email addresses. You can leave it on your merch table. (You can get people to "like" your page or enter a contest right there at the gig on their smartphones—but a strong email list is worth its weight in gold).

Print Posters—and get them into places where there could be possible fans. At the same time, print up some attractive cards with your bio and contact details—and hand these out to everyone at your gig—and leave it on that table you just used at the library.

Harness Free Publicity. Put it in the newspaper, school newsletter or any kind of community calendar. For that matter, contact your local public radio with news of your gig—and offer to do an interview about how you will be giving part of your proceeds to local charity X.

Use Mouth Power. Did you realize that your Aunty Mary has 30 friends? Your job is to communicate to her how much your gig matters to you and how great it would be have familiar faces there. Do you suck at doing this? Be bold, be enthusiastic and show them that you care about your music—without guilt tripping anybody or whining. They may even be upset with you if you don't extend that invitation.

(… and make sure Aunty Mary knows that she can book a table for her friends …)

—The Ultimate Team

I know many artists who only sell via digital downloads but in my experience, most people who turn up to gigs tend to forget to go online and order your latest release when they get home; they're more than happy to buy a CD at the end of the gig. CDs also make you more money than downloads and let's face it, for most musicians starting out, cash is something that's often in short supply.

***—Chris Kennedy:** principal product reviewer for VoiceCouncil Magazine, singer-songwriter*

Action 9: Steer Clear of These Promo FAILS

Leading experts give you their own "fail blog" of stuff to avoid when you're promoting yourself online.

#1 Overselling.

It's a mistake to spend all of your time online selling: watch my video, see my show, buy my merchandise. Nobody ever wants to be sold—especially fans of an entertainer. They want to be entertained! A good rule of thumb is to create one selling post for every ten entertaining posts.

—Jay Frank, leading author and Owner/CEO of DigSin

#2 Begging

When you beg people to re-tweet or to share your post, you lose credibility, becoming a "used car salesman" of the Internet. It is the quality of your content that should be driving the sharing of your posts and tweets. So, just let people see what you are about, the music you like and the culture you relate to—and don't reveal any desperation for interaction.

—Greg Isenberg, Founder of 5by, Venture Partner at Good People Ventures

#3 Blah Messages

Don't send out messages & updates that are nothing more than web links with generic messages like "Follow me on Twitter" or "watch my video, http:// … ." Instead, be personal, engaging and positive. Make people want to click.

—Clifford Schwartz, President and Co-Founder of NuMuBu, the global music industry network

#4 Stuck On Your Own Music

When you look at acts that people love, they remember not just the songs, but the stories. Rihanna's dramatic dating life is a part of the story of who she is. Lady Gaga is as much her music as the clothes she wears, the causes she supports and the crazy things she might say next. Everyone who has succeeded has a personality that comes out. Social media allows any artist to bring out that story, every day, for no cost at all. 75% of the artists I see online don't take advantage of this—they think that their online communication is all about their music. It's not.

—Jay Frank, author of Hack Your Hit and Hit DNA

#5 Crap Photos

Please only post your best photos and videos. If I see a bunch of garbage, then this suggests unprofessionalism. Your success depends on others picking up on what you are doing and helping you to drive things to the next level. If people look at your pictures and videos and nothing resonates for them, this is a quick way to lose an opportunity.

—Steve Eggleston, award-winning law professor, artist manager and best selling author

#6 Being Prey to the Predators

Beware of people who charge you hundreds or thousands of dollars to do online marketing or radio promo, making big promises. There are a lot of rapacious predators preying on the hopes and dreams of musicians, promising marketing packages that they are often unable to deliver. The onus on social media promotion is on the artist—after all, there is no one who can better interact with their online community.

—Brian Felsen, President of CDBaby, BookBaby and HostBaby

#7 Whining

Don't use your Facebook page to express your personal frustrations or to pressure people to come to your gig. Sounding needy or negative on line is unprofessional and it's a turn-off. Instead, try to put some effort and personality into all your posts. Find a clever or creative twist to make your gig sound more appealing. Tell everyone that you'll be trying out some new tunes out or that the venue has the most incredible chocolate cake.

—Emily Braden, award winning New York City Jazz Singer

#8 Ignoring Fans

I have a bone to pick with elitist artists who won't follow their fans on Twitter/Tumblr/Facebook—I follow everyone who asks me because it makes their day. You have no reason to not follow your supporters when they ask you. Who cares if you end up following 15,000 people—you can easily make your own lists of family and friends to keep things separate. I follow my fans—it makes them happy and, after all, I'm in the music business to inspire people.

—Peter Hollens, Pop Singer & Producer/Youtuber with over 175 million views

#9 Hashtag Fests

Don't write Twitter messages with just loads of hashtags slammed in: "!Video Alert! Watch this for my song 'Ripples In The Sea' #np #music #indie #folk #rock #musicmonday #mm RT http://youtu.be/GZZLGktR_78"

You might hope to gain attention in search results, but it just looks like spam! Make it clear, positive and engaging for your fans and casual browsers e.g.: "Find hidden ref to my fav artist in my new song 'Ripples in the Sea' 4 chance to win tkts #indie #rock http://youtu.be/GZZLGktR_78 "

—Susanne Currid, social media consultant

#10 Endless Inane Updates

Endless daily Facebook status updates about your musical exploits quickly become tedious.

"Today, I'm singing on a jingle out at xyz studios."

Next day: "Still singing that jingle at xyz studios for country singer Joe Schmo!"

Next day: "Taking a break from that jingle with Joe Schmo at xyz studios."

Next day: "God, I still love singing backing vocals with country singer Joe Schmo at xyz studios!"

I am a firm believer in not blowing one's own horn; humility is one of the greatest human traits. Let your work speak for itself. By all means, if you want to express your gratitude for being involved in a really big project, or if you want to let folks know about an upcoming concert—put it out there. But don't make it your job to tell everyone, all the time, how busy and how great you are. The people who might be in a position to hire you will think you are desperate. The show biz irony has always been, and will always be, that you can never let people know that you need work. It's a heartbreaking irony but it's real.

—Fred Mollin, veteran record producer, film and TV composer, musical director and songwriter

Frequently Asked Questions

> Why do some people get 30,000 hits on their YouTube vids when I get 300?

Answered by Jay Frank, leading author (Hack Your Hit and Futurehit.DNA) and Owner/CEO of DigSin

There are several things that an artist can do to ensure that their music videos get noticed. First, pay close attention to those who are closest to you: friends, family members and a few others who became big fans quickly. They will give you an indication of how well your song is going to do. However, you have to read between the lines; if they say your music is "good," it is merely OK. If they say it's "great," it is "good." If they say it's "one of the best," then you have a song that may make some waves. If your song isn't making much of an impact, then take stock and be honest with yourself about it. You can lose a lot of time and energy trying to promote a song that doesn't have a resonance with the public.

The second most important thing to increase your views is to recognize that marketing a song is an extremely long process. Many artists who see videos of others going viral believe that if they can just get their own video online, they will have hundreds of thousands of views in just a few weeks. You can win the lottery with better odds. The reality is that songs by new artists that succeed do so because people continually promote them for months and months—if not years. Just take a look at the videos by some recent artists such as Foster the People, Ellie Goulding and Gotye. After releasing their songs it can take anywhere from nine months to two years before it reaches its popularity apex. If it is going to take a major label (which has lots of money) nine months to two years, then it is going to take an independent artist that much longer.

All of this means that you have to be willing to remain firm in your conviction of the value of your song. You need to really dig into your efforts to continually and aggressively promote your best song over a period of months: reaching out on blogs, social networks, live performances, talking to fans and asking them to help you promote it—you will constantly be finding new people to like your song. Advertising might work in some cases, but nothing can replace your unwavering belief in the song and your focused energy in promoting it.

> How do you deal with a bad comment at a concert or on a website?

Answered by Jenn Bostic, award winning US singer-songwriter with a #1 album in the UK

Not everyone is going to like you. That's life. No matter what you do, someone somewhere will find something bad to say about it. Your performance is about rising above the naysayers and catering to your heart and the people who like what you're doing.

If a comment on one of my social networks can pass as constructive criticism, I'll leave it on the page, often thanking the commenter for their honesty. If the comment is offensive, disrespectful, or critical of other fans, I will delete it. I used to let those comments hurt my feelings, but I've since learned that doing this only slows me down. Take those hurtful or negative comments and channel the energy into drive and determination. Then, you've won. My all-time-favorite quote is by Judy Garland, "Always be a first-rate version of yourself, instead of a second-rate version of somebody else."

> I tweet, post pics on Facebook and update my status, but it seems that no one is watching ...

Answered by Greg Isenberg, Founder of 5by, Venture Partner at Good People Ventures

Keep in mind the 80-20 rule: 80% of your tweets, posts, up-dates, etc. should be about the music you like and cultural themes you relate to. The other 20% should actually be about self-promotion. The reason this works is because when you tweet about the work of others ("This really cool article in Rolling Stone Magazine said that ..."), you are likely to get re-tweets. When you promote only your own stuff, people are less likely to share it.

You also need to invest in getting some communication going—ask for replies from people. If you want to build a following, then you need to build relationships. Think of some of the famous musicians in your genre, reach out to their fans and interact with them. Let's say your music shares some similarities with that of Katy Perry; you might ask her fans, "What do you like about Katy's latest track?" When they answer you, you have a link. The best example of the power of building connections is Gary Vaynerchuk, a lone blogger who tweeted at just anyone who reached out to him. He himself reached out to 100 people per day and made connections very, very quickly. He now has 1,000,000 followers on Twitter.

An effective way to create interaction is to tweet or post an item about something that is on the hearts and minds of many. Just last week someone shared a picture of the hurricane in New York City with the Statue of Liberty in the background. The caption said, simply, "What do you think about what is going on in NYC?"—There was a huge response to this. Marry your content with thought provoking emotional themes.

Never forget we human beings talk about content—TV, movies, music, pictures ... As you marry your content with a "wrapper" that speaks to me, then you'll not only find that someone is watching, but that someone is actually following.

> What is the difference between promotion, sharing and distribution?

Answered by Charles Chemery (a.k.a. Charlie Sputnik) DJ, artist, and head of the Independent Artist/DJ Performance and Production programs at The Musician's Institute, Los Angeles.

Promotion garners exposure for something you intend to sell. It attracts attention to a new record, a tour, a new video or collaboration. An example might be that you offer a bonus track for free to draw attention to your new album.

Distribution The purpose of distribution is to put your music somewhere where users can find it and pay to hear or own it. Often a third party—an aggregator—helps you. Digital distribution platforms include iTunes and Spotify among many others.

Sharing is not about money, it is about letting your fans know that you care. Sharing feels organic and intimate and it builds good will and personal connection. Sharing can even go both ways. An example of sharing is offering an exclusive download of a new track to your fan club three weeks before it is available for streaming.

> What are the most important digital tools and platforms for promoting and distributing my music?

Answered by Charles Chemery (a.k.a. Charlie Sputnik) DJ, artist, and head of the Independent Artist/DJ Performance and Production programs at The Musician's Institute, Los Angeles.

Music careers are do-it-yourself now, and oftentimes there is not a lot of benefit in being signed to a label.

The most powerful platform for promotion among the social media and streaming services is YouTube. Just go to a party and you'll see people using YouTube to discover, enjoy and share music. It is free, it has everything, it contains the all-important video element, and with the ubiquity of high-speed internet, audio quality is satisfactory. Unfortunately, content copyright owners earn little or nothing from YouTube, although this is slowly changing.

All your social media channels (Facebook, Instagram, SoundCloud, YouTube, Twitter) can be harnessed for promotion and sharing, but don't miss the power of music blogs such as Stereogum. Find one that features music similar to yours, and send them your music in hopes they may feature it. Powerful blog aggregators such as HypeMachine are important "tastemakers" who scour the internet for great blogs, significantly influencing the public on who to pay attention to.

When it comes to distributing your music, the most important platform today is Spotify. The other important streaming services are Apple Music, Deezer, Rhapsody and Tidal.

"Non-interactive" streaming services—where users don't pick individual songs—like Pandora and Sirius Radio offer a great advantage for the unknown artist because your audience is already targeted for you. Your song gets shuffled together with songs of a similar type and will get heard by people already looking for that style.

Some artists don't like the miniscule amount of money artists and content owners receive via streaming services, while others are happy to have the exposure. Tidal boasts the highest royalties paid to its artists.

Buying songs for your own music library is a disappearing concept in a world where people want music for free, but iTunes, Amazon Music and Beatport are digital outlets where many still buy music.

To distribute your music via a streaming service or online store, independent artists must pay an aggregator such as ReverbNation, TuneCore or CDBaby. Aggregators also help you collect a certain portion of your royalties.

> People seem to like my songs, so why don't I have more fans?

Answered by Steve Eggleston, award-winning law professor, artist manager and best selling author

The self-evident explanation is that not enough people are listening to your songs. You may have family and friends and neighbors in your local club listening and giving you great feedback, but that's not enough; at the very least, you need to market yourself to the outside world via extensive social media and, if you can arrange it, club/pub-level touring.

If you're already doing that, then the likely answer is that your music is not as compelling as you think it is. In this case, you should be honing your skills as an artist, constantly practicing, rehearsing, writing, performing and recording new music. Dig deep into your soul until you find the gold. You need a song that stops people cold when they hear it, that compels them to listen to it time and again. Brandi Carlile's "Story" is a perfect example. See the hundreds of thousands of downloads on YouTube, many long preceding her rise to fame.

> *I know an artist who, when he receives a message from a fan ("my god, I love your new song!") will write back and use that fan's name: "Thanks so much, Jamie, that means a lot." He's responding as a human being who cares—not a robot. These kinds of acts are not forgotten!*
>
> **–Chris Maltese:** *artist manager, formerly a senior producer for MTV*

When you get the music right, really kick your social media into full gear. Be especially active in Facebook, Twitter, Pinterest, etc. Engage Facebook and Google+ ad campaigns in support of your mixed and mastered releases and shows. Start building an email list and sending out periodic newsletters informing fans of what you're doing. And as soon as you can afford it (or trade with someone), build an artist website where you post your songs, show schedule and other interesting things about you and/or your band. Until then, use ReverbNation.com.

In the end, if your song is good enough, then it will get shared. No one will be able to stop you.

> What is the secret to getting my Bio statement read?

Answered by Fred Mollin, veteran record producer, film and TV composer, musical director and songwriter

Whatever you do, keep it short and to the point. Give people the high points of your career, your background and what you are shooting for—that's good enough for an introduction. Remember, people don't have all the time in the world and appreciate it when you keep things lean. Two to three paragraphs are often all that's needed. Then, make sure it doesn't sound "flat"; make it enjoyable to read. A list of credits is always important to include.

> Should I invest in a MTV-quality music vid?

Answered by John Kjøller, member and vocal director of the hit vocal a cappella group Basix

We've created a polished music video to help create some "buzz" prior to the release of our new album. But this doesn't actually do much for the live-booking aspect of our PR.

You see, bookers and promoters need to see what we look like, how we do things, how we sound "for real," and how the audience responds to us—a live video is much more relevant for this purpose. So, the polished video is for our fans, to give them something that they can share with others.

Don't get me wrong, it has been a lot of fun to make a proper music video—and I love the result. I even think we may do it again! But I'm not sure how much we actually gain from this—the jury is still out. If you take this route, ensure you have a strong idea, a plan and a storyboard.

If you are focusing on getting more live performance gigs, I would encourage you to spend your money on good live video material—rather than a flashy, "MTV" video.

> OK I get it that social media is important. So, how do I get going with a successful strategy?

Answered by Bryan Kim, Director of Business Development at Tracksby / Hipset

Without getting lost in the specifics of best practices per respective social network, your general approach should be one of genuine interactions. Show a bit of your personality. Tell micro stories about micro events in your life, reveal what's meaningful to you. Don't just promote an iTunes link with some variation of an antiseptic "check it out" message. Instead, tell a mini-story about what the song or album meant to you. A promotional approach to social media is decreasingly effective in a world where fans can smell out the overly generic PR messaging. The rules have changed, and more fans demand meaningful online interactions.

If you're just starting out, dip your toes in the water, give it a spin. One of the best things about social networks is the instant feedback and engagement. With consistent effort, it's almost impossible not to learn how to use social media to your benefit.

> How can I make a good YouTube video when I'm not a technical person?

Answered by Gregory A. Barker in conversation with Tiffany Jo Allen, singer-songwriter and YouTube star with over 30 million hits

Some of the most frequent questions I get are from people who want to know about the "high-tech" devices I am using. Well, I have been using a very old camera with the inexpensive external microphone that was included in the package. I'm sure I will be updating this equipment, but it has served me well.

I say this because I don't want vocalists to think there are insurmountable technical obstacles that have to be overcome in order to share their art on YouTube. However, to ensure that you present your material well, there are some things every singer should consider:

1. Lighting. It's so important that you are well lit. I do most of my recording in my bedroom; when I started, I just experimented by turning different lights on and off and then looked at the results on video. The aim is to end up with a good, clear image—and I think I have achieved that without a professional lighting kit. I'm sure you can as well.
2. Mic Placement. I have had to work to get the right balance between guitar and voice for live performance. I've recorded lots of vids where one or the other is too loud. So, I've just re-recorded, working it out along the way.
3. Getting the Room Right. Different rooms have different acoustics depending on carpet, tiles, how high the ceilings are, etc. At the beginning, I went around to different rooms in the house, making my recordings and then checking the sound quality—there may be a more "scientific" way to do this, but it worked! I've found a location where the sound just naturally works without annoying echoes etc.

> *It takes a bit of acting, and a LOT of courage, to perform passionately to "nobody" (your camera).*
>
> ***—Mister Tim:** viral video star, voice artist, composer and sponsored kazoo player*

Remember: uploading a video is something anyone can do—YouTube has made it really easy for everyone. Just do it—you don't have to be a sound engineer to do this. Just experiment with your sound, lighting and location—and go for it.

> Should I pay for my promotion? What should I pay for?

Answered by Emily Braden, award winning New York City Jazz Singer

For each gig I ask myself the pivotal question, "Should I do this with just my personal fan base—using my online media tools? Or do I want to splurge and pay to get it into a certain magazine or pay for a publicist who can get it into a bunch of magazines and on the radio?"

If I am doing a gig to promote a new album, it has often been worth it to me to hire a publicist and a graphic artist. A publicist knows exactly who to call at the local newspapers and magazines in their city and how to get my song on the radio or my gig mentioned on the local news program. I use a graphic artist to design my poster. If you don't know the city very well, it may be worth it to you to hire a poster company to put up your posters in the key spots of that city for your type of gig. In smaller cities and towns, the money you spend on promotion may go much further than in a huge city like NYC, because those cities simply have less going on and fewer avenues for musical promotion.

I have sometimes considered paying to advertise my gig in a local magazine or newspaper. Paying for an ad is one option, but many local media will post your gig in their calendar for free. I write a press release for every major performance, and send it to the media in that city that I think are best for my type of show and my type of audience. This takes a bit of research. As a jazz musician in New York City, I might choose media like Hot House Magazine. There is always the chance, especially in a smaller city, once you've sent in your press release, that someone from that newspaper or magazine might call you for an interview.

What's the next step? Of course, I'll keep building my personal fan base through Facebook, Twitter, Tumblr and good old-fashioned email lists. Outside of this, my goal is to hire a booking agent, and eventually a manager. It's a lot of work managing my own bookings, the following up, the constant contacting—a booking agent would be much more efficient because of their contacts and knowledge of the business. I'm watching many independent artists enjoy great success in their singing career without being signed; many have just a booking agent or just a manager.

CHAPTER 4

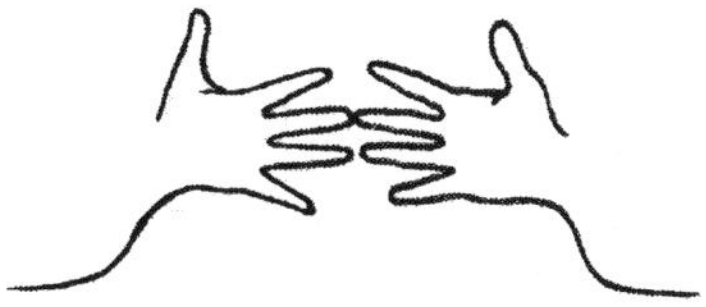

Take Charge of Your Performance

Be wickedly cool.

Singers are nothing less than medics distributing wholesome medication for a needy group of patients.

—Mark Baxter: acclaimed vocal coach with Aerosmith, Journey, Goo Goo Dolls and many others

Your gut never fails you. When it comes to artistic choices—ask yourself, "does this feel right?"

—Louise Rose, Entertainer and educator, has worked with Aretha Franklin, Oscar Peterson and Duke Ellington

Take Charge of Your Performance

Be wickedly cool.

Actions:

1. Shape Your Set.
2. Case Out the Joint
3. Don't Overdo Your Warm Up
4. Figure Out Your Look
5. Make the Sound Check Work for You
6. Create Continuity Between Songs
7. Tell the Venue What You Need
8. Remember: Nerves Are Good for You

Frequently Asked Questions:

- » *What can I demand from the venue—and do I need a contract?*
- » *I'm tired of being ignored as background music—how do I get people in to actually listen to me?*
- » *What is vocal masturbation?*
- » *I'm afraid I'm going to go off pitch—help?*
- » *When will I get paid?*
- » *The sound person isn't paying attention—he's texting during the whole gig.*
- » *The club's second act cancelled—now I have to sing for three hours—how do I do that?*
- » *What gear should I bring with me?*
- » *How can I put emotion into my performance without being fake?*
- » *I want the audience to be impressed—how can I ensure this?*
- » *What is a backline, stage plot and technical rider?*
- » *I can tell my audience hates me—what do I do?*
- » *I know I can sing, but the pressures of both the stage and the studio are getting to me. How can I sing my best?*
- » *When should we put our breaks and how long should they be?*
- » *How do I get past a mistake in the middle of my performance?*
- » *When I'm singing a cover, I find it hard to get all the vocal riffs to sound right.*
- » *My venue says they have everything—should I trust them?*
- » *Are there smart phone apps that singers are using at their gigs? What are they?*

Action 1: Shape Your Set

Plan your performance and stay flexible as you read your audience. We'll show you several ways prominent artists present material.

So there I am, just before walking out on stage, scribbling some notes on the back of a crinkled-up piece of paper.

My set list.

I'm trying to assess the "feel" of the room—trying to match what I'm going to do with where the crowd is at. At least that's what I do for one of my solo performance shows.

However, if you were to bump into me before one of the theatrical shows, where I am singing with my group, you wouldn't find me scribbling—that set list is worked out long in advance. When other singers, musicians and technical people are involved in a show, they just have to know the list well ahead of time. But even then there's still room for spontaneity, through what we will do in the improv sections, for example.

The set list: it's there to be followed, ignored, transformed, thrown out, slavishly adhered to and changed at the last minute. The main thing is that you have one. But how do you construct a set list?

There are many ways to do this, of course. You might choose a narrative approach, shaping your songs so they tell some kind of story—or you might tell some kind of developing story in between the songs. You could arrange your music so that there is increasing intensity, or have many points of increasing intensity—a roller coaster. Other singers choose a thematic presentation where songs are grouped around themes. Start thinking now about which approach can match your music and your audience. Try it out—and evaluate afterwards.

I want to share some questions that I use to help me figure out how to shape my sets.

What's the room like? How full will the venue be? What the mood of the audience likely to be in that night? Are you the first act on—or are you following a group? If following another act, what is the musical state they might be left in by that group—and where might you want to take them? Do you want to have a back-up list to cool an audience down—or to suddenly get them up and dancing? What are the variables you can easily change, drop and rearrange on your list?

By simply asking the questions—and using your answers to create a set list—you will push your performance ahead.

—Shlomo, World Loopstation Champion and Guiness World Record holder

Action 2: Case Out the Joint

Asking key questions about your venue before you even arrive can make all the difference to your time on stage.

It sounds like a minor point, but I always like to know where to park. If the venue is in a suburban area parking usually isn't a problem. But if I'm performing in the middle of Chicago and driving the van with a trailer, then parking could be a headache. I want to know, "Will I get a parking pass?" "Where do I load my stuff in?" and "Is it up two flights of stairs; is there a freight elevator?" Sometimes a venue is such a logistical nightmare that—all things equal—it might be worth choosing a different venue.

It's also good to know if there's a "green room," a separate place to wind down, warm up and tune up. Sometimes smoking is permitted in the "green room." If that's the case, I ask the guys in my band to not smoke in the room in order to protect my voice.

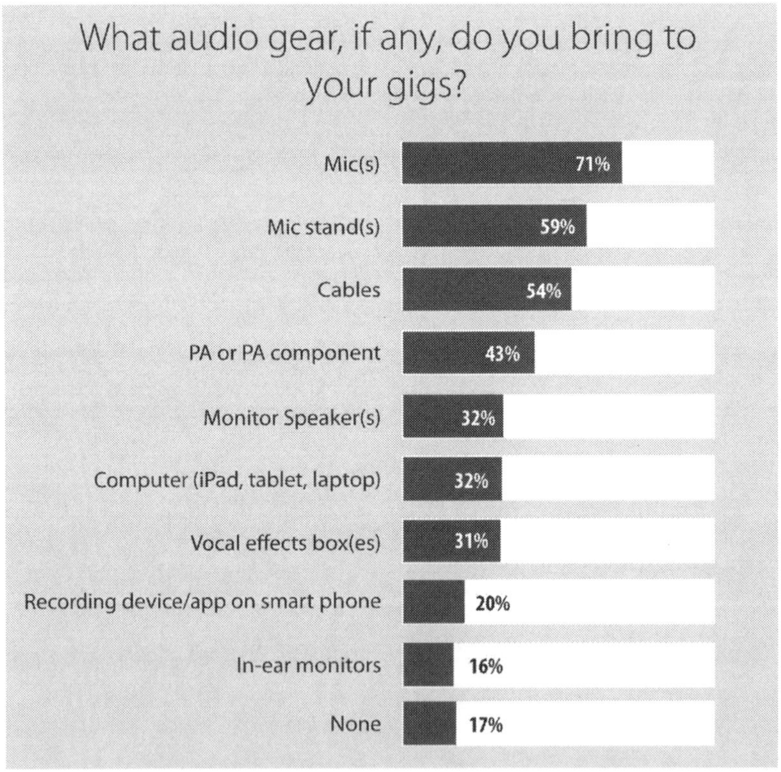

–from the 2012-2013 TC-Helicon survey of 1,000 singers

There are certain things I want to know about the sound system. "What sound system do you have?" "What will the monitoring situation be for my vocals?" You don't want to barrage a promoter or booker with tons of questions, so pick and choose what's most important to you. It might be better to reach out to other artists you know who have played the venue before and ask them these questions. But do ask the venue if you're able to get a sound check or simply a line check. If I'm told I'm only going to get a line check, I'll ask nicely, "If we get there early, can we have a full sound check?"

I need to say one more thing about the monitors, since that can be such an important factor in a performance: at a big venue with a nice system we can put guitars, backing vocals and my voice into the monitors, giving me a full sound on stage. But if I'm in a little club and the monitors are looking old and weak, I won't put anything in the monitors but my voice—and just have them crank up the monitor as loud as it will go without feeding back. This means that the rest of the band who are at the front of the stage will just have to monitor their own instruments via their amps. For keyboardists who like to go straight into the soundboard, this is sometimes a problem. That's why my band brings along a keyboard amp just in case.

I try not to over-indulge in the perks that a venue offers. I just want some un-chilled water and perhaps some beer for my guys (and some beers for me at the end of the night). Meals and/ or snacks are great. But my main goal is to be invited back, so I don't want to come across as too demanding. After all, I'm trying to build up my fan base and may want to return every few months. When I step through the doors I always say, "Thanks so much for having us." And then I wait for them to say to us, "Hey, do you guys need anything?" When we leave I say, "Hey this place is great! Who should I contact when we're back in town next?"

—Val Emmich, singer-songwriter, hailed by the New York Times as "a rocker who rocks to his own beat"

Action 3: Don't Overdo Your Warm Up

A warm up is not a work out. We'll show you time-honored ways vocalists through the years have gotten ready for their gigs.

I've encountered singers with tired voices who, for some reason, have the impression that a protracted "warm-up" regimen with vocal exercises is essential for performance. However, if you spontaneously sing lightly throughout the day and add the sound check, you're already putting your voice through its paces. Running through your song repertoire mentally in "real time" at night can also reinforce memorization of the lyrics while lulling you to a good night's sleep.

On gig day, you should be especially aware of how you use your voice, easing into your first vocalizations of the day. Humming, lip trills and yawn-sighs over a steaming mug of hot water for five minutes will get you off to a gentle start. Good vocal hygiene also entails avoiding annoying phone calls or projecting over ambient noise that can result in the voice being fatigued before you utter a single word in song.

Your eating habits can affect the condition of your voice and therefore help (or hinder) your vocal warm-up. I keep my diet free of irritants on gig day, such as spicy, tomato-based or greasy foods, chocolate and alcohol. I limit my intake of caffeine, which can dehydrate. I usually have a meal (protein and salad) at 4:00pm. I bring water to the gig, and if the venue is air-conditioned, I may even bring a steamer to keep back stage.

If you perform self-accompanied, warming up on your instrument separately from the vocals allows you to enjoy the tactile sensations of the guitar, piano, or bass. This also reinforces muscle memory that enables you to feel secure once you add the vocals and assemble the complete package for presentation.

Don't exhaust your voice and energy at the sound check. While you might want to run through some selections, be sure not to over-rehearse.

If you are singing regularly, the best, most effective warm-up may consist of simply running briefly through songs, "wearing them" just for the fun of it, and buoyantly freeing the voice with the coordination and energy that comes from the joy of making music. That same energy will be there for you as you transmit it to your audience during performance.

—Rachel L. Lebon, PhD, author, vocal coach and educator

Action 4: Figure Out Your Look

Every piece of clothing is a costume that communicates.

The first time I was ever written up in the paper the blurb said, "This girl (they didn't know my name!) sounds like a contemporary of Rosemary Clooney and she was sporting dreadlocks and Birkenstocks". I had been thinking of cutting off my dreadlocks but this report made me realize that they were helpful in having people identify me. So, I kept them. Now people say all the time, "You know, that girl in Nashville who sings jazz and has dreadlocks … " It helps them remember who I am—it is a point of identification. So, I am the jazz singer who has dreadlocks; it's not something that people expect but it has become a part of my brand.

Maybe you have something like that: tattoos, flaming red hair, a certain vintage or retro look or item—it helps to create a buzz. Don't despise it. Use it.

Of course your clothing will depend on your style. My advice is to wear clothes that suit your genre and then go slightly more extreme. In other words, have your appearance relate to someone in your audience—but don't look exactly like someone in the audience.

I think you have to remember that this is your business and you are selling a brand. You're still "you," but you can also view your image as something that is a role you play—so, notch it up a little. There are also psychological benefits from viewing your image as an aspect of your brand—if you are out there selling your brand and you get rejected, it is not as disappointing!

People look at me and they expect to hear Reggae. I sometimes wondered if I should have just looked "pretty" like Diana Krall. But my dreadlocks have people talking.

–Annie Sellick, internationally renowned jazz singer

Action 5: Make the Sound Check Work for You

You might have all the time in the world—or you might have five seconds after the previous act. Whatever case, follow these steps to testing and tweaking your set up.

Whether it's a sound check for yourself in a small, solo gig or you're in a larger venue complete with PA and sound engineer, a few simple steps will help your voice to prevail.

When you are doing the sound yourself, make sure that your gain level is not off the charts–you don't want to turn up the mains and have things start squealing. Also, I would never do a gig–even a tiny one–without a monitor. Make sure the monitor is where it needs to be for you to have a good strong signal. This will greatly reduce the chance of vocal fatigue.

Now take some time to check out how you sound. No matter how much you've rehearsed with effects at home, every space is different. For example, I'll tweak the reverb so that it suits the coffee shop setting without it sounding like I'm in a cathedral. This "test run" is especially important if you have a vocal effects unit. Check out your most dramatic effects–I've found the megaphone sound especially important to adjust as it can easily get out of control.

All of these principles apply in a larger venue. However, you now need to put energy into bringing the sound engineer on your side. Find out their name and don't forget it (this goes for the bartender, venue owner and any other staff). If they seem impatient with you, remember this may be for many reasons: they may be getting paid unfairly, have little knowledge of the gear, or may be trying to deal with several bands. You will only sound worse if you piss off the engineer.

Insist that you get enough of what you need through your monitor–no matter how impatient the engineer may be. It's your voice, after all. If you can't hear yourself, you will strain and your performance will suffer.

Everyone has different needs and preferences for their monitors, yet be clear with what you want. Instead of saying, vaguely, "I can't hear myself," think about communicating how your tone sounds. You could say, "I'm sounding a little muffled; could we try cutting the mids or lows?" or, "I'm hearing just the beginning of a little ringing (feedback) and my s-sounds are very strong; could we try backing down the highs?"

Finally, be careful when using hand signals to the engineer during your performance. You may think that a "thumbs up" means more volume, whereas your engineer may think you are congratulating him for the excellent sound! If you have to use a hand signal, point an index finger at your throat and then point up.

—Laura Clapp: singer-songwriter and Marketing Manager for TC-Group Americas

Action 6: Create Continuity Between Songs

Bring honor to yourself, your genre and your audience by mastering the transitions of your performance.

About 12 years ago I sat in at a gig where I hadn't been introduced to all the players. I took the stage, turned to the piano player, whom I didn't recognize as Linton Garner, a local jazz guru and the brother of the late jazz legend Erroll Garner, and asked, "Do you know, 'Misty?'" He gave me a funny smile and said, "Yeah, I know that one." I had just asked him if he knew his brother's most famous composition! It turned out to be a great performance and I now have an interesting story to tell whenever I introduce that song.

Whether I'm introducing a song, singing, talking, counting in or being silent, I want my performances to be a continuous stream of communication between me, my audience and the musicians on stage. The biggest thing that helps me do this is my personal relationship to my material.

The stronger your connection to your music, the easier it is to not only deliver a great interpretation, but also to talk to your audience. Remember, not every song needs a spoken introduction. Sometimes it's best to say nothing and let the music speak for itself.

The next thing that helps me create continuity is feeling at ease with the musicians on stage with me. For example, everyone must be comfortable with who is giving cues. Sometimes I'm the one counting in and giving cues, other times I work with an MD (musical director—often my piano player) who cues the rest of the players.

Lastly, I try to create a great relationship with the audience. Early in my shows, I always greet everyone with, "Hi" and "How is everybody doing?" I try to treat it like a family gathering. I sincerely thank the audience for coming out to see me—after all, I wouldn't have a job if it weren't for them. Here are some other things I do:

1. In my banter with the audience, I always avoid topics such as politics and religion.
2. If I am covering songs by a well-known artist, I often ask if anyone is a fan of that artist.
3. When I'm ill and have to perform, I'll say, "You'll have to forgive me, I'm sick tonight."
4. If we play a request despite not being prepared, I say, "That was our attempt at … "
5. At the end of my show I say, "I hate to love you and leave you … "

I find a positive attitude and little honesty always bring out more support from the audience.

No matter what the vibe is, I believe it is always possible to work with it. I always have an encore prepared and I always end up doing it. The one thing I try to do in every aspect of my show, is to have fun.

—Diane Pancel: LA Based singer, has shared the stage with David Foster, Nelly Furtado and Matt Dusk

Action 7: Tell the Venue What You Need

You are a business and one of your jobs is to make sure that you don't starve.

I tend to give people what they want without making any demands. After all, more than anything, I want people to listen to my music. However, my husband has come with me to some of my gigs and made some important observations like, "They are only paying you 40 bucks for this? That's ridiculous!" Or, "You drove six hours to that gig and they didn't feed you?"

You have to remember that you are a business and one of your jobs is to make sure that you aren't starving. This means asking some questions and letting the venue know some of your needs without sounding too demanding.

Be sure you know the exact amount that you are getting paid and what their compensation policy is about food and drink. Ask these questions up front—after all, it's your gig and you are the manager. Move onto other questions about how early you can get there to set things up, what the access to power is like and if they are providing a "backline"—this is gear that they already have on stage such as a drum kit, piano, etc. (A lot of clubs have a backline, though many restaurants and bars won't.)

> *You want to be wearing something that sets you apart. When I walk in to the venue, there is no doubt that I am the one going on stage. There is something extraordinary about me. Having said that, I could still perform, if I had to, wearing no make-up and my tracksuit.*
>
> ***—Katherine Ellis:*** *hit dance music songwriter, vocalist and performer*

I just played a gig at a vineyard and they actually had an "artist agreement" that dealt nicely with all of these issues. You might consider having a simple performance contract that outlines a few of the things you need. Just say to the venue, "Could I send you a copy of this contract so that we are on the same page?" If they freak out about this, and you still want the gig, you can let it go. However you still need to ask those questions.

As your career develops, and people start demanding that you play at larger venues, you can ask for a green room before the performance—but perhaps hold off on asking for a bowl of green M&M's.

—Laura Clapp: singer-songwriter and Marketing Manager for TC-Group Americas

Action 8: Remember: Nerves Are Good for You

Your challenge is not to get rid of those butterflies,
but to get them to fly in the same direction.

A big part of being a performer—whether a singer, an actor, or even a sportsman—is dealing with nerves. They're natural: it's part of the excitement of performing—especially live. Many performers even say that if you're not nervous, something's missing.

So, you need to recognise your anxiety and overcome it; even embrace it. "You won't experience this level of excitement in any other walk of life," one of Britain's best-known ballroom dancers told me. "The buzz, the nerves, the adrenalin is something you must learn to enjoy and use to heighten your performance, take it to a new level."

Visualise and prepare. That's not to say there aren't a few tricks you can use to make you more comfortable. "If you fail to prepare, you prepare to fail" is one of the oldest maxims, but no less true for that. So, visualise your performance. Picture in your head the space you will occupy, where you will stand, your relationship with your audience, what you will see.

When preparing for appearances on national chat-shows like the *Parkinson* show, alongside stars like Kevin Spacey, Judi Dench or Robbie Williams, I would set up two chairs in my dressing room at the exact angle they would be on the set and run through the answers I might give to the host sitting opposite.

Three-time world motor-racing champion Jackie Stewart once asked to spend time in a company's boardroom the day before making a big presentation to the directors. He wanted to feel comfortable, to know the space, to visualise his pitch.

Keep it simple. A sports psychologist told me (in addition to confiding that the greatest Olympians doubt themselves, often before their greatest challenges), that when tennis players or cricketers are out of form, it's often because they're not moving their feet. So, he told them, instead of cluttering your mind with too many thoughts, simply say to yourself "happy feet."

It worked on two levels: it reduced a lot of anxious thoughts into one simple positive message. And it put a smile on my face.

And one final thought … don't forget to breathe. Strange as it may sound, at moments of tension we often forget to breathe normally and naturally. Take a moment to breathe deeply, relax and focus.

… and ENJOY IT!

—Rory Bremner: Britain's foremost satirical impressionist with his own TV series

Frequently Asked Questions

> What can I demand from the venue—and do I need a contract?

Answered by Ron "Bumblefoot" Thal, lead guitarist, Guns N' Roses, songwriter, recording artist and producer

Every time you work with people, you are rolling the dice, which means things can go wrong—with or without a contract.

With small local gigs, you usually don't need a contract. In fact, a contract can be a turn-off because in a casual environment such as this, a contract makes it feel like "us against them" instead of a bunch of friends working together. You will need to carefully sort out the money and all the details of the gig, of course, but there is a certain accountability that comes from playing in your own town which means you can trust you'll get paid at the end of the night, and they can trust that you will deliver on your end.

Contracts are a good idea when you are touring, especially if your tour takes you out of your own country. Before you ever accept a gig like this, I suggest you check over the travel arrangements very carefully to ensure that the journey won't leave you exhausted before you even step on stage. Your contract will need to outline the basics of your gig: where and when are you playing? How long is the set? What backline is available? How do you get paid and when? What kind of security is available when a drunk guy climbs up on stage during the show and starts swinging his elbows around? If you want to appear more casual despite using a contract, you can always blame it on your manager (even if you don't actually have a manager, you can make one up—your favorite uncle will do). Just say, "I know this is a bit cheesy, but my manager is a real stickler and wants a contract."

Many lawyers out there spend their days settling contract disputes, which means even with a contract, there can be problems. This is why you have to listen to your gut and look for red flags, like when the venue owner is sitting there in his '70 suit, laughing and telling stories of when he chased the band out with a baseball bat.

Even if you are wronged, keep your cool. If you show up late for your gig because of travel delays, you have technically broken the contract. On the other hand, if the venue didn't do the promo they'd promised and no people show up, then they've broken the contract, and what's worse—they probably can't pay you. Don't retaliate and turn it into a war. Be the better human and trust that you will be rewarded in one way or another. When the promoter begrudgingly gives you your 300 bucks that was guaranteed by the contract, you can give him back a hundred and say, "Let's hope it goes better next time." Handle it with class, and others who hear about it will want to work with you all the more.

> I'm tired of being ignored as background music—how do I get people to actually listen to me?

Answered by Angela Kelman, Canadian Juno Award winning recording artist and veteran of thousands of gigs

We've all had gigs where we felt like wallpaper. We were creating ambience, but no one was paying attention. These kinds of gigs can be energy draining, so here are my secrets for getting and maintaining the audience's attention.

One way to engage your audience is to tailor your set list to them. When you get the call for a gig, ask about the age demographic of the audience, special guests and the nature of the event. If the event is for someone's birthday, and you find out their favorite band is Train, maybe you can work "Hey, Soul Sister" into your set somewhere. If it's a 40th anniversary party, learn a few songs from the era when the husband and wife were teenagers—this always evokes great emotional memories.

It's easy to go inside yourself at a gig when you feel that no one is paying attention. Instead, try to keep your energy up as if you are playing to an attentive crowd of thousands. Zero in on those people, no matter how few, who are paying attention to you. Interact with them. Ask them questions or get them to sing along by teaching them a background or call-and-answer part. Find a way to get them involved in your show. If you can engage a few people and they start having fun, other people will soon follow.

As a last resort to get attention while on stage, pull out your best move—and I don't mean lighting your hair on fire. As a vocalist, I have taken a big breath, and launched into a diva-like a cappella note for as long as I could. People will start to pay attention one by one just out of curiosity—"what is that woman doing?" Always do it in a spirit of having fun and you will be amazed how your audience will suddenly "wake up" and join the party.

Okay—those are my secrets. If you find yourself playing a "wallpaper" gig, and you've pulled out all these tricks and still no one pays attention, look at it as a paid rehearsal and move on to the next gig. There will be many more that will be memorable.

> What is vocal masturbation?

Answered by Peter Bach, member of the hit vocal a cappella group Basix

When you over-embellish your singing with riffs, licks and melismas, it can become self-indulgent to the point that some musicians have called it musical "masturbation."

For each vocal interjection you use to decorate your song, ask yourself the critical question: Why are you doing it? If the answer is, "because it sounds cool" or, "because I can," then I say: you can do better.

You can sing all the high notes you want, you can cover the melody in fast melismas, you can moan, you can groan, you can huff and you can puff, but if your only intention is to show us how much you can do with your voice, I promise you: we will get bored with you.

Try speaking the lyrics instead of singing them. If at some point in the spoken version of the song, you feel like moaning or screaming or crying, then you have found a good spot for vocal decoration of some sort.

We need to feel your necessity. We need to feel that the words coming from your mouth are real words coming from a real person that has something important to share with us—something that you just can't keep quiet about.

The best way to express raw emotion in your song (happiness, fear, rage, despair) might be through a sweet melisma, guttural moan or passionate high note. Here are two very different songs with different but strong emotions:

Just search for "Keep it Simple" by Kier and "Hurt" by Christina Aguilera

You can clearly feel the emotion in both songs, but one is simple with no vocal decorations and the other uses melismas. For my taste, I don't usually like a lot of melismas, but in "Hurt," the vocal decorations are well-placed and make the frustration and regret of the song even more powerful.

If you always sing with that sense of necessity, then you won't be just pleasuring yourself with your vocal interjections, the audience will get something too: they'll share in the experience of your honest expression.

> I'm afraid I'm going to go off pitch—help?

Answered by W. Timothy Gallwey, million selling author of "The Inner Game of Tennis, co-author of "The Inner Game of Music"

I want to introduce you to a very simple technique: change a command instruction to an awareness instruction. Let's say that you are told (by a teacher or by yourself) to stay on pitch. This command introduces doubt: "Maybe I am not on pitch." Doubt always negatively impacts your potential.

So, what you can do is to change the instruction from a "do" to an "awareness" instruction. Be aware of your pitch; it is very simple to be aware. There is no judgment in it. Actually, I encourage you to begin being non-judgmentally aware with all of your activities. Just observe without judgment. This doesn't mean that you don't hear when your voice is high or low, just that you stop judging your voice. As you become aware you will automatically make adjustments. There is a part of yourself that wants your voice to sound beautiful and on-pitch and it will make the necessary adjustments. The key is to trust your voice.

The most difficult aspect of the "inner game" is to trust. You need to trust your voice because you don't have a choice.

But think about it: you are intelligent. Your potential is there. I really don't think you are going to get anywhere judging your pitch every minute and telling yourself that you are too high or too low.

Don't believe in the fear that you will be off pitch. Simply listen and see what you can hear. In other words, take the command to stay on pitch as an invitation to listen more closely. The more you are non-judgmentally aware, the more the best part of yourself can make its best expression.

> When will I get paid?

Answered by Jennie Sawdon, singer, pianist and vocal tutor, voted "Wedding Singer of the Year"

In my experience, pubs and clubs tend to pay you on the night—in cash. Some will even make a direct deposit to my account before the night of the gig. However, there have been times that places said they were going to pay me later but then went bust. One time I was owed about a thousand dollars—all lost. So, it's always better to be paid on (or before) the night of your performance. I strongly suggest that you discuss this aspect before you do a gig. Musicians generally prefer cash to other kinds of payment, not, I might add, to dodge tax, but because it is easier to divide up money with other musicians on the night rather than having to pay them through your bank account.

For special events it's a little different. If I were going to sing at a wedding with a substantial fee, then I would send a contract. The most important aspect of this contract is to protect both parties. If the client pulls out of the agreement I will still get a percentage of the fee. Of course, this all depends on how early they pull out. For example there may be no fee due if they pull out up to six months before the date, a 50% fee up to three months before and a full fee if they pull out any time in the last few weeks. It took me years of getting stung before I realized that I needed this. This agreement also protects the client—if you are ill, you promise to provide a deputy of a similar standard or allow them to exit the contract with no penalty. Clients actually like to have a contract; it helps them to feel that the process is professional.

> The sound person isn't paying attention—he's texting during the whole gig.

Answered by Elliott Randall, legendary guitarist, formerly a musical consultant for Saturday Night Live

Who knows the reason your soundman is texting? Yes, he might be texting his girlfriend—but he might be texting the rest of the crew who are on their way up to the venue. You just can't assume that he's bored and not caring. If it were me, I would send the most diplomatic person in the band over to him to say, "We'd really like to achieve a great show tonight—if you need a few minutes, no problem, or would you be ready to help us out now?" It's all about non-confrontation. Everybody has to work together and feel they are on the same team.

It is a very good idea to have your own soundman—it is worth taking a cut in pay to be able to sound best.

I remember during the first part of my tenure as musical consultant for *Saturday Night Live*; Boz Scaggs was rehearsing on set and his needs were being ignored from the sound department. So he just stopped everything cold and said, "I am just going to stand here until you are all ready." I liked this response because there was no bullying involved, just a simple declaration of intention.

> The club's second act cancelled; now I have to sing for three hours—how do I do that?

Answered by Jeannie Deva, celebrity voice and performance coach

You can do this by being a PEP (Prepared Expert Professional). The PEP has these pieces in place: a vocal technique that eliminates strain, a large repertoire, a set strategy, a proper vocal warm-up and a vocal cool-down. I'm not going to say much about technique as Chapter 10 is devoted to this. However, I do want to emphasize that correct vocal technique means that you can sing for hours without injury or damage. If this is not the case for you, find a good coach and work on this area.

Here are the four ways to achieve this:

Broaden Your Repertoire. Start enlarging your list of songs now, before the need to do so is thrust upon you. I encourage singers to keep a loose-leaf notebook with a table of contents and their repertoire of song lyrics for easy reference.

Strategize Your Set. Two hours of actual singing equals three hours of performance once you include breaks, banter and applause. Depending on the type of music you sing and whether you're performing solo or with a band, construct longer sets with intimate moments that permit singing at a lower volume. One or more instrumental numbers or some sung by a band-mate will give you a vocal rest during your show. Pace your set appropriately if your voice can't support many powerful numbers in a row.

Warm-Up Properly. A proper warm-up is like an athlete or dancer gently stretching and limbering muscles in preparation for use. That's why I recommend that you don't simply sing through your songs. With a proper warm-up done, you'll easily sail into your first song with vocal freedom, confidence and a voice that will last.

Remember To Cool-Down. After performing, your vocal muscles are pumped-up. So if you don't do this, your voice can become hoarse. I've designed a number of effective cool-down exercises: one of them is a simple low-volume hum as you slide your voice up and down just a few notes like a tiny roller-coaster. Repeat several times. Then start a little higher and again go up and down a few notes. Continue for a few minutes. You'll feel the result; your voice should feel more vibrant.

> What gear should I bring with me?

Answered by Jeannie Deva, celebrity voice and performance coach

A few pieces of gear may make the difference between a catastrophic gig and a distraction-free stage performance.

Absolutely bring your own microphone. If you use the club's mic, you're going to be sharing dried spit, lipstick and germs with all the other singers who've used it. Additionally, the mic you use needs to match the personality of your voice. Otherwise, the sound design of the mic can alter your voice. This usually causes unwanted subconscious muscle manipulation as you try to get your voice to sound the way it does acoustically, but, it's being changed by the mic!

To deal with unexpected mic failure or a surprise guest singer showing up at your gig, bring an extra mic, a mic clip and cable.

You might need to bring monitors. Hearing yourself at a gig is imperative to not straining, singing on pitch and not blowing-out your voice. If the club doesn't have monitors (some smaller clubs may not have them), you'll have to be positioned such that you can hear yourself adequately through the PA speakers or … bring your own monitors.

If you perform in clubs, bring extra heavy duty extension cords and surge protectors (power strips) because the venue will almost never have them and your vocal effects pedals will be useless if you can't plug them in. And lastly, the most general purpose fix-all is Gaffer's tape (duct tape). It can be used to secure cables so you don't trip on them, but also for temporary repair of mic or music stands—and even holding a loose cable in place.

Finally, I give you my Gigging Musician's Mantra: Knowledge is Power—Plan Ahead—Arrive Prepared! This is why you need to obtain detailed information about the venues where you'll be performing.

I've heard stories of bands not knowing what gear the club had only to arrive and find that their needs couldn't be met. Know if the venue has a PA system and how many monitors. Either you or someone in your band should know if the PA mixing board has enough channels to allow everyone to be miked or amplified. Do they supply cables, mic stands, a drum shield or any other equipment your group needs to perform? If not, you'll have to bring it with you.

Be prepared and you'll have a blast!

> How can I put emotion into my performance without being fake?

Answered by Daniel Bedingfield, multi-platinum selling artist, BRIT Award Winner, Grammy Nominee

There are two choices that I've come across for any performance. In the first, an artist fakes their emotion by way of "substitution." They try to remember an old memory, trying to bring that up so that it is real in the moment. These artists are trying to get back to an earlier place, perhaps the place they were when they wrote the song, making themselves sad or happy. This is not the kind of art I want to listen to. I think it comes across as old, tired and fake.

The other choice is to create an emotion from scratch and experience it as one is singing the song and feeling the lyric. It is like creating life where there is no life. You can stay in this emotion and intention for the whole gig. It is as if you are channeling another reality from somewhere else; you are creating a little hole in the universe through which that reality can enter the room. See yourself as the creator of worlds ... of an entirely new thing.

Every mother looks at her children as unique and precious; that is the attitude that you need to bring to your performance.

You create your emotion, giving eye contact to the audience and pushing your space out to fill the whole room. Or, if you are more introverted, create this space just where you are standing with your mic and have the audience come and join you in your world—making them long for it.

I think that this is more important than everything else. Technique and singing in tune have their place to be sure, but look at Bob Dylan. We are speaking about creating something that is so real that everyone is desperate to be a part of it.

As an exercise, close your eyes and imagine that each person in the room is a pinprick of light. Imagine that you are seeing their soul as a little torch or flame. What you are attempting to do is to fill yourself with the world you have created and then expand that world and your awareness until it fills the room, until the boundary of yourself and the world you have created has reached the edge of the room and every pinprick of light is now inside of that.

When I do this and I am singing as strongly as I can, I can feel this flame flooding through my chest; it fills my whole body. I open my eyes and I usually see physical emotions in everyone's face and there is this kind of calm, like a huge wind blowing through the room. In this moment I hope that I have helped to transform the realities of the people who are listening, taking them away and out of the stressful day they have had, to somewhere calming, peaceful and exhilarating.

> I want the audience to be impressed—how can I ensure this?

Answered by Peter Hollens, Pop Singer & Producer/Youtuber with over 175 million views

There's the normal, boring answer to this question: pour time and energy into your craft before you ever get on stage. If your knowledge of the music and lyrics is rock solid, then you can be fully in the moment on stage.

We are living in a day and age when the general audience is more interested in your personality and your ability to be genuine and interact with them on a personal basis than they are on the musical perfection of your performance. So, interact with the audience if your personality allows this and it doesn't detract from the song. I was classically trained and had to learn, as I moved into the pop genre, that it's about delivery. I think that there's been so much movement in this direction because we're living in the reality TV era—people want to be a part of who you are and through YouTube and TV we've allowed them in. So, you need to show as much as possible of yourself.

I urge you to go beyond knowing your lyrics and songs and into the territory of being genuine. Be more interested in showing off your dorky self to your audience than trying to sing the highest note—they don't care—they are along for the ride (I am excluding the top 2 or 3 % of singers who are so absolutely musically gifted that audiences do come for that high note).

You have to be genuine—the audience will smell that out—whether it is on YouTube or in a live performance. Singers always feel naked on stage; your job is to embrace that nakedness and go for it. Then, the audience will respond to you. On YouTube they have the luxury of hiding behind a pseudonym. But, often people are honest in their reactions; it will help your craft if you can pay attention to what is really helpful and discount the trolls.

> What is a backline, stage plot and technical rider?

Answered by Ron "Bumblefoot" Thal, lead guitarist, Guns N' Roses, songwriter, recording artist and producer

The backline is all the gear you use at your gig (originally, "backline" referred to just the audio equipment that stands behind the band on stage, but it has expanded now to include musical instruments too).

Before you show up for a gig, you need to sort out which part of the backline will be provided by the venue, and which gear you will bring yourself. You would ask the venue, "What backline do you have?" They might say things like, "We have a cabinet but you bring your own guitar head; we have drums but you bring your own cymbals." Keep in mind that the PA, or the audio gear used to distribute the sound to the audience, is not part of the backline. I guess that makes it the "frontline," but I haven't actually heard anyone call it that.

A stage plot is a simple little drawing of the stage seen from overhead. Bands and artists use it to communicate how they would like the stage set up, when they are not doing it themselves. It shows where you want everyone to stand and where you want the gear to be. It includes things like squares for the guitar amps, rectangles for the monitor wedges and various symbols for the mics and drum kit.

The technical rider usually goes with the stage plot. It is the list of all your technical needs (the backline plus even more detail) and specifies the brands and models you prefer. You might ask for things like a direct line for keyboards, or if you sing with your own effects box, you'll need a line-out that goes to the front of house PA. At bigger venues and events, you would request a specific mic you prefer for the kick drum, for example.

> I can tell my audience hates me—what do I do?

Answered by Mary Black, leading Irish singer, renowned for her pure voice

It was my first tour as a solo artist. I was performing contemporary Irish music outside of Chicago. However, the crowd was not responding well—they were expecting me to do more traditional Irish songs. I could feel the discontent, the rumble. Finally some irate notes were handed to me on stage: "Sing something Irish!" This got my back up and I had to respond.

I told them that music didn't get more Irish than this, that I was Irish and that these songs were written by Irish writers living in Ireland and were permeated with Irish themes: immigration, famine, turmoil ... I promised them that if they could hear the words that they would connect with the music.

I wasn't rude. I feel you have to treat your audience with respect but I felt very strongly.

I went on with the performance and there was a huge turnaround—the evening ended with a standing ovation.

This brings to mind when both Bob Dylan and Joni Mitchell turned to electric music—people found it hard to embrace that change. I feel change is a good thing, though people will criticize you for changing (and for not changing!). In the end you have to be yourself and follow your heart.

I always place the emphasis on my lyrics, considering my music as poetry set to song. And even if the audience cannot understand the lyrics, if I am emotionally engaged then they can enter into the music on that level. So, if I am engaged with my lyrics and their underlying emotions then my audience has the best chance of entering into the heart of my performance.

> I know I can sing, but the pressures of both the stage and the studio are getting to me. How can I sing my best?

Answered by W. Timothy Gallwey, million selling author of "The Inner Game of Tennis, co-author of "The Inner Game of Music"

Remind yourself of your purpose for singing.

A course on music may tell you many sub-goals of music but the reason you want to sing is the big question that only you can answer.

So, why are you singing? Are you singing to get people's approval? To become famous? To share meaning and beauty? To be a star? To show off? To touch people? A combination? You have to ask yourself deeply "Why am I doing this?" Asking the question and reminding yourself of your answer is the strongest defense against the voice of fear and doubt.

Human beings are naturally purpose driven and feeding that purpose is essential. Your purpose is your own—no one can judge it.

I was coaching a professional golfer; she was the best in the country at the time. In fact, if she won three more tournaments she would be in the Hall of Fame. But she said her hands started shaking when she was approaching the last few holes on any tournament that she was in the contention of winning. So I asked her, "Why do you play this game?" She gave three beautiful answers:

a. I enjoy expressing a God given talent,
b. I really appreciate the beauty of the environment of golf and
c. I love competition.

I said, "So far your hands aren't shaking—is there anything else?"

She said, "Yes. Golf has made me somebody. I was nothing and now I am something. My fans are depending on me to win tournaments." And then she looked at me and said, "My hands are shaking now aren't they?"

They were.

I explained to her that nothing could take away her enjoyment of appreciating the first three reasons but being famous and having fans are things that can and will be taken away from her. She could be afraid of that if she wanted. But she began thinking, "Is all of this fear and doubt really worth what I am going through?" She also looked at the nonsense that she was "nobody" and now she is "somebody" and realized that she was somebody all the way along. The only thing she wanted was to be somebody in someone else's eyes. You need to ask yourself, "What do I want that for?" and "What do I get if I actually get that?" And it begins to shed light on the motive.

I now want to lead you back to the question, "Why do I want to sing?" You are the captain of your own ship and you are the one who gets to set sail in the direction that you want to. You just have to make sure the direction is what you want and not what other people want for you.

What happened to that pro golfer?

She actually didn't win the next tournament but she won the next one after that. And I saw this incredible picture of her in the paper just after she won jumping for joy into a lake—with all her clothes on. There she was flying through the air. That's the joy you get when you've gotten what's in you out. That's a joy that resides in that part of you that is free from fear and doubt.

And this joy takes precedence over the amount of applause you get.

> When should we put our breaks and how long should they be?

Answered by Katherine Ellis, hit dance music songwriter, vocalist and performer

When I am headlining at a dance club, I don't like to take a break. Building up energy throughout the set is important to me, and putting a break in the middle can take away from the momentum. On the other hand, if you are playing as background music at a restaurant or club over 3–4 hours you will certainly need some breaks. In this case, I suggest you aim to sing for no more than two hours total, breaking it up evenly across the evening.

A break should be about 15–30 minutes and not longer, so you don't lose the momentum from your previous set. Each set you play will usually be about 45 minutes. Even though I don't like to break up my show, if I am required to do so, I make sure each half has some of my big numbers in it. Remember, you may not have the same people listening to both halves of your show, so make sure each set contains something big and exciting.

One thing I do that is a sure fire way to end my show on a high is to pretend I've finished, then proceed to play several encores. People love to feel like they are getting extra. They don't know I planned to play those encores, and they walk away totally satisfied with their night. Shhhh don't tell anyone!

> How do I get past a mistake in the middle of my performance?

Answered by Donna McElroy, Grammy nominated vocalist; Associate Professor or Music at Berklee College of Music

Even when we're relaxed, well prepared, and totally focused, mistakes can happen. Many performers become embarrassed and distracted, and find it hard to concentrate on continuing through the performance. They often telegraph the mistake with their eyes, or make subsequent mistakes due to the distraction.

When I make a mistake I remind myself that it is more apparent to me than anyone else. Most of the time, the mistake I made was noticed by no one but me or the keyboard player, or possibly the songwriter if they're present; in other words, the whole gig didn't fall apart because of that misbegotten phrase.

Even in those very rare cases when a mistake is apparent to the audience, the audience will easily accept it and move on if they can see that you have done the same. Sometimes a glitch can even bring out more support from your listeners if it is handled quickly and honestly.

I remind myself that there's really nothing I can do about the previous song, and I certainly don't have to let the rest of my show suffer just because of any lapses in concentration.

I've also learned at the end of the gig to accept any and all compliments with grace and a smile (I've practiced this in the mirror!), and not to correct the audience members.

> When I'm singing a cover, I find it hard to get all the vocal riffs to sound right.

Answered by Donna McElroy, Grammy nominated vocalist; Associate Professor or Music at Berklee College of Music

Countless times I see the look of horror or devastation in the eyes of a singer when the passage didn't come out with the original artist's perfect execution. Firstly, remember that a recording is the result of perhaps several attempts. Who knows how many times the artist had to sing this passage to get the correct embellishment. All those "takes" the artist does are akin to practicing.

"Practice makes perfect" is an adage that cannot be overlooked in performance excellence, especially when it comes to a lick, run or other embellishment you are trying to "nail." No one in the audience has to know how long you spent repeating that passage. Only you know how hard you had to work to make it look effortless.

In the actual performance, that passage you rehearsed may come out differently. I may be a stickler for perfectly covering tunes, but singing a different idea should be thought of as artistic diversion, not a mistake. Do not give the variation away as an error by reacting frantically and losing your concentration. Tell yourself, "I've done all the studying of this passage I can; now I'll let the music take me where it wants to guide me!" Hearing it back, you might be surprised that your lick or run was even more soulful or emotional than the original artist's. Try to see your performance as a trailblazing new brand you're putting on the song, and go with the flow.

This will help you to make each song you learn your own. Taking risks and letting the creative juices flow will give you confidence, build your artistry and help you discover your personal sound.

> My venue says they have everything—should I trust them?

Answered by Chris Henderson, singer-songwriter-guitarist of Bronze Radio Return

We have been burned so many times in this area. There have been some very brutal shows where the monitors were distorting our sound—or not working at all. Or, the balance of our instruments was totally out of whack with how we wanted it to be. We're a six piece band with harmonica, organ and lots of guitars and we have a sense of what we want to cut through the mix at any given time—which may be completely different to what the sound guy is doing.

Some venues have great sound guys, but in other places … well … All of this led us to make the decision to have our own "front of house" person who travels with our band—he is considered an equal member of our band.

If this isn't an option for you, don't throw in the towel. If you run into a jaded sound guy, remember there may be a lot of reasons why they're rough around the edges. Perhaps they've been there too long, with bands never appreciating them. That's why, when we show up at a venue, we'll say something like "We appreciate what you're doing—is there anything we can do to help?" Make a personal connection—buy them a beer, help them set up and thank them for what they are doing—I bet they'll be less likely to have a smoke break when your set is on.

> Are there smart phone apps that singers are using at their gigs? What are they?

Answered by Kathy Alexander, singer, vocal coach and staff writer at VoiceCouncil Magazine

The answer to your question is a resounding "Yes"! There are three types of apps that come up when we talk to singers of all genres from Jazz to Metal—they're used not only at gigs but also in rehearsals.

The Recording App. It's not only innate talent that separates the "good" from the "great," but the courage to evaluate one's performances and make changes. Recording your performances is critical for this. Sometimes great ideas happen in rehearsal, but they are forgotten by the next day. So, every time you or your group has a great idea, get out your smartphone and record it. I use the "recorder plus pro" and find that the quality is good enough for me.

The Piano App. Practicing your music in the correct key not only saves your voice from strain due to singing out of range, but strengthens your "muscle memory." That's why I use my piano app constantly when I practice—if there isn't a pitched instrument around. This means I can capitalize on any chance I have to practice, even while I'm waiting in the car. There are a lot of apps available such as "Virtuoso." This is better than a pitch pipe for me because instead of just getting a starting pitch I can easily give myself the first few pitches—or a whole chord.

The Metronome App. A sense of timing doesn't magically descend from heaven; it is a quality that can be learned ... through the metronome. The metronome makes you aware of the spots where you unconsciously are slowing down and speeding up. I use "Metron"; I just turn it on at home or on the road when I am practicing to keep me consistent with my tempo. But whatever metronome app you use, make sure it does NOT have a pitch; a "click" or drum sound is always better than a "beep" or "ding."

There's so much more than I've mentioned: tuner apps for singer-guitarists, getting lyrics via the internet and being able to listen to all your mp3's for inspiration. So, the next time you reach for your smartphone, remember you just might have everything you need to push your vocal work ahead.

Engage.

What do *50 Shades of Grey*, bungee jumping, a Dickens classic and Susan Boyle's performance on *Britain's Got Talent* have in common?

They engage.

… right to the final, juicy, revelatory scene, sentence or musical note.

Our lives as performers hinge on achieving precisely this.

The contributors to this book have mastered the art of engagement. How? They have naturally or strategically connected their personal lives and passions with many of their every day habits. In other words, their involvement in music hasn't been a "hobby" separated from spending patterns, contact lists, entertainment routines and social media activity. Successful artists have found a way to bring together everything they do in the service of connecting their music to their audience. When was the last time you connected your habits to your music career?

Let's start with your money. If I were looking over your shoulder at your bank statement—or credit card bills—what would I see? Subtract the essentials: food, rent, mortgage, heat, lights, marshmallows … What's left? There is nothing so revealing about us as what we choose to spend our money on—even if it is just a few small, inexpensive items.

Let's drill down even deeper: in the last month or two what music-related purchases have you made? You may have heard a lot of music for free—but did you pay for a download, buy tickets to a concert or listen to music on a pay-for account like Spotify? Now we are getting to the juicy stuff: your musical passions. You may say that you love all kinds of music and appreciate all kinds of performers. Great (zzzzzzzz). But what is the stuff you would actually lay down your cash for? That is what you are truly engaged with. It is the music of *your soul.*

Is this music influencing your musical choices and emotional connection to the music you perform? Your own engagement to your songs is the cornerstone of truly reaching an audience. Allow your music to involve the genre, themes, sounds, or "feel" of the music you actually love. If you've been at the gigging life for a while, it may be time to make changes so that you are again excited about your set list. It doesn't matter if you are singing on YouTube, in a studio, on stage, in a box with a fox, or in the rain on a train. You must please yourself with the songs you are singing.

Now, pull out your address book (or Facebook contact list, email addresses, LinkedIn contacts). In a star-crazed world where we all hope to get discovered, we sometimes miss the gold hidden in our pocket. That's why I need to tell you the story of your Aunt Mary (or, whatever her name is …).

Once upon a time, there was an Aunt Mary. She was one of those nice, innocuous relatives who gave you a too-juicy kiss at Thanksgiving and kept sending you those sparkly-flowery cards on your birthday. You never thought to tell her that you were going to do a gig at the local pub—you didn't want her to pinch your cheeks and say "My what a wonderful young person you are turning out to be!" But she found out from your mother. What you didn't realize is that Mary is a nurse at the local hospital and, more importantly, the ringleader of the Friday night outings for all of her colleagues. She phones you up and asks, "Could we book a table at the pub where you are playing? There will be about 20 of us." You say, "yes" (because you are not an idiot) and you begin to see Aunt Mary as a potential fan. One of her nursing friends is impressed and has a son who works at the local paper and ...

Do you see where this is going?

If you are at the beginning of your gigging career your job is to put your music out there in your community—start getting performance experience, feedback, and building your fan base. Yes, you can benefit from more rehearsal time. Yes, you can spend time choosing more songs, refining your riffs and taking more lessons. These sound like "good" things to do (in fact, they are crucial to your career)—but they can be rationalizations that allow you to escape and procrastinate. Get the hell out there and use your contact list to do so. You're going to push yourself into some job experience, imperfections and all.

If you're further along, take a deeper look at that contact list and select a few promising loose threads. In the process of researching for this book, managers, agents and producers kept telling us that the singer who sends off one email to one promising contact may be left hoping forever. The singer who sends off five friendly, funny, tasteful and positive emails to the same busy contact just may eventually get the response they want.

Now let's take a look at the stuff you click onto on YouTube. Ever watch a Fail Blog? Yes, you have. Admit it. The fat man who jumps from the upstairs room into the tiny kiddie pool, the rope swing that detaches at just the wrong moment (over the inevitable pit of mud—or cow pies), the driver who can't parallel park if their life depended on it, the news reporter at the local farm who gets butted in their butt by a butt-crazed goat, the drunk 7-11 criminal who broke into the store but can't break out ... *ahhh* ... what a blessed *relief* to watch *other people* f*** up. Kind of makes me feel better about my life. Hmmmm...no wonder these clips are society's new addiction.

The truth is that we all have our personal list of Fail Blogs—most of us are just lucky we haven't got 17,798,563 views. After all, you are putting yourself in front of other people, exposing a vulnerable part of your soul though your voice and relying on technology to deliver. So many things can go wrong in the process. And they do.

It's time to reveal what separates the pro from the amateur. It isn't musical genius (well, sometimes it is). It isn't the silky quality of their voices, the star quality of their looks, the lucky breaks (this doesn't hurt) or the fact that they married a famous producer (ok, yes, it happens)—it is that they can watch *their own* Fail Blog, figure out what there is to learn, move on and never wallow in that video again. In other words, they engage with what went wrong, evaluate it, make some changes and keep going.

One of the fascinating discoveries of interviewing all 135 participants of this book was that whether they've been lucky to achieve star status or not, they all are *pros* for this reason: they've engaged with their mistakes, learned from them and moved on without meditating on them. They've also bothered to take into account audience reaction to their performance—live or virtual. They haven't rolled over onto their backs, exposed their belly button and begged the critics to walk all over them until they were a pulverized mess. But they did stop, look, listen and decide on how to best tweak things. This is what you must do with your own singing. When you have a flop (not "if"), learn from it and be *damn* persistent about getting back out there on that next balcony to jump into that kiddy pool (except that this time you will have purchased a slightly larger one ...).

Now we are going to take our last look at your secret habits—your web browser. What are the web sites you return to, the news stories you actually read to the very end, the posts and pictures that make you laugh (or cry), the tweets you like to follow? I bet you don't linger over the:

- Tweet with three words and eight hash-tags
- Facebook post announcing your friend's dinner choices
- 10th email in 10 days telling you to "buy this album now."
- Endless messages saying "check this link out" (with no reason why you should ...).
- Banner ads
- Messages that beg, harangue or whine.

No, you glossed over *all* of this—and you lingered over (and shared!) the material that moved you.

Are people doing this with your posts, tweets, blogs or announcements?

There is *no cookie cutter formula* to engaging your audience online or on stage. But there are some time-honored principles that come up from every sector of the Music Industry:

- As a singer people don't want you to sell; they want you to entertain. There should be very few selling messages in relation to your many entertaining messages.
- Bring your personality and values to your messages—and it doesn't have to be only about your music—it can be about your life, the issues you care about or stories that are important to you.
- Facilitate discussion rather than being at the center of it all. When fans start interacting with your posts, insights, pictures or messages, you are really moving forward.

We're not only talking about social media—but on stage as well. Don't sell; sing! Let your personality out and create interest in themes that engage your fans before, during and after your show.

Are you still with me? I'll be finding out when readers start responding to this book (or not). In fact, this little essay LIVES OR DIES on whether it kept you engaged until this point. If it didn't, I will revise it (or write a new one) for the second edition. If there is no second edition, I will apply what I've learned to the next writing gig. I'm not a world-famous author, but I am a *pro.*

Engage. Engage some more. Never stop engaging.

—Gregory A. Barker, PhD, Author and Commissioning Editor, VoiceCouncil Magazine

Mastering Your Gear

CHAPTER 5

Your Mic

Find it, own it, love it, trust it.

"No two human voices are the same, and no mic will be the perfect fit for every voice."

—Matt Houghton, Sound On Sound

"Having your own mic is key to taking control of your sound—besides, you need to know that it hasn't been dropped, licked or barfed on."

—The Ultimate Team

Your Mic

Find it, own it, love it, trust it.

Actions:

1. Choose Your Mic
2. Sing into It
3. Practice with It
4. Know Your Mic's Sonic Personality
5. Avoid These Mic No-Nos

Frequently Asked Questions:

» *I'm not enjoying my voice now that I'm amplified—help!*

» *I'm afraid of using those wireless mics—isn't it safer to stick with the traditional mics?*

» *Should I just buy a Shure SM 58? They seem to be everywhere ...*

» *There's always feedback. What do I do?*

» *How far should I go with owning my own gear—mic stand, cables, speakers, amp—where does it end?*

» *Does it hurt the mic to clean it?*

» *Can I lay down a high quality vocal track on a mobile device?*

» *Can my mic get too old, cold, damp—how do I know when it's dying?*

» *Do I need one of those expensive large diaphragm condenser mics (like a U87) to record vocals?*

» *What is one piece of gear I might want to own, after a mic and effects processor?*

Action 1: Choose Your Mic

Know the key things you need from your most crucial tool.

Tired of using that dirty mic that's been kicking around the venue? You know, the one with the cruddy buildup on the mesh that is so full of germs it gave you the flu? No more of this! Your mic, after all, is an extension of your voice and a key ingredient of a great performance.

So, you're going to choose your own mic and you are NOT going to be paralyzed by tech talk. You're going to get out there and develop your own opinions on how different mics sound with YOUR voice; use our "Top Ten Mic Testing Tips" (just below). But, before you run to the store, let's go over a few basics.

A key question is: what kind of environment are you singing in? If you are rocking in small, raucous venues, you'll need a dynamic mic that is very good at rejecting sound. But if you're a part of a jazz trio playing in a hushed, candlelit restaurant, then the issue of sound rejection isn't as critical. Some other mic options open up—you might even consider a condenser mic.

> *There I was, about to sing at the NAMM show—a cavernous, cacophonous room. What would I do about a mic? I decided to keep it simple: a standard dynamic mic. The key was to not set the gain so high that things squealed. If you're in a loud room, a dynamic is a good place to start. If you're in the studio or a quiet venue, you can branch out to try something more sensitive.*
>
> ***—Laura Clapp:*** *Singer-songwriter*

Each mic will have a slightly different response to your voice qualities and range and a different emphasis on proximity effect (the increase of bass frequencies when you get close to the mic). In other words, one singer's mic which gives him or her an airy, silky sheen may sound muddy on another's voice—this is why some testing will help you find just the right mic. Of course, the mic chain, PA and monitors will affect how you hear your voice—that's why it's good to test several mics out on the same system.

Finally, don't neglect cosmetic concerns. How you feel about a mic's color, weight and mesh shape are factors that will affect your performance—remember, in the end, it's all about your performance.

—The Ultimate Team

Top Ten Mic Testing Tips

Don't take the salesperson's word for it—do your own test in the store.

1. **Many**. Choose several different mics, setting these up in the in-store sound system (if you can sweet talk them into taking them home, all the better!).
2. **Flat**. Keep the volume and EQ settings the same between mics - or test them "flat" with no EQ or other effects.
3. **Perform**. Use the mic the same way you would in a performance—handheld and/or in the stand.
4. **Variation**. Sing a song (or parts of songs) that shows off variations in range, tone and volume of your voice.
5. **Noise**. Ensure you sing some strong P's and B's—mics handle popping noises differently. Also test for handling noise—does it rumble when you take it from the stand?
6. **Listen**. Ask yourself what specific quality you are listening to. It might be "low end response" or "popping". Now, sing - and listen for this quality across the mics.
7. **Proximity**. Test the proximity effect—the increase of bass frequency as you get right on the mic. Also, how does your voice sound when it is further away?
8. **Record**. If possible, record these tests to listen to them later and/or bring along a trusted friend for an additional point of view.
9. **Feel**. Don't neglect the "feel good" factor—look, color, weight and shape.
10. **Expense**. Don't equate expense with quality—at the $100-200 range, there are many potential candidates from reputable companies.

Action 2: Sing into It

It's not rocket science, but there are some basics to using a mic that will help you achieve what you want with your sound.

It may be tempting to think your sound is at the mercy of that dark, hooded figure at the back of the venue twisting knobs and punching buttons. Never underestimate your potential to control your own sound–it starts with how you use your mic.

Your basic starting point, especially for louder music, is to stay right on the mic. If you take your mic apart, removing the mesh and the foam windscreen, you'll see that the capsule looks like a little speaker inside. We all know that the best situation for listening to a speaker is to be right out in front of it–not above it, below it or to the side. It's the same with singing into your mic.

How close should you be to your mic? Listen to the effect on your sound if you sing far away from your mic–and then with your lips brushing up against the mesh. When you are 3–6 inches away from your cardioid mic, you will likely have a natural representation of your low-end tones.

These are boosted when you sing closer to the mic. This works to your advantage in intimate passages, but could work against you if you get too close during a loud phrase. Some singers need to be very close to their mic to prevent feedback or a muddy signal when there's a lot of stage noise. If you sing across the top of your mic, holding it vertically like you might hold an ice-cream cone, you'll boost your low frequencies but lose your high-end, leading to a dull signal.

So, stay close to your mic, usually within a few inches—pushing your lips against the grill from time to time so you know exactly where it is.

You'll hear experienced singers speaking about "mic technique." This means evening out your own signal by pulling back a little on your loud notes and coming forward on your soft notes. Getting in close on your mic not only allows the audience to better hear your quiet passages, but it also boosts your low fre-

> *The vocals just weren't loud enough when my daughter's new band played—despite there being a sound tech and good PA. Evidently, the tech had told the singer, "Don't you dare put your lips on the mic!" He was concerned about lipstick getting on the grill (it's an all-girl band). Fair enough, BUT the genre and venue really needed her close to the mic. Good sound techs are pleasant and businesslike; the other kind are busy burying your vocal. So, sing close—and project!*
>
> ***—Tom Lang:*** *singer-guitarist*

Do you own your own microphone?

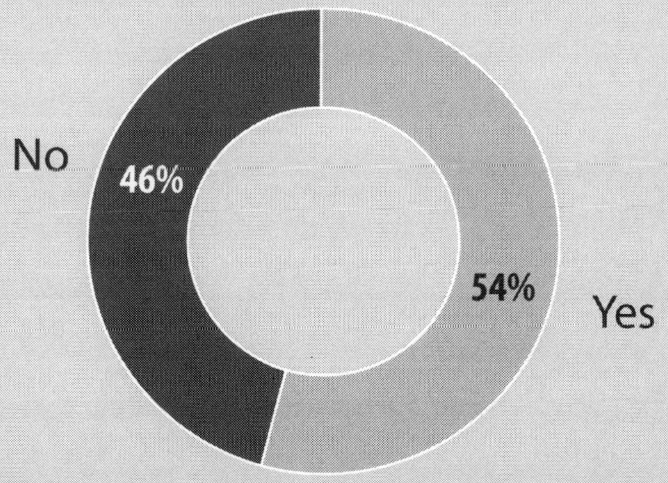

Playing the field?
69% of those who own a mic own more than one.

–from the 2012-2013 TC-Helicon survey of 1,000 singers

quencies. This is called proximity effect, and many singers use it to their advantage. To see great mic technique in action, check out any live performance YouTube video of Celine Dion, Adele or Michael Jackson.

Learning good mic technique is important: if your signal peaks on a loud note, the sound engineer will pull your level down—and he might not bring you back up for the rest of the show! Two caveats: (i) be careful about too much mic movement since you can drive your engineer crazy and (ii) singers who also play guitar or piano need to be rock solid about staying on their mic before working on this area. You see, it's just too tempting to pull away from the mic when you are glancing down at your instrument. All of these issues are easier to learn (and hear) if you have good monitoring—so make sure you look at the Actions in Chapter Six.

Finally, don't focus all of your energy on your mic. Your job is to sing, sending your energy out to the audience, letting your mic in on the deal.

—The Ultimate Team

Action 3: Practice with It

We'll introduce you to some techniques and exercises so that you will never have to have a "cold start" on stage.

Guitarists have long been in on a secret that singers are now discovering: it's great to practice with gear. In the "old days," singers would be thrown up on stage, a mic thrust into their hands and expected to get on with it. Meanwhile, the guitarist in the background brought his beloved amp from home, adjusted it to his familiar settings and propped his foot up on the cabinet for the millionth time, feeling that the stage was just an extension of his basement.

> ***How to Listen To Your Amplified Voice at Home:***
>
> *You don't need to be an audio specialist, a computer technician or a producer to hear how your voice sounds through equipment—just get:*
>
> *1. A mic & XLR cable*
> *2. A powered speaker*
> *3. A small mixer or vocal processor (sometimes a mixer is built into the powered speaker)*

Times have changed. Increasing numbers of vocalists want the same experience as guitarists—so they are in their own basements practicing with their mics, monitors and effects units. Why?

One word: Confidence.

There will always be a number of things you can't control in a live show—why make that number bigger than it needs to be? Your comfort with gear and amplification will translate into confidence onstage.

Of course there's the "I sound weird" hump that you'll need to overcome, similar to the feelings you had when you first heard your voice played back to you. Persist. You want the emotional investment

> *The soloist mentioned to me that she was using her own mic, an SM58. But when I looked at her mic, it was actually a Beta 58! They look similar but have very different sonic properties—The Beta 58 has a supercardioid capsule vs. the SM58's cardioid capsule. This told me, among other things, where to best place the monitors. If I didn't discover this before the performance, there could have a lot of feedback.*
>
> ***—The Ultimate Team***

going into using your gear and instruments to feel like *NOTHING* compared to the emotional investment in the words of your song. This takes more time for singer-instrumentalists. You'll know you're there when people don't even notice the gear—or instrument—while you sing.

Mix things up in your home rehearsal. After all, so many things can happen in a live gig: a mic stand can fail or seize up. You might be called up to sing a duet on a shared mic. A monitor can sound tinny. Simulate all of these situations. Record yourself—better yet, video yourself. When you play back your video for the first time, keep your eyes closed. Does your voice ever go quiet? Open your eyes and you may see that you drifted from the mic; if so, you've discovered a lapse in your mic technique.

Of course you can—and should—practice your singing without a mic. But when it comes to practicing for your performance, work your mic into the deal as often as you can. It's time to even the score with those guitarists.

—The Ultimate Team

Action 4: Know Your Mic's Sonic Personality

Match the way your mic "hears" with your genre, style and venue.

If you sing rock or pop, you'll be looking at mics that have a cardioid type of pick up pattern. These mics are great at rejecting sound from the back of the mic, but not as good at the sides. This is why singers using this mic place their monitor directly behind the mic.

If there is a lot of stage noise (thus feedback is a clear and present danger), you'll want to consider a supercardioid or hypercardioid mic; these mics reject even more sound at the sides (a hypercardioid has the most rejection) but do let in some sound at the back—which is why singers with these mics put their monitors slightly to their sides, at about 120 degrees. These mics are great if you are using a vocal effects processor, since they are so effective at preventing the "bleed" of noise other than your voice—a quality you need to create great vocal effects.

You would NEVER consider an omnidirectional mic (picking up sound from all directions) for a live performance since these would feedback easily—though they are used in a recording environment to pick up room ambiance and/or to capture several voices and instruments at the same time. Bidirectional mics also suffer from the same tendency to feedback, but can be great at capturing the intimacy of backing vocalists in a studio.

Most cardioid and super/hyper cardioid mics for live performance are dynamic mics. These mics use a technology that strikes a compromise between sensitivity and feedback rejection. Condenser mics, which are more sensitive to the complexities of the human voice have, until recently, been the sole province of the studio environment. However, many new condenser mics boast of excellent feedback rejection for live use. If you go down this road, then remember that these mics use a small electrical current in order to pick up and amplify their sound. This current called phantom power (about 48v) and needs to be switched on at the mixer.

> *When travelling, you could place your mic in a dedicated hard case or you could do as many gigging singers do: nest it in the midst of coiled cables in your cable case. Simply put, you don't ever want your mic banging around with hard metal objects that could dent its mesh.*
>
> ***—Tom Lang:** singer-songwriter*

Those are the basic "personality profiles," but every mic will have its own unique way of picking up and emphasizing different frequencies in your voice, with one mic merely sounding "like you" and another sounding "like YOU."

—The Ultimate Team

Action 5: Avoid These Mic No-Nos

It's time to make sure that you're not plagued by these mic maladies.

Cupping Your Mic. Yes, it might look cool in some genres, but it increases the risk of feedback and distorts your sound. On a dynamic mic there are some vents on the back of the diaphragm; close those vents and your mic becomes omnidirectional (picking up sound from all directions), causing serious feedback problems. In this state, it can no longer be relied upon to accent the highs and lows of your voice as it was designed to do. The long and short of this is that doing it usually makes your voice sound like crap. Simply grasp your mic on its stem, with your hand not too close to the mesh.

> *Did you know that your mic's mesh can be unscrewed and put in the dishwasher? You can also wash out the little foam windscreen right behind the mesh and above the capsule (taking great care, of course, that no H2O ever comes into contact with the capsule or other electric components). Doing this has the added advantage of removing that stale smell left by your friend who borrowed your mic after his smoke break.*
>
> ***—The Ultimate Team***

Mic Pick Up Patterns

Cardioid pattern

Note that this mic does not pick up sound from the "back", but does pick up more sound from the sides than the two patterns below.

Super-Cardioid pattern / Hyper-Cardioid pattern

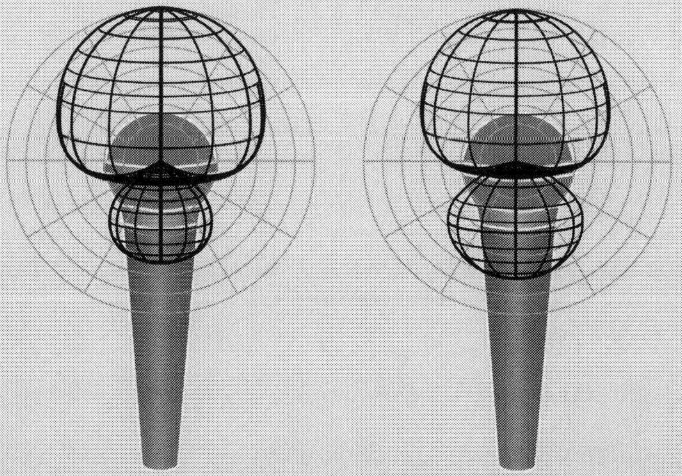

These patterns are approximations meant to highlight the difference between these types of microphones.

Mic at a Weird Angle. Standing or sitting with good posture will mean that sound will emerge from your mouth in an ever-so-slightly downward direction. Your mic needs to be right next to your mouth, also angled down slightly at a 30–45 degree angle. Holding your mic at a 90 degree angle, or holding it so that it is pointing down to your mouth (even if the mesh is close to your mouth), will have the effect of losing some of your high-end sound, creating a duller signal.

Oh God, please let someone notice and come up here and save me! My mic had started sinking lower and lower in the middle of a particularly moving song. I started hunching over—lower and lower—to sing into it, looking like a total dork. At the same time I was playing a very intricate piano part and there were no other musicians backing me up. Damn those who carelessly reef on the boom, stripping its threads!

–Kathy Alexander: *Singer, vocal coach and staff writer at VoiceCouncil Magazine*

The Low Mic. It's all too common to see singers–whether they are sitting or standing–hunch over their mic, rolling their shoulders forward or even bending their knees in to ensure that their mic reaches their mouth. All of these gymnastics compromise your vocal technique, breathing and stamina. The solution: raise the mic stand a few inches. Can't do this? Mic stand wrenched too tightly? Keep a can of WD-40 in your gig bag or ask a strong stagehand to adjust the mic. Oh, and if you're wearing running shoes for your sound check but you usually perform in high heels, take that height adjustment into account before you start performing.

The Unruly Boom. This one's a particular affliction of singer-pianists. Besides making sure your stand is tightened (but not over-tightened), a good trick with a tripod based boom stand is to have the boom parallel to one of the tripod legs; this will give you maximum stability. It sounds obvious, but it's worth saying: check that your mic isn't too far away from your mouth and that the boom does not obscure your face–it's all about keeping things as open as possible between you and your audience.

–The Ultimate Team

Frequently Asked Questions

> I'm not enjoying my voice now that I'm amplified—help!

Answered by Jaime Vendera, vocal coach renowned for his wineglass-shattering voice

Many people freak out when they finally hear their own voice, especially when amplified. Chill, rock star. You're just having "vocal image issues"—all singers do, because we all have LSD (lead singer's disease). The security of the choir allows you to blend in and not take the forefront. I suggest you keep singing in the choir to keep your voice strong and your ability to sing harmony intact. But you should also be that that front-man (or woman).

So, let's look at the amplified voice. Time for a list, so grab a pen and paper. Listen to a recording of yourself singing while coming through a sound system. What DON'T you like about your amplified voice? Too thin, too husky? Write it down. Now, what DO you like about it? Write it down.

Now, record yourself on a small, handheld recorder singing the same song and then listen back and re-check your list. Does your list reflect exactly the same likes/dislikes or are a few things different? Many times, the EQ and effects can wreak havoc on your ego. Maybe the mic has thinned out your tone, or it could be that it pointed out some little quirk, like a few flat spots you need to work on. By listening to both an amplified and hand-held recording of yourself, you'll be able to differentiate between what you need to work on and what is simply a fault of the EQ/effects setup. When it's an EQ/effects issue, simply take control of your own sound so you get the sound you want—you can use a vocal effects unit to "own" your own sound, then spend some time on your vocal exercises to strengthen those weak spots.

> I'm afraid of using those wireless mics—isn't it safer to stick with the traditional mics?

Answered by Klaus-Michael Polten, Director of Customer Relationships at Sennheiser

The highest end wireless mics used by A-list artists in live shows have a completely uncompressed digital transmission—but these mics are pretty expensive and out of the price range of most singers. I'm sure you can find a wireless mic that you like for way less money than uncompressed systems.

When wireless mic technology first appeared, you might have been right to be afraid. There were real issues with battery life and with competing signals coming through the system. All of that has been sorted out. The batteries on most mics last for a minimum of eight hours and new technology means that transmitters automatically choose clear frequencies without you having to touch or adjust anything. Of course, a wired mic will save you from spending money on batteries, but many singers are willing to pay that price for the freedom of a wireless.

There are still some crappy products out there, including some cheap knock-offs. However, most well known name brands can be trusted to give you a mic that has dealt effectively with the battery and noise issues.

I think the main reason that wireless mics are becoming more common is that audiences are getting used to singers freely moving around on stage. You should be aware, however, that not all wireless mics are the same. These mics involve compressing your voice so that it can transmit it through the air—and then decompressing your voice when it hits the receiver. This process (and the different technologies used to accomplish it) changes your audio signal. Sometimes you will not notice the change. Other times you will notice but you may even like the tonal result. You see, it is not just about technology but also about taste. This is why it is imperative that you test different wireless mics to see if you like their tonal qualities.

Finally, one tip for those of you with a wireless system: always turn your receiver on first, giving it time to search for a clear frequency. Then, turn on your transmitter (which is usually in the mic).

> Should I just buy a Shure SM 58? They seem to be everywhere …

Answered by Kevin Alexander, CEO of TC-Helicon & VP of Business Management at TC Group

Don't get caught in the trap of hearing someone singing and sounding fantastic and deciding you've got to get that mic. That mic will only help your sound if you have a similar technique, range, and tonality to your voice. Because different mics make your voice sound different, be sure that you check out all of the guidance at the beginning of this chapter on choosing a mic.

Where you sing, what you sing, how your sing—and your personal preferences for the "feel" of that piece of metal in your hand—will all play a part in your decision. Of course, the SM 58 became popular because it's a good mic, but it's definitely not the mic for everyone. Many singers swear to having achieved their desired sounds in live performance with different mics.

One thing to watch for is that many microphone manufactures have multiple versions of similar microphones. For example, many know the SM 58, but fewer people know about the Beta 58. Sennheiser has the popular e835, but there is also the e840, and e935. These mics have very different tonalities and isolation properties, but they look almost identical, so make sure you know the specific one that works well with your voice.

One of the most important things for a live performance is how much feedback rejection you want. If you've got a lot of stage noise, then there's the potential of that noise getting into your mic and causing a nasty feedback loop. An SM 58 isn't brilliant at rejecting feedback; a Beta 58 is better. On the other hand, this issue may not matter if your stage noise is low due to everyone in your group using in-ear monitors or if you are in a relatively quiet jazz trio.

Then, there are your personal feelings. How does the mic feel in your hands? Some singers like a heavier mic; some like a lighter mic. Some vocalists who sing close to the mic do not like the mesh to be rounded and prefer a flat mesh. Some singers like the tapered design of the 58, but other singers want a place where their hand naturally rests. Some mics even have an indented area for your hand. Some microphones offer on-off switches. Sennheiser and TC-Helicon both have technologies that allow you to control effect devices from your microphone. Whatever the case, your feelings about the mic are important when you are up on stage and there's nothing between your mouth and your fans except the mic you've chosen.

> There's always feedback. What do I do?

Answered by Klaus-Michael Polten, Director of Customer Relationships at Sennheiser

This comes down to basic physics: if your mic picks up sound from your speakers, it recycles this noise over and over again very quickly, becoming louder and louder. If you really want to see this in action (and you usually don't ...), then stand with your mic in front of your main speakers! Actually, if you have a guitarist behind you with a huge stack of Marshall speakers, this will do the trick.

What you need to do is to reduce the amount of sound from your speaker coming into your mic. Your first step is to get that speaker stack out from behind your mic, and make sure that you are singing from behind the main speakers. If you absolutely have to have speakers behind you then you want to be out of their "line of fire"; elevate them or place them at your sides.

This won't always be enough to reduce the amount of sound from your speakers bleeding into your mic, as you may have monitoring speakers pointing at you. So, make sure you are using a cardioid or super-cardioid mic—these are good at rejecting noise coming from the back or the side of the mic. Place your monitoring speakers so that their sound hits the area of the mic which is most insensitive to sound.

Famous Live Mics

- ***Adele:*** *Sennheiser SKM 2000-XP wireless with MMK 965-1 capsule (2012 Brit Awards & Grammy Awards performances)*
- ***Mariah Carey:*** *Shure KSM9 (Adventures of Mimi tour)*
- **Caleb Followill (Kings of Leon):** Sennheiser 935 (Only by the Night tour)
- ***James Hetfield (Metallica):*** Audio-Technica AE5400 (Death Magnetic tour)
- **Whitney Houston:** Sennheiser SKM 5200 (*Many live performances—also used by Beyonce, Rihanna & Cher*)
- ***Michael Jackson:*** Shure WBH54B Headset Mic ("This Is It")
- ***Jack Johnson:*** Neumann KMS105 (*Most festival appearances in 2010 including* Glastonbury, Hurricane, *and* Kokua)
- ***Norah Jones:*** Neumann KMS104 (*Most live performances*)
- ***Frank Sinatra:*** AKG C535 EB (Custom *gold version used in many concerts in his later years*)

After this basic step, you will want to consider the quality of your mic and speakers, as this can have a significant bearing on feedback. Many vocalists have moved to in-ear monitoring precisely because of this challenge. With in-ear monitoring, your signal comes directly into your ear, reducing the stage noise that enters into your mic. Your stage sound becomes clearer and your monitor sound is very consistent.

A final tip: it also helps to get close to your mic when you sing—this makes it more difficult for other signals to get into your mic.

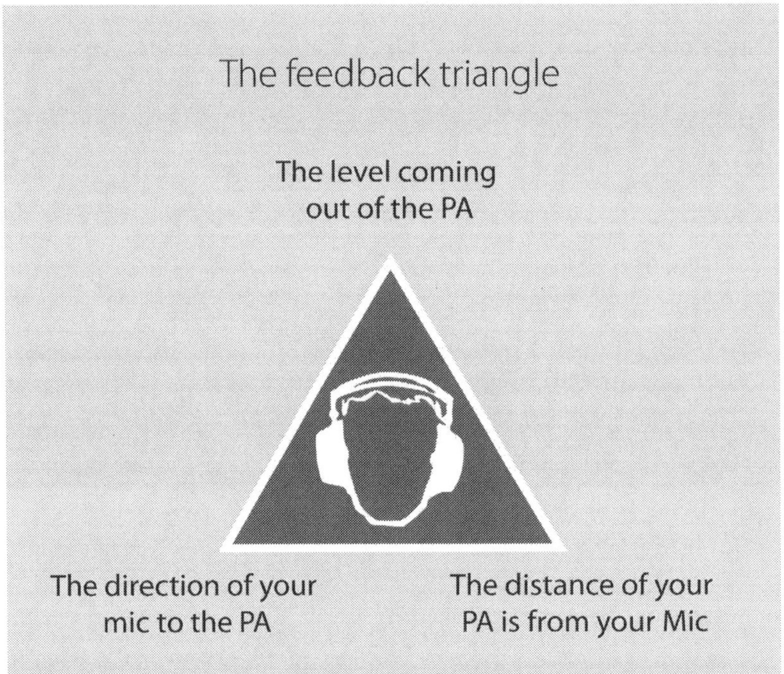

Any one of these corners of the triangle doesn't cause feedback on its own; together they do. The worst case is a loud PA, a mic pointed directly at your PA and the mic is very close to the PA. Change one part of the triangle (for example move the mic further away from the PA) and feedback is reduced.

> How far should I go with owning my own gear? Mic stand, cables, speakers, amp—where does it end?

Answered by Val Emmich, singer-songwriter, hailed by the New York Times as "a rocker who rocks to his own beat"

I've moved from one extreme to the other on this. Now, I have almost nothing when I do a live show. The key question is: "how much gear do you need to feel comfortable putting on a great show—*without feeling distracted*"?

I used to be obsessed with reproducing the sounds on our albums. So if there was a tremolo pedal in a brief part of our recorded song, I would make sure to have that on stage. My pedal board ended up being stacked with everything imaginable. I'd have a second guitar to get a specific sound quality on a certain song. All of this extra gear jeopardized the momentum of my live show for the audience. That's the wrong focus.

The audience simply doesn't care about your gear. They just want you to be "with them." The more gear that you have, the more that can go wrong: batteries running out, cables getting kinked, strings breaking, a pedal getting lost from your extensive collection. It's about reducing risk. If you're a germ freak, then have your own mic and stand—no problem. But constantly question the amount of gear that you have.

It took me a while to really understand how an album is a different beast from a live show. A recording is a statement that has to last through time; a live show is just a moment. My live audience is paying attention to the song as a whole, not the tiny details. So now I bring the least amount of stuff possible, and I want my entire band to follow the same mantra. I don't want my guitarist bending down to fix things in the middle of a song. I will often ask my band, "What are the bare essentials we need to get this song slamming?" We go with that.

In a live show, people really pay attention to the vocals. So if there's a choice between my guitarist playing a complicated guitar riff or adding a vocal harmony to emphasize the vocal sound, I'll choose the harmony every time. Strengthen the part of the music that people can relate to, sing along to. Be slaves to the song—the song is master. No one cares about the rest of this shit. It's hard for us music freaks who labor over every little nuance to get that through our thick skulls, but it's true.

> Does it hurt the mic to clean it?

Answered by Klaus-Michael Polten, Director of Customer Relationships at Sennheiser

A dynamic mic is normally very robust. You should never touch the capsule itself, but there is no problem with removing the metal basket and cleaning it. You can also clean (or replace) the foam inside the basket. In fact, this cleaning is necessary to reduce infection and to slow down the process of crud building up inside your mic.

You may lose some of the high end on your mic due to dirt accumulating on or below the membrane. This can take years to develop, and given the relatively low price of dynamic mics, you will normally just replace your mic. For expensive condenser mics used for recording, you might send your mic in for servicing. You'll notice that you are losing your high end when you go to your mixer, add more treble via the EQ and just get noise instead of a clear signal.

The reason you would not touch the capsule is because this is the sensitive part of the mic. The air from your voice moves a precisely placed membrane of polycarbonate that then converts your sound into an electric signal.

Your Mic's Demise

There are usually only three causes of your mic's demise:

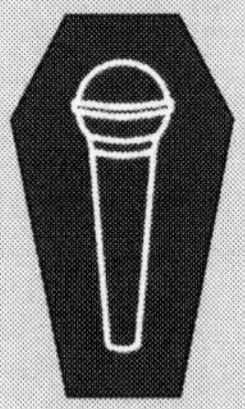

1. **Dirt buildup (this usually takes years to affect performance)**
2. **Connections getting tugged past breaking point**
3. **Being dropped**

Of these, dropping is common cause of mic death. However, some mics can be dropped many times without affecting their performance — though we don't recommend you try this.

> Can I lay down a high quality vocal track on a mobile device?

Answered by the Ultimate Team

Many viewers thought we were cheating with the sound on our "VoiceJam" looping-on-a-smartphone video—but we weren't. Of course there were rehearsals and multiple takes, but we managed to get excellent audio. However, these mics still have some way to go. Let me explain why.

Typically, the mic or mics in your phone are "omni-directional" (picking up sound from all directions) and loaded with processing that is designed to accentuate speech rather than produce a nice tone. One of these processors is an automatic gain control (ACG) that makes the gain swing higher when your voice goes quiet. Then, when you increase your volume, the gain swings lower, cancelling out background noise. These swings lead to an uneven vocal signal with background noise appearing and disappearing throughout the recording. Also, the sound from these mics tends to lack "low end," which means that your voice lacks warmth at best, and sounds tinny at worst. You also have to watch out for popping, which can be dealt with by singing at an angle to the mic.

These challenges can be overcome by using an external mic—there are some ingenious devices currently being designed for smart phones, and mobile field recorders come complete with XLR inputs for external mics. Perhaps the most dramatic developments have been in the area of USB mics, with leading brands developing high-quality mics that plug directly into your computer or offer an interface so that traditional vocal mics can easily be made digital.

This external mic solution is especially relevant for singers who want to make an impact through YouTube videos. Your best sound will be picked up by a mic that is close to your mouth—impossible to achieve with an inbuilt cameral mic. The right room can help with your sound quality, but the best solution is to either find a camera which allows you to plug in an external mic or to pick up your sound on a separate device and sync it up later.

> Can my mic get too old, cold, damp—how do I know when it's dying?

Answered by Wes Maebe, Recording-Mix-Mastering, FOH engineer for Sting, New Model Army, Yusuf Islam, Ellie Goulding, Elliott Randall

Microphones cannot get too old at all. In fact, the current trend is that the older the gear, the "cooler" it is.

Like anything older, it will need a lot of care. Quite a few of the in-vogue vintage microphones tend to be tube/valve and ribbon mics and, by default, these are quite delicate.

Mics are core units of your stage and studio work; obviously, you're going to look after your equipment. Dusty, smoky and damp environments are to be avoided at all times.

If your microphone's capsule gets damp or dirty, it will no longer perform correctly. Bad cases can manifest themselves as hissing noise or no sound at all. Crackling can also indicate that something's wrong; a capacitor or valve may be on the way out and may have to be replaced.

When you're not using your mics for a while, store them in their cases or cover them up. Ribbon mics are the most fragile of them all. Because their capsule is made out of an extremely thin piece of metal, dropping them or exposing them to a sudden blast of wind can result in a damaged diaphragm and repairing this can be costly.

Tricks to Tweak Your Smartphone Recording:

If you haven't purchased a smartphone or tablet yet, read people's opinions on brands and models that sound best.

Consider an aftermarket stereo mic with pop filters.

Get the best headphones or buds you can afford but don't fall for the hype: the most expensive "hip" headphones are more about style and overabundant boom than true reproduction.

Purchase an 1/8th" adaptor cable to go to audio gear. Generally the other ends are ¼" jacks. This helps you play your performances through the big speakers for maximum impression value!

Tube mics may require a little warm-up time; especially after you've switched them off, let them cool down for a little while before you move them around or pack them away.

> Do I need one of those expensive, large diaphragm condenser mics (like a U87) to record vocals?

Answered by Dirk Brauner, founder of Brauner Microphones

I can tell you this: singers who have moved from cheap to more expensive recording mics never go back. The U87 (and I would add the U67 and U47) are terrific recording mics, but they are far from the only ones. In fact, some singers feel strongly that other large diaphragm mics serve their voices better—it's an individual thing.

Cheaper mics sometimes tend to sound "muddy," have a limited dynamic range and frequency range and can produce strange resonances, peaks and noises due to the construction of the housing and the circuitry. Having said that, there are a few arguments for using cheaper recording mics. First, if you were to start out playing violin with a Stradivarius, you might never learn to value a great violin. That's why I like it when people have an experience of cheaper gear; they really develop sense of awareness when it comes to technical quality. It's the same with your first cheap guitar where the strings are high above the frets. Then, you move to a quality instrument and feel how sweet it is to play. If you start with cheap mics and then move to quality ones, you will notice that the difference is phenomenal.

The other thing that has to be said about cheaper mics is that sometimes you might get lucky. The main issue, after all, is the end result—the recording itself. Compared to when I started working on recordings, the standards of cheaper mics are rising. Try out several mics with a dealer who has a mic closet. If you find a cheaper mic that sounds great with your voice, then stick with this particular mic, even if the dealer insists on a mic off the shelf because they're supposed to be identical.

Enough about cheap mics. If an excellent recording is your priority, you will want a well-built, large diaphragm mic. Any large diaphragm mic worth its salt will make your voice sound like it has been rendered precisely, giving it a natural and detailed sound. This may take some time getting used to because you hear all of the details in your voice. When you are new to this, it is astonishing and may feel uncomfortable at first. So give yourself some time to develop a feeling for it. With more expensive mics the sensitivity is usually very high, so when you plug your mic into the preamp, you might be pretty hot. What you have do to is to lower the level on the preamp in order to find the right range to work in. This is something you have to get used to doing, especially if you are coming from a cheaper mic.

> What is one piece of gear I might want to own, after a mic and effects processor?

Recorder. Assuming you've already apportioned funds for singing lessons and cables etc, the next thing you could consider is a little portable recorder like those made by Zoom. Sure, you could use a smartphone but at the volume most bands play at, those sound pretty mushy and distorted while being too valuable to leave around. The mini recorders can take the higher volume and they record in stereo which lends a nice ambience to the proceedings. This is important because you need uncritical, unflinching feedback on how well you are singing as well as what you're saying between songs. If you haven't saved up for lessons, a mini recorder may increase your desire to do so!

—Tom Lang, product manager at TC-Helicon, singer-guitarist

Monitor. Invest in a powered monitor speaker that packs some punch. This gives you the ability (along with your mic and effects unit) to rehearse with amplified sound. Once I showed up to a gig and something was wrong with the venue's sound system. I just put my little powered monitor up on a stool behind me, pointing out to the audience. It became my monitor and my Front of House PA at the same time. The rest of my band had their own amplifiers, so we were able to do our show. Sure, it wasn't ideal, but I love being self-sufficient. And I don't even need to ask my band mates to help me carry anything—my mic, cables, effects box and speaker go in a bag in one hand, and my mic stand in the other.

—Kathy Alexander, singer, vocal coach and staff writer at VoiceCouncil Magazine

Mic Preamp. In a nutshell, a preamp raises the level of your voice's signal from mic level to line level. Mic level is the signal strength at the output of the microphone, typically 30 to 60 dB below line level. Line level is the strength of the signal that the internal mixer circuitry needs to see. The output of an outboard preamp plugs into the mixer line input, not the mic input. What is especially important to note is that the preamp can affect the sound and personality of your voice in the sound system. That's important for two reasons: firstly, if you find a preamplifier that works well with your voice and your microphone, your vocal sound will better off. Secondly, if you rely on the built-in preamp in the mixer, it might sound good or bad. This is a worthwhile investment, especially if you're playing smaller shows and are in control of your vocals in the mix.

—Bill Gibson, producer and author of more than 30 books on technology

CHAPTER 6

Sound System Basics

It's time to "friend" your PA.

"When I turn up at the gig, they tell me to set up 'over there.' Why is it that 'over there' is always 10 meters away from the nearest power outlet?"

—Phil King, singer-songwriter

"My guitarist husband actually required me to be able to roll mic cables up properly (the alternating figure-eight method) before he'd marry me—how's that for a pre-nup condition?"

—Kim Chandler, top session singer and industry coach

Sound System Basics

It's time to "friend" your PA.

Actions:

1. Plan Your Signal Path
2. Connect Your Mic
3. Set Your Input Level
4. Tweak Things to Perfection, Part I
5. Tweak Things to Perfection, Part II
6. Master Your Monitors
7. Get the Right Monitor Mix
8. Be a Cable Snob
9. Match the System's Power to Your Needs
10. Keep Your Perspective

Frequently Asked Questions:

» *What do I do if the sound stops working during my show?*

» *I can't hear myself!*

» *Do I need solid gold/nickel/titanium cables?*

» *There's too much stage noise and people are telling me that I'm singing a little off the beat.*

» *Whose job is it to make sure I sound good?*

» *Why do sound guys and girls always look so grumpy?*

» *What am I allowed to say and not say to a live sound guy or girl?*

» *Should the vocals be the loudest thing in the band?*

» *Some bands "cut through" but ours sounds "muddy"—is it just our sound system?*

Action 1: Plan Your Signal Path

Picture how your voice will reach the audience in your mind's eye so you can make it a reality for everyone's ear.

Here's a simple definition of a sound system: ***all of the gear that stands in between your voice and the ears of the audience.*** Some people call this a PA (public address system). What you are most concerned about is the "path" your voice will take though the system.

On one end of the system you have a mic that turns your vocal vibrations into electrical signals. These signals go to a preamp, a device that raises the power of these signals before ("pre") it flows through a mixing board. The mixing board is the intelligence center where you can adjust the tone, volume and other aspects of your signal—and combine and mix your vocal signal with other signals (like a guitar). Your signal is now sent to an amplifier which adds that heart-stopping power before it is outputted to the speakers. Of course the term "speakers" includes monitors (so you can hear yourself) as well as mains, those big black box speakers that ensure everyone else hears you too.

Mic—Preamp—Mixer—Amp—Speakers: these are the basic components. These might be separate pieces of gear, or certain components might be integrated into one piece of gear, such as a powered speaker that combines the amp and the speaker in one unit.

Let's say you are doing a gig where you will be using someone else's sound system. You don't need to be intimidated by new equipment; just imagine the system from the point of view of your voice. When you arrive at the venue, you'll want to:

- Plug your mic into the system (see Action two).
- Set the gain on your effects box and on the system (see Actions three and four).
- Tweak your level, EQ and effects, making sure things sound right in the monitors and that there is a great mains mix. There may be an experienced sound engineer to assist with this—if there isn't, Actions four and five will tell you what you need to know.
- Now, perform like there's no tomorrow.
- After your gig, deepen your knowledge about some critical components of your PA, or consider purchasing some gear—check out Actions 6–10.

The incredibly rapid pace of technological evolution has placed quality gear into the hands of musicians everywhere. It's now within your grasp to understand and be in control of your sound more than ever before—this chapter gives you the knowledge to do so.

—The Ultimate Team

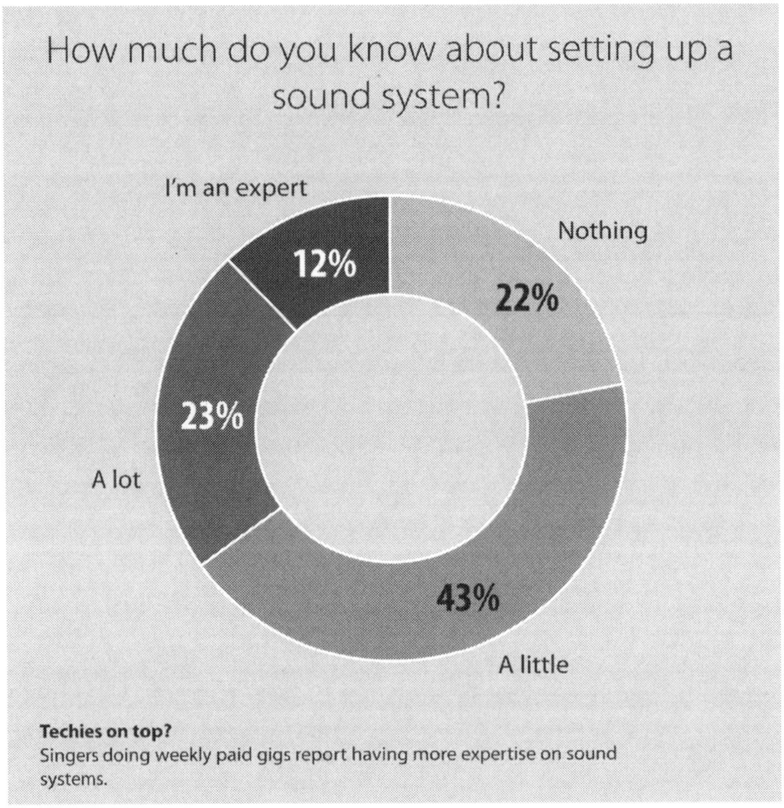

–from the 2012-2013 TC-Helicon survey of 1,000 singers

Action 2: Connect Your Mic

Proper mic etiquette goes a long way toward maintaining your gear and putting on a great show.

Professional mics come with an XRL connector; a ¼ connector likely means you have an amateur/karaoke piece of gear. XLR is short for Extra Long Range; it involves a system of three wires that allow you to run long cables so that there won't be interference with other devices or loss of audio quality between your mic's signal and the rest of the equipment. You are going to insert the "female" end of your mic cable into the stem of your mic and then the "male" end into your vocal effects processor, mixing board or "active" speaker (speaker with amp/mixers built in).

You'll always want to have your channel muted when you plug in your mic—this avoids pops and feedback loops, which can be dangerous for your gear (and your bandmates' ears). This is especially important when using mics with phantom power. This little bit of power flowing to a condenser mic can cause a massive sound when you plug your cable to the channel and your system is on.

While we're on the subject of muting, make sure you mute all the mics during your break between sets. You'd be surprised to see how many performers don't do this; they find themselves at the back of the venue having a drink when an inebriated stranger goes up on stage to have some fun. There's a mute switch on every channel of your mixing board—and sometimes an overall "break" switch on your system. You can have all of the channels muted but still have the capacity, on most mixing boards, to play an MP3 through the system to provide some background music on your break (and further deter that drunken yahoo from running up on the stage to fill the silence with his antics.)

Now some final tips on plugging in your mic: always hold it while you plug in the cable—this avoids the all-too-common occurrence of mics on stands falling over. Sometimes singers shove their connectors together without aligning them, followed by some twisting and turning to get things into alignment. This isn't a good idea since the connection can weaken and fail. Simply look at the alignment first before plugging in. Finally, many XLR cables have a spring-loaded pin that presses into a groove in your mic to make it lock. So when you connect your mic, you should hear a little "click" if you have this feature—and remember to depress that pin when disconnecting your mic.

—The Ultimate Team

Action 3: Set Your Input Level

It's about those green and amber lights—and the dangers of the "red-light district."

The next thing you will want to do—with your channel still muted—is to set the gain on the mixing board channel for your microphone. There are different terms for this function: level, gain, attenuation, or trim. Basically, when you connect your mic to the system there is a little amplifier in the mixer (a pre-amp) that adds some power to your signal so that it can work in the sound system. What you need to do is to match the vocal power you are sending into the mic with the mixer.

This is where those little green, amber and red lights come in. What you are trying to achieve at this stage is a signal which doesn't distort on the one hand (the red lights) and which is too low on the other hand (just a few green lights). If you have it set so that there are often red lights showing when you sing, you will hear distortion in the system. Engineers call this distortion "clipping"; if you study a sound wave pattern at this moment, it is as if someone has clipped off the tops of all of your sound waves so that they go up, ending in an abrupt, flat plateau rather than reaching a nice rounded peak.

The ideal setting for you will be to set your gain knob to a place where you are going amber, but not red when you sing passages that are loud and strong (though sometimes you only get green and red—or only red lights). If you are using a vocal effects processor, you run through this process twice, once with the processor and once with the mixer.

Now remember, setting the gain isn't getting the volume right for your audience; it's about getting the equipment working right. You are being a mechanic when you do this step—not a producer. You will set the volume after the gain. For systems that don't have separate gain and volume controls, you just have to work out a compromise.

We don't want to make you too afraid of the "red light district." The fact is that different manufacturers set those red lights at different audio levels. With some boards, if you see a red light, you are actually clipping or distorting while on other boards you are about to distort. So have a look at your manual. Better yet, just experiment with this so that you have a good, strong level.

—The Ultimate Team

Action 4: Tweak Things to Perfection, Part 1

Now it's time to make your sound sizzle through the entire system.

Getting a great vocal sound begins with vocal technique, choosing a mic that compliments your voice and mastering mic technique (see chapter five)—but it doesn't end there. You'll want to ensure that your signal is the best it can be at every point in the signal chain. Here are some tips to guide you:

Get the gain right. Remember that setting your gain on your preamp, effects box and/or amp is not the same as setting your volume. With gain you are adjusting the amount of power in your signal—not the volume leaving the system through the speakers (that's adjusted with your channel fader and mains fader) A good rule of thumb is to sing one of your more powerful passages and watch the meter (some preamps have a single red "clip light"). Turn the gain up until your signal clips and then turn the knob to the left a bit. Think in terms of the hands of a clock: if you are clipping at 2 o'clock, set it at 1 o'clock. Keep your eye on this in performance as you may get excited, sing more loudly than you did in the sound check, and need to back it off a bit more.

Control your monitor mix. It's important to know that the signal coming into your monitors does not need to be the same sound the audience is hearing through the mains. The auxiliary channels on your mixer allow you to hear a completely independent signal from the mains mix—and even to set effects (such as EQ) differently. We deal with monitors separately in this chapter, but the main thing is to ensure that you have clear rhythm and pitch references—and that your voice is set loud enough so that you don't over sing to compensate for a weak vocal signal on stage.

Learn to use tone controls. EQ is short for equalization; these tone controls allow you to cut or boost different frequencies in your sound. We're covering EQ in more detail on the next page, but it's important for you to know that EQ isn't the only way to tweak your tone. Your mixer's pan control allows you to move sound between Left and Right channels in a stereo system. Lead vocals are panned to the center along with, usually, the kick drum, snare and bass—but other instruments and backing vocals may be panned to the left or right. Panning these other sounds can actually can remove an "intruder" from a problem frequency area—and stop you from using too much EQ to solve it.

—The Ultimate Team

Action 5: Tweak Things to Perfection, Part II

It's time to face up to the limits and possibilities of EQ.

The ideal situation is for your voice, mic and sound system to work together to produce a great tone in the venue—without needing to adjust any of your frequencies. That rarely happens in live situations! The reality is that you may sound "muddy" in one room and "tinny" in another room of the same size.

With the EQ knobs on your mixer (sometimes called "tone control"), you can boost or cut specific frequencies of your sound. Many singers who are new to EQ simply turn up a certain frequency that they want to hear more of. For example, their voice sounds a little dull, so they boost the high frequency. Now, it's less dull but sounds a little harsh, so they turn up the mids and lows. Eventually, all of the EQ settings are turned up and the signal is distorting. Subtracting EQ is usually better than adding it because problem frequencies can hide behind other frequencies. This means that you sometimes miss the frequency you need to adjust by simply turning things up.

How do you set your EQ? On many mixing boards you will have knobs that control highs, high-mids, low-mids and lows. If you're lucky, you'll have a mixer with two sets of knobs for each main frequency (this is called parametric EQ)—one knob selects the frequency you are going to adjust and the other knob selects how many dBs (Decibels = the relative change in sound level) you will be cutting or boosting. Setting the EQ is an art, so allow time for experimentation and, if possible, watch an experienced sound engineer at work. Yet here are a few things to watch out for: if you are singing close to the mic, you are boosting your lower frequencies and this could cause you to sound muddy (in some venues). Try turning down the low and mid ranges a bit. If you then find that you want a little more clarity in the high end, you might try a little boost in the 3–6 kHz area; this will add a little "shine."

Perhaps there is a low rumble in your signal—your mic may be picking up street noise or the sound of the furnace in the venue. You can use the "high pass filter" in your EQ settings to cut out these frequencies. If your console is sophisticated enough, you can actually set this function rather than rely on a preset frequency. While singing, sweep the low frequency knob up to perhaps 300 Hz, until your voice sounds a bit thin—you've removed some of the fullness of your voice. So, back it down (perhaps between 150–200 Hz) and set the level. No more rumble.

Experienced engineers know that changing one set of frequencies affects others, which is why they will spend time sweeping their knobs and trying different solutions before deciding on EQ settings for your voice. These engineers also always use one word when referring to EQ: "moderation." These "tweaking tips" introduce the fascinating and complex area of live sound engineering; if you want to get into more depth with these issues, we recommend you pick up a guide dedicated wholly to this area such as *The Ultimate Live Sound Operator's Handbook* by Bill Gibson, one of the contributors to this book.

—*The Ultimate Team*

Action 6: Master Your Monitors

The key to a great performance can lie with the monitoring ...
and we aim to make you an expert.

If you can hear your voice well in your performance, then that is the end of the story when it comes to monitors—you can skip this section.

> *Monitors can be your best friend or your worst enemy. I've gone over to in-ears. In Thrash Metal music we're always fighting stage volume. Instead of having to battle with three different loud stage monitor mixes, in-ears put the mix I want to hear right into my head. Plus, you don't have to lug monitor boxes around. But they're not perfect. They won't help you sing better. There can be interference with wireless units and you still need a good engineer.*
>
> **—Joey Belladonna:** *soloist and former lead singer of Anthrax*

Oh, wouldn't it be great if life were that simple? The fact is that having the right monitors, getting what you need to come out of them, using them without feedback and knowing where to best place them are perhaps the most critical areas to get right for your live performance.

The good news is that hearing yourself while singing has never been easier with many different kinds of reasonably priced monitors on the market. So, let's start with learning about different types of monitors—for a handy overview see our chart below: "Monitors—Advantages and Disadvantages."

The most common monitors are "wedges." These are the wedge-shaped black boxes you see on the floor of many stages. Many singers, however, swear by their in-ear monitors. These are either wired or wireless and have the advantage of bringing the exact mix you want directly into your ears—at the volume you select. A newcomer to the monitoring world is the mic stand monitor, also known as the "near-field" monitor. These handy units stay close to your ears and are within your reach so that you can change the volume and tone to your liking. Of course, you can always go without monitors, trying to place the mains in such a way that you can hear yourself clearly. But hearing yourself clearly while you perform is the key. It's difficult to make mains work for both the audience and those on stage without causing feedback, so most singers have come to rely on monitors.

Electric guitarists would never be caught dead without their amp in the trunk of their car—even if they are playing a gig with a sound system in place. If something goes wrong, then they have the assurance of knowing they can always plug into their own gear and get their sound out. Should it be any different for vocalists? The fact is that many singers are buying their own set of monitors not only so that they are ready for any emergency, but also as their main component of their rehearsal PA or as a component of the system that they take to small venues. These will typically be wedge or near field monitors that have a variety of mounting options—including being able to put them on stands (or "sticks") for use as main speakers.

If you're going to buy yourself some monitors, keep in mind the general rule that expensive isn't always better. Still, you need to watch out for some cheap monitors (especially cheap wedges) that distort easily and make you sound awful. High quality monitors can be a singer's heaven. Made of only high quality components and run by someone who knows about monitoring, you will feel that you are getting a treat—you may even find that you need less volume out of your monitors because you can hear your voice so clearly.

—Tom Lang: product manager at TC-Helicon, singer-guitarist

Your Guide To Monitor Types—Advantages

Wedge Monitors	In-Ear Monitors	Mic Stand (Near Field) Monitors
A good quality set can double as your PA in small venues and your rehearsal equipment at home.	Personalize your mix.	Lightweight, small, easy to transport.
Some types can have a variety of mounting systems	Less chance of feedback.	Closer to your ears than wedges; therefore less volume required.
You are not isolated from other sounds on stage.	Protect your hearing by eliminating loud sounds and setting a level that is healthy for the long-haul.	Less chance of feedback than wedges from mics other than your own.
Sound quality is improving on mid-range wedges all the time.	Move around the stage with great ease (especially with wireless in-ears).	Less expensive than wedges.
	If using the same system in different venues, you can easily set up your mix, especially on digital systems which memorize your settings.	Can use with both regular and boom mic stands.
		Volume control within reach.
		Some units have tone controls.

Disadvantages

Wedge Monitors	In-Ear Monitors	Mic Stand (Near Field) Monitors
Consume stage space; less freedom to walk out in front	For a good mix you need all of the instruments mic'd. This many mics and cables may be impractical and may require a larger mixer with more capabilities.	Not all systems have conquered the "wobbliness" factor re. the mic stand.
Heavy to carry and transport	There's a potential for ear damage (i.e. someone knocks over a mic) – if your system does not have a limiter.	If you're in a louder band, these might not cut it.
Spread sound all over the stage; feedback possible	Having a stereo mix in your head may be disorienting when you turn around and look at your band and the sound is coming into your ears from a different direction.	
At high volumes there can be a "roar" at the rear, broadcasting annoying sounds to the audience.	Isolation: you may not hear some of the subtle but essential cues the audience or band members are giving you about their performance. That's why some singers mic the stage and the venue and add these elements into their mix – this is more work, however.	
	For a good quality in-ear experience, you need these custom molded – this is expensive and time consuming.	

Action 7: Get the Right Monitor Mix

This is where you try to eliminate the competition—the competition for your frequency, that is.

The ideal monitor mix involves hearing your voice clearly with at least one rhythmic instrument. If you are lucky enough to have reached this, you may not need to tweak anything.

If you aren't feeling happy with your monitor mix, notice the sounds that are conflicting with your voice. Maybe it is the guitar or the synth; try less of these in your monitor mix before you turn your voice up. You see, we singers will often ask for "more me" in our monitors, but that doesn't always solve our problem. Sometimes this actually works against hearing ourselves blend with the band. Instead of "more me," try less of other things. This also has the advantage of protecting our ears.

Now, sing a few things in the higher part of your range and in the lower part of your range. You'll want to hear a good, clear sound of your voice, something that sounds natural (unless you are using certain effects). In other words, you'll want a signal that is neither too "boomy" nor "bright." This is related to your frequency—if you're sounding too bassy, boomy and muddy, then turn down the lower frequencies a bit. If your voice is sounding "shrill" or "tinny," back off the high frequencies. Have some fun experimenting with this. In rehearsal, sing and create some boom by turning the bass knob all the way up. Then, turn this knob down and hear your voice thin out. Try the same with the mids and highs—listen to the extremes to help you feel your way into a good monitor mix. You'll also be learning about what those tone controls do.

Of course, a good monitor mix is all for naught if you are getting feedback. You'll want to make sure that your mic is in the "right" relationship to your near field or wedge monitors. This requires you to know a little bit how mics pic up sound—since the best scenario for avoiding feedback is to have the sound coming out of your monitor hitting a "dead" area of your mic.

> *Because I'm a woman often the sound guy turns my highs up. But, I often ask him to turn my highs down and my lows up so that I'm not irritating people with my voice and the "ee ee ee" the whole time. I need some "boom" in my sound.*
>
> **—Divinity Roxx:** *former musical director and bassist for Beyonce's all female band 2006–2011*

The average dynamic mic for live performance has an audio pick-up pattern shaped like a heart (cardioid) with the point of the heart representing the "dead" area at the back of your mic's mesh—where the "ball" of the mic meets the stem. Thus, this mic can be directly in front of the monitors with little chance for feedback. However, your ears will hear your monitoring better if your monitors are placed at your side. This means that you will want to experiment with monitor placement and make some sort of compromise between the potential for feedback that comes from having your monitors pointing at the side of your mic and the relative safety of having your monitors directly in front of you.

Other mics have different pick up patterns (see Chapter five, Action four) and different feedback rejection levels, so you will want to take a look at your mic's manual and then experiment with monitor placement so that you feel confident as you rock down the house.

—The Ultimate Team

Don't settle for a poor monitor mix. A lot of singers don't want to impose or they might feel insecure in asking the sound operator for help but this is important for the quality of the vocal performance. Keep working to get the monitors right—that's really the most important part of a singer's sound check. If the monitors aren't set correctly, the singer's pitch, rhythm, and emotional delivery will suffer dramatically. If the monitors are set correctly, the singer will feel comfortable and relaxed and will be capable of providing the best possible performance.

***–Bill Gibson:** President of Northwest Music and Recording*

Action 8: Be a Cable Snob

It's worth risking the criticism of "anal" when it comes to your cables and their care.

Life is just too short to deal with bad cables. We're talking about the cheaper cables or the ones that come free in your microphone package. These can crease, kink and break easily because they have not been engineered with high quality wrappings. In fact, it's not uncommon to find a permanent crease in cheap, factory-wrapped cables–this later develops into a break.

You're likely not going to be able to hear the difference from the quality of metal used in the cable, but a higher priced cable will be less likely to kink and break when you are wrapping it up. That's because there's a strain relief system in the cable sheathing that uses various fabric or plastic wrappings that allow your mic a few more tugs before it breaks. Remember that XLR cables are the opposite of Apple's "MagSafe" connectors–they take the full strain of any tug, pull or trip.

You will extend the life of your cables for years (not to mention endear yourself to the rest of your band members) by developing good cable wrapping technique. This involves being aware of the cable's "memory"–the natural way it wants to go after having been wrapped up so many times before. Do not twist it tightly around your elbow and hand as I see many people do! This will give you a cable that falls in a lumpy zigzag on the floor that'll be a tripping hazard and will break sooner. You want the coil to lay flat in your case and unravel easily during setup so you can afford to sip a cool beverage while your bandmates struggle with their respective rats nests as gigtime approaches.

How do you do this? First, make sure the cable is straight. It shouldn't be kinked or feel like it needs to unwind. If it does, take it to a sandy beach in the sun and feed it a cool beverage. At the risk of sounding obsessive, you can now choose between two methods:

1. The natural loop: hold one end in your right (or strong) hand. With the other hand, create coils that are around a foot in diameter. I give each coil a tiny twist as I wrap it and this

helps it to fall better. When the coiling is done I shake it a bit to further let it settle then place it flat in my gig bag.

2. The "official" loop used by theatre companies—this is the same as above, except that every other coil is reversed in direction. A caveat: I've tried this one but find that it tangled during uncoiling just as much *though it's supposed to uncoil more easily.*

If it feels weird or is not coiling right, start all over again. Really. Nicely coiled cables at setup make life so much easier.

Final tip: if I don't need the whole length to reach the receiving piece of gear, I leave the cable coiled and only pull what I need. This makes teardown faster and smoother as you only need to wrap a couple of coils. The very last thing you need is a little Velcro cable tie so that all of this careful work doesn't come undone.

—Tom Lang: product manager at TC-Helicon, singer-guitarist

Action 9: Match the System's Power to Your Needs

Don't let the sexy specs seduce you—ask yourself some key questions before you spring for a new piece of equipment.

Don't fall prey to marketing hype about equipment power. There's no one standard way for measuring the power of speakers and amps; manufacturers use different methods that can set you up with false expectations. For instance, you may be told that a speaker has an SPL (sound pressure level) of 120 dBs—that's loud! Yet what you aren't told is that this number is often not a measurement, but a theoretical calculation; in reality the SPL is often lower. If it was a true measurement, what frequency was used to measure that tone? It's easier to produce a high volume on mid frequencies than on bass tones. At what distance was the SPL measured? Sound pressure drops by half when you double the distance. Let the buyer beware!

Or, you may be told that a certain amp or powered speaker has 800 watts of power. That sounds promising until you discover this is a peak measurement, not a continuous average. Things can get even worse if you set your "powerful" equipment up and find that the resistance between your passive speakers and amp means you're only getting half (or sometimes even a quarter!) of the power stated. Finally, let's say you get the volume you want but the signal is distorting. Is the power worth it if you don't have clarity?

The only way to truly deal with these issues (other than getting a degree in electrical engineering) is to find a way to use the equipment before you buy it. Rent, borrow from friends, try it out in the shop and read user comments before you determine if the gear is up to the task.

Singers who are happy with their equipment purchases have also asked themselves hard questions about the purpose of their gear. When it comes to warming up your voice and practicing your vocal exercises, you need nothing other than a pitch pipe. But then your friends come over

Going to Invest in a System?

- *Thinking of a mini? There are some excellent portable mini PAs on the market, but don't assume that they will be enough for larger venues. Many bands are buying a pair of mains that have their own amp built in. You put these up on a "stick" (a stand). You would also need a mixer with a built in preamp and then, adding in the monitors you purchased for use in your home rehearsals, voila—you're ready to rock.*
- *Looking for more punch? Basically, any mains that are up on sticks are going to hold you back if you want to add that bass "thump" to your music. So, you would want to either add a subwoofer to your system—or invest in more powerful mains, with larger drivers.*
- *Is your motto "always be prepared"? Having a back-up system is easily possible by purchasing a mixer small enough to put into your gig bag, using this in conjunction with your powered monitors or some medium sized powered mains.*
- *Lusting after huge speaker cabinets? Let the buyer beware. Manufacturers cater to this lust, but if those cabinets aren't filled with quality components, they won't deliver the sound you want. Bigger is not always better. Check out the offerings in a specialist music shop rather than a general electrical retailer, as they will have a better selection and more expertise.*
- *Want to choose your configuration? The components of a PA system can come in many different forms. If you're going the portable route, you may want to check out getting active speakers which also incorporate a mixing desk with mic inputs on the back of the cabinets.*
- *Have you talked to the dealer? Your local dealer can be a great resource, go into the shop, get her or his recommendations and then check these systems out online to see what users are saying.*

with guitars, amps and a drum set and you can no longer hear your voice. Should you rush out and buy a PA?

You may find that a great place to start is with a near-field monitor for live performance or a floor monitor (see Action six). It's simplest if these are powered units with a mic input so that, like your guitarist friends, you can plug in and play. This also has the advantage of giving you a system to practice with your effects processor at home. If you purchase quality gear, then you won't need to crank your monitors up all the way to hear your voice AND you can take these units to your gigs to act as monitors, or even as PA for very small venues.

When you get out of the home and start gigging, it may be that the venues you will play in have their own systems. If they don't, check into rental prices in your area—you may find that this makes much more financial sense.

—The Ultimate Team

Action 10: Keep Your Perspec-

tive

Asking three all-important questions will ensure your system is delivering what your performance needs.

You may be hearing every little flaw in your singing and in your band's audio presentation. However, your audience may actually be less sensitive to what is going on with sound than you are.

You may be wondering if the sound waves are reaching that far corner, if your monitor mix is correctly balanced, and if you've purchased the right mic. These are all-important considerations, but remember the questions that are first and foremost for your listeners:

- Do I like the song?
- Does the vocalist look like they are having a good time?
- Can I hear the words?

Your first priority is to meet these questions with a resounding "YES"—only the final question deals directly with your sound system (though you will certainly find it easier to be happy with your music if you are confident about the technology you are using).

In a way, your audience's response to your music is "digital" (it is either on or off) while your response is "analog," flowing through many states and assessments. The good news about your "digital" audience is that if your mix isn't just right, there's a bit of "fuzz" in your system or you've forgotten a few words, your audience will still be "ON"—you just need to make sure you keep them that way with your emotional investment in your music.

You can hide a lot of flaws in a smile.

—Tom Lang: product manager at TC-Helicon, singer-guitarist

Frequently Asked Questions:

> What do I do if the sound stops working during my show?

Answered by Katherine Ellis, hit dance music songwriter, vocalist and performer

I was singing at a gay club in Melbourne once, and the sound suddenly stopped—in the middle of my show. How did I handle it? I very theatrically "fired" the DJ and proceeded to do a whole song *a cappella*. I got everybody clapping and they loved it. Later in the show, when the sound was working again, I magnanimously forgave my DJ and made it all into a big joke.

By putting yourself on that stage, you are saying, "I am in charge." The audience will always look to the person holding the microphone—that's you. Regardless of mistakes, illness or horrible sound problems, there is always something you can do to handle it.

> *Find out what the nature of the failure is in the first place. Did I trip a breaker? What else is on that circuit? If it is a club, am I sharing a circuit with other equipment, like the ice machines?*
> ***—Ed Simeone, front of house engineer:*** *ELO, James Taylor, TOTO, Stevie Wonder*

What if you get a sound guy who is not paying attention during your show? Take charge. Ask someone near the stage (a promoter, a DJ or someone assisting you) to go and tell the soundman what you need. Even if he is sitting there texting the whole time and you hate him, you cannot look annoyed or worried.

I once showed up to a venue that holds 1,000 people and due to some botched publicity, there were only eight people in the audience! I knew I had to have fun with it, so I dramatically shouted, "Hellooooooo London!" Earlier, I had met two fans in the ladies room who were really excited to see me. During the show, I invited them on the stage to sing background vocals. I found a way to entertain myself and my tiny audience.

If someone has made an effort to get dressed up and come out to see me, he or she deserves to be entertained. Inevitably some gigs are better than others, and an unforeseen circumstance can leave you feeling disappointed. But if one person has had a good time, then it's worth it.

> I can't hear myself!

Answered by The Ultimate Team

It's great you are voicing this concern! The stakes are just so high; with this issue unsolved, you'll lose your musical edge and your performance will suffer—not to mention putting you out of commission with a strained voice. So, let's run through a few of the usual suspects:

- **Not singing close enough to your mic.** Singing on a dynamic mic in a fairly loud setting often requires that you have your lips within an inch or two of the mesh (See Chapter five Action two). Oh, and if you have a mic that uses "phantom power," make sure this is on!
- **Gain and/or volume haven't been set properly.** There's an important relationship between gain and volume—we go over this in Action three of this chapter. If you're using an effects box, you need to work through these settings twice.
- **Not singing with a monitor** (see Action six), **don't have a good tone in your monitor** (Action seven), **don't have the right monitor mix** (Action seven).
- **Too much stage noise.** Create a better "audio space" for yourself by turning instrumental amps away from your area, asking instrumentalists to turn down their volume and/or reposition themselves on stage. Get a Plexiglas drum shield.
- **Main speakers are pointing directly at the walls** at the back of the venue and the resulting echo is drowning you out. Try changing the angle.
- **PA is under or overmatched for your venue**—see Action nine.
- **Your ears need to be trained to "focus in" on your amplified sound.** Picking out the sound of your amplified voice within a complex soundscape is not easy. That's because the real sound of your voice is different from the way it sounds to you. Amplify it and it sounds even more foreign. Making matters even more challenging is the fact that your *real* sound resonates in your head and ears, causing "interference." You can learn to hear your voice as you practice with amplification. Give yourself time to develop this ability.

> Do I need solid gold/nickel/titanium cables?

Answered by Tim Goodyer, founder and director of the Fast-and-Wide news site

The principal argument for gold-plated connectors is that gold doesn't oxidize—this means that you never get a buildup of unwanted material on your connection. Conversely, a steel connector oxidizes, building up resistance and causing contact problems over time. However, apart from being a relatively poor electrical conductor, gold is soft and, if you keep plugging it in and out of gear, it will wear away. So, though gold connectors are used in some telecoms and home hi-fi applications, it doesn't make sense for singers who will be gigging six times a week. Overall, I wouldn't place much store in gold connectors for live sound applications.

What you do want for your cables is a good-quality copper conductor (silver and oxygen-free copper belong in the world of hi-fi) and robust physical construction. Be careful about spending money going down a road where you will not hear the result in a live environment. And it doesn't make a lot of sense to overspend on cables when you could use that money to purchase a better mic. In the world of hobby-land people don't mind spending money on extra features so that they can boast having the best equipment—like golfers purchasing special socks to cover their clubs. However, these features often make no difference to their game. For the gigging singer, silver, gold and titanium are overkill.

In a live performance the biggest challenge you are going to face is not your cables, but the room itself. It is important to understand how the sound is behaving in a particular venue. You can begin by pointing your speakers in different places; beware of pointing the speakers directly where the sound will be bouncing straight back at you.

Of course, it is no good having great songs if a lead is going to let you down—so do make sure that your cables come from a reputable company and that you take care to handle them so that they don't get kinked or pinched.

> There's too much stage noise and people are telling me that I'm singing a little off the beat.

Answered by Bill Gibson, producer and author of more than 30 books on technology

In a situation where a Plexiglas cage isolates the drums, the guitar amps are isolated and the keys and bass are running direct into the board, huge problems for the singer can arise when it comes to singing in time. If the singer isn't hearing the monitor well or at all, he or she will sing in time with the reflection off the back wall, which might be 50–200 ms behind what the band is hearing and playing—sound travels at roughly one foot per millisecond. So in a 100-foot long room it takes about 200 ms (almost a quarter of a second) for the sound to get to the back wall and reflect back to the stage!

The issues of delayed reflections can cause the singer to sound extremely behind the beat to the audience and the band. The lack of a clear rhythmic element for the vocalist can result in a rhythmic mess, along with a frustrated singer and band. So, there must be a rhythmic instrument in the vocalist's monitor; if that instrument isn't loud enough to dominate the reflected sound, the singer will always be rhythmically behind the band.

> Whose job is it to make sure I sound good?

Answered by Val Emmich, singer-songwriter, hailed by the New York Times as "a rocker who rocks to his own beat"

I just assume that the venue is going to sound like shit and that the engineer will be, at best, only minimally engaged in my set. Ideally the audio should be a team effort between the artist and the venue, but this is wishful thinking. If you want to reduce the risks, see this as completely your responsibility.

I want everyone in the band to be extremely nice to the engineer, even if secretly they don't like how things are going. The engineer controls our destiny but try to take control of your own dynamics. In fact, we try to self-mix and we practice this art in our rehearsals. If there's a passage where my voice is going to a lower volume, I can't expect the engineer to bump my vocals up. So, my band will get lower in that moment. It's the same thing for a solo guitar section: the guitarist will click on a pedal that can boost his individual volume over the band's volume.

> Why do sound guys (or girls) always look so grumpy?

Answered by Ed Simeone, front of house engineer: ELO, James Taylor, TOTO, Stevie Wonder and many more

The expectations placed upon the sound person at a live show are enormous. First there are pressures from artists and fans who want the band to sound like their album. Granted, this is a little easier to do these days with a variety of digital consoles help to produce consistent sound night after night, but this is still challenging.

Then, there are the pressures and complexities of using so many audio and visual components at the same time. Large-scale live shows can exceed 50, 60 or more channels. Real singers don't employ lip-syncing, but the pressure of a pop show that features exhausting dance routines, such as a Britney Spears concert, means the engineer must squeeze every ounce of performance out of a headset mic or rely upon a backing track.

> *"Never have a fight with your doctor before you go into surgery." Try your very best to establish a good rapport with the Front of House engineer (and the Monitor Mixer, if there is one) before you hit the stage. This applies to everyone involved in the production—the stage manager, stage hands—anyone who can help to make your show better. Making friends and allies can only enhance the effectiveness of your presentation.*
>
> ***—Elliot Randall:** legendary guitarist, formerly a musical consultant for Saturday Night Live*

There are also pressures from management who judge the "quality" of the show from the audience reaction, not accepting the band might be having an off night. And then there are the nights when the bass player's brother-in-law tells him, "I couldn't hear the bass guitar."—the engineer is called on the carpet.

All of these pressures may translate into whether or not the engineer has a job the next day!

My most challenging show was when I was mixing Journey who were opening for the group Boston in the spring of 1977 at the Cobo Arena in Detroit. It was Boston's first tour and they were feeling a little intimidated by all the talent in Journey; even without Steve Perry, they were known as a "musicians' band" at the time. Journey got up on stage to open the show, and the system engineers had "left some headroom for Boston" during Journey's performance! We did not get a sound check, so I did not discover it until the moment I reached for a bass control knob in the console and it didn't do anything—the subs were turned way down, maybe off! Talk about a challenge ...

Having said that, I actually enjoy doing live shows. These shows place constraints on artists that they do not normally have to live with in the studio and you have to work together to make things happen. It is a great feeling to achieve a great sound in the midst of all of these pressures.

Another reason that the sound guy may be grumpy is that he's stuck in a club. These engineers have many of the same pressures I've spoken about above without the excitement of travel and high profile bands.

So, have a little compassion for the sound engineer. But more than this, you should think of the pro sound engineer as the "fifth Beatle"—one who translates what is happening in the moment to the audience. If he's going to do a great job at this, there needs to be cooperation, communication and understanding.

> What am I allowed to say and not say to a live sound guy or girl?

Answered by Divinity Roxx, former musical director and bassist for Beyonce's all female band ... 2006-2011

Here's the first rule: learn your soundman's (or woman's) name. Next, understand these two realities of a live show:

1. Your sound guy is not out to sabotage your show and make you suck.
2. But he *is* in control of your show.

This means that when you step on to the stage, it is not your stage yet. It's the sound man's stage. Don't let your band walk on stage for the sound check and start playing all at once. Stop the sound. Listen to your sound man. Give him what he wants. Professional sound guys have a process they use to get the best sound out of you and your band.

As the sound check progresses, it is important to let the sound man know what you need in your monitor. Politely say things like, "Can you turn me up (or down) in my monitors?" or, "There's feedback," or, "Can I have more (or less) guitar in my monitor?" You may also want some reverb in your monitor. I must hear my voice, my bass and the kick drum in my monitors. Those three things will keep me in time, in rhythm and on key. Your preferences may change depending on the show and the venue. With experience, you gain a better idea of what you like and how to ask for it. Recording all your shows and rehearsals will help with this.

If a band mate has gone out into the house and has noticed that your voice sounds tinny or that the band is drowning you out, you can say so—politely. Remember: the front of house (FOH) is more the soundman's domain. I would say, "I notice that I sound better when I have more lows in my voice—can you give me more lows?" See how respectfully I put that?

Here's my final advice: Never criticize the sound man, never interrupt your show to point out a sound issue and never shout at the sound man. You can always use hand signals or quietly ask someone nearby for what you need in between songs.

> Should the vocals be the loudest thing in the band?

Answered by Ed Simeone, front of house engineer: ELO, James Taylor, TOTO, Stevie Wonder and many more

"Loud" may not be the right word, since the drums and bass might be equally loud but at different frequencies. I would prefer to put it this way: the vocals always need to punch through the mix. This is because the lead vocal is the anchor element of the show. Technically, it may not be the loudest element. For instance, you may have a lot of sub woofers at the low end producing more decibels than the vocals, but the audience will not perceive it that way.

It's so different with some pop music such as Norah Jones—with an artist like her, the vocal is the primary sound, the anchor element without a doubt. All the other instruments are secondary. It all still has to gel, but the rest of the band is in a clear support role.

However, with a "busier" rock, pop or metal sound, the key thing is that the lead vocal punches through. Now, this can be difficult with other instruments fighting for the same frequencies, such as mid range guitars (screaming girls are another competition for that frequency range). This is why vocalists who want to take a more active role in their sound may want to look at some of the vocal processors now on the market that employ intelligent frequency enhancement that helps the vocals come through.

These effects boxes represent such an important development. In the mid-70s, vocalists like Linda Ronstadt, whom I toured with as a keyboard tech in the early 80s, were using the Aphex Aural Exciter on their album vocals to help them cut through the instruments (just listen to her 1976 album, *Hasten Down the Wind*). Today there are different tools: more advanced mics, better EQ, multiband compressors and, of course, effects processing tools with intelligent analyses of the lead vocals. Not only are these tools much better than what we were using years ago—they are affordable. Of course nothing replaces a great sound person operating a console.

But I need to say one more thing about vocals and conflicting frequencies. The most important thing to remember about using EQ is that it's not about the frequencies you boost—it's about the frequencies you cut. I suggest you look at one of those charts you see in audio magazines that show a piano keyboard relating the different notes to all the different instruments. Know what is in competition with the vocals and make sure you leave room for them to come through.

To do this, you have to identify the primary frequency of your singer so you can know the "competition." If you just boost, boost, boost, you soon run out of things to boost.

> Some bands "cut through" but ours sounds "muddy"—is it just our sound system?

Answered by Chris Henderson, singer-songwriter-guitarist of Bronze Radio Return

Yes, it can come down to the quality of your sound system, but one thing that has helped us immensely is keeping our stage volume low. If you can keep your amps lower, then the sound that is coming out of the main speakers won't need to compete with your amps. It's this "sonic competition" that can create a muddy sound in the venue—no matter the size of the space. It's really best if you can get as much of your sound as possible to come though the monitors rather than blasting out of your own amps on stage.

Many of us rock musicians have an inherent desire to blast the sound out. Fighting against this desire a little will go a long way to cleaning things up. Now, if you were to cut your stage volume down by half, this may turn you off what I am saying. Instead, just try taking it down a little, say 20%, and get used to that. Then lower it a little more at the next performance. You are looking for the threshold where the stage volume is enough for you to play but where the sound guy can do his thing to make you sound great in the venue.

CHAPTER 7

Your Live Effects

Create your signature sound.

"A well-placed effect could take your vocal interpretation to a new level, causing your voice to be remembered over the many other singers in your genre."

—Tom Lang, product manager at TC-Helicon, singer-guitarist

"The key is to use effects so that they do not call attention to themselves, but enhance the emotion of the song."

—David Frangioni, technical consultant & engineer, works with Ozzy Osbourne, Aerosmith, Shakira, Bryan Adams and many more

"We've created amazing tools to enhance all aspects of our modern life. Is that cheating? My answer is also a question: why not improve things if you can?"

—Dot Bustelo, internationally recognized music producer and music technology strategist

Your Live Effects

Create your signature sound

Actions:

1. Realize You Are Already Using Effects
2. Get the Volume Right
3. Set Your EQ
4. Work Out Your Compression
5. Add Some Icing
6. Turn Some Heads
7. Know Presets and Play with Parameters
8. Stay on the Cutting Edge
9. You Can't Polish a Turd

Frequently Asked Questions:

» *Do effects need to be controlled by the sound person, and do you have any additional tips for working with sound engineers on this?*

» *How do I actually use an effects box when I show up to a venue?*

» *Are effects legitimate?*

» *Can effects "fix" my voice?*

» *Do singers who use pitch correction just have crappy voices?*

» *I get it that effects are supposed to be used with thoughtfulness, but I'm still scared of misusing them and sounding like a nerd.*

Action 1: Realize You Are Already Using Effects

Make sure you are driving your effects in the direction that best suits the sound you want to create.

Every voice is "effected"—even if it's just the unique sound created by your voice in a certain kind of room. For that matter, if your singing voice is at all different from your speaking voice, you are affecting your voice. The important thing for you is not whether or not to use effects, but whether or not you are in control of the effects possible with your voice.

So, let's get away from a false division foisted on contemporary singers—that there are singers who sing with their "pure" voice and singers who use effects. This simply isn't true. Every time you pick up a microphone, your voice is affected by the particular frequency of response pattern of that mic, the PA's response to the mic and the characteristics of the room in which you are singing. When it comes to vocals in the studio, you'd be hard-pressed to find a recording that hasn't been modified electronically—even if it is only compression and EQ.

Now, of course, it is entirely possible to create a sound that is "too effected"—one that doesn't suit your presentation, that detracts from your interpretation of the song, that is out of place for your

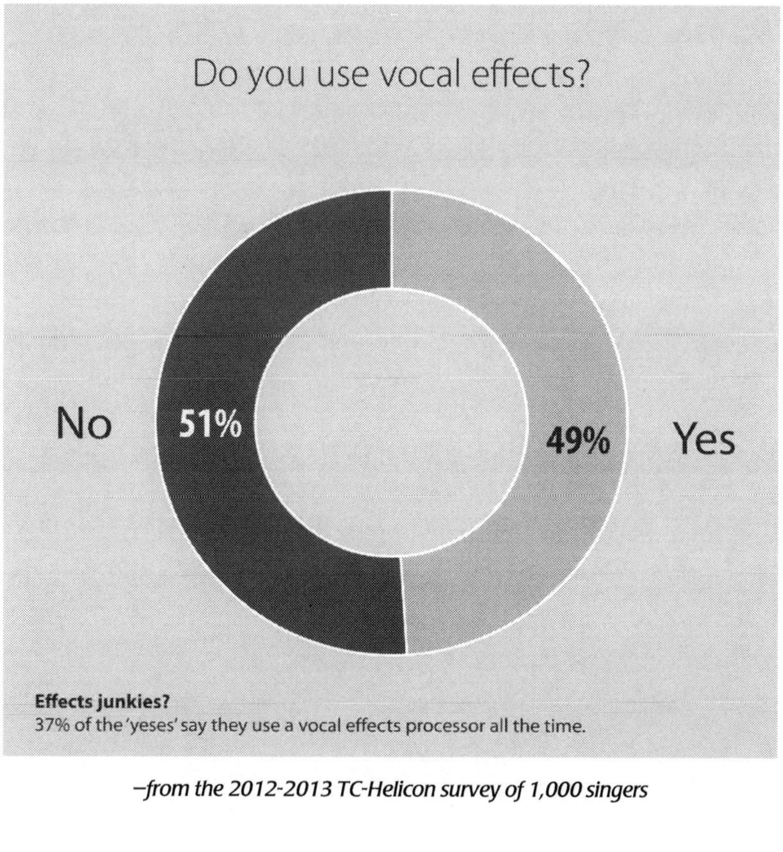

—from the 2012-2013 TC-Helicon survey of 1,000 singers

genre or that hides rather than highlights your voice. It's also possible to miss adding a well-placed effect that could take your vocal interpretation to a new level, causing your voice to be remembered over the many other singers in your genre. When the Beatles recorded their early albums, they cranked up the treble on their EQ—not because they needed to, but because they felt that particular effect enhanced qualities already present in their singing. A little "tweak" of their gear and we've never forgotten it.

That's what this section of the book is about: achieving a greater mastery with effects. Knowledge is power and knowledge about vocal effects is vocal power.

—Tom Lang: product manager at TC-Helicon, singer-guitarist

Action 2: Get the Volume Right

Two variables have to be right for you to communicate to your audience: volume and EQ.

Yes, even your volume is an effect—perhaps the most important one. When the microphone was invented, it allowed singers something that had never been possible before: the ability to sing using tones that had previously not been a part of the vocalist's world: whispers, a soft speaking voice, grunts, groans, moans, whimpers and cries. Before this, a singer's volume was a function of one's ability to project in an acoustic space; now it has become the label on a knob! How you handle that knob in live performance is a critical factor in the impact of your music.

We could give you a vague warning about being too loud or too soft in relation to the level of your instrumentation. But that's too obvious. How do you achieve this? When you've set things up in your venue or your rehearsal space, your first task should be to check your volume. Resist the urge to fiddle with the EQ (or Tone) controls for now. Leave the EQ off. At this stage your EQ should be "flat" (knobs turned down all the way). Get a long cable on your mic and step out in front so that you can hear your voice through the main speakers of the PA. Sing some quiet phrases. Then, sing some louder phrases. Does it sound OK? Do the same while accompanied by your instrumentation. Is your voice getting lost in the mix? Make some volume adjustments. If your band is too loud, then you'll either need to raise your volume, or get them to chill out when you are singing (this is, after all, the sign of a professional band—down in the verses and up in the chorus!). Over time you'll get used to setting your volume in a way so you can be heard well in relation to your overall mix. And you'll need to do this every time you perform, especially when you're in a new venue.

—Tom Lang: product manager at TC-Helicon, singer-guitarist

Action 3: Set Your EQ

Learn to tweak your tone without pushing your controls to their limits.

Now you are ready to think about EQ. EQ is short for "equalization," and it is also referred to as Tone Control. EQ is the way to modify the volume of different frequency bands of your voice. For example, more low, more high, more mid range. Why would you want to do this? Because not all mics, rooms and PA systems respond to your voice in the same way. EQ allows you a measure of control so that you maintain consistency with your tone in spite of these variables.

Let's say that a female singer has a high, bright voice AND is using a mic that is extra sensitive in the bright area. The result can sound shrill. So, you would "equalize" the high frequency by turning down the treble (or "high frequency" EQ) knob. Or, let's say you have a big "bassy" sound and are singing into a typical dynamic cardioid mic 2–3 inches away from your mouth. Typically, that mic will amplify the bass section—adding additional bass frequencies to your already "bassy" voice. The result is a muddy tone that causes your voice to be easily lost in all of the other musical sounds accompanying your song. You would then need to turn down your base tone on the mixer (this is often called "rolling off the base"). Now, your bass has been "equalized." This last example is called "proximity effect." Most mics at close range boost the low end; this is why, if you are singing with a mic right on your lips, you will usually want to turn down the bass EQ knob, not turn it up.

We could easily say that the EQ is unique for every singer in the context of his or her venue, mic and PA. But we're trying to be practical, so here are some things you should do: typically you'll roll off the bass ("low frequencies") a little and turn up the treble a little (to make up for a muddy PA or a mic that is boosting your lows) and not touch the mids. If it is just you and a single instrument (guitar or piano), you may not want to modify your tone that much. However, if you are singing with a full band, you may want to "brighten" your vocal (bass down, treble up) to compete with the accompaniment. Typically, instruments occupy more area in the "lows."

—Tom Lang: product manager at TC-Helicon, singer-guitarist

Action 4: Work Out Your Compression

Smooth out your tone, organically or inorganically.

For the daring among you, there is the area of compression. There are times when a loud vocal may overwhelm the overall mix and cause discomfort to an audience. There also may be quiet syllables that might otherwise be lost to your listeners. Compression deals with both of these situations, making your vocals more consistent so that your message comes through.

Many singers have developed "organic" ways to achieve compression: think of a crooner in front of a big band constantly moving the mic around. He or she is practicing a form of compression, moving the mic further away when he or she is belting and closer when he or she is creating a sense of intimacy through hushed or whispered tones. As a vocalist, you should be doing this—to

Don't fall into these three common traps.

- ***Trap 1: Thinking More EQ Is Better.*** *The singer wants their voice to cut nicely through the mix of sounds (that's good). But to achieve this, the singer boosts the bass frequencies a little, the mids and the high as well. The singer can now hear their voice better and decides that "more is better" (that's bad). All the EQ knobs eventually get maxed (i.e. turned up all the way). Not only has this modified your vocal tone in ways you may not want, but it may be ignoring a more simple solution—volume!*
- ***Trap 2: Louder, Louder, Louder.*** *Sometimes you feel your voice isn't cutting through the mix, so you just keep on turning up the volume. When, in reality, it is a certain frequency range that needs to be turned up. You may get what you want by boosting a certain frequency instead of turning everything up.*
- ***Trap 3: Ignoring the Mains.*** *Thinking that what you are hearing through the monitors is what the audience is hearing through the PA. If you are in a large venue with an experienced sound engineer, you will need to exercise some trust. But, in a smaller set up, where you have more control of your sound, you should, again, step in front and listen to yourself through the "mains" as well as the monitors.*

a degree. If you have a quiet passage, you can be more "on your mic" and move away from your mic for a screamed or belted note.

As an effect, compression can be very difficult to set well, but at its simplest level isn't too complex. There are two basic parameters. The first is "threshold" which is the level you set for compression to begin. The other parameter is "ratio" (for example 2:1) which results in turning down the level by two times the amount that your level is louder than the threshold (the higher the first number in the ratio—the more it will compress!)

If you are going to tinker with compression, you should be aware of two unwanted side effects:

1. Increased sensitivity of your sound system to feedback.
2. Uneven sounds when singing with others who do not have compression on their voices.

You can deal with (1) by experimenting with different parameters in your rehearsals. To deal with (2) you'll have to try harder to match their levels. Other singers without compression will have peaks that are higher than your peaks, whereas your average sound will be louder than their average. Practice will be key.

There's good news: some products now contain automatic compressors for voice that set all this automatically to just give you a bit of compression to smooth out your voice.

—Tom Lang: product manager at TC-Helicon, singer-guitarist

Action 5: Add Some Icing

Create a professional and memorable "sheen" to your voice—without sounding "corny."

Volume and EQ are the basics because getting these areas right is all you need to communicate effectively to your audience. But why leave your effects journey there? Reverb is a powerful quality that can augment your singing in just the right way to create a memorable performance.

Reverb adds a sense of space to your voice. Imagine clapping your hands in your bedroom compared to clapping them in an empty gymnasium. Your bedroom is relatively "dead"—the carpet, the bedding and the nooks and crannies created by all of the furniture cause the sound to get "lost." But the gymnasium is "live," adding an ambience to your voice. Reverb is that quality which makes singing a "la" sound like a "lahhhhhhhhhhhh." In the old days, this effect was simulated using springs—the spring would mimic the sound of your voice and add a lengthening effect to your voice. In our digital age, this is possible both through mixing boards and vocal effects processors. Your reverb settings are based on small, medium and large sized rooms and tonal characteristics of that room (i.e. "bright hall," "dark hall" etc.).

> *Are you decaying well? Decay is the length of time it takes for the sound of the reverb to disappear. On songs with longer vowel sounds and a lot of time between consonants (ballads) a longer decay can fit nicely in the mix. But you may want to avoid a long decay on songs with short vowel sounds and a short time between consonants (rap or the chorus to "Are You Gonna Go My Way" by Lenny Kravitz)*
>
> ***—The Ultimate Team***

Of course reverb can sound "corny" if it is used in excess and doesn't match your vocal intentions—but you would truly be surprised how many songs use a touch of reverb to add ambiance to a vocal. Even your favorite songs which you thought were "unaffected" are using a hint of reverb to contribute to the glue that holds the song together.

Typically, you will set the reverb and leave it there for the duration of your song. If you are singing in a "dry" room, a space that sucks up your vocal sound up without returning it, you will want to turn up the reverb. Your reverb settings will usually need to be higher in a carpeted banquet hall filled with soft surfaces such as table cloths; it will be lower (or, off completely) in a gymnasium. As with volume and EQ, step out in front, sing, and listen to how your voice sounds with various reverb settings.

There's another way to add space to your voice—delay (also known as echo). Whereas vocalists tend to set the reverb and leave it in place through the song, many vocalists like to use delay as a temporary attention-grabber, turning it off and on within a song in order to highlight specific phrases.

Think of singing to a mountain range. Your sound travels freely and then it hits a wall, bouncing back to you. If you are far away from that mountain range, your words appear to come back as separate, distinct words—they have been "delayed" quite a long time. Think of Pink Floyd's "Us and Them" (check it out on YouTube); they've set a long delay for their key words and have these repeating exactly on the beat of the song. Note that this is only done on specific words in order to draw attention to the message. But delay can also be set very short, slapping parts of words back in a millisecond (also known as "tight delay"). You'll hear this in a rockabilly style as well as in certain rock, pop or metal songs which want to "hit" a word hard in order to jolt the audience's attention.

Which forms of vocal processing or effects have you used in a live setting?

Effect	Used by %
Reverb/Delay	82%
EQ	53%
Compression	50%
Harmony	40%
Doubling	34%
Pitch Correction	22%
D-essing	21%
Distortion/megaphone	15%
Flanger	10%
HardTune™ / Auto-Tune™	8%

In the dark?
One out of every 10 singers who use vocal effects have no idea what they are - someone else is controlling them.

–from the 2012-2013 TC-Helicon survey of 1,000 singers

If you're using delay in a live performance, you'll need to remember that the sounds of your instrumental accompaniment will be audible in an echo (especially a snare or cymbal crash). Thus, you'll want to rehearse this effect with your band so that you avoid unwanted noise in your delay. With a good floor effects unit, you can simply set the delay and then punch it with your foot at precisely the time you wish. It may be that just doing this once in your song will cause your performance to stand out in the minds of your listeners.

—Tom Lang: product manager at TC-Helicon, singer-guitarist

Action 6: Turn Some Heads

You can enhance your voice in "organic" ways such as doubling, chorus and harmony OR through the gloriously "inorganic" sounds of flanging, telephone, megaphone, stutter, and pitch correction/hardtune.

Now we move on to effects which can provide added contrast, intensity and excitement to your music. You might think of them as vocal "detours," or sounds that take your song in a different direction for a moment. It's easy to overuse these effects, though in some rare cases this "works." Mostly, these effects are best used as occasional "punctuations" of your musical ideas. You'll recognize many of these effects as time-honored vocal practices. Others are new to the effects scene. As you face the task of fashioning your unique sound, you'll want to know about all of these effects.

In the past, these effects have only been possible in the studio. Now, they can be used live on vocal effects processors. These units are becoming increasingly more sophisticated and affordable. Of course, there are many more effects (and combinations of effects) than we'll run through here, but knowing these main ones will help you understand the many derivative sounds available to today's vocalist.

- **Doubling** is your voice "doubled"—singing the same exact vocal instantaneously in order to add "thickness," power and emphasis (and perhaps also to save money from not having to surround yourself with other singers!). This was originally done in the studio by re-recording the singer's voice and laying this on top of the original vocal track. Now, this effect can be achieved "live" without that "electronic" sound that was a part of earlier attempts back in the 90s—or even a few years ago. Listen to your favorite tunes and you'll likely here some doubling. Justin Bieber and Gotye (pop), Linkin Park and Green Day (modern rock), Eminem and will.i.am (hip hop) and Sheryl Crow are all examples of artists who employ this effect well.
- **Chorus** is another way to simulate a vocal "thickness"; unlike doubling, the effect simulates many other people (not just you) singing the same notes. The name of this effect comes from Broadway where a lone vocalist is suddenly surrounded by the cast who join in on the melody in order to drive home the message of the song. However, the "effect" version is not a faithful recreation of these natural origins.
- **Harmony** also adds intensity to your music and, now you no longer need to wait for just the right voices to accompany you—you can use your own! Using harmony on a vocal effects processor can include anything from a brief harmonic punctuation of a single a syllable, word or phrase to an entire chorus of your song.

The effects we've discussed so far are aimed at enhancing your voice in an "organic" fashion. That is, they are designed to sound like you. Many vocalists, however, have engaged a form of artistry where they have attempted to sound anything like themselves; they've experimented with "inorganic" effects.

- **Flanging** began in the tape era with the simple act of touching a finger to one of two tapes playing your voice simultaneously. The sound produced from the two machines—one playing just slightly behind the other—has come to be known as flanging, a smooth, swooshing, "modern" sound. The Doobie Brothers did this on "Listen to the Music." A more contemporary example is "Believe" by Lenny Kravitz.
- **Stutter** makes a "loop" of your most recent syllable and links this to the tempo of your song. You would just say "yah" and stutter turns this into "yahyahyahyahyahyahyahya-hyahyah." This is a great vocal attention-grabber but would drive people crazy if it was used in an entire song. Check out many tunes by Niki Minaj (including her feat. with Bieber, "Beauty and the Beat") as well as Party Rock Anthem by LMFAO.
- **Telephone/Megaphone** is an intentional attack on the quality of your vocal sound through rolling off the base and distorting your vocals in a manner that is consistent with how your voice might sound over a telephone or megaphone. Current effects processors give a range of options. These sounds are currently popular in the pop world, but will they survive as popular sounds? That's anyone's guess. Still, many artists have rocketed to popular acclaim through the careful use of these effects.
- **Pitch Correction** is a hotly debated effect in the music world. While it is valid to debate whether or not singers should employ a subtle pitch correction in order to ensure they stay on pitch, that's not what we are talking about here. Pitch correction (sometimes called Auto-Tune™ or HardTune™) has also been cranked up and used as an effect across the genres of contemporary music. It was first used by Cher in "Believe" and people have been drawn to its "vocoder" or "robotic" sounds ever since.

—Tom Lang: product manager at TC-Helicon, singer-guitarist

Action 7: Know Presets and Play with Parameters

We'll show you the path to creating your signature sound—and convince you that all of this technology doesn't mean an end to originality, but a new beginning.

Watch interviews with the "old guard" of contemporary music—those who became famous because they caught the attention of millions through their unique sound. They will often say something like this: "Back in the old days, we didn't have all of this gear, but we knew every inch of the gear we did have and we got creative. We hooked things up backwards, hung things from the ceiling, placed stuff in tiled bathrooms ... until we got our sound." Many of the most popular digitally produced effects today originate from these early experiments.

But times have changed, and now you live in a gear-permeated world. Literally millions of different high-quality vocal sounds and effects can be produced live or in studio with a flick of a switch. The "old guard" would be astonished by what can be achieved today at a low cost. But the question is, how will you discover your own signature sound in this technological world?

Your first step is to familiarize yourself with the presets of your vocal effects unit—really, this is your best education in the world of effects. A "preset" is simply a collection of parameter values under one name. It is a single action for you so that you do not need to set all of the individual commands that go into making a type of effect. You can simply hit "flange 1" or "megaphone 24" and listen to how you sound. Setting hours aside for this experimentation is not only fun, but you will also begin to form judgments about what works and doesn't work for your voice.

Now you will be ready to move onto how today's unique vocal sounds are going to be discovered: playing with the parameters yourself. Let's say that a certain preset sounded intriguing to you, yet wasn't quite right. Now you can create that same parameter with more bass, less flange, some distortion, and added delay. You are now the creator of a new effect blending with your unique voice. This may seem like a far cry from the "old days" when a vocalist discovered his or her sound by singing through a guitar amp in a bathroom on a train. But it is, really, the same process: you are taking the tools available, learning them inside and out, making your own discoveries and arriving at your signature sound.

—Tom Lang: product manager at TC-Helicon, singer-guitarist

Action 8: Stay on the Cutting Edge

Stay on top of the ever-changing world of vocal effects—
and even have fun at the same time.

Vocal effects processors are becoming more complex, compact and classy. Mics with buttons that can drive effects boxes have just been introduced. What's next? Imagine showing up at your gig with only a mic and smart phone that connect wirelessly into the venue's PA and produce effects they could only dream about at Carnegie Hall. We're almost there.

There's a revolution happening with singers taking control of all aspects of their sound assisted by some handy technology. But how do you find out about the latest developments? This question is more important than ever since the industry is rapidly changing; there are new possibilities than ever before at lower prices. The sound you believe will make the most impact is within your reach.

There are, in fact, several ways to stay on top of things. The easiest way is to visit some virtual music stores. Try Googling "apps for singers" to check out the latest software. Then, you can Google your favorite online retailers, take a look at the latest gear and find some quality YouTube reviews. After this, you can visit your local shop and rent or buy a vocal effects product, testing it out over the weekend. Of course, before you rent or buy a piece of gear you'll want to check out some quality reviews on the web, on YouTube and on the shop site.

But if you want to go even further, we have a suggestion for you. Music trade shows drive the entire industry and companies time their product development for introductions at these shows. If you're lucky enough to get a ticket to NAMM or Musik Messe, then you'll really be on top of things. If you're at one of these shows, you'll see aisles and aisles filled with large booths representing industry giants; you'll also see some tiny booths where someone has created an innovation that hasn't quite caught on yet. These hidden corners in the convention hall can sometimes introduce you to some of the most exciting developments in music technology.

In an age of Twitter feeds, vlogs and blogs, you can stay at home and can pick up invaluable information from people who are walking around these shows providing commentary for their own audiences. Just Google the name of the show or any of the companies that are there, and you can be just as savvy as those attending—or maybe even more so, since there is no way one person at these shows can discover everything.

At the same time as you are checking out the latest products, you'll also want to watch what your favorite tech-savvy artists are doing and check out what vocalists in your area are using—not so you can merely imitate them, but so you can see how they are pushing their equipment to new limits.

Why make these efforts? Because you are on a quest to control your sound. When you can take the tools that are available and use them to craft your own vocal vision, then you'll become the one others are trying to keep on top of.

—Tom Lang: product manager at TC-Helicon, singer-guitarist

Action 9: You Can't Polish a Turd

It's not about having a "good voice." It's about having the best possible voice as the foundation for your effects. We'll show you how.

There are all of these incredible technological possibilities out there—but you also have to take the time to hone your singing craft. Learn to sing better. Even the slickest technology can't give you the satisfying feeling that you are a part of what is sounding good, even if you're using the tech to cover up sloppy technique.

We're not being elitist about this. It's not about having a "good voice" by some objective standard. It's not about having the pipes of Michael Jackson, Christian Aguilera or other singers who can belt tunes while thousands swoon in stadiums. Let's face it: there are some singers who are just the lucky ones with a beautiful tone, style and sense of rhythm that just a little training will send to the stratosphere. Then there are guys like me who have to struggle much more to sound great. I still engage in that struggle, partly because I have to—I'm compelled to be musical and

I LOVE it—but the other side to this is that I'm committed to my craft. When Saturday morning comes along and I would rather be out having a coffee than going to my vocal lesson, I go to my vocal lesson.

The dedication to my singing work helps me to get more out of my effects. You see, singing is essentially about establishing a connection between your voice and your listener's ears. If you were to type some lyrics in an app and click a few buttons to turn those words into a processed voice, this would not be singing—it would be a third-person experience. Similarly, if you are not singing at or near your vocal potential, you'll find that you are distanced from your audience and that that the technology you are using is a substitute for, rather than an enhancement of, your voice. With a good strong vocal base layer, you'll find that you will have more confidence and scope in using effects.

OK—so you're working on your voice and you are using technology. Great. But watch out for these effects fails!

Top Effects Fails:

1. **The Over-done Effect.** Don't leave a distinctive effect on for an entire song, set, or performance. Remember that contrast is king; you need to vary your sound to keep people engaged. You would never go to hear a writer read the same word over and over again—think of your effects as words you do not want to overuse. The most common mistakes are to keep your harmony processor on through an entire song, or to crank up your reverb or delay and never crank it down.
2. **Trying to be T-Pain.** Constant pitch correction from song to song is an epic failure for almost anyone. With the exception of T-Pain and others who effectively use pitch correction as a defining effect, many vocalists make the mistake of turning pitch correction up too much so that the voice sounds just beyond authentic.
3. **Cranked Up Reverb and Delay.** If these effects are cranked up too loudly and for too long a duration, your vocals can come across as "mucky" and "muddy," like you are singing at the bottom of a well. Now, there are exceptions to any rule; you may be intentionally be trying to create a certain sound for your performance—but, in general, you would be wise to be careful with these effects.

—Tom Lang: product manager at TC-Helicon, singer-guitarist

Frequently Asked Questions:

> Do effects need to be controlled by the sound person, and do you have any additional tips for working with sound engineers on this?

Answered by Tiff Randol, singer-songwriter, creator of IAMEVE, over 100 TV/film placements

If you have a very simple sound (a little reverb and delay), most live engineers are perfectly capable of controlling your effects. Just let them know how wet you like your vocals and give them a little direction.

If you have created your own specific vocal sound, you must control your own effects entirely just like any instrumentalist. I recommend finding a portable effects unit that gives you the ability to control your vocal effects anywhere you go. It puts you in the driver seat with your sound and adds dimension to the live show.

Not all engineers may be used to working with a vocalist who controls his/her own sound. Give him/her your setup sheet, and let him/her know to keep your vocals dry in his/her mix and the EQ flat. It's possible that the sound engineer is used to controlling the overall mix and may not be pleased that you are running your own sound. The best thing to do is just thank him/her often for helping and be professional and respectful. Don't be a diva until you start singing.

Another tip: never feel pressured around sound check. If you need a few more minutes to get comfortable or mentally prepare, take your time. The stage time is yours to do with as you please, so if the engineer is pressing you, kindly let him/her know that you need more time and will play a shorter set if necessary. It's better to be comfortable with your sound/headspace and play one less song.

Finally—is your gear insured? Your insurance company or audio supplier most likely has an affordable insurance plan that protects you at all times with your equipment—a must have.

> How do I actually use an effects box when I show up to a venue?

Answered by Emma Hewitt, top of the charts singer-songwriter, videos have reached over 25 million views

It's really simple and easy to use: plug your mic in and run a cord to the sound desk. That's it.

I usually ask the sound engineer to patch my effects unit in direct line with the mic signal as you would with a guitar pedal. The tone button is always engaged to provide some crispness and a touch of "mastering" to the vocals and just makes everything sound brighter and better. For me, performing live vocals to a mastered dance track, there is the issue of bridging the separation between the mastered track and the live vocal, and the tone function is essential for that.

Quite often sound engineers want me to use the effects on their desks, but I like to control the effects I use—which are the same as on my recordings. I understand their effects may be amazing, but if I can control my own delay, reverb and modulation it allows me to experiment on the fly and make that part of the performance and I also know exactly where I want the long delay to trail over and when I want the vocal to flange … I can tap the tempo and switch effects off when I am speaking to the audience, that type of thing.

Most of the time engineers are actually grateful that their job is made easier once they hear how the unit sounds during sound check.

I've performed in some clubs that aren't set up specifically for live vocals—when you introduce a microphone into these types of acoustic environments, the feedback can be horrendous! You hope there's a capable sound engineer at the desk who can remove the EQ on the problem frequencies—which are usually the high ones. But once this happens, my tone can sound muddy. This is when I take control with my unit, making things sound brighter—there's even an adaptive gate on my VoiceLive 2 that reduces feedback.

My unit has been a lifesaver more times than I can remember; once I turned up for a show in Egypt and the sound guy came over and asked ME how to turn the sound system on! It turns out that he was in charge of the lighting and the venue thought he could also manage the sound as well! So, I just turned the system on, plugged in my effects box into my mic channel and my mic into my box. I was able to manage the sound myself.

> Are effects legitimate?

Answered by Mister Tim, viral video star, voice artist, composer and sponsored kazoo player

People tell me all the time that I'm cheating with my *a cappella* acts because we use technology!

But think of it this way: You never hear a "pure guitar" sound in a band; the audio is always processed and people accept that one instrument can be used to produce a variety of sounds.

When singing in rock-oriented, all-vocal groups, we work toward a distinctive sound which has everything to do with technology: heavy compression, reverb, and delay. This is similar to the way guitar players use reverb, delay and other effects to achieve their unique presentation.

When mic'd or plugged into a direct box, even the "pure" sound of an acoustic guitar is actually the result of processing, compressing and equalizing technology.

Likewise, the "pure" vocal sound we associate with great live and recorded singers is processed: reverb, delay and electronic tricks make the voice sound natural … when in fact it is anything but.

> Can effects "fix" my voice?

Answered by Wes Maebe, Recording-Mix-Mastering, FOH engineer for Sting, New Model Army, Yusuf Islam, Ellie Goulding, Elliott Randall

It seems to me that a lot of performers use effects to hide behind them. It's like when you pick up a guitar as a kid and you need to have the biggest amp, the flashiest guitar and a pedal board the size of an airport terminal to sound good. Then you look at the big hitters and you see there's a cable running from the instrument to the amp and that's it. And, hey, what do you know, it sounds amazing and hits you right in the gut!

Your focus needs to be on writing killer tunes, performing them in front of people and making the hairs on the backs of their necks stand up without the aid of a myriad of effects to hide behind.

Once you have mastered your instrument (and that includes your voice), you then have the power and the control to start experimenting with effects for creative reasons rather than corrective reasons.

Budget reasons can come into play here as well. When you're traveling the country to play your shows, it's not always possible to take a full production crew and backing band with you—certainly not in the early stages of your career. This is where a nice choice of effects can help you create a more interesting show for the punters to watch and listen to.

Effects boxes that add a little reverb, delay and chorus can thicken your voice up nicely and the various harmonizers that are available will allow you to put together a nice block of backing vocals.

Obviously all of this relates right back to the studio as well. Make sure all the material has gone down to tape or hard drive properly before you start swamping them in effects. It is always so much more powerful and effective when you can touch people's feeling with raw and honest music. Drowning everything in effects does not necessarily make for a good song; we just have to look back for about 30 years and see how overuse of effects can date your music.

> Do singers who use pitch correction just have crappy voices?

Answered by Dot Bustelo, internationally recognized music producer and music technology strategist

Is it crappy to fix your hair with a blow dryer or put on lipstick or mascara? Is it wrong to add a box of premade Stove Top stuffing to your roast chicken entrée or use a mix for chocolate chip cookies you bake and serve warm out of the oven?

We've created amazing tools to enhance all aspects of our modern life. Think of the beautiful filters in iPhoto that can change the hue of a picture so that you look a little suntanned or mask any lines or blemishes in your face. Is that cheating? My answer is also a question: why not improve things if you can?

Of course, it is an art, a craft and a responsibility to improve and not to overdo. This applies to everything from lipstick to pitch correction—unless you decide that overdoing things is actually a part of the art form you are creating, like T-Pain, who created a genre from overusing pitch correction. How about KISS? They completely overdid their makeup—nothing "natural" about their look! In fact, they made their make up a part of their art form. You can choose to take any of these tools to slightly enhance, or make "more natural" (I use the term "supernatural"), your appearance, your performance or your recorded music. It's about getting across your unique message and art.

> I get it that effects are supposed to be used with thoughtfulness, but I'm still scared of misusing them and sounding like a nerd.

Answered by Tiff Randol, singer-songwriter, creator of IAMEVE, over 100 TV/film placements

It's easy to go overboard with effects, so "less is more" is a good rule of thumb. Effects should enhance your vocal sound, not drown it. At the same time, don't shy away from experimenting. Worst-case scenario: you get off stage and realize you went too far—it's not the end of the world. One of the things that makes a live show magical and human is how we recover from our mistakes, so why be afraid of making them?

It's a good idea to have someone in the audience record your performance, so you can listen later on and assess the show. I also like to ask a few of my musician/producer friends for feedback.

When you are at home or rehearsal, it's a perfect time to go crazy with effects. There's no limit and no right or wrong way to go about it. Of course, experimenting is not everybody's thing. Just have fun and express yourself in whatever way makes you feel good. If you want a unique sound but don't like to experiment, then find someone who does and have them set you up. Ultimately, an effects unit is just a toy. Either you like playing with it or you don't.

CHAPTER 8

Recording Your Voice

Create magic that will last.

"Be alive—don't be a machine. Perfect singing in the recording studio is not necessarily interesting."

—Toke Wulf, Basix, "Best European Album"

"Once I'm in the recording studio, I imagine who I'm singing for. Just remember this motto: shut your eyes, see the crowd and sing."

—Katherine Ellis, hit dance music songwriter, vocalist and performer

"You will hear people say, 'We'll fix it in the mix.' In the pro studio scene, many of us laugh about this. If you get things right from the start, everything falls into place and makes the mixing process so much easier.

—Al Schmitt, legendary engineer and producer with more than 150 gold and platinum albums

Recording Your Voice

Create magic that will last

Actions:

1. Get the Environment Right
2. Work Your Mic & Headphones
3. Know When to Rely on Tech for Your Recording
4. Make the Most of Your Bedroom
5. The Basement Studio: Consider Some Gear Under $500
6. The Basement Studio: Record Your Voice into Your Computer
7. The Basement Studio: Know What Your Audio Software Can Do for You
8. Do This Stuff When You're Paying for Studio Time
9. Get a Producer
10. Take a Final Walkthrough

Frequently Asked Questions:

» *How come there's a buzz/noise/hiss in the silent parts of my song?*

» *What's the cheapest way I can record my voice and post it on my site?*

» *I just can't relax when I'm recording. Help!*

» *We want to make our first CD to sell at our gigs—is it worth all the money to go to a studio or should we try to do this on our own?*

» *I'm not an engineer—can I get a recording that is anywhere near as good as a professional one?*

» *I've got a good recording mic at home—if I were to spend money on just one thing beyond the mic, what would it be?*

» *What's the most important thing to keep in mind when we record our first album?*

» *I've got a basement full of great gear. What does a pro studio have that I don't?*

» *How do I choose the right studio for my first album?*

» *Can I talk the studio down in price? To what degree is the price negotiable and what factors come into play with that?*

» *I want to bring some of my own gear to the studio, like my effects box—will I get in trouble with the engineer?*

» *After the session is all done, how much can I defend my vision for the mix without being a neurotic artist and driving everyone crazy?*

» *Is there any etiquette I need to know in the studio?*

» *Should I record my voice on one of those expensive large-diaphragm condenser mics (U87/M149)?*

Action 1: Get the Environment Right

Arguably the greatest producer in history reveals the path to a great vocal recording.

There's a lot we can learn from Quincy Jones—a man who has probably been responsible for more mega hits than any other producer. He produced *Thriller, Off the Wall, Back on the Block* and worked with incredible artists such as Michael Jackson, Barbra Streisand and so many others. One of the themes that struck me when working with Quincy in his book on producing is the respect he gives to each singer—indeed, to each person he works with.

There's a lot more to leading a person to a performance than beating it out of him or her. In the studio, Quincy doesn't stand there and yell at the singer in order to make him or her sing it his way. Instead, he fosters a relationship that releases a performance that is better than it would have otherwise been. He is just so supportive; he genuinely loves the people he works with. The great vocal performances he's been behind have been influenced by this love and respect.

Thus, it's crucial for singers to develop trust with the people around them in the studio—their producer and engineer. This adds a huge value to their performance. Quincy wouldn't have been able to have a positive impact with Michael Jackson if Michael couldn't express his opinion in the context of a solid and creative working relationship.

There are also some things that singers can do for themselves. When you're going to sing, make sure you have adjusted the lighting and temperature that are most comfortable for you, and that you've created an ambiance that is inspiring. Standing in a cold, blank room with fluorescent light is not inspiring. Someone needs to create an environment that supports a heartfelt performance, whether it's the producer, engineer, or the artist. I've produced a lot of recording sessions where singers have walked in with their candles, Christmas lights, photos, lamps, and whatever it takes to inspire them to a stellar performance. If you're

Famous Studio Mics

- ***Adele:*** *Rode Classic II ("Rolling in the Deep")*
- ***Mariah Carey:*** *Sony C800G ("One Sweet Day")*
- ***Caleb Followill (Kings of Leon):*** *Shure SM57 ("Sex on Fire")*
- ***James Hetfield (Metallica):*** *Shure SM7 ("St. Anger")*
- ***Whitney Houston:*** *Neumann U87 ("I Want to Dance with Somebody")*
- ***Michael Jackson:*** *SM7 ("Billie Jean")*
- ***Norah Jones:*** *Neumann M49 ("Don't Know Why")*
- ***Jack Johnson:*** *Telefunken U47 ("Sleep Through the Static")*
- ***Frank Sinatra:*** *Telefunken U47 ("Come Fly with Me")*
- ***Bruce Springsteen:*** *Telefunken ELA M251 ("Born in the USA")*

bashful about doing this kind of thing, you need to move past that and do whatever it takes to give your best performance.

One of the stories that Quincy shared with me about his work with Michael Jackson involved this very concept. Michael liked all of the lights off in the studio and control room with a single, very narrow spot shining straight down on his microphone. Between lyrics or musical sections Michael would be dancing in the dark and just on cue, he'd step up the mic for his lines! Even Michael Jackson, arguably one of the best studio singers ever, did whatever it took to support his best work.

—Bill Gibson: co-author with Quincy Jones, "Q on Producing"

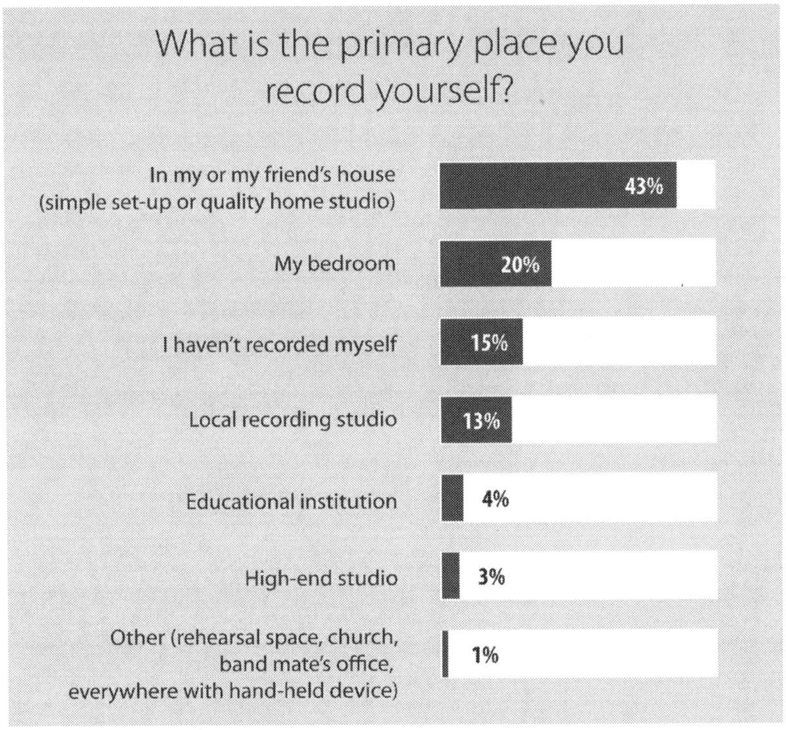

—from the 2012-2013 TC-Helicon survey of 1,000 singers

Action 2: Work Your Mic & Headphones

The sensitivity of recording gear might throw you off on the first go-around—learn these tips for optimizing your technique.

When I was 18, I was playing guitar and singing at home using a cheap dynamic mic with lots of effects. I thought I sounded pretty good. The studio I was working in wanted to add some backing vocals to a song for which I had done some keyboard arrangements. I thought, "I sound great singing through my gear at home—I can do the backing vocals myself, no problem!"

The engineer had a little smile on his face when we walked into the recording booth. I soon found out why.

The recording revealed every weakness in my voice—things that were covered up by my cheap gear at home. I was shocked by the high resolution, three-dimensional fidelity of my voice. Everyone in the studio had a good laugh. I was convinced to go and get a vocal coach to work on my singing. At the same time, this experience began a love affair with high fidelity sound that surely played a major role in me becoming a manufacturer of such gear.

When you are first getting used to working with a recording mic, there are several things you can do to optimize your experience. First, make sure your recording space doesn't have any distractions—this should be the case with any professional recording booth. You should be able to focus easily on your most important task: singing. If you're not in a professional recording booth, you'll want a space that is not overly reverberant-and that doesn't build up too many resonant reflections. An example of the kind of space you wouldn't want to record in would be a bathroom. (Unless you would intentionally want to use it for FX reasons.)

You'll also want to make sure that your headphone mix gives you a sense of control over your singing. A great headphone mix gives you a sense of your voice being supported by the instruments rather than singing against them. Imagine that you are singing in a room accompanied only by an acoustic guitar; you are supported by the sound and

Top Tips to Capture a Great Recording

- ***Go in early.*** *The ideal situation is that you go into the studio before your recording session to try out two or three different mics. A good producer or engineer can listen and make suggestions. It may be that the engineer says, "You know, I just tried this mic out with artist X—you might find that it will really work for you."*
- ***Relax.*** *Make sure you have a relaxed atmosphere in the studio. As an artist you just have to minimize stress and be able to approach your recording knowing you have the right mic and headphone mix.*
- ***Be with supportive people.*** *A good producer is aware of what might be going on in your head and therefore can help you relax. When someone has confidence in you, it makes your work all the easier—thus, one of the signs of a good producer is that they share how much confidence they have in your abilities. That always helps an artist to "perk up," especially new artists. If, in turn, you have confidence in your engineer/producer, then your burden is lessened.*

Al Schmitt: *legendary engineer and producer with more than 150 gold and platinum albums* not singing against it. You want this same feeling with the instrument sounds coming through your headphones.

In addition to this, watch the amount of reverb. Too much reverb in your mix will mush things up, making it more difficult for you to relate to your music. (Reverb and other effects can all be added later on.) A hint on using effects: You should not be able to tell that an effect has been used, but you can tell if it is missing. Also make sure that you don't overdo the bass level in your headphones. You see, the bones in your head always make a resonance in the low frequency. You don't want to add too much energy to the bass that is already present in your head—doing so will cause you to have to work against this force in your mix without eventually noticing that you have to. Overall, you want your perception of your voice in your head giving you the sense that you have control over your music. Don't be afraid to ask for changes in your mix—this does not affect your recording.

Then, you'll want to learn to "work the mic," coming in close for your low-volume, intimate moments and backing off for louder, more powerful passages. Every mic behaves differently to your distance, so expect to spend a little time figuring out the patterns that work the best. How much you move towards and away from the mic also depends on the amount of compression being used in your recording. I wouldn't use much compression on the headphone mix. You'll want to discuss all of this with your engineer, getting his or her feedback on mic placement. If you are recording at home, where you do not have a perfectly treated recording space, then your position to the mic is especially crucial. You see, uneven sound reflections in the room mean that just changing your position by an inch gives a different sound. Make sure you experiment to find the "sweet spot."

—Dirk Brauner: founder of Brauner Microphones

Action 3: Know When to Rely on Tech for Your Recording

Today's technology gives singers more options than ever before—but be careful not to make it a crutch.

The game has changed for vocalists in the recording studio. Even up to ten years ago, one of our main quests was to capture performances with higher fidelity. Now we've moved on to a vast array of possibilities for actually altering those performances. What can now be done in terms of timing and tuning is just incredible. There are almost unlimited editing opportunities.

In the past, great singers that I've worked with like Steven Tyler and Ozzy Osbourne entered the studio without expecting to fix things "later," meaning that they sang it until they got it right, punching into the track where necessary. This is to their credit. They knew what they wanted before they entered the studio—and they would do as many takes at they needed to get their vocals sounding great, perfect.

Now, one can take more liberties in the studio and fix it later. But should vocalists avail themselves of these technological opportunities? Is it right to think that one can "fix" things in postproduction? That's actually a complex question and I want to make a complex argument.

Let's step back for a minute and look at the relationship between technology and art. There has never been a time when technology hasn't influenced art—even before any electronics existed. It may have been a more sophisticated paintbrush or a new kind of canvas that opened up new artistic possibilities. Now, we are living in an era where technology is interacting with the creation of art more than it ever has. We can accept and celebrate this.

> *Don't think that you will always have the same quality on plugins as you will on original pieces of gear. There is no plugin, after all, that can equal a Fairchild compressor on a vocal.*
>
> ***—Al Schmitt:** legendary engineer and producer with more than 150 gold and platinum albums*

Singers today will want to know what is possible in terms of timing, tuning, layering vocals and all kinds of other effects—not to lower their standards, but to increase their options.

Every singer who has been in the studio knows that time is money; time can also be the enemy of the creative process. If it takes you three hours to nail a single phrase of your song, you could be sacrificing parts of your album. However, if you know that you can get the "feel" of that line down perfectly but have a hard time reaching the note, fixing that single note will take a minute in postproduction. You can draw upon this knowledge for picking and choosing how you will approach your creative process in the studio. In other words, if your time is limited, but you know the technical possibilities, you have more resources to reach your goals.

Here's an extreme example. There was a famous female pop singer-whose name I cannot mention who said to me, "You have these two takes and then I have to be on a private jet. Two passes in real-time, that's it." Now, I am not suggesting that you choose this method for your recording! But that was the situation I had to work with and technology ended up being the deciding factor in producing a quality vocal track. At the other extreme you have vocalists who want no Auto-Tune on their vocals and the engineering work is largely limited to punching and crossfading, because they are singing it all without auto-tuning.

I come away from all of these experiences with this piece of wisdom: *understand the technological options AND push yourself for the best performance.* Don't use the options as a crutch; expand your range, develop your sense of pitch and timing—give the song your best performance. Then, consider how technology can help you reach your goals.

Aim for an organically satisfying vocal performance. Then realize that technology can enhance it—as well as shorten the time it takes to achieve it.

—David Frangioni: technical consultant & engineer, works with Ozzy Osbourne, Aerosmith, Shakira, Bryan Adams and many more

Action 4: Make the Most of Your Bedroom

These six cheap and easy ideas will improve your sound when you're doing your own recording on your computer, smartphone or camera:

Experiment with Mic Placement. Experiment with the distance between your mic and mouth—as well as the mic's height in relation to your mouth. This is critical whether you are using the mic on your smartphone or something more professional. You will be surprised when you play back some examples of having done this in different ways. No matter what you choose, aim the mic at your mouth. If you are playing a guitar, you must be careful to place the mic in a spot where it will pick up more of your voice than the guitar. Your mic needs to be absolutely still, protected from very low frequency sounds in your room (such as the rumble of that truck driving by). Pro mics come with a dedicated suspension mount. Short of this, putting a foam pad or floor-polishing disc from a industrial floor cleaner under circular based mic stands can do the trick.

—The Ultimate Team

Find the Best Room in the House. Don't just set up your mic in your bedroom because it's convenient—it could be that your brother's bedroom will make you sound better. Why? Because his walls are plastered with football jerseys that act as acoustic panels absorbing the sound and preventing unwanted audio reflections from infiltrating your recording. Besides, your bedroom has a window facing the street and you can hear every passing vehicle. Or, you might find that your kitchen, with its hardwood floor, gives you a tasteful reverb that makes your YouTube video sound wonderful. Experiment in EVERY room in your house before you settle into your recording.

—The Ultimate Team

Consider Some Modest Gear Under $100. For improving your home recordings, first spend some money on how you pick up your sound. Before drooling over expensive pro-studio mics, consider a budget studio mic. Some of these cost far less that their sound quality would lead you to believe. Then you'll need an interface with phantom power to connect it to your computer—there are many simple and affordable options (which will also work great with live mics). Or, you could consider a USB powered microphone. Just plug this directly into your computer and start recording your voice and other instruments.

If it's the visual element you're looking to improve, then check out some of the inexpensive webcams popular among YouTubers. Keep in mind that the in-built microphone on your webcam (or video camera) will not offer the same sound quality as a dedicated vocal recording microphone.

For the best results, record the audio part of your video using your studio microphone into your recording interface while you are filming and then synchronize this with the video afterwards.

When it comes to your recording software, it's hard to improve on some of the programs that you may already have bundled with your computer—even entry level versions of some programs give you all you need to produce great results. I know I'm supposed to stick to devices for home recording here, but don't forget some cool peripherals like the drink holder I just purchased: you clip it to a mic stand and this forever solves spilling your drink on stage—or in your bedroom!

—Chris Kennedy, principal product reviewer for VoiceCouncil Magazine, singer-songwriter

Recording Gear Under $100

Equipment	Product	
XLR Mics	**Audio Technica AT2020**	**MXL V63M**
USB Mics	**Samson C01U**	**Behringer C1-U**
Interface	**Blue's Icicle**	**ART USB Dual Tube Pre**
Webcams	**Logitech's C920 HD Pro Webcam**	**Microsoft LifeCam Studio**
Software	**GarageBand on Mac**	**Steinberg's Cubase Elements 6**

Eliminate Hum and Distortion on Home Recording Equipment. There can be many sources of hum. If all you have is a microphone connected to an audio interface, try a different mic cable. If you have a microphone connected to one or more device before the audio interface, try plugging the AC power of everything in the set up to the same power bar. If that doesn't work (and don't tell anyone you heard this from me), move from a 3 pin to a 2 pin plug (this is often called a "cheater plug") power bar and plug everything into this except the computer in the signal. Finally, try different cables. Distortion is usually caused by "clipping," which simply means that something is turned up too much. Make sure that you set the level or gain on the mic input so that loud passages don't exceed -9dB as monitored in the recording program. This gives you 9dB of "headroom," which means that you can go even 9dB louder than the loud passage before distortion will occur.

—David Hilderman, Chief Operating Officer of TC-Helicon Vocal Technologies

Build Your Own Vocal Booth. Watch that you are not picking up too much of your room's ambient sounds when you record. Once you record a vocal take with room ambiance, this is virtually impossible to remove later in the process. This is an inexpensive issue to deal with: get a little vocal foam enclosure that attaches to the mic stand and/or construct your own recording booth.

I have a million dollars' worth of recording equipment; yet I've built my own vocal booth out of PVC pipes and curtains–for a total cost of $45.00.

–Mark Needham, Grammy nominated producer and mix engineer

Action 5: The Basement Studio: Consider Some Gear Under $500

You now have a dedicated room for rehearsals and recording—and a fair amount of gear. Line it all up so that your voice gets the best deal possible.

There are a few components in the chain to splash out on to help you capture a great vocal performance: a microphone preamp, headphones and studio monitors.

Mic preamps can range from just over a couple of hundred bucks to a few thousand. Check out manufacturers like API, Cranesong, D.A.V., Focusrite, Rupert Neve Designs and Tubetech.

This is the box that will carry and transform your microphone signal to your mixing desk and recording device. All these different units will bring their own character to the plate so try some different mic preamps in combination with your microphone to discover different tonal characteristics. You may have the best sounding microphone in the universe, but if you stick it through a crap preamp, it's not going to record well. You can spend a lot of money on a good pre-amp–but best place to start is to experiment and see if you get a sound for your voice that you like.

Headphones can make or break an artist's performance in the studio. They need to be comfortable, sound nice and have fantastic isolation properties. Some artists love to have the backing track pumping away in the cans in order to get into the vibe to lay down their performance. Now you're standing in front of a very sensitive microphone that will pick up a mouse dreaming in the studio. When you have the music blasting and a click track thumping away, this could all leak out of the headphones straight into the mic and potentially ruin your vocal takes.

The classic studio headphones that are famous for their isolation are the Beyer DT-100. Unfortunately they sound quite "honky" and *a number of* artists now refuse to use them. AKG 240, Beyer DT-250 feel nicer and I've had some amazing results with Audio Technica's ATH-M50. Again, these things are very subjective and people will react differently to different headphones. Use whatever you need to get the job done.

Studio monitors are super-important. These speakers are going to tell you what you are capturing to "tape." If you ask ten engineers and/or producers about their monitors, it's very likely you'll get ten different opinions. Monitors will interact with the room you're in, so you'll need to shop around for a bit to find those that work best for your taste and within your acoustic environment.

Learn your monitors, get used to them and find out about their quirks and peaks. Once you know exactly how they behave, you'll instinctively know what to tweak, where to put the microphone and how the material will translate on various professional and consumer systems. Monitor manufacturers to take a close look at are Genelec, Dynaudio, sE Electronics, Focal, KRK, Acoustic Energy and PMC.

– *Wes Maebe: Recording-Mix-Mastering, FOH engineer for Sting, New Model Army, Yusuf Islam, Ellie Goulding, Elliott Randall*

Cost of a Basic Home Studio

Darrell Smith, an experienced studio producer and co-founder of the AVL company Kung Pow Productions, offers his recommendations for the gear necessary for a start-up home studio. In his words, "This is what it's going to take to get a quality recording of your voice."

The Cost of a Basic Home Studio

Item	Name, Brand and Information	Approx. cost (USD)
Mic Stand	K&M or DR heavy-duty, straight mic stand with folding legs	**$60**
Microphone	Shure SM7, Audio Technica 4040, Audix CX112	**$300**
Acoustic Reflection Filter (reduces sounds from the room; without this, you must treat the room or create a 4x4 recording booth)	SE Reflection Filter, Primeacoustic Vox Guard	**$99-$299**
25' Mic Cable	Proco, Rapco, Monster	**$50**
USB Audio interface	Apogee Duet 2, Focusrite Scarlett 2i4, MOTU UltraLite	**$500**
Audio production software (also called DAW, or Digital Audio Workstation, software)	Avid ProTools, Presonus Studio 1, Reaper Ableton Live	**$500**
Headphones	Sony MDR7506, Sennheiser HD280 Pro, Shure SRH440	**$99**
Laptop	(relatively modern please. No G4/G5!s) (updated OS, latest driver installed from company website, recording software installed – before connecting your audio interface!)	**$1000**
Digital files of backing tracks/ karaoke tracks	Your favorite karaoke tracks or a band track you or your friend recorded	**$2-$4 per digital karaoke track**
Studio Monitors	Tannoy Reveal or Yamaha HS80M	**$300-400**
Total		**$2900-$3200**

Action 6: The Basement Studio: Record Your Voice into Your Computer

It's never been easier to translate your vocal gold into your hard drive.

It all starts with the mic. Great vocal performances are often captured on large diaphragm condenser microphones costing from $1,000 to $4,000. Legends like Ella Fitzgerald and Frank Sinatra were recorded on Neumann and Telefunken's U 47s and U 67s, and still today many artists choose these brands. Here's the thing: start with a Shure SM7 for $400. Then, wait until you've worked with a producer whom you trust and who has tried a few different mics on your voice. If you are happy with the end result, go and invest in whatever microphone that producer picked for you.

Next, you need a mic pre-amplifier (preamp, or "pre"), which takes the very low output level of your microphone and brings it up to a usable level for recording. It is crucial to set your preamp correctly—too much gain and you will introduce noise and distortion into your sound; too little gain and your signal will be too weak to record. Your preamp greatly affects the tone of your vocal recording, so consider your genre when you choose your preamp. API's preamps are preferred for American rock, while Neve's are preferred for Brit rock. GML and Avalon attempt to be more transparent. Preamps cost $1,000–4,000 per channel.

There is one last necessity. A microphone turns the sounds of your voice into an analog signal (audio as electricity). Your computer can only understand digital audio signals (audio as bits and bytes). This is why you need an analog to digital converter (A/D converter). An A/D converter takes thousands of snapshots of your sound every second. Be aware that not all A/D converters are created equal. Universal Audio, Apogee, Avid HDX, and other boutique brands offer excellent convertors, but these cost over $2,000.

Some good news: A/D converters and a few preamps can be packaged together in one piece of gear: an audio interface. The Apogee Duet 2 ($550) is a great choice for a simple but pro set-up. Make sure you have updated your operating system and have installed the latest driver for your audio interface from the company website *before* you connect it to your computer.

When you are ready to invest further in your signal chain, you will want to buy a standalone, high-quality microphone preamp to increase the detail and character of your vocal signal chain. But for starters, an Apogee Duet 2, an SM7 and some cables will get you a complete signal chain for $1,200. For the time being, everything else you need can be done with software or hardware that you can invest in later.

—Darrell Smith: audio professional and owner of Kungpow Productions

Action 7: The Basement Studio:

Know What Your Audio Software Can Do for You

More than just a fancy acronym, your DAW can produce studio-quality vocal tracks.

The Digital Audio Workstation (DAW) software package running on your computer brings the core recording, signal processing and mixing capabilities to your vocal studio. When you are just getting started, you can buy less costly software such as Reaper, Mixcraft or Garageband. Later you can choose one of the big industry standards, such as Avid ProTools 10.

Getting started in your DAW software involves adding the necessary tracks to your new session, dropping in your backing track (a karaoke track or a previously recorded band track) and getting the levels right in your headphones. It is crucial to set the mic level on your audio interface so that the meter on your vocal channel doesn't go into the red when you make your loudest sound. When you sing, remember to keep your mouth about 3–6 inches from the mic and try to "work the mic" (see action two).

When you play your first recording back, it's going to sound a bit stark. Don't worry. You can change this with signal processing (equalization, compression, de-essing, reverb, etc.) You may eventually buy some standalone gear, but for now, you will use plugins—pieces of audio gear in software form that enhance your sound. You'll find most plugins you'll need included with your software. Read FAQ five to find out what each of these plugins does, then start applying them to your recorded vocal. Experimenting with these will help you learn how to get the sound you want.

I recommend recording a bunch of songs as complete takes before you read the next paragraph. Focus on emotional connection over technical perfection. Only once you are achieving this consistently should you start experimenting with the following overdubbing techniques.

Let's say you've got a great take but there were a few moments that didn't quite go down how you had hoped. You are now ready to switch your software into overdub mode. *Overdubbing* is the process of re-recording a certain word or phrase to replace your previous one. *Comping* is the process of choosing the best passages from a number of takes and creating a composite track that incorporates the best bits of each. Be aware that many people lose perspective trying to fix the tiniest things. Remember: beauty has its imperfections.

Once you've tracked and comped a great take, your next step is tuning or pitch-correction. Celemony's plugin Melodyne preserves the nuance in your pitch performance while allowing you to adjust the note centers for pitch accuracy. Another good tuning plugin is Antares' Auto-Tune or Waves Tune.

Now you can go back to all the plugins you experimented with before and do your final signal processing (see FAQ five again) to make this a killer track.

—Darrell Smith: audio professional and owner of Kungpow Productions

Action 8: Do This Stuff When You're Paying for Studio Time

Master the new sphere of the Pro Studio with these five suggestions from engineers and producers

Know Your Albums. You don't want to be discussing the intricacies of sound when you're on the clock in the studio. That's why it's a good idea to be able to point to a couple of albums that you all think you want to sound like. It's not that you're trying to mimic those albums (even if you try to mimic, you'll always sound like you). It's about having a tangible "thing" you can show your producer and engineer (and each other!), to be on the same page and using the same language. After all, talking about music can be such a vague exercise! You might be describing a sound as "wobbly" when the other person is using the word "punchy"—give yourselves some mutually understood reference points from other recordings. Also, you can easily demo your recordings on your own, getting used to how you like things to layer (or not layer) before you ever get to a studio.

—Val Emmich, singer-songwriter, hailed by the New York Times as "a rocker who rocks to his own beat"

Catch Your Vibe with the Mic. Studio singing involves capturing your voice in an enclosure where you have to stand still—this is a real difference from the live environment. However, like the live environment, it's great if you can control the dynamic of your mic a little on your own, pulling your head back slightly on the loudest notes and leaning in closely in for the quieter sections. When singers first come to the studio we'll spend some time experimenting with all of this. We always try things the normal way first, with the mic mounted and the singer standing still. However, if you're a really active performer and it turns out to be too difficult to keep still in the studio, then we sometimes revert to something closer to a live setup, letting you hold a mic. After all, the key thing is to do what it takes to catch your vibe in the studio.

—Ian Stewart, co-founder and co-owner at Blueprint Recording Studios

Relentlessly Pursue Your Vision. You can and should share your ideas for the overall "feel" you are trying to achieve with your voice and your music. Los Angeles based producer and engineer Tristan Leral tells vocalists to keep stating their vision, especially since it may change slightly or develop during the session. You might find it helpful to name an artist or a specific song to help describe the sound and vibe you want for each song. Regardless of your level of confidence or experience, remember: it is your recording. No matter how many opinions come into play, it has to feel right to you.

–The Ultimate Team

Keep Talking To The Engineer. The engineer is the technical force behind everything that is happening in the session. Many of us wear different hats as well, such as vocal producer, producer and tea maker. Communication is key: be clear with us about what sounds right or wrong in the headphones. Also, develop a common way of articulating certain terms so that neither of us is confused. If you want to "punch-in" a vocal, you might be saying "pick it up" or "drop it in"–just come to an understanding of the terms. Singing in a professional studio with great mics/gear can actually be intimidating because you may not be used to hearing your breathing and your voice so clearly. It can feel like some mics "swallow you up." Talk with the engineer if you get that feeling. We can use reverb/delays/FX in your headphones while you record to help in the process. This is less intimidating than listening to a dry vocal.

–Mark "Exit" Goodchild, Grammy-nominated producer and engineer

> *Just look at all the great artists: they don't produce themselves. Why? There are just so many aspects to making an album. When you self produce you put so much of a burden on yourself that you can't concentrate properly on what you are doing. Your number one priority should be to get someone you are comfortable with—and compatible with—to take some of the burden off you and provide another point of view.*
>
> ***–Al Schmitt:** legendary engineer and producer with more than 150 gold and platinum albums*

Get the Headphone Mix Right. Every singer I work with uses the headphones a different way. Some people want every vocal deadpanned in the middle or to have all sound delivered to the left ear so that they can take one of the phones off their ear and hear the room's reflections. If you're in a professional studio setting, communication is the key–talk to your engineer about how you would like things to sound ("more of this, less of that"). If you are by yourself and if you have just one phone on your ear, make sure that the other side is muted so that extra background noise isn't created.

–Mark "Exit" Goodchild, Grammy-nominated producer and engineer

Action 9: Get a Producer

Free yourself up to focus on getting the best sound possible.

There are two excellent reasons to consider a producer for your recording—the first is that no one in the band has complete objectivity. The second is that everyone in the band has their own territory that he or she needs to be watching. A producer takes the pressure off the band, releasing them to focus on their music.

> *Cooperative bands can be very tricky. In 1969 I was with Seatrain; we were recording an album—self-produced. There were five of us and an engineer—that made for 12 hands on the console! It sounded ... not great. Sometimes creative decisions are best left in the hands of someone else who has earned the trust of the band. Before I left the group I suggested that they have a producer, George Martin (who worked with the Beatles). A few months later they hired him—and they had a hit album.*
>
> ***—Elliot Randall:*** *legendary guitarist, formerly a musical consultant for Saturday Night Live*

There is always some natural chaos in any group of people. At best you are brothers with different ways of seeing things and at worst you are warring siblings. Those are just the way human dynamics are. So, you need someone who can be objective and tame the lions. This is the "fifth member" of your band who has the objectivity and talent to make sure that the best material gets recorded and that the arrangements and production are at their best.

At the very best you will have a George Martin figure (of Beatles fame), someone who is a gifted member and helps your band to achieve success. Quality producers will immerse themselves in all of the dynamics of the band and are paid very well for doing so. Everybody can always profit from a great producer whom they can really trust.

Sometimes bands use an engineer as their producer. This makes a lot of sense as it is one less person in the chain. You just have to make sure that your engineer has the people skills to pull this off. "Expensive" is not necessary—you just need someone who can facilitate the band's vision and work with the chemistry of the band. You can find that individual in every stratum of the industry.

If you have someone who possesses emotional stability and is a good team leader, someone who wants to fulfill everyone's vision in the band, then that can only benefit you.

—Fred Mollin: veteran record producer, film and TV composer, musical director and songwriter

Action 10: Take a Final Walkthrough

Make the recording environment as familiar as your favourite pair of jeans.

The first thing you must know when recording your voice is that things get better over time.

There is an enormous difference in the way that you hear yourself in the studio as opposed to a live performance. As much as you want that magic to occur in the studio, you simply have to take into account that studio singing is a craft that takes some time to develop. So, take the pressure off by giving yourself that time to get used to this new environment.

First, take time to listen and make notes on what you would like to hear in your headphone mix. The first question you will want to ask is, "How am I hearing myself—am I getting enough of 'me' in the headphone mix?" Then you will want to ask yourself questions about the quality of sound coming through: do you want a little or a lot of reverb? Do you want any particular instrument in—or out—of the headphone mix? Basically, you are working at customizing the sound to your taste.

If you are having pitch issues, try taking one headphone off and putting it behind your ear. This allows you to hear your voice in the room. For my own singing, I do this all the time—and many vocalists I work with do as well. There are no hard and fast rules you need to adhere to—just some principles that can help you get comfortable.

There's no single "right" path I can prescribe that will ensure that you connect emotionally to your song. Every singer is different. The overall principle is for you to tap into the emotions of your song in the same way that you would in a live performance, or if you were singing for a loved one. In other words, once you have gone through the steps to feel comfortable with the "craft" aspect of studio singing, then it is a matter of accessing the emotional resources that were there when you wrote the song, heard the song, or performed the song in a live setting.

Solving one more issue may be important for your studio performance: do you want to see people in the control room when you are singing? Personally, I don't—and most artists I work with don't either. Many singers find it best to sing with the control room window at the side—this allows you to not be distracted by people walking around the control room and to more easily lose yourself in the performance. Nine out of ten singers I work with want it this way—but a small minority of singers like to sing to the control room. Again, there are no hard and fast rules. The main thing is that you feel you are not distracted and can enter into "living" the song as you sing it.

—Fred Mollin: veteran record producer, film and TV composer, musical director and songwriter

Frequently Asked Questions:

> How come there's a buzz/noise/hiss in the silent parts of my song?

Answered by Mark "Exit" Goodchild, Grammy-nominated producer and engineer

This could end up being a long answer about "noise floor" (the sum of all noise sources), but I'll make it easy: that buzz and hiss is there the whole time—it's just being masked by the music. The buzz could be from an amplifier or a bad cable connection. Hiss, in the analog world, would be the sound of analog tape rolling. But I highly doubt that's the instance here. Generally, if a mic is recording, it's going to pick up room noise no matter what. Sometimes that noise you hear could be the microphone track that is still on. To eliminate noise and hiss, in analog or digitally, use gates. In the digital world you can also edit the actual audio regions so that if there is no actual audio playing, the region is deleted in that section. I do this a lot—ProTools has a function called "Strip Silence" for this.

> What's the cheapest way I can record my voice and post it on my site?

Answered by Chris Kennedy, principal product reviewer for VoiceCouncil Magazine, singer-songwriter

If you already have a computer, one of the simplest recording solutions is a USB condenser microphone. Unlike typical condenser microphones that require a separate interface with phantom power, these mics are powered by your computer via a USB cable. They also need no separate preamp, specialist sound card or mixer to record with—so they are great for recording on a small budget. An added bonus of USB condenser microphones is that they are usually quite capable of producing reasonable results on acoustic instruments as well as vocals. This makes them a particularly good option if you're a singer who also performs on acoustic guitar.

> *Go into your studio session with at least three songs, even if you are aiming for a single. There is always at least one song that doesn't go as planned. It is great if you have originals, but you can certainly choose covers. I recommend you turn covers on their heads—your version should bring a whole new perspective to the song.*
>
> ***—Tony Harnell:*** *award winning lead singer of TNT*

If you already have a good quality mic that you use live, an even cheaper option would be to get a low-cost USB audio interface that enables you to connect your existing microphone to your computer. Remember that using a live microphone may not be as optimal as using a dedicated studio mic and you'll likely not be able to record other instruments such as an acoustic guitar at a satisfactory level. However, if you are just recording a demo of your vocals, then there is no reason why you could not get perfectly good sounding results using this method.

Once your vocals have been recorded into your computer, you will then need some software to enable you to edit and mix your vocals. There are several free options available; Audacity and Reaper are among the most popular. These programs will also allow you to use freeware VST effects that can add extra polish to your recordings, such as adding reverb and compression to your vocals. When your track is finished you can then export it as an MP3. The final step is to get it online. One of the easiest ways is to set up a SoundCloud account that allows you to stream your music online to whoever wants to listen to it. You can even embed their player on your own website.

> I just can't relax when I'm recording. Help!

Answered by Judy Rodman, award-winning vocal coach and chart-topping recording artist

Even veteran performing artists can experience vocal booth anxiety—anything from a vague sense of self-conscious insecurity to full blown "red light fever"!

Let's face it: recording can feel strange. It can cause guarded body language resulting in breath issues as well as a tightened throat and loss of vocal control. Good news: there are things you can do to help make the vocal booth feel more familiar and to help diffuse your tension.

First of all, singing with your hands and arms hanging limply at your sides can cause all kinds of breath and throat problems. This is unfortunately a common vocal booth error. The most confident singers use their hands!

I witnessed a great example of this some years ago when I was singing background vocals on a Johnny Cash record. We were recording "simul": the band, the background singers and Johnny were all cutting at the same time. Talk about pressure! Then I saw something odd ... the engineer handed Johnny a guitar with no strings. Turns out, having his guitar in his hands caused Johnny's head to be balanced farther back at the mic, opening his throat. And it caused his arms to be open and lifted, widening the bottom of his ribcage. This is absolutely vital for good breath control. Johnny just knew he was in a more familiar stance and that he could sing much more confidently.

You don't need to hold a guitar to achieve this—just talk with your hands, communicate with your eyes and ensure you don't become too "tight." A technique that I have developed for difficult notes and phrases is to press fingertips from each hand into each other so that the ribcage expands and the head is balanced over the tailbone. The shoulders should stay relaxed.

My Top Relaxation Tips:

- **Choose the right production team.** Positive reinforcement along with intuitive correction can go a long way toward helping you relax.
- **Be very clear to whom you are singing!** Focus your mind to sing to one heart—the person to whom the lyric is directed—not to the people in the control room.

- **Keep the critic out of the vocal booth.** Be the child creator at the mic; avoid perfectionism and excessive concern about vocal technique. Save your critical hat for when you listen to playback.
- **Employ these preparation strategies:**
  - Your physical and vocal stamina should be in top form.
  - Eat a good healthy, protein rich meal and drink plenty of water days before.
  - If you are singing leads, know your material inside out (memorize if possible).
  - Wear studio-appropriate clothes and shoes.
  - Come in calm and centered. Limit stressful conversation, phone calls, hyperactivity and chaos prior to your session.
  - Be sure you have everything you need … lyrics, water, directions to the studio, checkbook, etc.

One final thought: the fewer the people in the control room, the better. Save the party for the mix!

> We want to make our first CD to sell at our gigs—is it worth all the money to go to a studio, or should we try to do this on our own?

Answered by Ross Pallone, Emmy nominated independent recording engineer and co-producer

Have you considered an online recording process? Send a rough mix of your song to a drummer—or other instrumentalist—who records it in their studio and sends an audio file back to you for you to import into your mix. There are studios everywhere who offer this service. Check out studiopros.com, themissingtrack.com, onlinesessions.co.uk and onlinerecordingmasters.com

—The Ultimate Team

This is a good question for young artists. I have been recording and mixing for over thirty years. I have heard some very good home recordings and some very terrible ones. Of course, not everyone can afford to go to a commercial studio or even a small home studio.

There is some very good inexpensive gear out on the market now that can make an excellent recording. If you decide to spend the money to hire an engineer to record and mix your project, I would suggest that you listen to projects that they have done and compare the sound to good professional recordings of respected artists. It probably will not sound like an expensive record done by real pros, but the difference should not sound like night and day either.

One good option would be to have someone record your project in a decent studio and then send it out to an experienced mixer. If you are not in a big rush to get it done and are willing to wait for the mixer to have some down time, you may be able to get a very good mix engineer to mix your project for a reasonable price. The recording engineer should record the tracks with very little to no EQ and compression, as you will get a better result in the mix. A good mixer may also be able to master your project for you and make it ready for duplication.

You most certainly can try to do the recording yourself if you have enough equipment and you're somewhat knowledgeable. There are books available that can teach you the basics. Again, you could do the recording yourself and send the files to a good mixer to finish it.

If you decide to go this way, you may need to still go to a studio to record the drums because you will need more mics, mic stands, mic preamps, etc. that you probably don't own. A lot of excellent pro drummers I know have studios in their homes and will record for you at a reasonable price.

> I'm not an engineer—can I get a recording that is anywhere near as good as a professional one?

Answered by Darrell Smith: audio professional and owner of Kungpow Productions

There is no reason that you, a singer, cannot create recordings in your home studio that will stand up to professional standards—but it takes some time. What a pro engineer can do in a few minutes may take you weeks or months to master. These signal processing tips will get you started.

Every voice interacts differently with the backing track, which is why you need equalization (EQ). There are many frequencies present in your voice—not just the one your ears perceive when you sing a certain pitch. Your EQ allows you to either boost or cut back certain frequencies or groups of frequencies, thus shaping your tone so your voice sits more prominently in the mix (see my chart below for quick and dirty tips for setting EQ).

A high pass filter (HPF) is an equalizer of sorts. When you set your HPF to a certain frequency, such as 160 Hz, it eliminates the muddiness of your vocal by "turning down" the bass frequencies that unnaturally build up when you get close to a microphone (for more about proximity effect, see Chapter Five Action 2). This brings clarity to your vocal, but if the HPF is set too high, you will lose the fullness in your voice. "I Will Always Love You" by Whitney Houston shows a judicious use of a HPF.

A compressor levels out the loud moments in your vocal to be more in line with the quiet ones. Consider that plosives (T's and P's) can be 6 dB louder than your vowels, and you can see why we need compression to help your vocal hold its position in the mix. Setting your threshold so that there is no more than 6dB of compression is a good place to start.

De-Essing reduces the sibilance ("s" sound). Generally, you'll need about 10–12 dB of de-essing, but reduce that amount if you sense a loss of clarity.

A doubler increases the perceived width of your vocal by duplicating your vocal with a touch of pitch shifting and delay. Keep the doubling effect back 8–12dB from your main vocal.

Reverb adds depth and space around your dry vocal. The space can be a big hall (long reverb), or a small room (short reverb or ambience). A great place to start is a "vocal plate" pre-set. You can then set the reverb level according to how prominent you want it. Always exercise restraint with reverb, delay and doubling—you'll thank yourself in five years.

The final step of vocal processing involves automating the vocal level within each section, or even within each phrase, of the song so that the vocal always stays above the track.

Darrell's Quick and Dirty Guide to Setting EQ

It is impossible to EQ a voice without listening to it, so be aware that this chart is meant as a safe place to start. Resist the temptation to boost everything—sometimes it's what you cut that matters most.

Quick and Dirty Guide to Setting EQ

What:	What to set it to:	What it should do:
High pass filter (HPF)	160 Hz	**Minimize 'wooliness' of vocal**
EQ - low	Cut 125 Hz by 2 dB	**Even out the bass**
EQ low-mid	Cut 600 by 1-3 dB	
EQ high-mid	Boost 5,000 Hz by 3 dB	**Increase intelligibility, help vocal cut through mix**
EQ high	Boost 12,000 Hz by 2-4 dB	**Increase airiness of vocal**
EQ low-mid (advanced)	Boost a frequency somewhere between 160-500 Hz by 2 dB	**Bring warmth to your vocal. Find the right freq. to boost by adjusting as you listen to your vocal.**

> I've got a good recording mic at home—if I were to spend money on just one thing beyond the mic, what would it be?

Answered by Dot Bustelo, internationally recognized music producer and music technology strategist

I can't limit my answer to just one item since your mic is only the beginning of the signal chain to your computer. There are two other steps: the mic preamp and the converter—the device that converts the analog signal of your vocal into a digital format for your computer.

I work with a singer who had little experience setting up studio technology herself, so I gave her an all-in-one box to get her started on recording her vocals, an Apogee ONE. This contains a mic, mic preamp and a converter in one box the size of an iPod. There's obviously a value to a dedicated mic, preamp or converter, but some of the innovative and professional ways these are now combined are worth checking out. The Apogee ONE is being used on a lot of hit records.

Another thing you should invest in is a decent pair of headphones. This doesn't need to cost a lot of money—there are a lot of industry-standard units that cost $80–90. You owe it to yourself to have a pair that you can have on your ears for a long period of time and through which you like how the music feels and sounds. Ask your pro studio friends which ones they use—and try a few out.

Finally, get a decent pair of speakers for your home studio—you want to be inspired when you are listening to your music at home; it should sound good. Speakers are a professional tool that will form a part of your inspiration to write and record your music.

> What's the most important thing to keep in mind when we record our first album?

Answered by Ross Pallone, Emmy nominated independent recording engineer and co-producer

Well, there are many important things to keep in mind. From a recording point of view, you will want quality mics and mic preamps. The recording environment should be quiet and the recording room should have sound treatments to make your recording sound good. It should also have a clean signal path with no hums or buzzes. A pro studio will have excellent monitoring and the control room will have acoustical treatments if necessary. Recording in your basement can be OK if you know what to listen for.

The most important thing a pro studio should have is an experienced and competent engineer. Whether you are recording at home or in a studio, the most important thing will be the engineer.

In the golden days of the recording business, almost all recordings were done in a professional studio. Most of those studios either had competent engineers or artists would hire independent engineers with good reputations and a list of impressive credits. Now, too many people think that they are capable of doing a professional recording and mix at home. While some do have the talent and can do a good job, there are plenty of bad sounding records being made because the people recording them are not spending the money in the right place.

With that being said, I do understand that many just don't have the money to hire a good engineer. So for those of you who must do it yourselves, get some help from books, seminars, magazines and friends. Some of the pro retailers have free seminars at their stores. There is also free info on-line. Get some good studio monitors, listen to pro recordings on them and try to make your mix sound in line with them.

However you decide to record your project, the bottom line will be the songs and the vocal talent. No matter how good your record sounds, it will not be successful without good songs.

> I've got a basement full of great gear. What does a pro studio have that I don't?

Answered by Wes Maebe, Recording-Mix-Mastering, FOH engineer for Sting, New Model Army, Yusuf Islam, Ellie Goulding, Elliott Randall

I can sum up the answer in four words: Expertise, Acoustics, Vibe and Focus.

Recording studios cost millions to build. The planning of the layout, the aesthetic and acoustic design of the recording and control rooms, silent air conditioning, doors, windows, cabling, equipment, catering areas, recreation areas—everything has been carefully thought through to maximize the artist's comfort and recording experience.

All of the equipment is cared for, inspected and fixed on a regular basis by highly skilled technical staff who are on site as long as you are in the studio to make sure that everything is in perfect working order. If anything breaks down, it will be fixed instantly or replaced by another unit to keep the flow of the session going.

> *I've heard so many recordings that reflect a great performance but are marred by poor sound quality. So, be careful about working in a cramped home studio with less than optimal equipment. Everything now is done at 96K or 192K on Pro Tools, but the quality of the room, the mic and the preamps are critical for your audio quality.*
>
> ***—Al Schmitt:** legendary engineer and producer with more than 150 gold and platinum albums*

The variety of acoustics you get in a recording studio is something you just cannot achieve in your basement.

First of all, your basement will most likely have four parallel walls that will create a phenomenon known as standing waves. These are sound waves that create a loop of themselves between your walls and generate a resonance. Because of these resonances, you'll listen to your material and instinctively reach for the EQ to tune these things out; this may result in bass-light recordings or material with lower mid frequency dips.

Studios have been designed not to have these problems. Different recording rooms will have different characteristics that make them suitable for different styles of music or even instrumentation. You may record your drums, bass and guitars in one studio and all the vocals in a different room or in a completely different studio. Studios may have iso (isolation) booths, which allow you to record at the same time as other band members, but will have the instrument amplifiers separated so as to minimize spill onto the other microphones.

Obviously the recording rooms and control rooms are separated from each other to allow for accurate monitoring behind the console. My guess is that your basement will contain all the recording equipment and the band's back line in all in the same room, so you all would have to work on headphones.

No answer to this question would be complete without a word about studio staff. The studio bookers are angels who will bend over backwards to make sure that your time in the studio is the best time of your life. For all the amazing consoles and microphones in the world, nine out of ten times it is the studio booker who will be responsible for you wanting to come back!

"I want a weird African choir to sing on this pop track." "We need a specific 70s drum kit in this color." "Our engineer requires gluten/wheat and dairy free food … at 4:25 in the morning." When you make the most out-of-this-world request, they'll somehow make it work. And studio assistants know every bit of the studio and are there to make sure your engineer and producer can focus on the task at hand, record your material and make it sound phenomenal.

If you try to produce, engineer, write, play, and have fun all at the same time, you're going to fall short somewhere.

The professional recording environment is a microscope that allows you to really zoom into your material and performance.

> How do I choose the right studio for my first album?

Answered by Kevin Wesley Williams, producer and engineer for Marilyn Manson, Megadeth and many more …

Remember this: a studio is only as good as its engineers. This is why your choice of studio should be based on its engineers more than anything else.

There are more recording studios out there than ever before, and just like finding a good car mechanic or a dentist, the best way to find the right people to record your album is to ask other musicians for recommendations.

Once you have a list of names, set up meetings at the studios so you can go talk to the engineers. You need to make sure that your engineer excels in the type of music you want to record. Ask engineers to play you examples of music they have recorded as well as projects they are currently working on. Ask about the processes they would use for your recording. For example, you can ask what type of microphone and preamp they would recommend and why.

You want to find an engineer who makes you feel comfortable, especially since your first album has the potential to be stressful. By choosing a professional studio with highly trained engineers, one assurance you are paying for is that these guys have the confidence and expertise to put you at ease.

Budget plays a big part in what a studio can offer you. Be careful of the studio whose rate seems too good to be true. You might just get what you pay for. A studio with high rates may indicate that the studio is more in demand or has better tools available, but that does not necessarily guarantee a better outcome. Be honest with the studio regarding your budget and ask them if there are ways to get a better rate, such as if you book larger blocks of time or if you come on certain days or at certain times.

> Can I talk the studio down in price? To what degree is the price negotiable, and what factors come into play with that?

Answered by Mark Needham, Grammy nominated producer and mix engineer

All studios are flexible on budgets these days. Budgets vary widely from project to project—even for major labels. The best approach is just to come in and say, "Here's what I can afford. Can you make this work?" Having this in writing is important—a "deal memo," contract or even an email. This memo will say something about how much time you expect to be given to work on your songs and the price. Putting this in writing may save you a lot of grief down the road.

I have a friend in a very well known band that had done a deal with a studio and its engineers; it turned into a nightmare. He lost $15,000 of studio time because the studio's engineer had health/substance abuse issues, and they had to start the recording process again—from scratch. There was no deal memo and, thus, no way to hold the studio to its side of the bargain.

So for your deal memo, just write out one paragraph, based on what you agreed to verbally. Basically it is a statement that says, "I will give you X amount of money in return for X (the studio's commitment in terms of time and personnel)." Do this before you put your money down on the table.

> I want to bring some of my own gear to the studio, like my effects box—will I get in trouble with the engineer?

Answered by Mark "Exit" Goodchild, Grammy-nominated producer and engineer

You will absolutely NOT get in trouble. Any good engineer will encourage this. They'll want to see what you are working with and how you are working with it. In fact, we engineers can probably show you better ways to use your own gear. After a client shows me how they are using their gear, I often find that this can be kept in the recording process.

> After the session is all done, how much can I defend my vision for the mix without being a neurotic artist and driving everyone crazy?

Answered by Tristan Leral, engineer and producer for major artists

You all know "Billie Jean" by Michael Jackson, right? They created 91 different mixes of that song. In the end, do you know which one they chose? Mix #2. What this means is that when you are aiming for that perfect mix, you can sometimes lose perspective. You have to go back to the basics and ask yourself, "How do you relate to the song as you just heard it?"

The process of mixing can be absolutely endless partly because these days, technology makes it possible. Today, it takes 30 seconds to load up a session and revert it back to the way it was six months ago. You have the luxury of changing your mind 50,000 times on how the tambourine should sound. There comes a point where the producer's role is important. The producer is the one who says, "The vocal is right. The vibe is right. Let's stop worrying about the tambourine."

If you are losing perspective, it helps to take a break and listen to the mix in a different setting. Sometimes you have to relax and trust that what you had was great from the get-go.

Perfectionism aside, the artist's opinion always plays a key role in the mixing process. The only exception is for what I call the "grunt work." I don't know any artist who would want to sit and listen to me play with the bass drum track for three hours! Once the grunt work is done, I want the artist to be a part of it. The artist has to feel that the mix reflects their vision. I usually send the artist 2–3 versions of each song—each with a different mix. He or she sends me his or her notes and we tweak it until it's right.

> Is there any etiquette I need to know in the studio?

Answered by Judy Rodman, award-winning vocal coach and chart-topping recording artist

The atmosphere in the studio matters. It's hard to get great recordings with distracting chaos, frustration or personal irritation affecting the singer, producer or engineer. Here are eight points of etiquette to make the studio a friendlier and more efficient place:

1. ***Limit talking in the control room.*** Lower your voice and keep talking to a minimum in or near the control room while producer and engineer are working. This will reduce stress on the production team who are trying capture your vocal magic while dealing with technical challenges—within a tight time frame.
2. ***Sing into and out of lines to be punched.*** It is usually best to start singing before and keep singing after the line to be punched in. This makes it much easier for the engineer to match sounds, rhythms and breaths and make the punch usable.
3. ***When singing scratch vocals on tracking sessions, don't make the band stop because you messed up.*** Instrumental tracking sessions need to focus on the playing—not the singing. If you think you might want to keep your scratch vocals as finals and want to re-sing, just ask the engineer to record you again when a musician does another pass.
4. ***Unplug your headphones when leaving the vocal booth if someone else will be singing.*** This simple act is courteous to the engineer when doing group vocals and keeps your headphones from bleeding into the mic.
5. ***Close doors, limit noise.*** Shut isolating doors behind you when entering the booth so the engineer won't have to. Don't allow anyone to open a door when you're recording. Remove noisy fabrics or jewelry.
6. ***Don't make ear-splitting noises on the microphone.*** Don't whistle, blow or yell into a mic, possibly frying it and the ears of everyone in the control room! Check the mic by clucking or scratching fingernails lightly on it. If you are going to change your volume significantly, alert the engineer so he/she can adjust levels.

7. ***Be willing to work as hard as your production team.*** Getting a great vocal takes focused effort. Be ready and willing to go the distance; keep a positive attitude when asked to correct or change something—save the drama for the lyrics.
8. ***When you are finished singing, pick up after yourself.*** It may surprise you how much this simple courtesy is appreciated by weary studio personnel.

> Should I record my voice on one of those expensive large-diaphragm condenser mics (U87/M149)?

Answered by Bill Gibson, producer and author of more than 30 books on technology

That's an important question. Let's look at both sides of this. Singers and engineers often like to record with large diaphragm condenser mics because the larger diaphragm captures a full and natural sound, which might not require EQ when good mic technique is used.

If the vocalist has a very dynamic and expressive voice with an airy sound at times and lots of emotional feeling in the performance, then a large-diaphragm condenser mic is an obvious choice. Beyond that, the singer needs to find the actual mic that sounds best for his or her voice—that might be a condenser, dynamic, or ribbon mic.

However, if the singer is one-dimensionally aggressive with little subtlety, the recordist might consider a dynamic mic for a couple of reasons: first, a constant "screamo" or "cookie monster" type sound just might work better in the recording if you don't capture all of its intricacies. Second, a dynamic mic might be better able to handle the sheer volume and moisture produced by an extremely loud and aggressive singer.

The grounds for this choice include your overall needs and the sound of the specific mic you choose. Sometimes—a small diaphragm condenser mic is the best choice, especially if you record a lot of acoustic instruments in addition to vocals. If you do more vocal recording with an occasional acoustical recording, a large-diaphragm condenser might be the best choice. Certain mics are known to exhibit characteristics of both the large and small diaphragm. The Shure KSM 32 and the AKG 414 are examples of good multi-purpose large diaphragm mics.

Neumann, a German microphone manufacturer, has produced some of the most commonly used studio microphones. There is no doubt that these mics give excellent results for many singers. Examples are the U 87 and U 67 (either the vintage or new release). The U 47 is a vintage Neumann mic that is known for its warm, smooth, balanced tone—it is one of the more frequently photographed studio mics. Neumann's TLM 103 should also be considered not least because of its reasonable price.

There are other large diaphragm mics that vocalists will want to try out such as the Audio-Technica AT 4047 (made to emulate the vintage U 47 at a fraction of the price) and the AT 4060 tube mic. Shure's KSM 32 and KSM 44 are also very nice large diaphragm mics. Many singers also have good results with Blue mics and the AKG 414 is also a popular choice.

CHAPTER 9

Looping

Transform your performance.

"To me, live looping IS the future of music. The way we make music will change forever. Live looping is a proto-version of what is to come: live production."

—Beardyman, beatboxer and looper, named "King of Sounds and Ruler of Beats" by the BBC

"Imagine the freedom of being able to play open mics, to open for other artists, to do solo shows—without having to coordinate schedules or having to pay the rest of the band!"

—Mister Tim, viral video star, voice artist, composer and sponsored kazoo player

Looping

Transform your performance.

Actions:

1. Use Looping. You May Win a Grammy.
2. Just Do It
3. Make a Solid Base Layer
4. Add More Layers—and Take Them Away
5. Use Looping in Solo and Ensemble Performances
6. Improve Your Musicality

Frequently Asked Questions:

» *Give me at least one good reason to use looping in my already successful solo singer-guitarist pop-rock gigs.*

» *Won't an audience get tired of you setting up loops?*

» *I tried looping on a song in my latest house concert, but things got out of sync and I had to stop in the middle of my song. Does this mean looping isn't for me?*

Action 1: Use Looping. You May Win a Grammy

Grammy award winning artist Kimbra reveals how looping can be an integral part of your vocal creativity.

At a time when I saw myself as just a singer with a guitar, looping challenged me to think of myself as an instrument. When I was 16, I borrowed an 8-track Boss recorder from the high school music room and experimented with overdubbing my voice multiple times. My voice had a whole new sound when layered as two, three or four voices. I also discovered I could loop up a bass part, then trigger it to come in at certain points with a foot pedal. I had found a way to create new textures, embrace more dynamics and turn the things I heard in my head into a performance reality.

Later, when I started performing with a full band and playing less guitar, my voice became the sole instrument for realizing the creative elements I wanted. Be it lush landscapes or poignant aggression, I wanted to find a way to achieve the complex sounds of the music I was listening to at the time such as Nine Inch Nails, Miles Davis and The Mars Volta. The product that best allowed me to do that was VoiceLive Touch. It was my playground for creating arrangements.

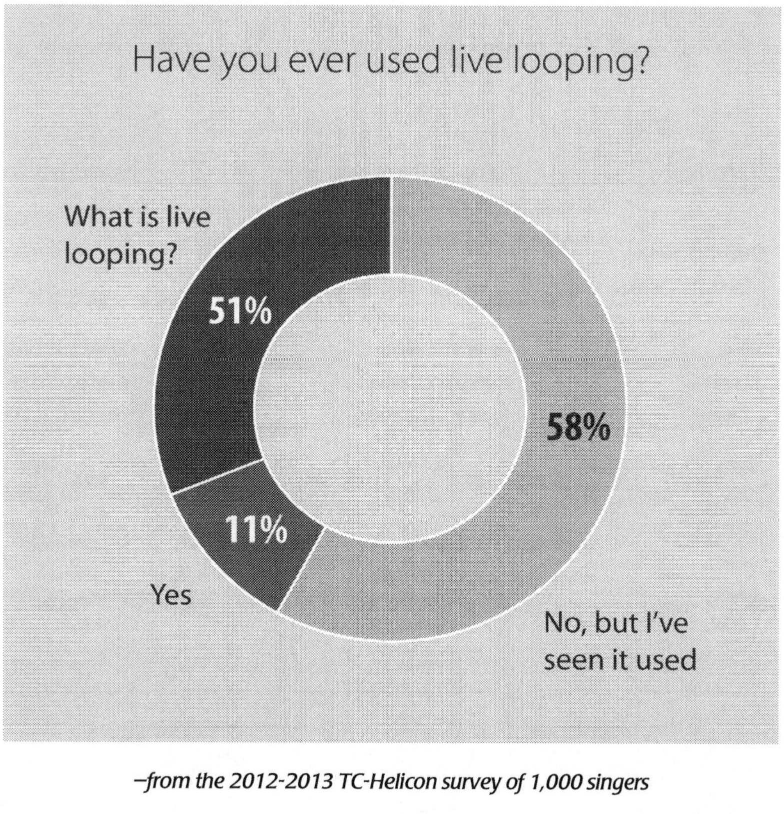

–from the 2012-2013 TC-Helicon survey of 1,000 singers

My challenge these days is to keep a balance with my relationship to technology—allowing it to illuminate the music and stretch the soundscape but not take over or distract from the essence and connection of the song. I use looping in moments where it adds a dimension that the band can't. The presence of multiple voices on stage acting as my backups is not meant to be a novelty and I am careful not to overuse it. Looping, like any instrument, can add texture and color. I sometimes use it to accentuate grooves like a beatboxer, only in a more melodic way—similar to a bass player.

Looping is an incredible writing tool. Instead of having to manually record separate parts to communicate an idea to a producer, I can do it on the fly as the idea comes to me. I can demonstrate an entire song by layering the various parts I hear or singing the harmony stacks in real time and setting them to triggers.

In the live context, looping lets the audience in on something wonderful: seeing the artist build a song from the ground up with the thrilling awareness that it could all go wrong at any moment. All it takes is a finger that misses a beat or a loop that is not quite right—and it's game over. This new and sometimes scary territory keeps me from becoming too comfortable on stage.

—Kimbra: New Zealand born songstress

Action 2: Just Do It

Layered loops can bring new dimensions to live performances, adding texture and complexity without the need for additional performers.

In just the last few years looping has moved from a fad on the fringes to a full-blown performance art. It's already changing the way many vocalists approach their singing and their gigs.

First, though, let's define the terms. A loop is a short phrase that is recorded and played back, repeatedly, as long as you like. You can add more loops on top of this, creating a rich, multi-layered vocal (or instrumental) fabric.

The first loop is usually rhythmic: you are setting down a pattern that will be the "foundation" of a multi-storied vocal building. So, you might make a "boom-chica-boom-chica boom" sound for four beats. This is your first loop. Your next loop might be your voice sounding a low note on beats 2 & 4, simulating a bass guitar. Then, you sing a captivating solo over these two loops. Sound cool?

It's actually more than cool.

Vocalists of all genres are beginning to use looping as a way to compose music, improve their musicality and create powerful performances without the need for other instrumentalists or singers. You might have thought looping was a fad limited to "tech-head" singers; it is actually becoming a way to save money, remember musical ideas, and make performances possible when your band has gotten the flu. Looping is earthy, relevant and practical.

So, don't skip the next actions in this chapter. We're not only going to tell you how you can loop, but we'll also look at applications of looping that apply to every singer.

What do you need to loop? Well, you probably already have looping capability—there are popular looping apps for your smartphone. Also, looping is becoming a standard feature on many vocal effects units, not to mention the proliferation of looping-dedicated devices. All you need to do is press the button and try it out.

—Tom Lang: product manager at TC-Helicon, singer-guitarist

Action 3: Make a Solid Base Layer

Just as in building a house, a strong foundation is key to a great looping performance.

Looping can build excitement in any vocal performance, but it is key to get the first loop—the "base layer"—right.

Let's say that your first loop is one bar, four beats long. There will be two button presses to make your loop. At the beginning of the bar you will have your first press—recording on—then at the end of your bar, you will have your second press—recording off. That sounds simple, but the trick to looping is to time your presses to be right on the rhythmic division of your beats. Expect this to take some practice. There's a technique that musicians learn in the studio called "playing to a click"—basically this is where everyone plays to the steady beat of a metronome through his or her headphones so that there is no slowing down or speeding up. For looping it's usually helpful to get your foot or finger tapping on a steady beat before pressing; press record on exactly your first beat, and "stop" at exactly the end of your phrase.

Some looping devices/applications are foot activated and some are hand activated—each one of these will need its own practice time. But remember, even the pros like Reggie Watts, Beardyman and Shlomo don't always get it right. Even in live performances with thousands of fans, loopers can be off their tempo when starting or stopping their base layer. When this happens, the looper has a choice—to keep going, adding layers that are built on this slightly off tempo base layer, or to simply stop and make a new base layer. Professional loopers tell us that the latter option, though sometimes slightly embarrassing, is always better!

You also need to make sure that your first loop isn't at full volume if you plan to add other layers to it. If your input LEDs are going red when you are recording the loop, you'll end up distorting your sound, and further layers may sound like a big vocal mess. So stay quieter on your fist loop. It might help you to imagine that other loops are like other musicians with whom you need to blend.

We already mentioned that the base layer is usually rhythmic in nature—this is because it acts as a guide for other layers to come. If you begin with something *rubato*, you're not going to easily know when the loop starts and stops. However, all rules are made to be broken: Imogen Heap does all kinds of vocal snippets as base loops. However, we suggest you begin experimenting with your first loop as a solid percussion sound.

–Tom Lang: product manager at TC-Helicon, singer-guitarist

Action 4: Add More Layers—and Take Them Away

Mastering the art of adding and subtracting looped layers will allow you to control your music's emotion—and keep your audience hooked.

The excitement of looping has to do with building musical energy to an apex though adding more loops ... AND then stripping these layers away again to ensure that your music stays dynamic. But remember: your loops usually need to repeat a few times before you will hear them well enough to be able to add more layers.

On an advanced piece of looping gear you will find a feature called "phrase looping," which allows you to define a set of layers—each with their own effects—and also allows you to stop or start any one of these phrases while others continue. For example, your first layer might be an eight measure percussion phrase. This is followed by a base phrase, in turn followed by your own singing, a guitar—anything. In normal looping when you peel the layers back, you can never return to just your base line (it was your second layer). With the phrase function you can choose to play any or all of your phrases.

Or, you can use the "undo" button. "Undo" removes all the layers that you've added to your base layer. This isn't as nuanced of an effect as the phrase function since the undo button always takes you back to your first layer. Undo is a "radical" move that is effective when you don't want to be subtle. Remember, when you build layers and then suddenly "slam" it back to only that first layer, this will grab the audience's attention.

Put Effects into the Loop

Looping doesn't have to be only about vocal sounds you create with your mouth, you can add vocal effects from your looper or effects unit. You can, for example, alter the octave of your voice to become a base, add echoes to the beat, use reverb on one layer and not on another layer. Playing around with effects can help you build a three dimensional mix. Some loopers even have the ability to add a stutter effect (or other quality) to any place within an established loop.

***–Tom Lang:** product manager at TC-Helicon, singer-guitarist*

Adding layers and taking them away isn't only about drama. When I am doing a solo acoustic guitar gig—and just before I know I am going to solo on my guitar—I record a loop. Then I solo over top of that. It is as if a band has suddenly appeared to support me! This effect is so subtle and seamless that it's rare for the audience to notice that I have even turned on my looper!

—Tom Lang: product manager at TC-Helicon, singer-guitarist

Action 5: Use Looping in Solo and Ensemble Performances

Looping in live performances allows soloists and ensembles alike to beef up their sound and add harmonic or rhythmic complexity.

Picture a vocalist alone on stage with just a few pedals on the floor and a mic. It can be incredibly rewarding: the satisfaction of relying only on yourself to produce a complex vocal performance with a rich and deep vocal ambiance. But it can also be fraught with danger! You are, after all, relying to a high degree on technology to achieve this. However, a growing number of vocalists believe the challenge is worth it. The obvious examples are people like Dub FX and Reggie Watts—the beatboxers who make incredible noises with their mouths and layer these into complex structures which dazzle audiences. But the more melodic singer is using looping technology to craft more melodic presentations that create climaxes though layering loops. The main idea is that you can use less people in your band to create more rhythmic or harmonic interest.

Singer-instrumentalists can create a larger sound through looping. One way they do this is through instrumental loops. If a singer-guitarist wants to play a lead break with his or her guitar, this has usually meant that he or she has to stop playing his or her chord progression—thus, the lead is played over instrumental emptiness. Now he or she can make the chord progression happen in a loop and be free to add his or her single line lead break over top.

If you are the sole singer in a band, a looper allows you to do your own backup vocals. Usually you would do this in live time with an effects unit on a harmony setting. However, with looping you can start and stop certain vocal loops and sing riffs over top. You can act, then, as your own backing vocalist section at the same time you are singing the lead vocals. The critical thing here is to practice with your band in order to ensure that everyone stays with the rhythm set when the loop was created. It's a challenge to have your drummer—whose job it is to lead with the beat—become a follower. Make sure your drummer can hear the rhythm of your loop clearly. Or, you can use your looping at the beginning of the song and kick the loop off when the drummer comes in.

—Tom Lang: product manager at TC-Helicon, singer-guitarist

Action 6: Improve Your Musicality

Compose music, practice harmonizing and flesh out new ideas—all without the need for a jam session.

Using harmonies on a looping device can really build your harmonic abilities. Imagine showing up for your band rehearsal or performance hitting those harmonies perfectly—your friends will think you've been taking lessons from a skilled music teacher, not realizing that you have been taking lessons from yourself!

> *If you're looping and make a mistake early on, I think it's vital to stop the song and say something about it. A "whoopsie" moment can make people smile, brings people together—and no one is going to walk out.*
>
> ***–Shlomo:** internationally acclaimed beatboxer*

In order to accomplish this, you will need a starting pitch reference. Let's say you have a base layer that is rhythmic–then you want to have the next layer contain a recurring note in order to establish the key. Then you would sing a melody on another loop. Because the melody is one of your loops, it will repeat and you can practice singing harmonies to your own vocal lines. You can then make your harmony into its own loop and add even more harmonies. It will be critical that your melody line is set at the right place in your range to allow you to easily harmonize above or below the line. Of course, not all harmonies are parallel thirds. As you experiment with making harmonies on your looper, you will also learn how differently they can intertwine with varying degrees of effectiveness.

But there's more than harmony training available with loops. Singer-songwriters will find looping a new inspiration and singers who haven't written music may now find doing so compelling. This is because using a looper can be like jamming with another musician. You know how a guitarist might be doing a certain riff, then you might sing a vocal over that riff which turns into a musical idea that evolves into a song? Well, with a looper you can lay down some musical ideas and then "compose" over these. You can capture your inspirations quickly and easily, dispose of the ones that don't work and keep riffing on the ones that hold promise. It's like having a musician friend come over to your house every time you want to explore some new musical ideas.

–Tom Lang: product manager at TC-Helicon, singer-guitarist

Frequently Asked Questions:

> Give me at least one good reason to use looping in my already successful solo singer-guitarist pop-rock gigs.

Answered by Beardyman, beatboxer and looper, named "King of Sounds and Ruler of Beats" by the BBC

Because you can add a novel dimension to your song. It's simple to use any of the already available commercial loopers to lay down a beat during your performance and then punch it in. For instance, you can just make some breathing noises and/or clapping sounds and you have an instant rhythmic backing. It's better than having an electronically created backing beat because it comes from you; it's unique and will sound different every time you create it. You can also layer up your voice for a chorus. Even though looping has been around for a while, people still marvel at using it in these ways in a live performance.

> Won't an audience get tired of me setting up loops?

Answered by Beardyman, beatboxer and looper, named "King of Sounds and Ruler of Beats" by the BBC

If what you're doing over the top of your loop is interesting and good, then the issue of monotony isn't so pressing. In fact, if you hear something iterate four times, you stop noticing it—any foreground object becomes a background object when it stays still long enough. Beyond this basic thought, the possibilities are endless. I'll give you a few ideas, though there are no hard and fast rules; there are different tactics for different genres.

Reggie Watts is an acoustic artist who works with eight bar loops—that's all his equipment can do. He holds your attention with his singing and his free-form lyrical presentation—as well as his characteristic voice and accents. The looping isn't what is most engaging here—he is simply laying down a simple bed, three layers, and does his magic on top of this. Imogen Heap sculpts beautiful and intricate songs with a creative use of technology—including looping. What keeps people engaged is her incredible singing and intricate songwriting.

Having said this, there are a few things you might try. It is easy to make something more engaging by simply cutting it out and bringing it back—such as stopping the guitar for just a second to give the song some space. This is a hip-hop idea—it breaks the trance and pulls in some attention. In fact, you could keep ducking out of different parts. Don't do this randomly—make sure it makes some sense. If you're using four channels you could take the volume down every four bars and do something on one or all of the channels—little changes keep it interesting. I've come to looping through the beatboxing and dance world, so what I will often do is to cut out the beat at the end of a 32 bar section for half a bar—some house DJs are surprised that I would do that, but it keeps things interesting.

If you are using a basic piece of looping equipment, have it record during the chorus (or any other section you know you will be returning to later on). Then, when you return to that section, punch in the loop. You are now free to add another live layer to your music—and your audience will be taken by surprise. It's really helpful if, when looping, you are singing into a mic that doesn't go into the looper. In other words, separate out your channels so that you can be singing while you are looping; the singing doesn't get recorded on the loop (and vice versa). Some sound will spill through, of course, but this gives you more options to be versatile in how you use your loops. An A/B switcher is the best way to do this—I have this built into my equipment.

> I tried looping on a song in my latest house concert, but things got out of sync and I had to stop in the middle of my song. Does this mean looping isn't for me?

Answered by Shlomo, internationally acclaimed human beatboxer

You may not want to give up on looping so quickly—there's a way to handle what happened to you.

Lots of vocalists are getting excited about looping—and rightly so: looping is an incredible opportunity for vocalists to be more in control of their sound. But looping presents a huge challenge, as you've found out. Especially if something goes wrong at the beginning of the loop—then it is there for the entire song!

If you're looping and make a mistake early on, I think it's vital to stop the song and say something about it. The crowd loves to think you are real and a human being that can get something wrong. A "whoopsie" moment can makes people smile, brings people together—and no one is going to walk out.

Not long ago I was on the big stage in Glastonbury and my loop station sent an error message: "Too busy press any key." I was shocked—here I was in the middle of a performance with 10,000 people watching and not only had my technology just stopped—it sent me an obscure message that sounded like something from an Atari computer from the 1980s!

I read the message out to the crowd and they thought it was funny. This turned out to be a happy accident: I pressed a random key and a weird tempo emerged which led to a new version of my song.

Little hidden evil monsters will wreak havoc in your equipment at precisely the wrong time. When that happens, don't be afraid to admit this to your audience—this will usually make them feel closer to you.

Listen.

One grey Monday morning in September, a class of sleepy audio engineering students filed into their first day of Mixing 101. Many of them had that "zombie look" people get when they haven't quite recovered from the weekend's pub crawl. Their instructor introduced himself and quietly swiped through some tracks on his phone. He played one through the sound system and asked them to identify as many distinct sounds as possible. They immediately recognized the famous intro lick on guitar, and could identify about six instruments: drums, bass, two guitars and lead vocal with harmonies. They also noticed the keyboard solo in the middle. For the rest of the term, they listened … and listened. The instructor helped them hear more detail in recordings than they had ever heard before.

On the last day of class, the instructor played that same recording from the first day. This time, the students felt like Neo in the blockbuster movie, *The Matrix* when he sees glowing green code on everything. They perceived a world of detail they had missed before. They could easily identify each individual component of the drum kit, including a tambourine that they didn't notice the first time. They could estimate the size and type of the tom toms, snare and cymbals. They realized that not one, but two instruments backed that opening guitar solo. They could hear a tremolo effect on the electric guitar and what today would be called a vintage reverb sound on the voices. There were more vocal harmonies than they previously thought, including "oohs" in certain sections. They noticed the absence of pitch correction—many thought this was refreshing. The most startling detail was the panning of the vocals: all the vocals were on the right! What? How did they not hear that before? The keyboard solo stumped them. They couldn't quite figure out if it was an acoustic or electronic instrument. This was an old recording, so how did they get that sound back then?

The famous producer, George Martin, was behind that keyboard sound. The recording was "In My Life" by the Beatles. The instructor congratulated the students for their astute observations and explained that George Martin himself had played the keyboard solo on a piano. He recorded it at half speed, and then doubled the speed in the mix.

Before taking the class, these students could pick out half a dozen sonic details in the recording. Now they could perceive almost 20 individual instruments and vocal parts, plus effects and recording techniques. The students realized how much the class had transformed them—more specifically, how it had transformed their listening.

The world-class audio experts in this book spilled their guts on everything about audio gear and how to use it, but the one thing they can't give you through the pages of a book, is their finely-tuned listening skill. It's not expensive gear or software that makes music sound great. It's the listening ability of the one who operates it. Every audio decision comes down to listening. Never on autopilot, a good sound engineer listens with fresh ears and responds differently to each situation. Our audio pros gave us great information, but it can only be of use to you if you take your listening to the next level.

If you can sing and perform well, your listening journey is already well under way. Every time you sing in tune you are using perceptive and active listening. To step it up even more, you are going to use that same skill, but with a focus on new and different sonic qualities.

Let's start with the basics—hearing the sound of your own voice. More specifically, the sound of your amplified voice through speakers or headphones. Some artists in this book have talked about sound checks and how to get good monitor mixes. Those same artists, however, have an almost telepathic ability to hear themselves under even the worst conditions. You can get there too, with listening.

Being able to hear the sound of your own amplified voice can be a complicated matter. There are actually three versions of your voice. First, there's the one that resonates inside your head. People are usually shocked the first time they hear a recording of themselves due to the *absence* of this in-your-head voice. The second version of your voice is the one your ears pick up from the outside as it comes out of your mouth and bounces around the room. The last version of your voice is the one coming from the speakers or headphones—your amplified voice. The reason it can be so hard for novice singers to hear themselves properly is that they haven't learned to locate the sound of their *amplified* voice amongst the interference of the other two voices not to mention the cacophony of musical instruments that back them at any given moment.

Locating your voice in the headphones or speakers requires focussed listening, which means you can't just stand there passively expecting the sound of your voice to knock you over the head. The level of your voice must be audible, of course, but the rest is up to your ears.

Tuning in to the sound of your amplified voice will not only help you monitor yourself more effectively, and therefore sing better, but it will also help your mic technique. Have you ever figured out what the proximity effect actually *sounds* like? Can you perceive the subtle change in tone as you come in close and then back off your mic? Have you tried to use mic technique to make your songs more vibrant? I have observed masterful singers in front of a recording mic and the subtle turning or pulling back of their heads as they sing. I like to call them "human compressors." Only listening will let you develop these skills for yourself.

How do you get better at picking out your amplified voice and hearing the proximity effect? Get your hands on some audio gear. I don't care how much of a non-techie you think you are. If you are serious about performing in contemporary genres, then you simply must have a sound system at home and a way of recording yourself—no matter how basic it may be. Some of the engineers and producers we talked to felt so strongly about this that they would probably criticize this book for not devoting more pages to it! Do you have a live mic? Who cares if it is not perfect for recording! Get yourself an audio interface, some recording software, a computer you can use, and start experimenting. Alternatively, go for an all-in-one vocal effects box into which you can plug your mic and a powered speaker.

With some basic gear at home, you can figure out what audio processing and effects *sound* like, and more importantly how your unique voice sounds under their influence. Reading about effects in this book is not enough. With your own software plug-ins, you can learn to hear what compression does. You can listen to what different reverbs sound like. Sometimes the easiest way to hear a certain effect is to crank it to the max; then you can go, "oh, so that's what too much high end sounds like." Listen to the balance of your voice against a backing track. Record yourself and listen for your mic technique. This experimenting will let you hone your musical skill, teach you how to hear more details in the soundscape, and let you develop your signature sound. The subtle influence of your mic, the vibe that comes from your particular reverb—these are all things that you will learn to hear, and then use to bring out the uniqueness of your voice.

Next on your listening journey is to give yourself a goal every time you listen to music. Try listening to one song multiple times, each time focussing only on one instrument. Try focussing on two instruments at once. How do they fit together sonically speaking? Listen for the effects on the vocal. What part of the tone is natural to the singer, and what part is heightened by the effects? When you feel an emotional response to the song, try to figure out which audio processes contributed to that great moment.

Don't take all this on by yourself. Lean on the listening insight of knowledgeable people. When you find an audio-savvy person who you can lean on for advice and help, do everything you can to show them appreciation and kindness. When I found my audio-savvy person, I married him! My husband was a professional audio engineer for many years, and I have enjoyed excellent live sound and monitor mixes thanks to him. I am at a place on my own listening journey where I still find it hard to hear the subtle influence of the recording mic on my sound. I know the right mic can highlight my voice better than a different one, so I lean on my hubby to help when I need to choose one. Whenever we go to a concert, whenever he is mixing a recording or whenever he does live sound for me, I ask questions. I try to tap into his superior listening skill, to help me understand and develop mine. How did they get the guitar to sound like that? Why did my mic feed back? Was it just me or was there way too much reverb on that vocal group? We often go over to the sound booth and spy on what gear they are using at a live show.

Engineers and producers have the most skilled ears of all, which means even with your improved listening skill you will still use these pros on your important projects. But never forget: no matter how skilled others are at listening, you are still the expert on your music and your message. Those pros can help you get the sounds you want much more successfully when you are able to communicate a clear vision that includes details about the audio processing and effects you desire.

It is amazing how many of the sound engineering experts we spoke to all said the same thing: emotion in a performance—recorded or live—is far more important than technical correctness. Our experts would not even begin to talk about technology until they made something very clear: an authentic delivery of the song is required before you even consider what technology can do to enhance it. When you listen to your vocal, the most important question you need to ask yourself is, "Does it make me feel something?" Without passion and truth in your delivery, you can't have a great recording or a great show—no matter how perfect it is or how many audio tools you employ.

As a contemporary singer, you know how powerful the influence of audio technology is on your music. You know that the right audio processing can heighten the impact of your song and allow your passion to reach your audience more effectively. Every time you listen to your own recordings, open your ears to the sound, and ask yourself, "Does every element of this song, including the audio processing, help to bring out the emotion and message I intend?"

Anyone would agree it would be silly for a drummer not to learn how to play the ride cymbal—to let it sit there, unused. The ride cymbal is a crucial part of any drum kit and one of several pieces a drummer uses to express her creative ideas. To a singer, audio tools are no different. Learning to hear and understand the world of audio is like learning to play an important part of your vocal instrument. Your listening journey allows you to claim maximum creative control over your art. Harness the power of audio. Do it by listening.

—Kathy Alexander, singer, vocal coach and staff writer at VoiceCouncil Magazine

Technique, Health and Relationships

CHAPTER 10

Technique in the Trenches

A voice that's as hard as steel and soft as silk.

"Singing should NEVER hurt. Not even when you rehearse. Don't think that it will be better in a little while."

—Anders Ørsanger, Basix, "Best European Album"

"The 'pain sound' is often the desired aesthetic—but it should be produced painlessly!"

—Dane Chalfin, Vocal Coach, Rehabilitation Specialist and Pop Pathway Leader at Leeds College of Music

"Believe it or not, your loudest voice uses the least air."

—Kim Chandler, top session singer and industry vocal coach

Technique in the Trenches

A voice that's as hard as steel and soft as silk.

Actions:

1. If It Hurts, Stop
2. Know Thy Voice
3. Distinguish Good Effort from Bad Effort
4. Develop Active Posture
5. Harness the Power of Breathing
6. Release Your Stress
7. Boost Your Volume and Range
8. Avoid Stupid Stuff
9. Understand Extreme Vocal Effects
10. Choose the Right Singing Teacher

Frequently Asked Questions:

» *What's the point of warming up?*

» *Is "proper technique" going to ruin my cool sound?*

» *Am I stuck with my range?*

» *What's the perfect vocal warm-up?*

» *I want to imitate my idol (Adele)—will this stop me from finding my own voice?*

» *Is it OK to mimic my singing teacher's voice?*

» *What's a good warm-up on the day of my gig?*

» *Are the classical technique snobs blowing putrid hot air?*

» *I keep hearing people say "head voice" and "chest voice"—what does this mean?*

» *How much time should I spend training my voice?*

» *How do I cope with the overwhelming vocal demands of gigs six nights a week? Help!*

» *Is there any secret to nailing a high note?*

Action 1: If It Hurts, Stop

Too many singers mistake a hurting throat for a badge of honor—a sign that they are working hard at their singing. It's time to knock this idea down.

The voice is not as complicated to use as many people think.

It is an instrument that everybody has and uses every day. Of course it requires practice to sing professionally, but when you know how the voice works, you will be able to learn what is required.

It is important that singers themselves take responsibility for their own development. Even the best teacher in the world cannot teach you anything unless you yourself pick up the teaching and work with it. Trust your taste, powers of judgment and senses. Experimenting brings renewal; individuality is also important. Feel, listen, and choose. Determine whether you are getting the sound you want. Why should you use a sound you do not like? Always be your own judge and decide whether you are getting closer to your goals.

In my opinion the taste of the teacher is unimportant. To me the teacher's task is purely to help a singer to achieve her/his desired way of singing in a healthy manner. The teacher can make suggestions about alternative sound possibilities, but it is the singer who should make the artistic choices.

> *This chapter gives you the essentials for unleashing your vocal power over the long haul. You can then expand your knowledge with good singing teachers, vocal coaches and other professionals dedicated to contemporary vocal technique based on solid research.*
>
> ***—The Ultimate Team***

Make sure you are on the right track when you practice. A correct technique should result in continuous improvements in your singing. There is no reason to take lessons for years if you do not think the instructions are making singing any easier or are bringing you closer to your goals.

The first thing a singer must learn is not to lose the voice. Once you lose your voice you have to stop working until it returns. Furthermore, it is difficult to experiment if you are hoarse, as the voice does not respond as it normally would. As long as the voice is in good condition, you can practice and experiment your way until you achieve your goals.

An important rule that cannot be stressed enough is that singing must never hurt or feel uncomfortable. If something does not sound right, if something feels wrong, or if it feels uncomfortable, your voice is telling you that you are doing something wrong. Always trust your sensations—they are better and more direct than even the best teacher's ear.

Singing must ALWAYS feel comfortable. The technique must have the intended effect immediately otherwise the training is not being done correctly. If an exercise hurts, feels uncomfortable, or feels wrong, it IS wrong. You are the only one who knows how it feels, so trust your sensations.

—Cathrine Sadolin: leading voice researcher and founder of the Complete Vocal Institute

We asked Cathrine Sadolin to share her singing journey:

When I first began singing, I had every issue imaginable! You see, I was not your typical singer. I originally began singing to help my asthma. Of course I fell in love with music, but was plagued by difficulties: I was constantly hoarse, had lots of air in my voice, a restricted range and no volume. My voice teachers were great with their suggestions of how to fine tune the sounds and harness the power of imagination, but none of this helped me. I needed more basic help and this didn't seem available.

I relied on my acting and interpretive abilities to pull me through performances; however, I was struggling very seriously. Finally, I decided to lock myself in a room with the latest books on anatomy and physiological research on the voice. I was determined not to emerge until I solved these problems for myself!

Soon, a basic insight emerged that unlocked the key to vocal technique: the vocal folds provide the vibrations necessary to make sound, but the tone of your sound is created in the vocal tract above the vocal cords. This means that, with proper support, it is possible to make any sound you want—in any genre you want—without hurting the vocal cords.

Action 2: Know Thy Voice

A little knowledge of how your voice works will give you the power to use it however you want.

"Voice" refers to a sound created in your larynx. A simple way to think of the larynx is as a shell or box that houses the vocal folds (or vocal cords). The vocal folds are like lips that can be set into vibration when air flows between them.

It is easy to vibrate vocal folds—babies do this from the day they are born. However, controlling those vibrations involves training. Think of that baby crying; it's an intense, attention getting sound. However, there is not much tonality, sound quality or variation. These factors have to be learned if we are going to make music.

Of course, not all of your sound variation is produced in the vocal folds. Much of your sound quality happens in the vocal tract, the area above the folds. It is in this area that you can produce a "ringing" tone, a "yawny" sound, or a "twang" quality—and any number of other modifications. Being an artist means learning to control these qualities. Your goal is to work with both your larynx and your airways to produce the sounds that you feel are most suited to your music.

Everything we do in music has to be intentional; we don't want to produce or listen to sound qualities that are an accident. That's why I differentiate between a singer who can introduce a "grind" or "dirt" quality into their singing when they want it and someone who always has it because they have a voice problem. The vocalist Diamanda Galás is an incredible example of vocal artistry. She has been described as "capable of the most unnerving vocal terror." She actually turns the lights down in performance and makes snake-like hisses, blood curdling screams and demonic sounding noises. However, she produces these sounds in healthy ways; she doesn't suffer from nodes, polyps or any other vocal issues. In fact, she can turn around and immediately produce a pure vocal sound. To me, that's art. If you have a large polyp on your vocal fold and it produces a "masculine" sound, with constant raspiness, then you are not harnessing your voice to its full potential. What you want is a healthy pair of vocal folds and the ability to create a wide spectrum of sound when and where you want.

Here's another way to say it: think of someone blowing on a brass instrument. That player can "overblow it," producing a rough and nasty sounding quality. But if used too much, this will be quite annoying to the listener. What this player needs to do is to produce a variety of sounds to express emotion. Actually, any constant sound quality made for too long is annoying to a listener, whether it's vibrato or "whine." Your goal is to develop your voice so that you can introduce certain qualities when and where you want them.

—Ingo R. Titze, PhD: one of the world's leading voice scientists and Executive Director of the National Center for Voice and Speech, Utah

The Voice

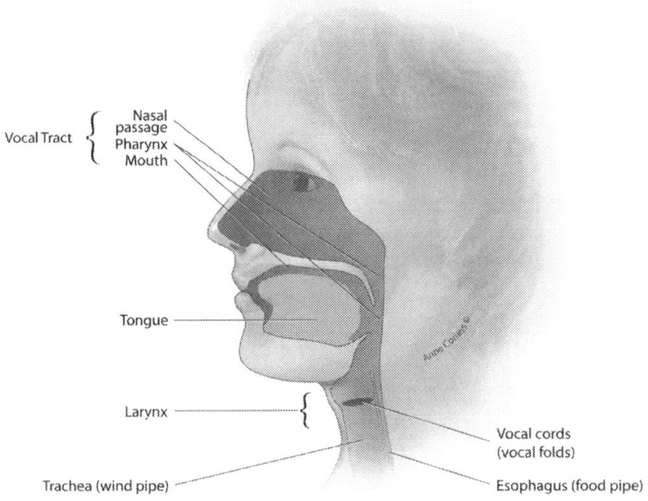

Artwork by Anne Corless RN, RM, BA (Hons) Design, MAA, RMIP, AFC

The Larynx
(view from above)

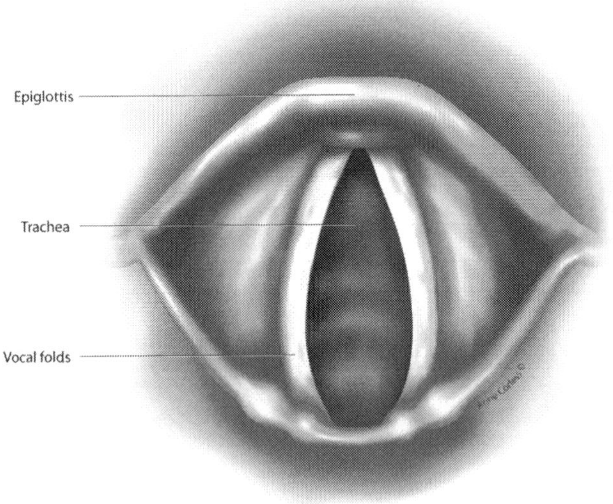

Artwork by Anne Corless RN, RM, BA (Hons) Design, MAA, RMIP, AFC

Action 3: Distinguish Good Effort from Bad Effort

There's some tension that you don't need—and some that you do. Become a master at knowing the difference.

Singing takes effort. You can't get away from it. *Physics for Dummies* tells us that energy is a constant: you can't create it or destroy it but you can move it around. The same process is true for singing: there is a certain amount of energy or effort that goes into the process—you can't escape it. Now here is the critical point: what you do have control over is how you ration your effort.

Most singers who seek coaching do so because there is some deficit with range, power or choice of voice quality. In other words, when they go to make the sound they want to make, something doesn't work and it is strained.

That sensation of strain is felt in and around the larynx. The larynx is probably best viewed as a valve; it regulates how much air can pass from the lungs and out of the body. Along this path, air is turned into vibrations that are amplified into sound and shaped into words and phrases. How much effort should the larynx be making? Not much. On a scale of 0 to 10 with 0 representing no effort and 10 representing all the strength you could possibly muster, you should not be feeling more than a 2 or 3 in the larynx.

So, if you are only using a 2–3 effort level in the larynx, where else is your effort coming from? Your added effort should be coming from a combination of the muscles of core stability and in the muscles of respiration. In other words, body support and breath support.

> *I've "fried" my voice too many times in the past. The main cause is over-compensation with the throat, which may be triggered by bad sound monitoring and/or an "over-emotional" state.*
>
> ***—Chris Baretto:** Metal singer, NYC*

Now it's time to feel how the "good effort" of core stability actually works. Try sitting on the edge of your chair. Get ready to stand up—but don't come off the chair yet. Feel yourself coming up and forward and hang on to that sensation. Then, as slowly as possible, move up to a standing position without locking the knees. Now come back down and sit, again, on the edge of the chair. Notice how much effort is going from the base of the neck down to the bottom of pelvis. This is a good way of feeling the muscles of core stability or "Active Posture." These are the same muscles you want to engage in your singing.

Now, it's crucial for you to experience how your voice works with your body: repeat the same thing: stand up, but now only let your bottom come 3 to 5 inches off the chair. Hold this position—but don't hold your breath. Breathe normally but hold the effort going into your body. Call out to a friend, as if they are across the street, using a sound like "Oy!" or "Eh!" Notice how much effort is going on around your larynx—we'll call this voice effort. It shouldn't be much.

Here is where it should all make sense: sit back down and relax your body completely and call out the same sound at the same pitch and the same volume. You will notice that the effort in the voice went up when you let the effort in your body go down.

You force your voice effort to increase as you decrease your physical stamina.

If your voice effort around your larynx is working at a "6" and you have an hour of songs to sing, you will struggle to get through your performance. What you need to do is engage your muscles—just as you did above in the "chair exercise." When you put this effort into your body to support your voice, your stamina will increase and your performance will be more likely to succeed.

—Dane Chalfin: Vocal Coach, Rehabilitation Specialist and Pop Pathway Leader at Leeds College of Music

Action 4: Develop Active Posture

Whether you are standing, sitting or leaping into the mosh pit, some simple work on your posture can help you improve your range and volume.

There are two good reasons for developing your posture. First, you'll sing with more power, volume and intensity. Second, you'll project confidence, looking like you own the stage instead of only renting it.

Don't worry: I'm not going to tell you that you have to be rigid, tight, unnaturally and awkwardly "square" in all of your movements. In fact, I am going to share with you what I call "dynamic stability" or "active posture." This is where you stabilize your trunk in order to let the rest of your body move freely and effectively.

The best way to think about posture is to do some boxing.

I box with my vocal students regularly. In fact, when I was training up the four male leads for the West End production of *Rock of Ages* (now a movie with Tom Cruise, Russell Brand and Catherine Zeta-Jones), I used boxing practice to help them face the relentless vocal demands of their show.

When you are boxing, you are constantly moving but ready to take a hit. Your trunk is stabilized, your knees are agile, and your feet are ready to move.

When my vocal students are in the boxing position, I put my hands up in a defensive position and ask them to hit me. Of course, they are always reluctant to take their best shot—but I want them to! Only then will they experience the feeling that it isn't the hand that is the main weapon—it's the trunk. Your hand is just the end of your battering ram that you bring forward through the power of your trunk.

It's the same thing in singing. Once you have a stable trunk, you can do whatever you want with your hands and legs while still singing effectively with power and control. You can put your leg up on a monitor stand, make sweeping gestures with your arms—even bend into a squatting position for a high note.

So, what does a stable trunk look like? It's basically about keeping your head, neck, back and pelvis in alignment through conscious muscle effort. In other words your head shouldn't be jutting out, your shoulders shouldn't sag and your back shouldn't be hunched. Rather, you should be able to draw a straight line down from the top of your head to the middle of your pelvis.

Why does this way of holding yourself work so well? When we slouch, the ribs collapse onto the abdomen restricting the natural movement of the diaphragm and the abdominal muscles. When the head and neck are sticking out we are putting greater pressure on the muscles of the neck and throat to hold up the head instead of leaving them free so that the larynx can do its work more effectively. When you practice "active posture," you remove all of the necessary problems and release the full power of your voice.

All of this happens because of a principle of muscle recruitment: if a muscle is in trouble and cannot do a job it will recruit help from its nearest and dearest neighbor. Poor posture means we end up recruiting a lot of help from muscles of breathing and voicing to stabilize our unstable frame. Active posture means that your entire body is ready to function at maximum efficiency and power.

Check out Action six for an exercise to help with this.

—Dane Chalfin: Vocal Coach, Rehabilitation Specialist and Pop Pathway Leader at Leeds College of Music

Action 5: Harness the Power of Breathing

Breathing is the secret to power and control—but you'd be surprised at how much, or how little air you actually need.

There is no completely "right way" to breathe as breathing will respond naturally to changes in posture and physical activity. However, singers under the pressure of performance sometimes breathe in ways that cause them a loss of power and control.

For example, a vocalist may take in too much air for what they need to do. You might instinctively think that taking a big breath will give you more power in your singing but "it ain't necessarily so." A large intake of air tends to build up too much pressure against your vocal folds (vocal cords), encouraging you to close them tightly to keep the air in. This can make it difficult to control how the first notes come out, making your voice sound tight or explosive.

Just try this now for yourself: take in a huge amount of air, hold it for a second or two, and then sing. Do you feel the pressure of air pushing to get out when you first start singing? Do you find it difficult to control your first few notes? Of course, you do need to take in a larger breath to sustain long singing phrases but singers are often surprised to find that they do not need as much air as they think they do.

Some singers take in too little air or try to sing until the air has run out. Just try singing a few lines on a very small breath. Pretty soon you will begin to feel the strain in your throat; your jaw may also start to feel tight. Too little air, or simply not connecting with the air, is likely to make you "push" your voice and develop extra muscle tension around the larynx. This is likely to be uncomfortable and will reduce your vocal power and control. What we want to develop is a good coordination between the breath and voice, that's all.

> *The quickest ways to hurt your voice are: to sing with a band and no monitors, push out too much air as you sing, and try to get volume by tightening the muscles in your throat rather than using resonance.*
>
> ***—Jeannie Deva:** Celebrity Vocal Coach*

Some patterns of breathing are physically easier than others. Think of your lungs a bit like a syringe on its head. Your diaphragm (the big dome shaped muscle that makes the floor of the lungs) is like the plunger; when you draw it down, it pulls the air into the lungs. In the case of our bodies, as the plunger (our diaphragm) moves down, it also pushes the squidgy contents of the abdomen downwards too. We can then use the lower abdominal muscles to gently push the plunger back up again to control the air smoothly in speech or singing. These abdominal muscles are the same ones you feel squeezing inwards when you giggle, cough or blow out a candle. Breathing in this way has the advantage of being natural, economical of muscle effort, and gives you better control over your voice.

Something you can do to feel what we have been talking about is to let your abdominal muscles go a little bit as you breathe in, as if you were taking a quiet gasp. You should feel your abdomen move sharply outwards and your lungs fill with air quickly and efficiently. You can use this to "top up" the air in speaking and singing so you can learn to take in just the right amount you need.

—Sara Harris: co-founder of the Voice Research Society and past President of the British Voice Association

Action 6: Release Your Stress

Here are some simple exercises so that you can actually feel healthy technique at work.

Life in the twenty-first century causes muscle tension. We may not even realize it, but we may be carrying a lot of stress in certain muscle groups. Releasing these muscles means we won't carry this tension and stress into our singing.

Here are three relaxation exercises—use them three times a day: "three times a day keeps the stress at bay." They should be a part of your warm up—and your cool down.

1. Relaxing

Relax Your Throat. Let your head drop forward and gently, slowly and fluidly roll your chin up to your shoulder and repeat three times each side. Move your shoulders up to your ears, hold and release. Repeat three times and make sure you don't hold your breath. Now do the opposite: pull your shoulders down towards the floor, release and repeat three times.

Relax Your Mouth. Polish your teeth with your tongue: top, bottom, front and back for one minute. This may cause a dull, aching sensation under the jaw. That's OK—keep polishing.

Relax Your Jaw. Imagine that you are chewing a piece of toffee that grows larger the more you chew it. Don't open your lips; make space for the "magic toffee" at the back of your throat. The more you chew, the bigger it gets. This should trigger a yawn. When it does, allow yourself to have the biggest, widest, longest yawn you've had in a good while (adults seldom allow themselves a full yawn). Repeat three to five times.

2. Re-engage Essential Tension

   Relaxing is only one stage of your preparation for singing. Vocalizing takes effort—but you don't want that effort to center on your head and neck. So, it's now time to engage your entire body.

   Every day do some general body stretching and then move into some swimming, walking or jogging. This will keep you fit, developing a physical edge for singing with power and intensity.

   Now you can do an exercise to build and reinforce the importance of your body in your singing. I suggest body-weight squats. This exercise takes some effort and could place some strain on your joints if not done properly—so do check in with your doctor to ensure you are up for this:

   Clasp your hands together in front of your body and keep your head, neck, back and pelvis aligned. Thrust your bottom out behind you and bend your knees as low as you can—keeping your bottom tucked in enough to avoid arching the lower back. Do this slowly all the way down into the squat position and back up. Don't lock your knees. Repeat this a few times. You should be able to draw a line of effort down from the base of the skull to the pelvis; it should feel solid, grounded and energized. Now try coming up from the squat without locking the knees and try singing a difficult passage from a song in your repertoire. Notice the level of voice effort compared to the level of postural effort. Relax your posture and try the same passage—notice that this feels more difficult without any postural effort.

3. Warm Up Your Breath Support and Get Ready to Sing

   If you've followed these exercises in order (and I hope that you have), you will see that you've done a lot of warming up without actually engaging your voice. Good. You see, your entire body is involved in singing.

   Now we come to your breath and voice. There are some fine vocal warm ups in this chapter; here is an exercise that warms up your voice and requires engagement with good breath support.

   Make a revving noise like a Harley Davidson "VVV VVV VVV." Notice the effort around the abdomen and lower back. Try sliding up and down your range on this sound. Notice how the "VVV" helps you build air pressure. If you release the support this can overwhelm the larynx, so be diligent!

   What should you do beyond this? It will depend on your demands for the day. It will also depend on how your body is feeling that day. If you have a show that is demanding you might check in with your support levels for your belt and then conserve your energy until you're on stage; if you have a quiet day but want to practice for an hour you might spend more time on vocal exercises—examples of which can be found in the work of contributors to this chapter.

   You'll always have unique demands, but you will never want to compromise on doing these basic relaxation and engagement exercises.

—Dane Chalfin: Vocal Coach, Rehabilitation Specialist and Pop Pathway Leader at Leeds College of Music

Action 7: Boost Your Volume and Range

Once you're ready to sing, don't forget these tips that will help you release your maximum singing potential.

Power and range are two of the hallmarks of impressive singing ability in any style. Technically, the goal is to be able to boost volume and have dependable high notes without necessarily harming the fragile tissue of the vocal folds. The good news is that it's not difficult to do this, but it does take a precision-approach rather than an "I'm going to go for it and hope I don't kill myself vocally" approach.

Let's start with power boosting—you'll need to make sure that you do this with proper support, using the action of the torso and abdominals to increase air pressure to the vocal folds. When you sing, keep your chest comfortably lifted; don't let it drop. Keep your ribcage expanded all the way around—don't let it collapse. Just below your sternum, you'll find a spot I call the "magic spot." This area of your upper belly should "firm" OUT for every note you sing, loud or soft. Your lower belly (navel and below) should gradually go IN for singing; relax it for breathing.

Your goal is to avoid neck-tightening, head lifting, head tweaking and a tight jaw and tight tongue so typical of unsupported loud singing. Remember, without the proper support described above, you'll end up pressing your vocal folds which can lead to swelling and hoarseness.

In addition to support, increasing ring and nasality will make you sound a lot louder. It's like turning up the treble on your sound system. You can amplify your ring easily by pulling up slightly on the sides of your nose (I call that "ick face") and imagine your sound is pointing out through the center of your face. Don't be afraid of being nasal when you need to be loud in pop, rock, R&B, and other commercial music styles. You'll just sound louder safely!

> *A singer may aggravate any current vocal problems to their voice by competing against a lot of background noise; singing in the car or getting into extended conversations in noisy pubs or clubs, for example.*
>
> ***—John Rubin:*** *MD FACS FRCS, Consultant Ear Nose and Throat Surgeon, The University College London*

Now, let's look at your range. Your vocal range is determined primarily by the size of your vocal folds—it's "preset." Yet, what you can do is to find your lowest and highest notes, then learn to sing more comfortably to these limits. So, I want you to sit at a keyboard and find the lowest and highest notes that you can sing with pitch (not just noise or air). I'm surprised by how many singers never do this! You'll likely find that your range is 3 and 1/3 octaves, more or less. Now your job is to vocalize regularly on ALL the notes of your range. That'll result in your ability to add more of those "at the edges" notes comfortably into your performances.

—Lisa Popeil, celebrity vocal coach and creator of the Voiceworks® Method

Action 8: Avoid Stupid Stuff

It's time to stop being your own enemy with a set of habits that get in the way of your voice being at its best.

I can't tell you not to do the things I've listed below (if someone tells me what to do, I often do the opposite!), but I can tell you that singing is your opportunity. For anyone who really cares about their work, there is a certain amount of discipline involved. That's why I ask you to consider the following points:

Practicing too loud is a common mistake. Be strong and tell your guitarist to play with the volume down, especially if the rehearsal space is not large. He may not like it, but explain that he can go and buy new strings if he wants—you can't—your vocal cords are irreplaceable. This same advice goes for your speaking voice, which is the same basic mechanism as your singing voice. Don't go for a long journey in a car and talk or sing over the radio. The background noise of the engine makes you speak and sing louder to hear yourself. If you arrive early for the gig you may be chatting over some very loud noise—shut up (literally) and save your voice for your performance.

Avoid alcohol, tea and coffee and smoking any substance. All of these have an adverse effect on your vocal cords, causing drying, affecting your chemical balance and even causing difficulty with your sense of pitch. You have to make your own choice how important your work is to you. However, you do not need to live a miserable life—just monitor what your voice feels like and make your own judgment. Peer pressure is sometimes the reason for wrong choices. Simple things like deciding not to drink or smoke when everyone else is can be difficult and even lead to confrontations. A glass of mineral water, pretending to be a gin and tonic, can shut people up and stop them pressing drinks at you.

Don't get a spicy meal late at night. This is often the cause of acid reflux. A simple explanation of acid reflux is that the acid produced to digest your food washes over your vocal folds causing a burning sensation in your throat and, consequently, hoarseness. You can get advice from a doctor, who will normally give you a lacto-acid product to neutralize the acid. To lessen the possibility of acid reflux, avoid eating spicy food, avoid eating late at night and try sleeping with your head at a higher level than your feet.

Finally, avoid wearing out your voice in practice. Be sensible and choose songs that are the right key for you. If you encounter a difficult passage in a song, don't keep singing the song over and over again hoping it will just get better. Instead, isolate the difficult passage and think through what is causing the difficulty. Then, apply different ideas to how you might work on that passage.

My list of what to avoid may sound negative, but the point is to be at a place where you can pour your energy into your voice. Singing is a great joy—remember why you started!

—Mary Hammond: leading educator and vocal coach for Coldplay and many other star acts

Action 9: Understand Extreme Vocal Effects

Read this before you sing with distortion or other "unorthodox" effects.

Effects are usually an indispensable part of a singing career. Effects are those sounds that are not connected to melody and text, i.e. sounds that underline the singer's expression or style. Today we have "step by step" instructions on how to master: Distortion, Creak, Creaking, Rattle, Growl, Grunt, Screams, Intentional vocal breaks, Air added, and various types of Vibrato and Ornamentations.

Effects must sound as if they are spontaneous, for example, as though the singer has made a huge emotional outcry without any consideration for the voice. In everyday life, these effects often occur without you having control over the voice, but for a professional singer they must be based on the overall principles for the correct use of the voice, both in order to avoid damage and to enable the singer to repeat the effect concert after concert.

Many singers have strained their voices by producing effects in an unhealthy manner. But it is possible to produce healthy effects and use them every day for many hours. The secret behind producing healthy effects is to not expect your vocal folds to do the work, or to take the strain, but to understand that effects are produced above the vocal folds in the vocal tract. Focusing primarily on working with the vocal tract reduces the risk of straining or damaging the voice.

Effects are technically demanding. It is essential that you are in control of the three overall principles of singing before you even CONSIDER working with effects. After that, you must be able to control the four vocal modes (Neutral, Curbing, Overdrive and Edge) as most effects are combined with one of these modes. Then control the sound color, and finally, control the chosen effect.

> *I just have to warm up because the stuff I do is so extreme—the "death voice" or "Cookie Monster" sounds permeate this kind of music.*
>
> ***—Chuck Billy:*** *lead singer, Testament*

As always when you work with the voice, and especially when you work with effects, it is essential to be aware of its healthy limits. If you become hoarse, stop working until the voice has recovered. It can be both difficult and unhealthy for the voice to practice when hoarse as the voice reacts differently to how it would normally. As long as the voice is healthy, you can practice and experiment until you succeed.

A main rule that cannot be stressed enough is that singing must NEVER hurt or feel uncomfortable. If something feels wrong or gives discomfort, your voice is trying to tell you that you are doing something wrong. Respect these warning signs!

—Cathrine Sadolin: leading voice researcher and founder of the Complete Vocal Institute

Action 10: Choose the Right Singing Teacher

Taking control of your sound means learning from the best resources.

Choosing the right singing teacher can be a veritable minefield! Vocal coaching is largely an unregulated profession, so anyone can set up as a vocal coach, whether they have the qualifications, skills, experience and temperament—or don't.

Remember, you are a paying client. You need to know that your hard-earned money is being put to good use and that your voice is in competent, caring hands. While not fail-safe, here is a checklist of six key question areas to help raise important issues with a prospective teacher:

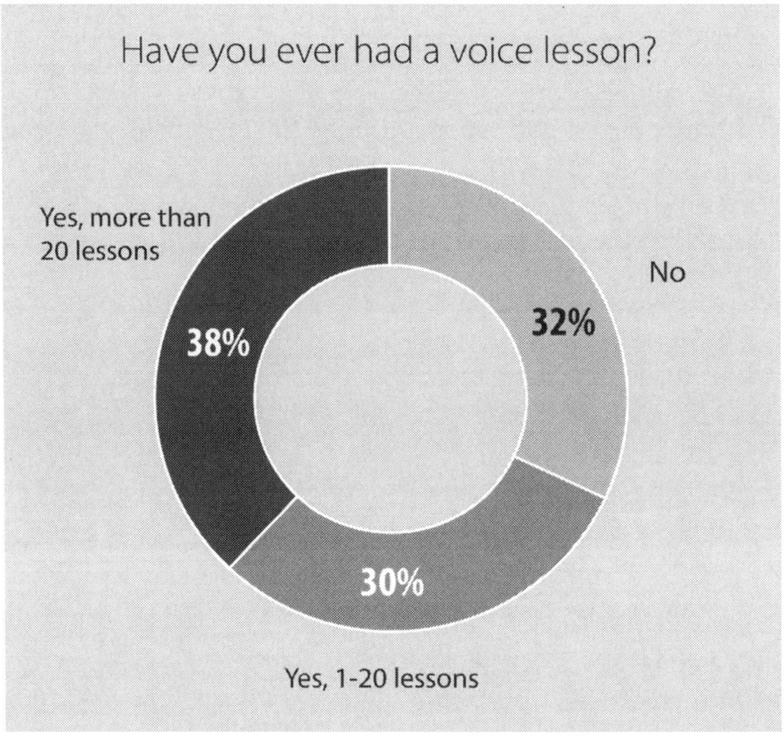

–from the 2012-2013 TC-Helicon survey of 1,000 singers

Musical Training. Do they have recognised music qualifications, e.g. a doctorate, master's or bachelor's degree, or diploma from a reputable institution? The higher the qualification, the better. Ask to see the certificates themselves if you need reassurance.

Vocal Training. What is the extent of the teacher's own vocal training? Which type of singing did they train in? Does this match your vocal style? Which particular vocal methodologies are they trained in or familiar with?

Performing Experience. What is the extent of their performing background? Does it match what you want to get into or are already into? Was it only in the past or are they still performing? Will they be an inspirational vocal role model for you?

Teacher Training. Do they have teaching qualifications? If yes, this should mean that they know how to structure and pace a lesson, how to put together an overall plan of vocal development, how to cater for different learning styles and how to communicate effectively.

Teaching Experience. What is the extent of their teaching background? How long have they taught privately? Do they also teach at any reputable institutions? Do they lead vocal master classes or workshops? Do they have any media presence as a coach?

On-going Training. Are they are committed to ongoing training and lifelong learning? Do they regularly attend reputable training days, workshops, courses, and/or conferences? Do they belong to associations related to music, singing or vocal health? Do they stay up to date with voice research?

There are other considerations, of course. You will want to explore issues related to location, facilities, rates, compatibility—but the bottom line is results. You should see improvement both straight away and steadily over time. If you don't, then question staying on with that person—their methods and approach may not be right for you.

—Kim Chandler: top session singer and industry vocal coach

Frequently Asked Questions

> What's the point of warming up?

Answered by Troy Sanders, bassist and vocalist of Mastodon

It took me ten years of being in Mastodon to figure out where the obvious weak link was—my vocals.

I'm surrounded by musicians that are on top of their game, you know. We've got a thunderous, talented drummer. We've got two guitar wizards on each side of me—and what I'm doing vocally is kind of shooting our band in the foot. I no longer want to embarrass me and my friends performing live, ever again. I vowed to take action and step up my game, not only for the sake of myself but for the rest of my band as well.

So I adopted a series of vocal warm-ups that I've done every single day that we've played music; every show day or recording day, or rehearsal day, for the past year and a half. I've got three different warm-up CDs from three different vocal teachers. I've kind of created my own thirty minute warm-up from bits and pieces of each one.

The two biggest advantages that I can plainly see from doing these warm-ups are, number one: you don't blow your voice out from getting on stage with over-elevated energy and passion (at least I haven't yet—knock on wood). And number two: I've been strong from the first note, instead of warming up during the show.

I take care of my bass guitar; I change its strings, I handle it with care, I clean it, I keep it polished. It's the same thing with vocals. This is the biggest thing that I've taken from vocal warm-ups or lessons. My voice is an instrument as well as my bass—and I need to take care of it and treat it properly so it will last a long time.

Handle with care!

> Is "proper technique" going to ruin my cool sound?

Answered by Juliet Russell, singer, composer, choir director and a vocal coach on BBC 1's The Voice

Not if it's proper technique! Technique should enhance what you do, give you more performance choices and help you optimize how you use your voice to ensure maximum durability, flexibility and consistency.

Personally, I love voices that have a lot of character and I think it is important to work with a singer's individual vocal style, but technique isn't only about supporting your desired sounds—it's about opening up more possibilities. Without exploring proper technique, you could be limiting yourself by playing safe and simply sticking to what you know.

As humans we have a rich palette of expressive sounds available to us and sometimes the key to establishing a wider range of expression is to find the emotional connection in the words and the melodies that you are singing. Naturally our voice reflects our mood, even temporarily: we feign disappointment by using creak; when we're tired our voice can be lower with less effective cord closure and when we're excited our voice can become higher and brighter. Don't be scared to experiment with the versatility of your voice.

Another good reason to explore technique is to prepare you for the rigors of extended voice use; for long days of recording, regular gigs and tours. Warm ups and cool downs, alongside effective technique can help to keep your voice in great condition. Getting into good, healthy habits early on ensures you are investing in your future as a singer. Even those blessed with an amazing, distinctive tone may have vocal or postural habits that are counter-productive.

I worked with a young singer whose individual tone and songwriting skills had secured her a management contract and UK tour, however the way she was producing her sound was unsustainable. She had developed nodules. She didn't need surgery, but was seeing a speech therapist to help reduce them and to learn better vocal habits. She came to me as she was scared of losing her "natural" sound and what she saw as the key to her success. We worked together to analyze what was working for her and where her existing habits were damaging her voice. She retrained her voice and body, replacing old habits with usable and sustainable new ones and an improved anatomical knowledge about how her voice actually works. Her voice still sounds distinctive and original, but now she also has stamina and choice.

Elite athletes work on technique with a coach because they understand that although they have natural physical ability, they can improve their performance significantly by working with someone with expertise. For a singer and vocal coach the relationship is similar, you need to work together to support your goals and help you to achieve your potential.

> Am I stuck with my range?

Answered by Leontine Hass, Artistic Director and founder of London's Associated Studios

If you would like to sing songs that have higher or lower notes than you are currently capable of singing, there is a lot you can do about it. In fact, working on your range gives you more command of your voice and more musical possibilities. It also keeps your voice healthy: you are stretching your folds out and keeping your vocal mechanism flexible.

First, get to know where your voice sits, where the notes spin and ring and sound broad and easy—that is where most of your songs should lie in terms of the range. Voices tend to sit best in a certain tessitura, i.e. the range of notes where the voice sounds and feels the most comfortable. Your voice "type," i.e. whether you are a Soprano/ Mezzo/ Alto (women) or a Tenor/ Baritone/ Bass (men), has less to do with your range, and more to do with where your voice "lies." This aspect is something you should work with rather than against. If you are a bass and have great low notes but sound constricted and tight in the upper range, by all means work on the top, but try not to sing songs that lie up there consistently.

Then, look at lengthening your long rope. An experienced vocal coach will be able to give you exercises to build on your range and show you how to access different voice qualities—I am going to give you one such exercise below—dealing with tongue root tension. But you will want many such exercises in your arsenal. This is because there are many valid ways to approach this issue. Also, not only can you learn to extend your range, you can also learn to use voice qualities that allow you to access notes you may never reach any other way. Many baritones for instance, access very high notes by using their "belt," rather than their head voice.

The most common technical challenge stopping singers from accessing their high range is tongue root tension. If you are finding that your tongue root (just under your chin) is rock hard and bulges outwards on high notes, then you have tongue root tension. A hard/gripped tongue root prevents the larynx from gently rising, which it has to do for higher pitches.

The answer is to stick the tongue out a lot, and, ensuring that your jaw is not clenched, say "sing." Keep your tongue in the forward position with the sides up against the upper molars, and to try to use the support muscles in your back and abdomen and sides, to support the voice rather than digging on your tongue root. Changing this muscle memory may take a few weeks, but it is more than worth it!

> What's the perfect vocal warm-up?

Answered by Kim Chandler, top session singer and industry vocal coach

Before I reveal my perfect warm-up, let's agree on what we mean…

A warm-up is not a workout. It is the short preparation phase before a workout, perhaps 5–10 minutes long. This means that more is not necessarily better. Singers shouldn't waste precious energy required to get through a gig by doing an excessively long warm-up.

My warm-up routine is an essential part of what helps me to survive an often hectic schedule which can include backing vocals for TV shows, singing on countless jingles, leading master classes for London artists, corporate gigs in & around London, etc.

Here it is:

1. Begin your warm up within an hour of your performance/recording session, preferably just before.
2. If it's feasible, take yourself through a full "toe-to-top" stretch. Remember your voice is housed in your body, so spend a couple of minutes checking in with your body and releasing it of excess tension.

3. Next, slide up & down the vocal range (a.k.a. "sirens") giving the voice a good stretch out, going lower and higher than you intend to sing. I like to start with trilling & humming as a gentle, user-friendly way to check in with the voice.
4. Finally, move onto some range extension & agility exercises in the genre you will be singing in. There are many reasons I recommend doing vocal warm-ups and voice building exercises in a style-specific manner, but the main reason is musical relevance. I want singers to be able to see the point of the exercises and enjoy doing them.

That's it. Now, there are some other things you may want to take into consideration, such as where to warm up. As much as it may be convenient, warming up while driving isn't ideal because of the seated posture; you're also competing with engine & road noise and more importantly, you should be giving your full attention to driving, not be distracted by singing.

Other than this you can be quite creative with where you warm up. Most singers warm up in their dressing room or band room. I've even seen singers resort to warming up in restrooms or going out to a parked car for privacy. I've also seen singers do loud warm-ups for rock gigs by singing straight into a cushion, towel or pillow to dampen the noise.

Finally, remember that your mind needs a warm-up as well. So, focus on the task at hand, believe in yourself and realize that your singing can make a difference.

> I want to imitate my Idol (Adele)—will this stop me from finding my own voice?

Answered by Tim Howar of "Mike and the Mechanics," currently starring in "Rock of Ages"

Robert DeNiro says, "Art is imitation" (stealing from Plato!) Imitating is often the road to finding our unique voice—not to mention kick starting a career—as Christian Slater did when he imitated Jack Nicholson.

But there is something that singers often miss when they are trying to sound like an artist: understanding that artist's own musical influences. Do some research; find out Adele's influences—where she is from? What has she listened to? You might even discover that you don't want to sing like Adele but like some of the artists that influenced her!

Everyone thought that Amy Winehouse sounded original, but she sounded like Billie Holiday. You can also hear Billie in Adele—there is also some Ella Fitzgerald and Julie London in there as well. Guys sometimes want to sound like Steven Tyler. Find out what his influences are—Beatles, Stones, and blues artists like Robert Johnson or Howlin' Wolf. Michael Bublé sounds a bit like Mel Tormé and Chet Baker with a dash of Hoagy Carmichael (and was luckily discovered by David Foster when he was singing at a wedding). Go back in time and expose yourself to your favorite artist's influences.

(Here's a secret: a great way to make an impression at any audition is not to choose a song that the panel knows well and hears every day—pick a song by an artist who influenced the song or artist they know so well. If I was asked to audition for *We Will Rock You* and Brian May was looking on, I might choose a Sparks or early Bowie tune instead of a Queen standard. Or, if auditioning for a Sinatra show I might pick a song by Bing Crosby or Tony Bennett—or something in that vein—maybe a wartime song.)

If you are imitating a rock diva who screams or makes other extreme sounds, remember that your voice is a muscle. Give it time to grow; learn the right techniques for this music so that you don't blow out your voice. If you want to climb mountains you have to start by climbing hills, using the proper exercises and allowing yourself time to recover after practicing and performing.

Listen to yourself. If you think that you sound a bit like Janis Joplin and that turns you on, then go for it! But give yourself time to grow, research, experiment and learn.

> Is it OK to mimic my singing teacher's voice?

Answered by Dr. Ronald C. Scherer, Ph.D, Professor in the Department of Communication Sciences and Disorders, Bowling Green State University

As dangerous as it can be to imitate the voice of your favorite artist when it causes pain or fatigue to your voice, there is a really important role for trying to sound like someone else. In our quest to develop healthy singing technique, sometimes the best thing we can do is to try to imitate our teacher the best we can.

This is qualified by the critically important aspect of the teacher being there with you when you attempt this imitation, so that whatever change you make can be immediately evaluated as to the direction it takes your voice, toward more healthy and effective technique or not.

A voice teacher will make sounds for you to imitate that are directed toward your next steps of training. Sometimes those sounds to imitate are strange, perhaps even seemingly dangerous, which is often the reaction a student has when the teacher gives you, for example, constricted and "snarly" sounds, because the teacher is attempting to directly change and improve how you use your larynx in conjunction with how you are breathing for singing. Each student is different, and rarely is imitation the only approach that is used. For some, however, imitation is powerful, immediate, and most efficient.

Imitation of sound quality and voice production techniques are actually used routinely in all fields that are focused on voice building. It is routine in voice therapy (speech-language pathology clinics) and voice and speech training (for theatre and public speaking), as well as the singing studio. The clinician, singing teacher, and voice and speech trainer offer laryngeal changes, pitch inflection, vowel change, stress, timing, resonance alteration, and many other aspects for the student/client to imitate. Imitation can be efficient because it lacks verbal instruction on the physiology of the intended behavior, and thus takes less "thinking" or cognitive requirements. But remember the context is for optimal and efficient change through guidance; this is far from just listening to a singer and trying to imitate that person without someone telling you that you might be hurting yourself. I do not want to indicate that you should not imitate others, but if you do, bring that imitation to your singing lesson to ask your teacher if that is a good direction for you to follow.

An added benefit to imitation is that you are usually asked by your teacher "How does that feel and sound to you?" when the imitation is moving your voice in the right direction. A common set of images and jargon will emerge between you and your teacher that will help you to queue yourself to produce the improved production behavior and also retain the improvements. This process may provide new insights, new behaviors, better skills, and more enjoyment on your road to becoming a vocal artist.

> What's a good warm-up on the day of my gig?

Answered by Jaime Babbitt, renowned jingle singer and backing vocalist, former Disney Records coach

I'll answer that, but first, this important announcement:

Getting a good night's sleep the night before your gig is a part of a good warm-up!

(Thanks; now, back to our regularly scheduled question ...)

Well, it's the warm-up you do EVERY DAY because we're singers and we warm up EVERY DAY, gig or no gig. Runners run, musicians practice, prizefighters train—you see where I'm going here. They become great (and remain great) at what they love because they DO IT. Hopefully you've gotten a warm-up from your awesome singing teacher. If not, find me!

Your warm-up should last approximately 20 minutes and be finished 60–90 minutes before your gig. Make sure you're awake for two hours before warming up (yes, wait two hours after waking from a nap!) and be finished eating at least one hour before warming up; heartburn is so not fun.

So, for an 8pm gig (give or take):

- 5:00pm—meal ends
- 6:30pm—warm-up begins
- 6:55pm—warm-up ends

Warm up standing. No ear-buds or headphones, please. Also, no warming up in the car on the way, either (okay, if you've done warm-ups for a while and are adept at singing while sitting with proper support, I'll give you wiggle room). In the shower is fine; just make sure you're not screaming over the water—find a reasonable volume.

You should also:

- Hydrate
- Stay indoors during allergy season
- Minimize extraneous talking
- Have a relatively stress-free day

Most importantly, know yourself: if things like alcohol, dairy, smoke, spicy foods or a super-challenging workout feel "wrong," steer clear. See, having a gig means it's already a great day, so do your best to keep it that way! Wow, I just rhymed ...

> Are the classical technique snobs blowing putrid hot air?

Answered by Mary Hammond: leading educator and vocal coach for Coldplay and many other star acts

I understand this reaction. Far too often "classical teachers" have been elitist, disparaging of the structure and content of pop music. There are even "classical" teachers who say that if you sing pop music you will ruin your voice! Thirty years ago I remember standing up at a conference for music teachers saying, "What about students who want to learn pop music?" I got shot down. Nobody took me (or them) seriously.

> *Our 8 1/2 hours of daily singing left me with nodes. I've since taken voice lessons to correct my technique, particularly lessons to build stamina, integrate proper pelvic floor support, and maintain muscle relaxation so as not to compensate for a tired voice. I can't over-emphasize the importance of doing this right away!*
>
> ***—Liz Ager:*** *Urban Method*

I don't even like the word "technique"—it implies that there is just one right way to do things. There are many ways of approaching how to make sounds. There isn't even one "classical technique," but several depending on the language and region! The essential thing is to produce sound without hurting yourself. How you then decide to use your voice depends on your musical interests.

What we can all agree on is that you need to train your voice muscularly, developing your control over your vocal mechanism so that you can improve your range and your ability to sustain your notes. But then you apply all of this to your musical interests and it is here that you will find your own sound—that is what you really want. The goal is to have your individuality emerge in your singing.

On this journey you can delve into many different ideas and styles. For example, when I am teaching contemporary singers, I will draw from a wide variety of styles—including classical. Sometimes I ask a singer to pretend that they are singing opera. This mimicking helps them to find a lower larynx position and then discover the energy to make some new sounds. It's fun and can lead to new vocal possibilities. Freddie Mercury, Elvis and others have used these very sounds to achieve their musical goals.

Finally, don't get locked into just one method—stay open to many ideas and styles in your quest to create sounds that are meaningful to you.

> I keep hearing people say "head voice" and "chest voice"—what does this mean?

Answered by Tim Carson, professional singer and vocal coach, founder of Vocal Artistry

Imagine if every instrument ever made was actually two different instruments combined into one! Every guitar was made with a keyboard built into the top, and every trumpet was also a clarinet with separate mouthpieces and levers for each—ridiculous, right?! These instruments would look like something out of a Dr. Seuss book and be impossible to play.

Yet this is the challenge that every singer is up against. The larynx or voicebox (the instrument you play as a singer) is able to change the shape of the vocal cords, creating two instruments that sound different and are "played" differently by the singer.

When the muscles in the larynx stretch the vocal cords out so that they are long and thin, the singer is able to sing high, and the tone becomes lighter and softer. It's the sound you hear when a woman is singing opera or like Snow White, or a man is singing like a girl ... or like the Bee Gees. We call this Head Voice or Falsetto.

The muscles in the larynx can also move the opposite direction, making the Vocal Cords short and thick. This gives the voice a fuller and louder sound. It's what we use when we talk, shout, and belt out a rock or pop song with force and volume. We call this Chest Voice.

Here's one of the most important "secrets" about singing: developing a strong Head Voice will help you sing higher in your Chest Voice than you ever have. It will also allow you to sing in your Chest Voice longer without getting tired or hurting your voice.

It is crazy that we have two different instruments crammed into our throat. But if you can learn to play both, and develop equal strength in your chest and head voice, you will be well on your way to singing at your best!

> How much time should I spend training my voice?

Answered by Jaime Vendera, vocal coach renowned for his wineglass-shattering voice

It's different for every person, but there is an easy way to calculate it: if it starts to hurt, stop. In actuality, you NEVER want your voice to hurt, but at the end of a good workout, you may feel a little tired or fatigued, just like your legs may feel after squats at the gym. But that tiredness will rapidly dissipate as long as you're using correct vocal technique. If the pain continues, you're doing something wrong and you'll need to evaluate your technique and possibly adjust your practice time.

To figure out the best time for you, I suggest starting with fifteen minutes of some sort of warm up/workout, followed by fifteen minutes of rehearsing your songs. If you feel great at that point, bump it up to twenty minutes each, then thirty each and so on. Find what time feels right for your voice. A good workout should make you feel like a million bucks. Remember, ALWAYS do a warm up/workout before singing, because, after all, the goal is to strengthen the voice and then sing, not spend all the time on vocal exercises. Over the course of a month, you should be able to calculate the length of time that works most efficiently for you. At that point, change the ratio of time between exercises from 1:1 to 1:2, meaning, if you exercise for fifteen minutes, you should sing for thirty. That way, you're a rock star in no time!

> How do I cope with the overwhelming vocal demands of gigs six nights a week? Help!

Answered by Dr. Robert W. Bastian, MD, Board Certified Otolaryngologist and founder of the Bastian Voice Institute

To continue being able to sing your heart out, you have to avoid injury to the surface layer of your vocal folds—called mucosa.

When you speak or sing, the mucosal layers of the folds vibrate—256 times per second, for example, when you sing middle C! Each one of these vibrations involves a tiny collision and a shearing force. Imagine these collisions by clapping an imaginary pair of hands that are one inch long; to "see" shearing forces, slide the skin on the back of these miniature hands back and forth vigorously. Thankfully, the vocal folds are designed for all of this.

To avoid injury from going "too far," first keep an eye on the amount of your voice use. Here I am not only thinking of during your performance—but also on your cell phone, interacting with fans, and so forth.

Then, become aware of the manner of your voice use. The way one speaks to a friend in a quiet room is much less taxing to the vocal fold mucosa than is shouting to be heard over background noise at a party. The same contrast can apply to singing style. Some singers learn to convey an aggressive style of singing using amplification, a brighter resonance quality, speech over-articulation, and even body language in order to "dial back" a bit on the aggressiveness of actual voice use. A good teacher can come to the rescue here.

You might also build "space" into your gig; boisterous backstage banter between sets creates "massed" voice use, while resting the voice during those breaks spaces it; you can also think of a series of especially taxing songs sung together as massing voice use as compared with interspersing difficult songs with less demanding ones.

Of course, other things can help, too. Consistently consume fluids (water is best) to keep urine pale. This practice keeps the vocal folds wet, and this wetness, like oil in a motor, is protective against the rigors of vibration. You can also experiment with management of a common condition called acid reflux in which stomach acid burbles upward at night during sleep into the throat, thereby irritating and "burning" the larynx (see Chapter Eleven, Action 4). Finally, take the swelling test (below) each day so you can monitor how you are doing.

The Worst Singing Advice Ever Given:

"There is nothing wrong with feeling a little pain, you can still sing through it!"

—reported by Simone Niles

"The vocal folds are so tiny that a warm up doesn't make any difference."

—reported by Daniel Borch

"Sing with a plum in your mouth."

—reported by Shlomo

"Constipate! Constipate!"

—reported by Kim Chandler

"When you have a cold, you just have to try to sing as loud as possible."

—reported by John Kjøller

Take The Swelling Test:

Like the smoke detector in an airplane lavatory, "swelling tests" are vocal tasks that help you detect swelling of the vocal fold mucosa (surface layer) when it is subtle or small—long before it has become a crisis. The idea is to take the following vocal test exactly the same way every day so that you become aware—early, immediately—if you have to exert any extra effort.

Using an extremely tiny, high-pitched voice, sing the first phrase of "Happy Birthday" several times, repeating the phrase at a slightly higher starting pitch each time, until you reach a pitch at which your voice falters—that is, at which the mucosa stops wanting to vibrate. It may help to use a keyboard to track your ascending pitches. Also, as you go higher, you have to resist the natural tendency to just get louder to "make" the folds vibrate. Doing this kind of 20-second swelling test twice per day—at the beginning of your first warm-up and just before retiring to bed—can "take the clothes off the voice" and keep you aware at all times of the condition of the surface of your vocal folds, so as to help you make decisions about schedules, sets, songs to cut, sharing of vocals with other band members so as to reduce wear and tear on your voice, whether or not to excuse yourself from social events, and so forth.

If, for example, you find one day that your "Happy Birthday" begins to falter (cutting out to air or otherwise not wanting to work) at a lower pitch than normal, stop for a moment and think about the amount and manner of your voice use in the past 24 hours. If you say, "hmm ... not surprising," that is, it makes sense from recent vocal use that your folds would be a bit swollen, even though your speaking voice is fine, then you need to back off on voice use in whatever ways you can until your "Happy Birthday" returns to your normal baseline.

> Is there any secret to nailing a high note?

Answered by Kathy Alexander, singer, vocal coach and staff writer at VoiceCouncil Magazine

Our natural tendency is to strain when attempting a high note. That tension makes singing a lot harder, which is why so many teachers have come up with exercises to fool our body into relaxing while we sing.

Working with a knowledgeable teacher is the best way to strengthen your technique, but the four exercises below will help you get started. Using the first few words of "Somewhere Over the Rainbow" or a phrase from your song that contains a high note, try these:

1. Sing your whole phrase on pure vowels (like "ah" or "ooh") or nonsense syllables (like "ya ya"). This will encourage you to open up your vocal tract. Try different vowels, perhaps using the vowels from the song—leaving out the consonants. Now put the words back in, but keep the open feeling of singing the vowels.
2. Sing "forward" or "down" into the high note. This requires you to do a little mime. Imagine you are holding a ball. Now sing your phrase. As you sing the high note, throw the ball either forward into the horizon or down into the floor. Try it in slow motion. Try it fast. See which movement frees your voice more.
3. Find a medium sized object that you must bend down to lift. I like to use the end of a small coffee table. Sing your phrase and as you sing the high note, bend down and lift that object. This will engage muscles in your core, distract you from your vocal worries and free your voice.
4. Imagine that you are drawing the sound in instead of forcing it out. Stretch your arms out to the side like an airplane. As you sing that high note, move your hands in towards your mouth as if you trying to scoop in and eat all the air in front of you.

Changing your song to a lower key may be the best way to eliminate strain while you develop your technique. Why not try it?

CHAPTER 11

Staying Healthy

Help, my voice is sinking!

"I'm still doing vocal gymnastics at the age of 56, singing five or six nights a week in one and a half hour sets—and we haven't changed the original keys from the 70s."

—Bernie Shaw, lead Singer of Uriah Heep

"We have to remember that the voice is our instrument—and this instrument is not like a violin that you can put safely away in a closet when you've finished playing. Singers walk around with their instrument—and expose it to wind, rain and all kinds of other factors that don't face that violin in the closet."

—Neil Sedaka, legendary American singer, songwriter, composer and pianist

"I can hear the taunts from the cheap seats now, but I steadfastly stand by my use of earplugs. The only drawback is that you have to be careful not to play louder as a result."

—Tom Lang, singer-guitarist and product manager, TC-Helicon

Staying Healthy

Help, my voice is sinking!

Actions:

1. Be Skeptical of Miracle Cures
2. Keep Your Wallet in Your Pocket—at First
3. Prevent Illness
4. Reduce Reflux
5. Drink More Water
6. Speak Well of Yourself
7. Steer Clear of Vending Machines
8. Protect Your Ears
9. Survive Singing When You're Sick
10. Get Some Sleep ... Then Get Some More

Frequently Asked Questions:

- » *Can I be a "bad boy"—smoke, drink and still sing well? It totally fits into my genre-lifestyle.*
- » *My voice has changed. I can't sing as high and everything takes so much more effort.*
- » *I've been told to rest my voice. What does that mean? Total silence?*
- » *I've got a sore throat and I just have to sing—will I destroy my voice?*
- » *Can't I just take a pill and sound better?*
- » *Is there anything I shouldn't eat or drink?*
- » *What is a node?*
- » *I have to get a scope—I'm terrified! What will it be like?*
- » *My ears are ringing from tonight's performance. Will they bounce back?*
- » *In my musical scene everyone smokes—what's the best way to prevent this from getting into my system?*
- » *My throat doesn't hurt, but my voice often gets hoarse and feels sluggish.*
- » *My voice has good days and bad days—what's going on?*
- » *My voice just isn't what it used to be—and no doctor can help—should I just give up?*
- » *Is getting surgery done on the voice "bad"?*
- » *Is Cortisone the miracle cure I've been looking for to get me through my next few performances?*

Action 1: Be Skeptical of Miracle Cures

Don't be fooled by the promises on the packaging—they're designed to part you from your money.

As an experiment to see how many helpful and unhelpful medications there are for the voice I arranged with the very co-operative local pharmacist to take one of every product that claims to help the voice from his store—lozenges, sprays, liquids—everything. I dropped them on a table, took some photographs and counted: around 300 different products. I emphasize that these were all from one small, local shop. In my opinion as a physician, only a couple of these products were likely to be of any significant benefit.

These kinds of drugs represent a multi-billion a year industry. Yet, there are significant risks associated with many of them. The promotional advertising for one of these products even suggested that you could sing your lungs out and this drug would take care of everything. I call this vocal abuse.

Most of these drugs are merely comforting in nature—they don't actually fix the underlying problem. Menthol, for example, simply produces a chemical "mirage," sending an icy sensation to your brain so that it "thinks" your airways are clear. This lasts only as long as you are actively inhaling the menthol and does not heal or change anything. If you have a "productive" mucussy cough, the worst thing you can do is to take magic pills to dry it up. You need a wet cough, it keeps your mucus moving, reducing chance of further infection. It may be worth taking medicine for a dry, persistent cough. However, you really need to get to a doctor to find out why you have a dry, persistent cough in the first place.

Medicated lozenges, sprays and alcohol can dull the pain and can actually mask further vocal damage and prevent you from getting an answer to the question of why you have this pain in the first place.

—Tom Harris: MA, FRCS, Hon. FRCSLT, Consultant ENT Surgeon

Action 2: Keep Your Wallet in Your Pocket—at First

There are many effective remedies for your voice that are actually free.

When singers are suffering with a cough, cold or upper respiratory infection, there are many things they can do that don't cost anything. The most soothing thing to do for the vocal tract is to steam it—this is exactly the same technique you would use for a child with croup. It really works and there are no side effects. You can just put some boiling water in a bowl and cover it—and your head—with a towel. Then you can inhale the steam for about five minutes. For a longer treatment you can go out and buy a steamer; this is basically just a kettle with a funnel on the side. You can take these anywhere.

If you have a load of mucus in your nose, you can use a saline douche or spray to get it out of there. The Do-It-Yourself method is simply to take a level teaspoon of salt and a level teaspoon of baking soda (bi-carbonate of soda) in a pint (about 500 mL) of warm water. You then sniff handfuls of this up your nose (douching). It will make you cough and can be messy! An easier method is to use a small spray canister of "Normal Saline" that is built for this purpose—and there are many on the market. I use one that has a mixture with exactly the same concentration as one's body salts. The essential thing for your vocal tract is to keep it damp—and to keep the mucus moving.

I want to say more about mucus. People often don't understand that the normal situation is for your body to be moving a half a gallon of mucous every day. This is normal and healthy—it is your body's way of getting rid of dust, germs and other things. The reason most people don't notice this is that the mucous is tasteless and odorless. However, as soon as you have an infection, the mucus dries out and becomes thicker and nastier, developing color and odor. This is why people assume that mucus is bad for you. It isn't—it just needs to be kept moving. The reason I am emphasizing this point is that so many singers rush out and get a decongestant; this dries the mucus and works against you in the long term.

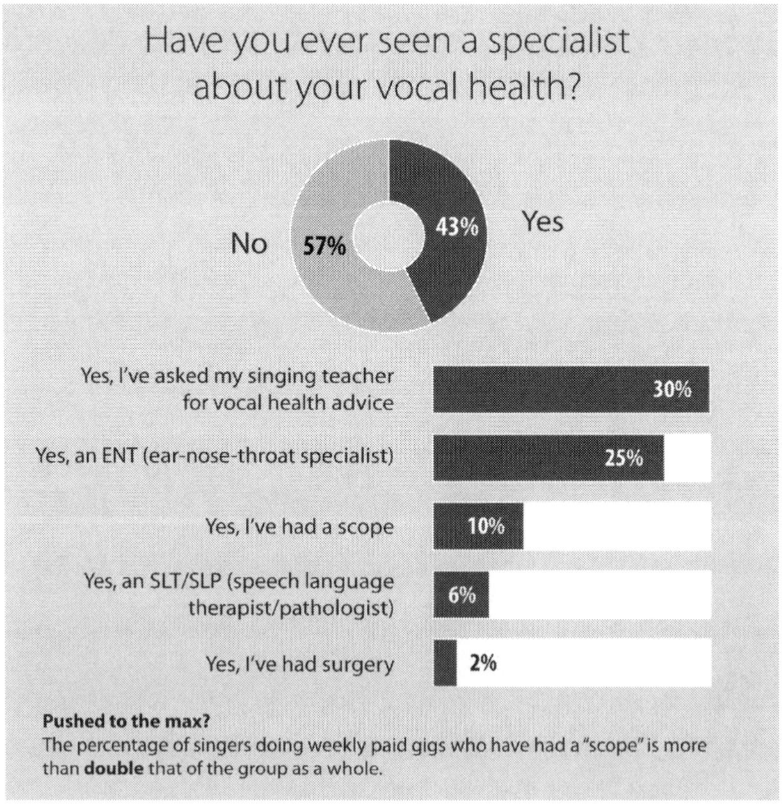

—from the 2012-2013 TC-Helicon survey of 1,000 singers

The bottom line is that the body is trying to produce a normal layer of thin, runny mucous that can still move over the membranes, shifting dust, germs etc. through and out of your system and enabling the transfer of oxygen and carbon dioxide gases on which our lives depend. However, a decongestant has a drying affect on your mucus, turning it into a "glue" which doesn't move well at all. So, you may get some short-term symptomatic relief with a decongestant, but then are left with things not moving. I would never recommend a decongestant. If you've got excess mucus in your nose, saline sprays are absolutely brilliant for moving it along—hence they actually reduce the likelihood of secondary infection.

—Tom Harris: MA, FRCS, Hon. FRCSLT, Consultant ENT Surgeon

Action 3: Prevent Illness

There's an invasion force heading your way—keep your defenses up and stand firmly in front of your (disinfected) mic.

Many people think that they get sick because it's cold outside and they haven't "bundled up." This is a misconception. It is true that most colds occur during the fall and winter. However, this is due to the opening of schools and the start of cold weather that causes people to spend more time indoors. This increases the chances that viruses will spread from person to person.

The most important factor for avoiding a viral or bacterial infection is simply good hygiene—wash your hands often. It's even more important if you are working with children. The average person will get 3–4 upper respiratory infections per year, but if you work with children it's 9–10 infections per year. Using anti-bacterial hand gel is just as effective—if not more so—than regular soap. It is also easier to

Top Tips on Vocal Health from Tasha Layton, backing vocalist with Katy Perry

1. **Eat well & exercise** *(It's also good for fitting into my costumes!)*
2. **Drink lots of water.** *Keep all of your liquids from being too hot or too cold.*
3. **Sleep.** *It's one of the only things that restores the voice. Getting enough sleep is a huge factor for successful singing.*
4. **Steam** *(or humidifier). A hot, steamy shower is excellent for the voice. I often place a humidifier in my room if I have an important session approaching.*
5. **Warm up properly***—there is never a time I don't warm up. Also: cool down after your performance (in the form of a shortened warm up).*
6. **Avoid dairy products** *and other foods that can create phlegm and acid reflux.*

*—**Tasha Layton:** LA based singer and backing vocalist with Katy Perry*

use and carry around. Some say that overuse of the antibacterial gel can be dangerous due to increasing the levels of resistant bacteria but this has not been proven and is unlikely. The wisdom that should prevail is: "everything in moderation."

The other thing you'll want to do is to be good to your entire body. If you're a singer you should act like a pro athlete: eat well, get rest, stay fit and avoid constant over-fatigue. Staying in good shape will also help decrease your chance of infection—and help you move through an infection more quickly when you get one.

There's a certain subset of people for whom infections frequently become a deep-seated sinusitis that lasts much longer than the average infection, sometimes weeks to months. For these patients we set up a preventative regime that involves keeping sinuses open as soon as one feels the onset of a cold. You see, when the membranes of your nose swell due to an infection they can close the drainage pathways of the sinuses. When this happens a simple cold or nasal infection can turn into a sinus infection, which is more severe and can last much longer. For these patients, I will often recommend both nasal steroids and nasal saline irrigation at the first sign of a cold. I prefer a squeeze bottle over a neti pot because it has more of a scrubbing action that really irrigates. Keeping open the sinus drainage pathways helps to prevent an infection from settling in.

Finally, keep hydrated—drink lots of water. The mucus in your throat is like oil in a car; it is thin and protective and coats the lining of your vocal folds and throat. Give it every chance to do its work for you by drinking 6–8 glasses a day.

—Michael J. Pitman MD: Director of the Division of Laryngology at The New York Eye and Ear Infirmary

Action 4: Reduce Your Reflux

You can be well fed—without reducing one iota of your vocal quality.

Acid reflux is one of the troubles that arise in a well-fed society. If you are singing, you will be using raised abdominal pressure to support your voice and, if you have a stomach full of food and acid, some of this may come bouncing back into your throat.

There is a related challenge that is less recognized but is still just as real, where stomach acid comes up but doesn't sit there very long—just enough to give you a bad taste at the back of your throat. Reflux irritates and burns, causing stiff, thick inflamed mucus membranes. This makes you take a long time to warm up your voice and causes your vocal muscles to become overly "tight," and may affect the range of the voice.

You see, your stomach has all sorts of clever mucus glands that protect the stomach lining from this acid, but if the acid flows back out of the stomach, it can damage the mucous membrane that lines your throat and vocal folds. In fact, if you look into the throat after reflux you will see the mucous membranes around the back of the vocal folds looking red and "angry."

As a doctor, I find it difficult to persuade performers to behave reasonably—they all like the after show parties with platefuls of pasta and wine. This is followed by going home and lying flat. So, now you have a stomach full of acid alcohol and some of it comes back up your throat. So when should you eat? Performers tend not to like breakfast, so meals start with coffee and then get bigger throughout the day. From the point of view of acid reflux, it should be the opposite. You should have a full breakfast, with your meals getting smaller throughout the day. Don't eat within an hour of the performance—and don't eat much afterwards. Singers may find this advice dull and boring, but it will really decrease reflux.

> *Reflux can occur without pain, yet cause inconsistencies in voice quality and vocal range.*
>
> ***—Dr. Ronald C. Scherer:*** *Professor, Bowling Green State University*

Also, if you have the symptoms of reflux (swallowing and burping with an occasional bad taste in your mouth), then you need to raise the head of your bed by about 4 inches. Don't think that more pillows under your head will achieve this as this can lead to neck-ache. Instead, just put a couple of bricks under the bedposts at the head of you bed. You see, you want your stomach lower than your throat. Putting gravity on your side is absolutely free.

—Tom Harris: MA, FRCS, Hon. FRCSLT, Consultant ENT Surgeon

Action 5: Drink More Water

It's not just any liquid that will do the trick. Attain greater vocal health with H_2O.

Drinking water is like making sure you have the right amount of oil in your car. Your car may still function if the oil is low or dirty—but it won't run as well as if you had maintained and changed the oil.

You'll want to be drinking water throughout the day. Keep in mind that your vocal folds don't get the benefits of your drinking water right away—so you want to be ahead of your thirst. For most people this means eight glasses of water a day. There are some people who can get away with a little less than this but there are many people who need more, especially if they're exerting themselves in performance. The way to judge if you are getting the right amount of water is that your pee should be pale. When you're not well hydrated, your pee is darker.

Stay away from too much caffeine—that can be dehydrating, making you pee more, getting rid of good fluid. It can also cause acid reflux. Alcohol also dehydrates you. You see, you want your vocal cord tissue to be moist. Your cords vibrate at incredible speeds: around 100 times a second for a man and 200 times for a woman during speech, increasing to many times more than this when you are singing. If they become sticky and dry it is much harder for them to vibrate—and strain/irritation will occur. Everyone knows Adele had a voice injury. Her issue was probably due to a crazy schedule and higher keys on her album than were sustainable in live performance over time. At the same time, many young singers want to be Adele! So, keep up your water—other than good technique, it is one of your main defenses against tissue damage. Keep your water bottle out there with you on stage. Room temperature is best; water that is really cold or really hot can affect your singing.

Many singers think that teas and juices can be used in place of water since they are mostly made up of water. To some extent this is true, but, remember, black and green tea have caffeine. Also, mint based teas can be irritating (even if you don't feel it) and can lead to reflux. Also watch out for eucalyptus (another possible irritant) and anything containing menthol as this can numb your throat and mask any damage that may be occurring. Other than these exceptions, most herbal teas should be fine.

When it comes to juices you'll want to avoid really acidic beverages such as grapefruit and orange juice before performance as they can lead to reflux and irritation. On a positive note, lots of singers report that papaya extract is excellent for reflux. But, remember: you can never go wrong with good, old fashioned water.

—Amy Lebowitz-Cooper, M.S., CCC-SLP; Director of Speech Pathology, Voice and Swallowing, New York Eye and Ear Infirmary

Your H_2O Checklist

- *Drink six to eight cups a day (but this is not a "magic number")*
- *Adjust the amount of water you consume to take into account sweating and caffeine*
- *Have enough so that you "pee pale"*
- *Room temperature is better than hot or cold*
- *Sip rather than glug*
- *Don't wait until you are thirsty to drink*

Action 6: Speak Well of Yourself

The key to unlocking the potential of your voice may not be singing practice, but talking practice.

The crazy thing about the speaking voice is that most of us aren't taught about it—though we speak all day long! In fact, when singers come to me for help, we often discover that their singing challenge came from a speaking problem.

All of us develop our own technique for speaking as soon as we start talking but we seldom ask, "Are my speaking habits good for my singing voice?" One way to make sure that this is the case is to do a daily speaking-warm-up early in the day—regardless of whether or not you will be singing later.

A speaking warm up is great for getting out of "glottal fry;" this is our low-creaky-husky-gravelly tone. It's often the way we speak when we first wake up or when we talk on the phone. It is a lazy way of speaking that doesn't require a lot of breath support or coordination. Furthermore, it is considered "cool" and socially acceptable—not to mention "sexy!" Try out glottal fry now. Imagine that you have just woken up and speak in a low, gravelly voice without much breathing. The problem is that though this kind of speaking seems "easy," it doesn't project well and can be fatiguing. It's also a lot to ask of the vocal folds to jump from glottal fry to a warmed up singing voice (which is often a couple of octaves higher).

In a speaking warm up it's not about how high or low you can go. It's about being where you feel comfortable, in your mid range. Start with some lip trills at a single pitch, around where you talk. Then try some little glides, making small pitch changes—these are therapeutic, like a massage for the vocal folds. Move onto some "yawn-sighs"—this is exactly as the phrase suggests: a fairly breathy yawn and release of sound. You can also do some humming, staying in the middle of your range. If you hum with your tongue hanging out then you will be helping to ease tongue-tension too. Finally, take a piece of junk mail and read it out loud in a "sing-songy" voice like a flight attendant or a reporter might use. Your voice doesn't need to stay in "sing-songy" mode all of the time, but it's important that you find that "place" early in your day as a starting place.

Finally, a word to singers who are on the road or performing regularly: you can often have 18-hour days when the voice is constantly in use. It's often the little things that can add up to voice fatigue. Public spaces often have a high degree of background noise that has to be overcome when you are speaking. Even if one has good speaking and singing technique, it is very important to recharge one's batteries. This means limiting one's speaking time. When I am working with busy professional singers who have any voice difficulty at all, I tell them to speak when they're paid and to be quiet when they're not.

—Amy Lebowitz-Cooper, M.S., CCC-SLP; Director of Speech Pathology, Voice and Swallowing, New York Eye and Ear Infirmary

Action 7: Steer Clear of Vending Machines

Have your food, glorious food without inglorious burps, growls, gas, acid reflux and other gross performance-inhibiting stuff.

Lord knows how long that stuff has been sitting there. Your body needs vitamins for the glowing skin on stage, and maintenance of cells within the body. Plants were put on this earth for a reason—for us to eat them. Choose apples, berries, baby carrots and salads.

Fried foods and sweets will leave you feeling bloated, tired, and craving for more. If something tastes too good it's probably loaded with salt, oil or sugar, so AVOID. Choose whole grains—yeah, that brown stuff that still has the speckles of the kernel, husk and germ from the seeds. Remember, you are what you eat. Avoid dairy and beans: they produce gas, and are high in acid content. You can get lean proteins from chicken, eggs, certain cuts of meat (eye of round and loin), poultry and tofu.

Food gives us energy. Think of your body as a car. It requires fuel to operate just as our bodies require food for survival. You wouldn't put cheap diesel in a high performance unleaded v6 engine. The same goes with how we nourish ourselves. I'm not here to put you on a diet but to teach you how to make informed choices and get back to the basics of eating as close to nature as possible.

If you do want to lose weight, remember to avoid the quick fix. You want to look good on stage so it's going to take some effort, otherwise we'd all be models. It's all about calories in vs. calories out. To get rid of that gut, avoid empty calories that come from foods that are high in sugar. Pastries, desserts, ice cream, even natural juices that you think might be healthy for you are extremely high in sugar.

> *I'm talking about made-out-of-cardboard sausage rolls or service station pasties, pastries or other fodder—there's nothing in these for your brain or your body.*
>
> ***—Shlomo:*** *World Loopstation Champion and Guinness World Record holder*

And don't be fooled by the "No Added Sugar" label: all that means is no sugar has been added to the original 40 grams that are naturally in there. Remember, we eat for fuel so put the natural form of fiber and protein in your diet; this takes longer to be digested, leaving you full longer. Most fibrous foods do cause gas so it's important for you to get in tune with your body to see how each food affects you.

Pizza, bagels, macaroni and cheese, beer, alcohol, juice, cookies, chips—these don't take much effort to be metabolized and go straight to the cells to be stored as fat. Fiber must be chewed thoroughly and gastric juices come into play so imagine how much energy you are using just to digest. Now, that's what leads to an increased metabolism. FIRE AWAY!

—Sharon Zarabi: RD, CDN, CPT—Registered Dietitian and Certified Dietitian Nutritionist

Action 8: Protect Your Ears

Earplugs and good monitoring are the equivalent of safe sex for your ears—learn why.

Always do what you can to protect your hearing—after all, how can you sing if you can't hear yourself?

Yet, the dominant ideology in the entertainment industry has often been that one has to sacrifice to make it—those who complain about things like audio levels have found themselves left behind in this dog-eat-dog environment. However, the last few years have seen huge changes in awareness of this area. Now, the care of one's hearing is on the agenda for many major training institutions for singers.

To keep it simple and cheap, one can simply download a decibel-meter app (like Decibel Ultra) on your smart phone. Become aware of the stage/studio noise level through this app and then look on the chart (below) to evaluate the dangers. You'll notice that sustained exposure to anything over 90–95 dB can lead to hearing loss—and most rock concerts are louder than this. They are actually the equivalent to using a sandblaster!

Should noise level be a problem, one of my recommendations is that you purchase special musicians' earplugs that reduce the amount of noise reaching your ears. I am not talking about those cheapo two-dollar earplugs: these won't protect your hearing at all frequencies evenly. You need a pair of earplugs that have been balanced to protect against loudness across the frequency spectrum in a balanced manner. It is not unusual for players in an orchestra and musicians in bands to wear such specialized earplugs nowadays.

If singers do not wear earplugs in a setting where the noise level is quite loud, they run the risk of hearing loss and ringing which may become a lifelong problem. So: wear earplugs whenever things get too loud not just in concerts, but even during rehearsals.

Noise Levels in Your Life

Sound:	dB:
Weakest sound heard	0dB
Whisper Quiet Library at 6' (2m)	30dB
Normal conversation at 3' (1m)	60-65dB
Telephone dial tone	80dB
City Traffic (inside car)	85dB
Jackhammer at 50' (15m)	95dB
Level at which sustained exposure may result in hearing loss	90 - 95dB
Hand Drill	98dB
Power mower at 3' (1m)	107dB
Amplifier, rock, 4-6' (1.5-2m) Symphonic music peak **Pain begins.** Even short-term exposure can cause permanent damage.	125dB
Loudest recommended exposure WITH hearing protection	140dB
Rock music peak	150dB
Death of hearing tissue	180dB
Loudest sound possible	194dB

Remember—you want to be in this business for the long haul. Hearing loss does not promote such longevity since you'll have trouble hearing your music director, other singing colleagues, and even yourself. Protect your ears!

—Christopher Chang, MD, Board-Certified Otolaryngology Head & Neck Surgeon

Daily Permissible Noise Level Exposure

Hours Per Day:	Sound Level dB:
8	**90dB**
6	**92dB**
4	**95dB**
3	**97dB**
2	**100dB**
1.5	**102dB**
1	**105dB**
0.5	**110dB**
0.25 or less	**115dB**

Action 9: Survive Singing When You're Sick

Some purists would say we should shut up now and go to bed. But you've got a gig that you just have to do and we're gonna help you through it.

If you are ill, the best thing is for you to lay aside your singing and have adequate rest so that you can recover. After all, that's what you would expect your doctor to say! However, if this is not possible, then I want you to consider modifying your performances rather than taking extreme strategies (pain killers and steroids) that will mask your pain and could lead to further damage.

When you get to the part of a song where you exert tremendous vocal effort, hold the mic out to the audience and invite the crowd to sing that passage. Also, change the pitch of some of your songs—and remove some of your top notes. You see, if your throat is already swollen and you are straining to sing, your throat will get even more swollen. This may actually be a great time to get band members to join in on the chorus and to lengthen instrumental solos—let some of the band members show off!

If you are in the middle of a tour or a run of regular gigs then you have to pace yourself. A good vocal coach can work with you on some specific strategies to reduce the impact of your singing in performance. From a medical point of view, I want to stress how effective and helpful these changes can be.

I recently worked with a professional singer who had been singing for over twenty years. She was in a demanding production and had developed nodules. I told her to have all of her songs transposed down two or three notes. The result was that the nodules actually went away! This reminds me of a time when I was watching a concert by the late Freddie Mercury—it was a long performance and I was wondering how he was actually going to get through it. He simply modified his singing to avoid some of the high notes that were on the recordings.

Of course it is absolutely critical that you can hear your voice well in performance—this means having effective monitoring. Make sure you check out chapter six on what constitutes good monitoring—but from my perspective as a doctor it is critical to have this in place to avoid straining and subsequent swelling in your throat.

If you have a career-making performance or audition then a doctor might pull out all the stops and prop you up with steroids. However, there are real dangers with this as the steroids will mask your symptoms and lead to vocal damage if you do not have adequate vocal rest after the performance. It's kind of like an athlete who might have a sprained ankle and takes a pain killer so that he can run the race without pain. There can be lots of damage—so much so that this strategy won't work for subsequent races.

—Gayle Woodson, MD, board certified in Otolaryngology specializing in the treatment of voice disorders

> *Sometimes we practice some "SOS management," acute treatments that keep a singer on track for the short term. However, we want the singer, over time, to adopt a lifestyle that will support their vocation—that makes economic as well as medical sense.*
>
> **—Dr. Ruth Epstein:** *Consultant Speech and Language Therapist*

Action 10: Get Some Sleep ... Then Get Some More

There's a secret weapon to getting a handle on a good night's sleep—and it has to do with your music.

As a singer, you have a secret weapon to help you slip into sleep but I'll bet you've never used it. The reason most people toss and turn all night is that they have unresolved emotional issues. It may not even be anything heavy—just the events of the day replayed on a loop in their minds. The problem is that your mind is not the place to process an emotional issue—your body is—but we live in a culture that frowns on reacting physically to a feeling. Just imagine a grown up collapsing on the floor crying because the line is long at Starbucks!

The reasons humans have emotions is to inspire an action (e-MOTION). Thinking all night about the actions you should have taken that day only raises the emotional alarms and doesn't provide an outlet for your brain.

As a singer, a song is a perfect way to replay the day and move the emotions from your head to your body. Yes—I'm suggesting you get up (you weren't sleeping anyway) and write a song—or sing an appropriate cover. Don't worry about the quality of your voice. It's merely the act of singing that counts, not the aesthetics. Once you are singing the emotion of the song will knock on the door; allow the feeling into your body. It will move through you without getting stuck as stress in your brain. That's why I've always slept well after a great gig.

Now, let's talk about improving your sleep. Getting proper sleep is all about creating a ritual so your brain knows it's time to shut down.

If you gig regularly then you should maintain the late schedule even on your nights off. As you get close to bedtime (whenever that is) start to wind down by dimming the lights and lowering the temperature to 68 F (20 C). When you lay down the bedroom needs to be pitch black and quiet with all electronics turned off. I mean OFF—not just on "quiet mode." It may seem harmless, but having a smart phone next to your bed chirping every time you get a hit on Twitter pulls your brain out of deep sleep. Also, the blue background on a screen tricks your brain into thinking it is still daytime and may make it more difficult to fall asleep. Each morning is when your biological clock is reset. You do this by bathing your face in sunlight—or exposing yourself to some bright lights for at least a half hour.

Unfortunately, it's easy to train your brain NOT to sleep by associating too many activities with a bed. So reserve your bed for just sleep and sex. That means no TV watching, reading, texting, songwriting or yapping on the phone. This can be a challenge when a bed is the only piece of furniture in the room (like in some of the cheap hotels I've stayed in). Even so, I am incredibly strict with this rule. I'll sit on my suitcase if need be—so once I do lie down on a bed, my brain knows that I am there for sleep.

Finally, I want to say a word about the "power-nap"—which is not a substitute for deep sleep but a great way to recharge. What defines a power nap is that it is no longer than 20 minutes—even if it takes you 18 to settle down. Anything over 20 minutes and you're flirting with deep sleep. The problem with deep sleep is that it triggers a change in metabolism and can negatively affect the quality of your voice when you wake up (which you do not want in the middle of your singing day). With practice you can get really good at power napping. I would always find a place after sound check—in the van, under a table, behind the drum kit—wherever you won't be interrupted. Those 20 minutes were critical for getting my focus back for that night's performance.

—Mark Baxter: acclaimed vocal coach with Aerosmith, Journey, Goo Goo Dolls and many others

Frequently Asked Questions

> Can I be a bad boy—smoke, drink and still sing well? It totally fits into my genre-lifestyle.

Answered by Amy Lebowitz-Cooper, M.S., CCC-SLP; Director of Speech Pathology, Voice and Swallowing, New York Eye and Ear Infirmary

The Rolling Stones certainly led very wild lives during the 70s. Now, when they tour, you can be sure a physio is close by. I would hope that every singer could afford the lifestyle option of personal medical staff (!), but it's unlikely. Take care of yourself now so that you don't have to travel with a doctor later on.

I could go on for pages and pages about health concerns when it comes to smoking—cancer being the biggest. However, you've likely heard all of this before so I think I'll tell you about one issue that especially impacts singers. When you smoke a cigarette, your oral cavity acts as a funnel that concentrates that heated air down a very tiny opening—the space between your vocal folds. This is a very small space through which all of that smoke moves. This causes the folds to retain water, swell and get irritated—even burned. The result is a voice that is deeper and huskier. For rock music it may be great to have that voice quality, and some singers may keep smoking to keep that sound. However, over time cigarettes destroy singing capacity. You can actually learn to make the "rough" sounds you want through healthy singing techniques; this is an intensive process that requires lots of discipline. However, that is a much better choice—especially if you want a long-term singing career.

With alcohol I could similarly go on for pages about the health risks, the dangers of addiction and the emotional disconnection it can create with the music you love. However, you've probably heard all of this before too, so let me zero in on one particular issue. What I want you to understand about alcohol is that when you're drinking, you are not monitoring your voice well. You will be less careful when you talk and sing which means it is much easier to do vocal damage. It's not that we don't want you to enjoy yourself, but if you are a singer, then you are a professional; singing is your work. When you treat your work with care, others will notice and you'll be giving yourself every chance to succeed in your genre—and life.

> My voice has changed. I can't sing as high and everything takes so much more effort.

Answered by Gayle Woodson, MD, board certified in Otolaryngology specializing in the treatment of voice disorders

If this has happened suddenly—and there is no cold or other illness—then I would want to look down your throat with a mirror or a scope. My main concern would be to determine if there was anything (such as bleeding) that would require you to stop singing for a while. You could also have developed a polyp that could require surgery. At the same time I would do as most doctors do: ask you many, many questions about your life in order to try to get a sense of the history and context of what is happening. Perhaps you have a new job, have taken on extra work, are in some kind of emotional or relational distress—all of these factors can affect your voice.

> I've been told to rest my voice. What does that mean? Total silence?

Answered by Sue M. Jones, B.Sc., M.Sc., MRCSLT, Speech-Language Therapist

There are two situations where complete voice rest is recommended: 1. After an operation on the vocal folds. 2. In the case of an acute laryngeal infection (laryngitis, or vocal fold inflammation).

Some doctors recommend voice rest if a singer is experiencing a voice problem that doesn't require surgery. In my experience rest alone rarely accomplishes a great deal unless there is laryngitis.

If a singer is experiencing voice problems they need a full diagnostic assessment since the issue is often related to muscle tension which will not improve with voice rest. If the singer has been busy with lots of performances, then reducing the vocal load may help. It is also wise to take more care with the voice when you have a cold or any upper respiratory tract infection. This means cutting down on voice use—not complete vocal rest. Remember, always avoid straining the voice.

When a vocal problem is due to muscle tension but no surgery has been required, therapy should be carried out by a speech therapist specialising in voice disorders. Following the voice therapy, further work with a singing teacher will also be of benefit. All of this is best managed in a multidisciplinary voice clinic. Singers should seek a referral to their nearest clinic.

> I've got a sore throat and I just have to sing—will I destroy my voice?

Answered by Christopher Chang, MD, Board-Certified Otolaryngology Head & Neck Surgeon

It depends which kind of sore throat you have—there are different issues for different kinds of sore throats. Some require a mandatory voice rest otherwise there is a risk of permanent vocal damage. Other kinds may have only a short-term adverse impact without risk of "voice destruction."

From a singer's perspective, sore throat issues can be divided into a vocal cord issue and a non-vocal cord issue.

If the sore throat is due to a problem not related to the vocal cord, singing may not necessarily injure the vocal cord. However, a sore throat can interfere with proper singing technique and introduce muscle tension to the voicebox leading to vocal problems including hoarseness and pain with singing. Once bad technique leading to bad muscle memory occurs, it can take a couple of months to "relearn" good singing habits. It is best to treat the sore throat (whether due to strep throat, reflux, pharyngitis or viral infection) before it interferes with singing technique.

Now, if the sore throat involves your vocal cords, then you could risk a significant vocal injury that may put you out of commission anywhere from a month to a year (or even longer). Sore throats due to a vocal cord source can be due to laryngitis, vocal cord hemorrhage, and even cancer if persistent. Vocal cord nodules, cysts, and polyps typically are painless. However, muscle tension to compensate for vocal cord nodules, cysts, and polyps can cause a sore throat indirectly.

If a singer has an upcoming performance, then an ear, nose and throat doctor (ENT) can evaluate where and what is causing a sore throat. If it is just a mild infection, you might receive antibiotics and decongestants. If there is redness and swelling then it will be time to evaluate the importance of the performance and discuss the risks involved. If there are millions of dollars at stake (not to mention a career opportunity), then you might be asked to consider steroids—if you do take these, then you will definitely need to rest your voice afterwards. The best option is that you forgo the performance.

In a worst case scenario a performance must be cancelled when there is the presence of a severe laryngitis with a large blood vessel present which risks vocal cord hemorrhage or the presence of a vocal cord ulcer.

My recommendation is that you see a good ear, nose and throat doctor and get your voice box examined. Skip the GP (if you can) and go straight to an ENT—they are the only ones qualified to actually look at your voice box.

> Can't I just take a pill and sound better?

Answered by Sara Harris, co-founder of the Voice Research Society and past President of the British Voice Association

I love the quote about a woman who asks a New York cabbie for directions, "Young man, how do you get to Carnegie Hall?" He answers: "Lady, you gotta practice!" There is no drug that can make you sing better because singing is like any other skill: It has to be learned. Learning skills involve creating new neurological pathways in the brain by repeating patterns of movement over and over again. It takes a lot of time to create new healthy vocal habits that are stable and that you can fall back upon in times of trouble.

In my work as a specialist speech and language therapist I try to help people avoid the need for drugs. Instead they learn to use their voices more efficiently to resolve problems when they've "lost the plot" and stop them relapsing in the future. It may be that infections, vocal fatigue or misuse have led to tension and a disconnection between the breath and the body. Frequently emotional distress will upset the voice and can sometimes even reduce people to a whisper.

When these things happen, I work to re-build their speaking technique from the ground up—this takes practice rather than drugs.

Sometimes drugs are necessary. I work with other medical specialists (my husband is a laryngologist) and there are times when a singer needs antibiotics or help with asthma, allergies or acid indigestion. In these cases it would be an ENT Surgeon or GP who would prescribe the necessary medicines. Occasionally singers with infections just cannot cancel a performance because there is no cover and their ENT surgeon may decide to prescribe a short course of steroids. However, these are only used in emergencies and should not be taken long term. Usually, if you take the time to develop good vocal technique you don't need to resort to medical drugs.

> Is there anything I shouldn't eat or drink?

Answered by Christopher Chang, MD, Board-Certified Otolaryngology Head & Neck Surgeon

As an Ear, Nose and Throat doctor (ENT), my big concern would be to avoid any food or drink that may lead to throat injury or dryness. The big culprits are caffeine and alcohol. I simply tell all of my singers, "Given you've chosen singing as your career, you unfortunately have to make changes to your lifestyle to avoid anything that might harm your voice—so no caffeine or alcohol." These both promote reflux and drying.

There are reasons, after all, that some swimmers place alcohol into their ears after swimming—it dries them out. Also, both caffeine and alcohol relax the lower sphincter of your stomach, making it easier for acid reflux to occur (see Action four). Of course alcohol helps some singers to feel more relaxed but if you are pursuing a professional career then you don't want to use drugs to maintain your performance; at some point such dependence will be more harmful than helpful.

Eat smaller amounts more frequently—this "grazing" style of eating is actually healthier than the usual three meals a day.

***—Dr. Anthony F. Jahn:** MD, internationally renowned otolaryngologist*

Taking care of your vocal apparatus involves drinking plenty of water. With this "engine oil" running through your system, your next task is to avoid any food products that exaggerate reflux—fatty, spicy, and acidic foods. Avoid eating or drinking anything within three hours of going to sleep. Singers who have a stomach full of pizza and coke when they lie down to sleep will find that their voice is "rougher" the next day with reflux. Having said this, there are many vocalists who do all the right things and still need to take extra precautionary measures against reflux such as tilting their bed so that their head is slightly elevated.

In terms of your performance, my basic suggestion is to not eat and drink to the point that you are full—treat yourself like an athlete. Athletes will never "pig out" on the day of their race—they may do so a day or two before, but on the day of the race they keep it "light."

> What is a node?

Answered by Ingo R. Titze, PhD, one of the world's leading voice scientists and Executive Director of the National Center for Voice and Speech, Utah

Nodes (or nodules) usually come in pairs. These are little bumps created by the tissue of your vocal folds colliding with each other. Think of hand clapping. If you were to clap continuously for 5-minutes you would develop a stinging sensation. You would actually need to find another way to clap, perhaps on your wrists or the back of your hands.

The skin of our vocal folds can actually take a lot of "claps." We've carried out extensive research in this area and have learned that for a busy schoolteacher in a public school, someone who may be speaking in monologue for six to seven hours per day, there can be as many as a million or more vocal fold collisions. As those collisions become stronger, there are ultimately reactions to it; tissues create their own protection. This protection begins as a calloused, thickened area with fluid in it. Later this becomes filled with a fibrous material. All of this is a natural way of the vocal fold protecting itself; however, the result is the production of an ugly unwanted sound.

Nodes shouldn't be confused with "polyps." A polyp is a larger growth and is only on one side of the larynx. These may originate from a blockage of a liquid or a ruptured blood vessel. When a part of the vocal fold becomes irritated, the body sends more and more fluid to that area; this fluid becomes an encapsulated bump that flops around on the vocal fold.

> I have to get a scope—I'm terrified! What will it be like?

Answered by The Ultimate Team

First, congratulate yourself. Instead of wandering around in a haze wondering what may be wrong with your voice, you are about to get some facts. We thought the best thing would be for you to hear from a singer who's had this done:

> When I had my first scope they put it down my nose. It's pretty uncomfortable! It's a thin, firm cable with a miniaturized camera on the end. They sprayed anaesthetic inside my nose to help with the pain. But even with this, it still felt painful, weird and my eyes watered. Mind you, I have pretty small nasal passages and other singers with larger passages may not feel pain at all.
>
> The ENT has done this procedure a million times before, so he coached me well: relax, breathe deeply, etc. I encouraged myself with some positive self-talk. The result: yes, I had nodules and I needed to take vocal rest. I took the vocal rest, went back for another scope (!) and was told that the nodules were gone. I was glad, of course, but my voice still wasn't sounding good. I asked about this, but this ENT did not have a specialization in the singing voice so wasn't able to give me any advice.

So, I asked him to refer me to a different ENT who was recommended by many singers I know. This time the scope wasn't put down my nose (hurray!) but was on a rigid "stick" that went to the back of my mouth. This ENT asked me to sing as he made a high-speed video; in fact, he "televised" what he saw for me! It was fascinating.

He had a better answer to my question; he said that my range was likely reduced because of stiffness and/or scar tissue on the vocal folds, perhaps exacerbated by some acid reflux (suggested by areas of redness). I did a test for reflux and followed this by seeing a speech language therapist.

> My ears are ringing from tonight's performance. Will they bounce back?

Answered by Anthony F. Jahn, MD, internationally renowned otolaryngologist with appointments at Columbia University, the Metropolitan Opera and the Lincoln Center

The short answer is: usually yes, but not always. Loud sounds, whether noise or music, traumatize the inner ears. One effect of such trauma is that the circulation to the inner ear goes into spasm, and the hair cells of the cochlea get less oxygen. They temporarily stop working, and you develop hearing loss and ringing (tinnitus).

If you are healthy, the traumatizing sound exposure is not too loud or prolonged, and you don't do it too often, both hearing loss and tinnitus should recover. However, if you do this often enough, the temporary threshold shift (hearing loss) and tinnitus may become permanent. Other factors, such as genetics and smoking may also play a role, so we don't know exactly how many times you can traumatize your inner ears before permanent changes occur.

Although there is some animal research on medications that may prevent damage from such noise trauma, the best current advice is to always protect your ears. Special musicians' earplugs which have a high fidelity (flat) frequency response can be used to effectively attenuate the loud sounds (either 15 or 25 decibel filters can be used) without distorting the music. I strongly advise you to protect your ears, since once tinnitus and hearing loss become permanent; there is no treatment short of hearing aids.

> In my musical scene everyone smokes—what's the best way to prevent this from getting into my system?

Answered by Dr. Anthony F. Jahn, MD, internationally renowned otolaryngologist with appointments at Columbia University the, Metropolitan Opera and Lincoln Centre

Short of posting a prominent "Do Not Smoke" sign, there are several measures you can take to reduce any irritation or damage to the voice from smoky performing environments.

First, try to breathe through your nose as much as possible. Obviously when you sing or speak, you will preferentially inhale through your mouth, so, unless you need to mingle with the customers, try to limit your non-singing vocal activities. If you have a quieter dressing room where you can retire between sets, do so—and while there, drink some water!

Second, use a saline nasal spray frequently between sets. This moisturizes the nasal lining and helps trap irritating particles in the nasal mucus, before they reach your larynx.

Next, stay well hydrated: drink lots of water to moisturize your pharyngeal and laryngeal mucous membranes; this also helps to clear out inhaled debris. Limit your alcohol intake, since alcohol dehydrates you and, along with loud social speaking and singing, increases possible damage to the throat (have you ever been to a quiet bar?).

Finally, you may consider inhaling some steam at the end of your evening, either from a vaporizer, or as part of a long hot shower. This again wets the mucous membranes, and allows the little hairs (cilia) to work more effectively to clear out any inhaled debris.

And, it goes without saying: don't hang out at the stage door with the smokers!

> My throat doesn't hurt, but my voice often gets hoarse and feels sluggish.

Answered by Michael J. Pitman MD, Director of the Division of Laryngology at The New York Eye and Ear Infirmary

There are so many things this could be—we might see twenty different people in a week who will say the same thing—and there could be twenty different answers! It could be allergies, voice overuse, reflux, nodules, polyps, atypical swelling—any of these and others. This is why I would want to see you and examine your throat and vocal folds in order to determine the exact cause and formulate a plan to treat it. What is important, as a professional voice user, is that you do not wait until you have voice loss or raspiness before you see a laryngologist. Any change in voice that lasts more than two weeks is not normal and should be checked. Such symptoms would include vocal strain, breathiness, fatigue or loss of range. To pick up changes early you should engage in self-monitoring by performing the same vocal warm up every morning. Because you perform the same vocal exercise at the same time of day, every day, you'll be able to detect small changes in the voice early and care for them before they become a big problem.

> My voice has good days and bad days—what's going on?

Answered by Tom Harris, MA, FRCS, Hon. FRCSLT, Consultant ENT Surgeon

Well, if you are having good days and bad days it is unlikely to be the result of nodes or a polyp. However, my first reaction as an ENT is that I want to see what is up with your vocal folds—so I want to stick a scope in your mouth to see down your throat and take a good look. You could be experiencing reflux, which paints your throat with acid from time to time (see Action four above). But your challenge could also be the result of a work schedule where your muscles are constantly tight. Stress and overuse of the voice often lies behind an inefficient use of the voice. Think of runners in a marathon. If you watch these runners pass by the 5-mile mark, most of them will be in fine form, their running technique appears refined and effective. But take a look at the same runners at the 20-mile mark—many of these will be running using whatever muscles are still functioning! This less efficient use of muscles leads to early exhaustion and possible injury. The same is true with the voice. If you can't relax between your vocal efforts, tired vocal muscles will produce inefficient voicing with early fatigue from which it will take a longer time to recover—this could be the source of your "bad days."

> My voice just isn't what it used to be—and no doctor can help—should I just give up?

Answered by Bernie Shaw, lead singer of Uriah Heep

A few years ago I woke up and was unable to hit my top notes. The top end of my voice is an incredibly popular part of my music and I couldn't reach it. It started vibrating with a weird oscillation. The usual symptom for this is nodes—but even the best laryngologists couldn't find any. Some medical specialists even said, "You're 35 years old and you've had a good run at this—perhaps you can consider another career." I thought to myself, "You're joking—I've got years to go!"

> *I start drinking water in the afternoon so I'm ready at nine to sing.*
>
> ***—Tom Lang:*** *singer-guitarist and product manager, TC-Helicon*

And then I found this excellent ENT surgeon—Tom Harris. He wouldn't give up. He gave me a laryngoscopy up the nose and down the larynx—I could barely breathe. He had me sing in my falsetto and this pulled my vocal folds up slightly and that is when a polyp could be seen. Then it was the matter of a small operation and a week's recovery. I was back on stage.

> Is getting surgery done on the voice "bad"?

Answered by Dr. Robert W. Bastian, MD, Board Certified Otolaryngologist and founder of the Bastian Voice Institute

Of course, the best strategy for singers is to avoid ever needing surgery through a kind of preventative maintenance: good technique, hydration, treatment of medical issues, self-monitoring, and appropriate periods of voice rest—all of the central themes covered in this chapter. However, there are times when a surgical intervention is not only necessary, but may be a career saving option.

I recently met with a singer (details have been altered to protect identity) who had worked hard for many years on her career—and she just had a major break: a tour in Asia that included a dozen performances and a recording contract. However, she had severe hoarseness and was diagnosed with a "hemorrhagic polyp." This is like a blood blister on the edge of the vocal fold. She felt that he was going to lose the opportunity of a lifetime.

To use an analogy, the hemorrhagic polyp is like a deep pothole containing a puddle. The "nonsurgical" option is to close the road for many months hoping that "naturally-occurring" dust, leaves, and litter will gradually repair the defect. It makes more sense to call out the road crew.

Some singers simply can't wait and rest the voice months and months—especially when they know that at the end of the wait, the polyp may still be there. That's why vocal fold microsurgery can be the best way forward, as it has been for the singer above. The problem can be repaired and performance can resume within weeks.

Singers naturally recoil from the idea of surgery, because they think that a scar will always result. But consider: do you have a visible or otherwise detectable "scar" every time you scrape a knuckle? That is the magnitude of the "wound" after expert microsurgery. Furthermore, it can be the case that not doing surgery can damage a career, due to cancellations and/or substandard performance capability. For otherwise irreversible injuries, surgery must remain an option! Vocal fold microsurgery is performed through a laryngoscope (a hollow, lighted cylinder placed against carefully protected upper teeth and base of tongue), while you are under general anaesthesia (completely asleep) in a day-surgery center.

Near-total silence for four days postoperatively is followed by gradual resumption of voice use on an individualized schedule, leading to return to performance in about six weeks (four in a pinch). The singer referenced above already has a dramatically improved voice, only one week postoperatively, and should be ready for her performance schedule in a few more weeks.

Obviously, the singer with a hemorrhagic polyp will also need a pre-operative session of voice therapy along with a few similar sessions postoperatively. This work teaches the singer what regimen to follow vocally as the vocal fold heals; basic ways of reducing risk of future injury; and how to monitor for the earliest most subtle evidence of re-injury long before it interferes with performance or even becomes another vocal "crisis."

> Is Cortisone the miracle cure I've been looking for to get me through my next few performances?

Answered by Daniel Borch, PhD, one of Sweden's most established vocal coaches, Head of the Voice Centre

Cortisone is often perceived by professional singers to be a wonder drug, but abuse is widespread. Cortisone is a drug that is used to suppress the reactions of the body's immune system. The body makes its own cortisone in the form of cortisol—a so-called "stress hormone" that is secreted by the adrenal glands and which plays an important role in our body's defence system. The natural reactions of our immune system in the event of allergies or vocal fold strain result in swelling of the skin or mucosa.

Cortisone is used to suppress this reaction. The dose prescribed is often many times higher than the amount produced by the body. If a singer's vocal folds are inflamed due to over exertion or allergies, cortisone can alleviate the symptoms and allow them to get through a vital performance such as a TV show, opening night or other important showcase. Cortisone is only available on prescription and is usually taken twice on the day of performance.

But we must remember that Cortisone represses the body's reaction to something it is not happy about. Swelling occurs for a reason. The body is expressing its displeasure with something we have inhaled, eaten or exposed our muscles or mucous membranes to. It is imperative that we listen to our bodies and avoid these situations in the future. If you have a cold, by all means use cold medicine to relieve the symptoms, but do not use cortisone. Cortisone represses the body's immune system—as we will no longer have all of our immune resources at our disposal, we may actually get worse instead of better.

The unpleasant side effects of cortisone use are many, not to mention that it may lead to vocal injury. Because the swelling has been medically alleviated, there is a risk that the vocalist will no longer feel when they are over-exerting themselves. This may lead to more serious swelling. Vocalists who take cortisone even though they are healthy and experience better sensations when singing, may be suffering from mild, chronic inflammation caused by the frequent use of their voice. In this case I recommend that they work on their vocal technique and get to know their limits.

In conclusion, I would encourage you, whenever possible, to cancel performances when you are sick. Few performances are so important that they will have a long term effect on your career.

Moreover, the goal is to be able to sing for many years so it is important to cultivate good vocal habits, know your limits and have the foresight to say "no" to gigs that are beyond your capacity or when you are sick or burnt-out. In the event of a major crisis such as a TV performance and where your voice is strained but you are not sick, you may turn to cortisone—as a last resort.

CHAPTER 12

The Unforgettable Vocal Connection

Be remembered after the show.

Get rid of all the stuff you are hiding behind and let me have the full experience: words, song—and YOU.

—John Kjøller of Basix, Best European Album

"All the greatest singers didn't just sing one way. At different times their voices were guttural, clean, whispering, torn up. They were in agony. They were in love."

—Ron "Bumblefoot" Thal of Guns N' Roses

The Unforgettable Vocal Connection

Be remembered after the show.

Actions:

1. Embrace the Moment
2. Embrace the Audience
3. Embrace the Song
4. Embrace Who You Are
5. Embrace Your Soul

Frequently Asked Questions:

» *People say, "Put your heart into it," but I'm just not sure what that means.*

» *How can I get the audience on their feet?*

» *When I perform I want to live on the edge! How can I get the audience to come with me?*

» *I feel like a fool when I talk between songs.*

» *I'm not getting much of a response when I perform. What can I do?*

» *How can I sing from my heart if I don't really believe in my song?*

» *I've been told I'm good, but no one's ever told me that my music has moved them. What am I missing?*

» *I always lose my connection with the audience when I've made a blunder.*

» *Is there really such a thing as an X-factor or indefinable star quality? If so, how can I get that?*

» *My voice sounds similar to a very well known artist—so how can I stand out?*

» *Some singers look so "free" and "fluid" in their performances. How can I be like this?*

» *When I go to a performance by my favourite artist, I'm just so moved—what is she doing that I'm not?*

» *I asked three people what I was missing in my music—one said it's my look. One said I was pitchy. One said my voice needed to sound more cool. Are all of them right?*

» *How do I get that powerful sound and presence of the greatest rock stars?*

Action 1: Embrace the Moment

Be as close to "magic," "God" and "perfection" as possible.

Singers and musicians are some of the most driven, courageous people on the face of the earth. They deal with more day-to-day rejection in one year than most people do in a lifetime.

Every day, they face the financial challenge of living a freelance lifestyle, the disrespect of people who think they should get "real jobs," and their own fear that they'll never work again. Every day, they have to ignore the possibility that the vision they have dedicated their lives to is a pipe dream. With every note they stretch themselves, emotionally and physically, risking criticism and judgment. With every passing year, many of them watch as the other people their age achieve the predictable milestones of normal life—the car, the family, the house, the nest egg.

Why?

Because musicians and singers are willing to give their entire lives to a moment—to that melody, that lyric, that chord, or that interpretation that will stir the audience's soul. Singers and musicians are beings who have tasted life's nectar in that crystal moment when they poured out their creative spirit and touched another's heart.

In that instant, they were as close to magic, God, and perfection as anyone could ever be. And in their own hearts, they know that to dedicate oneself to that moment is worth a thousand lifetimes.

—David Ackert: American entrepreneur, business development expert and actor

> *There is nothing that gives a fan a warmer feeling than when an artist speaks and jokes with them. I know one artist who, when he sees a fan get out a phone, invites them up on stage so that he can say "hi" to this fan's friend! Everyone has a laugh and thinks of the artist as "one of us."*
>
> ***—Chris Maltese:** artist manager, formerly a senior producer for MTV*

Action 2: Embrace the Audience

Love them—without showing off and without apology.

To truly engage an audience, you must do one specific thing: Love them! Love isn't merely a "feeling" you experience towards a person as much as it is an action towards a person that elicits feelings from the object of your love. Whether it be romantic, friendship, family or strangers, you must be vulnerable and risk rejection, ridicule and an un-requited love that can be crushing!

If you look at yourself when performing, rather than looking at your audience—really looking at them—you fall into the trap of self-absorption. This trap locks you into the coffin of your selfishness where you have little life to share with others.

Genuine and vulnerable! This is what audiences are begging for. Great vocal training will give you the confidence to forget about your voice, forget about yourself and focus purely on loving the people in front of you. This means giving yourself to them in a conversation that is in song form. Talk to them musically! This means that your songs are less "diva opportunities" and more "genuine opportunities" to have meaningful conversations to connect you with your audience. When you sing, you are essentially acting, only on pitch. The best actors are the believable actors.

Look into the eyes of certain individuals you connect with and paralyze them with passion. They want this and will thank you for making them almost nervous, or even better—giddy. They come to love you because you loved them first!

—Brett Manning: leading US Vocal Coach to many of today's top artists

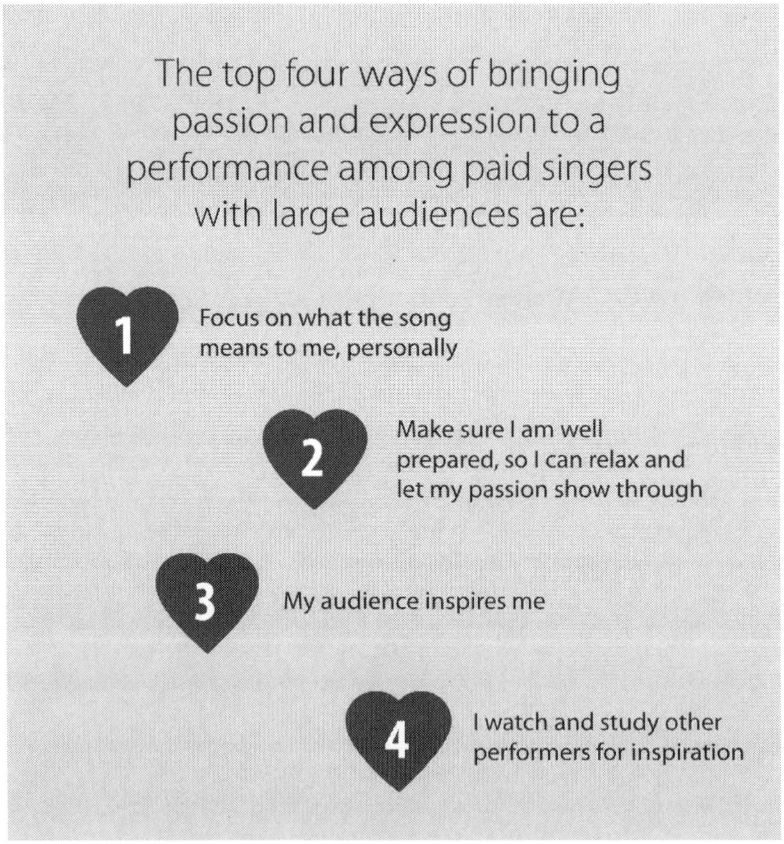

—from the 2012-2013 TC-Helicon survey of 1,000 singers

Action 3: Embrace the Song

You have a voice that can profoundly connect with every human being—and in which the faintest amount of bullshit can be detected.

When great singers get on stage something extraordinary happens: they don't think about what they are singing; they actually become the song.

I have seen this with all of the great singers I've worked with: Dame Shirley Bassey, Lionel Richie, The Bee Gees, Sir Elton John, Lady Gaga and so many others. All of them–automatically and without thinking–embody the song they are singing. They become the song for us. In fact, our love for the song is indistinguishable from our having been drawn into the personality of the vocalist who is singing it.

Now, how do these singers achieve this unforgettable connection? Vocal performance is a strange science. There is no simple system to ensure a powerful performance. But there are some things all vocalists can do to make this powerful identification more likely.

I always say to aspiring singers that the first thing to do when you are working on a song is to sit down in your favorite chair with your favorite drink beside you. Then, write down the lyrics (from memory if you can) with a wide space between each line. In the space between the lines, write the outline of a screen play that gives you a story, a narrative that could accompany these lyrics and which you can access at any point in time when you are singing the song. This helps you to place the song into your deepest memory.

> *An exercise: sing your song with nonsense vowels. Can you still convey its meaning? Its emotional tone?*
>
> ***—Mister Tim:*** *viral video star*

The wonderful thing about songs is that they are a fusion of lyrics and music; one can think of the lyrics as the specifics of the story and the music as the emotion that underlies this story. What you need to find is your own personal connection to this underlying emotion. That's what bringing your story to the song does.

You see, if you've memorized the words and the music without a deeper emotional connection, this is like having the music in your random access memory but not in your hard drive.

I was working with the singer Simone Simone, daughter of Nina Simone, and we were preparing for an audition for the Vegas production of the musical, *We Will Rock You.* She was actually going to be auditioning the song "No One But You" in front of Roger Taylor of Queen and Ben Elton, the writer of the musical. Can you imagine the pressure? We prepared by trying to connect with the basic emotion of the song–which is about the loss of someone dear. Simone's mother had recently died and I asked her if there was some way that she could access that emotion of loss and put it into the song. She brought up her raw feelings and sang the song with an exposed heart, crying buckets as she sang. It was such a powerful emotional experience that we actually had to discuss how to place some limitations on her access to that emotional reality. When she came to the audition and sang the song the following day, she was offered the part instantly. Sadly it didn't work out and she never performed in the show but Simone is definitely a singer who knows how to bring her deepest self to her music.

Of course we must remember that everyone has a bad day. I was watching the Live Aid concert in 1986 when Phil Collins was performing in London. And then he hopped on a Concorde Jet to New York to perform again on the same day! In the New York performance there was a point in his second song where he hesitated. You could see an expression flash across his face that seemed to say, "Oh shit—I've forgotten the words!" Next, he stumbled on the piano and you could see his expression now reflect: "Not only have I forgotten my words, but now I've forgotten my notes!" All of this happened in milliseconds; then he was back on track. His recovery was almost instant and the remainder of his performance was powerful.

I credit the speed of this recovery to the fact that he had done something more than memorize the words and notes to his music. Like all great singers, he had achieved a deep emotional connection with the song, too deep to be stopped by a challenge to his memory.

—Mike Dixon: musical supervisor, director, arranger and composer for TV and stage

Action 4: Embrace Who You Are

It's time to pay attention to the one thing you have that others don't: you.

> *Even in literature and art, no man who bothers about originality will ever be original; whereas if you simply try to tell the truth (without caring two pence how often it has been told before) you will, nine times out of ten, become original without ever having noticed it.*
> ***—C.S. Lewis (shared by Kimbra)***

No one else shares the same set of influences or even anatomy as you. It takes bravery and honesty to explore all of these aspects of yourself. You must even risk sounding a little odd at times if that's what the emotion of the song requires.

I enjoyed a lot of traditional Maori music when I was growing up in New Zealand. There is a certain percussive instinct in their style which likely rubbed off on me at a subconscious level and influenced the way I explored my voice. Everyone's unique environment and upbringing leaves a mark on the way they approach music.

Your voice is not limited, however, to only one way of operating or a certain "range." Becoming intimate with your own anatomy as a singer and broadening the spectrum of textures you can create will let you penetrate emotion in a truthful way.

It all starts with an exploration of your instrument. For me, this meant acquiring both influences and tools that allowed me to stretch myself vocally. At one time I listened to a lot of Jazz and Broadway music. Then I discovered artists like Jeff Buckley, Nina Simone, Mike Patton, Kate Bush, Elliott Smith, and Prince. These artists had distinct thumbprints to their voice and were tapping into something I'd never experienced before. I then discovered artists from Africa and Pakistan who also inspired and influenced me. Just like a guitarist who learns a Jimi Hendrix solo, when you copy the way someone else sings, it forces you to open up undiscovered facets of your own voice and new ways of using it.

Once you have explored all the influences that inspire you and have discovered the range of textures your voice can create, forget about them all. In order to channel emotion truthfully to an audience, you cannot consciously think about your sound or your identity. Embrace your own conviction and your own connection to a lyric and soundscape. Let go of any expectations that dictate what you "should" sound like and connect entirely with the song from your unique cultural and personal makeup—this allows for something "beyond" to take place, and will translate to the audience more effectively than any vocal trickery.

The journey may start with a study of great singers but it should always end with self-forgetfulness that only comes with a complete letting go of intellect. Only then can we embrace our true selves and find a conviction that is completely our own. And we do it without even thinking about whether it is original or not.

—Kimbra, Grammy award winning vocal artist

Action 5: Embrace Your Soul

Make the move from being an entertainer to being an artist.

You can be an entertainer any day, but to be an artist you have to be able to paint a picture. It is your interpretation that is key. It has to be YOUR interpretation; it can't be anyone else's. I'm not only talking about original music—you can take someone else's song and paint it your way. Remember: an entertainer gets on stage and does what they're told. An artist gets on stage and loses themselves in their music.

People have given me all sorts of advice over the years: "Don't wear a hat." (I wear the hat), "Move around on stage more." (I don't), "Sing more with your eyes open." (I'll keep my eyes closed if I feel like it). It got really bad when I was pursuing the major labels—they wanted to rob me of my artist's soul and leave me wearing a chicken suit. You see, there's a lot of greed in the music industry and labels will only want you to do what they think will make money—even if it's not authentic for you.

Yet, the stage is my special place. It is there that I get into my soul. I'm not worried about what other people are thinking, because if I do that, I'll mess up. Even when I've been depressed, I've just kept singing, digging down more deeply into myself. The funny thing is that sometimes the sadder I've been, the more people have felt drawn to my music. In those times, I would experience the stage as my safety net: people can't come up there—I can do what I want in that space and people can watch. And if I am really feeling my music, they are feeling something as well.

So get up there and dig down deep into your soul. Sing from your heart. The whole point of singing is to get something off your chest, to get out there what you've been through.

I'm not denying the importance of rehearsing—this develops your "muscle memory." When you have your song "down," you can really take it to the next level, the place where you don't need to think about your technique, where you are free to dig down into your emotions.

There will always be something special about someone who can dig down into their soul and pull out the truth. Be that someone.

—Michael Grimm: winner of America's Got Talent, Season Five

Frequently Asked Questions

> People say, "Put your heart into it," but I'm just not sure what that means.

Answered by Mark De-Lisser, vocal coach with The Voice, UK and the ACM Gospel Choir; has worked with Jessie J, Olly Murs and more

I think this story will help you.

I was once invited to an acting school to see if I could heighten the singing abilities of a young group of acting students.

There was this one guy who seemed to make no improvement from week to week. His notes were mostly out of tune and all of my technique and improvisational ideas did not seem to make any difference.

In fact, his singing was so bad that the other students would laugh under their breath every time he got up to sing. He was not making any connection with the music—and he certainly was not reaching anyone's heart.

Finally we came to our last session—it was also the last time we would ever be meeting before this student graduated. When it came time for him to sing, I had an idea.

I chose a female from the group, at random, and asked her to sit in a chair in the middle of the room. Then I asked this student to get up and sing a love song. I told him, "I want you to sing this love song to this girl. I want you to sing it to her as if you mean every word." I gave her strict instructions not to react to his singing or any of his movements, to just close her eyes and allow him to sing his song.

It's difficult for me to convey the power of what happened next. He opened his mouth and sang as he never had before. In fact, we all began to cry—even the guys in the group. He had tapped into an emotional connection, the depth of which we hadn't yet heard from anyone else in the group.

Was his voice technically perfect? No. His pitching and tone was better than it ever had been, but you wouldn't say it was a "great" voice.

It was, however, a "connected" voice.

The song ended and the room was still. I can still feel the power of that moment.

After the class, this same guy ran up to me and said, "I want to thank you for what you've done."

I told him that I couldn't accept thanks; it was all his own doing.

"No, you don't get it," he persisted, "You see, when I came to school three years ago, I fell in love with that very same girl you asked to sit in the chair. I have loved her every single day for three years and I longed to say something … do something … but never did—until today."

It turns out that he believed this might be the only time that he would ever tell her how he felt. So, he sang from his heart. And no one in that class has ever forgotten.

Singing from your heart means that you give your song everything you've got. This is the effort you would put into anything—or anyone—you really loved.

If you open up to the feelings and emotions in your heart, they will inform your voice.

> How can I get the audience on their feet?

Answered by Ben "the Verse" Mount, DJ, rapper, producer and MC of Pendulum

Getting a crowd psyched up and having a great time depends first of all, on your music. As the MC of Pendulum, I build on what the music is doing. I let the music do the speaking, and only speak up to the crowd when it is needed. Our music is so aggressive that "less" can be "more," when it comes to getting the crowd going.

It is also important to "read" the crowd. I look for a small group of people who are reacting well to what I'm doing. I call this a "pocket of violence." I focus my attention on one of these pockets and once they get worked up, I step back a bit. The vibe spreads and pretty soon the whole crowd is going. Remember to balance this out by focusing on the crowd as a whole—including the back of the room.

Your show must have peaks and valleys. No one can just go crazy for the whole time. You need the valleys where things calm down so you can make the most out of the peaks.

If you are not getting the crowd reaction you want, then I would say make some new music. It is the music itself that must induce the response you are hoping for. Each genre implies a certain crowd behavior. Metal has moshing and rap has the hand-in-the-air thing. If you want your crowd to dance, then the first thing you have to do is make sure your music is right for that.

No matter how raw and aggressive your on-stage persona is, you always have to stay in control. With all the excitement of performing live, you will be tempted to push your voice—but that won't sound good. Always remember your diction, your delivery and your physical presence. Be psyched up but be in control even when your persona isn't.

> When I perform I want to live on the edge! How can I get the audience to come with me?

Answered by Val Emmich, singer-songwriter, hailed by the New York Times as "a rocker who rocks to his own beat"

Live on the edge. Live with passion and authenticity. Champion causes and issues you really believe in. Bring all of this into your music and performances. People will find that irresistible. But not all people. You must realize that some people will be scared of it. But those who are drawn to your passion will be with you for the long haul.

I don't want to live in the "middle." You can find the "middle" in every art form. It's the place of business, the place where people sell. It involves compromising ideas so that they're palatable for the masses. It means making music that everyone can love—instantly. It involves thinking about what people like. "Think" shouldn't come into it. Your music should come from "feel." It's not something you're trying to scientifically compute.

Coming at your music from the "middle" becomes predictable and stale. You might do okay for a little while, but you won't be remembered. You have to decide, "Do I want to be remembered?" Or, "Do I just want to be in the game where most people seem to be playing?" The world is filled with so much content that it's easy to be drowned out. So, you could argue that the "middle" is the worst place to be. The edge is better!

> *It's the emotional connection that wins me over every time. I want the singer to make me hear the song like I've never heard it before. That's the difference between a good singer and a great singer*
> ***—Juliet Russell:** vocal coach for BBC 1's The Voice*

When it comes to performances, I feel that I have an obligation to give audiences an honest experience rather than a recycled one. I want those who see my show in Pennsylvania, for example, to experience a different show than the one I put on in Chicago. So, I'm open to going to "places" in a performance that aren't planned. I've stopped my band mid-song, changed the order of the set-list, decided all of a sudden to do one part of the show with just guitar and me—these reflect honest impulses, coming from a deep, internal place. Of course, I work very hard at rehearsing, but then you get to that place where you don't have to think any more—muscle memory is strong—and that's where the fun begins, the unexpected. Embrace your fears. Go to that place of vulnerability and people will respond.

> I feel like a fool when I talk between songs.

Answered by Mark Baxter, acclaimed vocal coach with Aerosmith, Journey, Goo Goo Dolls and many others

Then don't. I know that sounds cold. There are those singers who have the gift of gab like David Lee Roth, Bono and Springsteen. They go off on a 20-minute monolog and it's hilarious, righteous and brilliant. But there are many artists who say nothing in their concerts; they simply let the music do the talking. It can actually make your music more powerful. You see, if you're uncomfortable in any way on stage it spreads to the audience; so play to your strengths.

Singers who aren't good with the gab need to prepare a set where there's a three-song "medley" before any talking whatsoever. At the first break (or when a string on a guitar needs to be changed), keep your speaking simple: "Thanks for coming out tonight." I don't recommend asking questions like, "How's everybody doing tonight?" because the answer (or lack of one) may work against you!

Don't worry about some silence. When you're on stage a minute of silence can feel like an hour because adrenaline is pumping through you. It's the same response if you're in an auto accident—all of a sudden the world spins in slow motion. This is also why bands often speed up tempos when playing live. Just remember that's not the perspective of the audience—they'll be fine with some silence.

Have you ever gone to a concert and timed the distance between songs? Of course not! If a show feels like it's dragging it's always because you're not into the music. People that are into your band are anticipating the next song—so the dead space seems much shorter to them. Unless, of course, you succumb to your anxiety and start mumbling something awkward into the microphone. To avoid incriminating yourself just remember what cops always say as they slap on the handcuffs, "You have the right to remain silent. Anything you say may be used against you!"

> I'm not getting much of a response when I perform. What can I do?

Answered by Katherine Ellis, hit dance music songwriter, vocalist and performer

The audience actually wants you to tell them what to do. They want to sing, they want to clap, they want to be entertained. Take the bull by the horns and tell them what you want them to do. It is your job. I often start a show with, "Helloooo London!!!" (or whatever city I may be in). I throw my arms out so as to invite them to welcome me. If they don't, I will tell them, "This is where you clap, come on everybody! Yeah!" In my early days, I'd worry: what if they hate me? What if they don't do what I say? But they will. And if they won't—I will get off that stage and will go into the audience and make a spectacle of somebody. I will even say, "Don't make me come down there. Because I will!"

> How can I sing from my heart if I don't really believe in my song?

Answered by Mark De-Lisser, vocal coach with The Voice, UK and the ACM Gospel Choir; has worked with Jessie J, Olly Murs and more

I am a vocal artist with a strong Gospel music background leading a group of young white, secular, urban professionals singing gospel music. So, how can you sing Gospel music with power and passion if you are an atheist?

Your first step in this journey is to try to understand the writer. Your second step is to make our own interpretation of the song, to see the song reflecting your own truth.

Let's stay with the example of Gospel music. This music came out of the "spirituals," songs that reflected all of the oppression and suffering of the people at that time. When it moved into the churches, becoming "Gospel music," that original foundation wasn't lost—it gradually shifted to themes of overcoming evil and reflecting the struggle to do good instead of evil.

When I bring this music to my Gospel choir, I invite them to take a third step of interpretation. Most of my singers have never been to church and the concept of "God" seems airy-fairy. So, I ask them to find their own standpoint. Maybe "God" for them is a loved one, anyone who gives support or strength to get through tough things—your support network. I tell them, "Whatever your belief, put it into this song. If, instead of God, you really want to praise Allah, your wife, the Buddha, or your friend—put it into this song."

Your goal is to take the music you are singing right now, understand the writer, and then find a way for that song to reflect your own experiences and truths. Make your own act of interpretation.

Your voice understands your feelings. So, put your heart and soul into your song from where you are, rather than where other people expect you to be.

> I've been told I'm good, but no one's ever told me that my music has moved them. What am I missing?

Answered by Dan Bowling, Music Supervisor and Director in London and New York City, author of "Auditions Undressed"

Remember that it's about having a purpose and a clear direction with a song. I ask singers fundamental questions all the time: What are you trying to say with this song? Who are you saying it to? What is your reason for singing the song? Singers may impress me with show-stopping notes, but I can always tell if they haven't really thought about what it is that they want to express or the subtext or feeling that underlies any song lyric.

You can't be vague. Audiences intuitively pick up on this; they need to feel the core or the focus of what it is you want to express. Great singers are always connected to the thought behind the music and the lyrics. This same greatness can be yours as long as you remember to connect to the words as well as to the music.

A great exercise to help you connect emotionally to a song and audience is to separate the song lyrics from the music and practice both—independently of each other. If you can convince an audience of the truth of the words without the music or conversely, the beauty of the melody without the words, you'll instinctively be able to reunite lyric and tune in a new, cohesive and emotionally potent way.

> I always lose my connection with the audience when I've made a blunder.

Answered by Mary Black, leading Irish singer, renowned for her pure voice

I quickly realized that I had to be myself even if that meant tripping up over an introduction to a song or kicking over a glass of water mid performance. Audiences actually love the little quirky things that happen—even mistakes. These make the show unique, so find a way to work with whatever happens in your show and make sure you keep speaking and singing from your heart.

It is OK not to be perfect. To simply "be" your music and to be honest are what it's all about. Even now my voice is not the same as when I was starting out. There are some notes I can no longer hit. You have to remember that it's all about keeping the connection with yourself and your audience. That's the bottom line. If something beautiful comes out of your voice—that is the bonus.

> Is there really such thing as an X-factor or indefinable star quality? If so, how can I get that?

Answered by Brett Manning, leading US Vocal Coach to many of today's top artists

Some people are born with stardom but never actualize their true potential. They sound compelling with every syllable that pours out of them, but they lack discipline, desire and the training to take them to the next level. If you don't "want" what you have, you will never "use" what you have.

> *Singers always feel naked on stage; your job is to embrace that nakedness and go for it.*
>
> ***—Peter Hollens:** Pop Singer & Producer/Youtuber with over 175 million views*

There is however, a definitively learned element of charisma. This I know because I've repeatedly seen singers get this. What happens when you find your voice, explode past your limits and become the "boss" of your own abilities?

Charisma comes by way of confidence. Thus, the reason we see people change their personalities once they become stars. Suddenly they rise above their own personalities and no longer recognize the shy, timid and apologetic person they used to be. This process is done only when you coach the whole person—not merely the voice.

One thing you can do to get started on this process is to find a coach who knows how the voice functions properly, meaning: one who has the ability to find, build and stabilize your high notes—and a coach who connects with you on an emotional, spiritual and psychological level.

> My voice sounds similar to a very well known artist—so how can I stand out?

Answered by Brett Manning, leading US Vocal Coach to many of today's top artists

Typically, a singer gravitates towards their favorite artists. Therefore, multiple influences, a creative risk-taking personality and a diverse technique will allow you to have that mixture of tones that brings out the "cool-factor" that we all know is the true identity of every super-star. Either you're distinct or you're extinct.

One thing you can try out as you get on the road to your own voice is to vocalize closer to your own speaking voice. Avoid copying examples that are unnatural to your own propensities or make you feel insecure about your own "unique" sound. NEVER sing louder than you can comfortably and freely. Be confident in your personality and you will soar!

> Some singers look so "free" and "fluid" in their performances. How can I be like this?

Answered by W. Timothy Gallwey, million selling author of "The Inner Game of Tennis, co-author of "The Inner Game of Music"

There are so many similarities between performing in sports and in music. I learned this in tennis: where you doubt the proficiency of a particular shot, your muscles over-tighten and you tend to over-control the result. It is the same with singing. If you entertain doubts, your vocal apparatus will tighten in a way that makes the sound less pure and fulfills the prophecy of your doubt.

I was working on a PBS television special on the idea that the most important game is the "inner game," the ideas, thoughts and emotions that are going on inside our heads. I was working with a golfer who was expressing his belief in these ideas. Yet, he was obviously very tight as he held his club and there was this moment during his swing when, just for a quarter of a second, his face had a look of terror. I just asked him to be aware of the tightness of his grip and feel the changes in that tightness. He said, "I am trying to come around the ball." I said, I know what you are trying to do, but I just want you to be aware of the tightness of your grip. Getting that distinction between trying to fix things and the effort of being aware was such a huge thing for him; it took time to sink in. It is not just the intellectual decision but the willingness to let go and trust what will happen if you're conscious.

When it comes to singing, rather than trying hard to get certain things "right," put your focus on becoming aware of certain aspects of your singing. It might be worthwhile for singers to experiment with this approach in areas other than singing—in areas that have less consequence for you so that you get used to the process, such as your practice sessions.

In my family I would say, "Pay attention to your manners." And I meant just that. I just wanted my children to be aware. I was not saying, "Do this or that correctly." I just wanted them to pay attention. This was my way of communicating, "I trust that if you see what you are doing you will do what you need to do." One day my son asked me, "What's the point of good manners?" And I realized in that moment that I had never thought out the goal. The goal of singing is to sound beautiful, or bring the beauty of the voice into the world. What is the goal of manners? The goal of manners is to create a comfortable environment for eating a meal together.

You need to have a goal for your awareness if you are going to make an adjustment. In singing, the goal almost goes without saying. Focus on your goal and move from trying to be good to being more aware of certain aspects of your singing.

> When I go to a performance by my favorite artist, I'm just so moved—what is she doing that I'm not?

Answered by Noreen Smith, LA based singer, vocal technique instructor, choir director and music director

It takes most artists years to get to a place where they can totally transport their audience. It is a journey of working it out at open mics and developing musical maturity.

Ask yourself this question: what motivates me to perform? The performers that last are motivated by one thing: they want their audience to have the greatest time ever. Do you truly care about your fans getting lost in your songs and leaving their cares behind? Yes? Then your motivation is coming from the right place. In contrast, when artists only care about proving how amazing they are via the audience's affirmation, it leads down a path of desperation causing self-esteem issues, defensiveness, and emotional roller coaster rides. Healthy motivation means you are not depending on a big audience or lots of compliments. It means you are free to live in the moment—only then can you move your audience.

> *You have to dig deep to find what it is that moves you—once you are moved then you can transfer that to the listener and that is what it is all about.*
>
> ***—Mary Black:** leading Irish singer*

Having your motivation in the right place is essential, but not the only thing you need. A moving performance needs some layers. Play around with tone color (breathy/clear/cry), emphasis, vibrato, pronunciation and volume so you can paint mind-pictures with your voice. Carefully crafted layers allow you to tell your story and make an impact. Listen to Colbie Caillat's song, "Bubbly." She manages to deliver a moving performance despite the most ridiculous lyrics! How does she do that? Layers. When it comes to an artist like Adele, her lyrics alone can take your heart out and squeeze it like a kitchen sponge! Apply layers to those kinds of lyrics plus the right amount of vulnerability—amazing.

There is one final tool that helps you follow that north star of motivation and create those layers: vocal technique. The more knowledge and control you have of your voice, the more expressive you can be.

> I asked three people what I was missing in my music—one said it's my look. One said I was pitchy. One said my voice needed to sound more cool. Are all of them right?

Answered by Val Emmich, singer–songwriter, hailed by the New York Times as "a rocker who rocks to his own beat"

My answer: ask 100 people. It's great to get feedback, but you're really not learning much with only three pieces of feedback. Ask a lot of people and pay attention to the comments that keep coming back. Earlier in my career people kept saying, "Open your eyes when you sing." It was hard for me to do and it took me a long time to learn. It felt so fake and inauthentic at first. I didn't know where to look. I tried to justify my behavior by pointing to other artists who kept their eyes closed. But the comments kept coming and I slowly realized that people simply wanted me to engage with them.

The great performers have a way of drawing you in with their eyes. You can't chase everyone's desire about who they want you to be. Just absorb the feedback that comes in and try not to lie to yourself.

> How do I get that powerful sound and presence of the greatest rock stars?

Answered by Mike Dixon, musical supervisor, director, arranger and composer for TV and stage

One of the most challenging moments of my musical career occurred when I was asked to be the Musical Director for the very first stage production of *We Will Rock You* in London in 2002.

My challenge was to take a large number of musical theatre singers and actors and transform them into rock stars, who could faithfully produce the music that has been recognized across the world as among the most powerful tunes in rock music history. When I asked Roger Taylor of Queen for his advice on how to do this he said, "Just tell them to get out there and sing the song—simply sing it." I thought to myself, "That's easy for you to say because you don't even need to think about your process—it just happens for you. But these musical-theatre singers will not have your 'stuff' to draw upon."

One day, early in the process, I was rehearsing "Bohemian Rhapsody" with the cast—and Brian May and Roger Taylor themselves were at the back of the room watching. They recorded "Bohemian Rhapsody" in 1974, but whenever they performed the song live they never sang the middle section. You see, it was multi-tracked to the hilt and the technology just wasn't available in those years to create the effects they wanted for a live performance. For the musical, I told them that I could make a vocal arrangement for that section—and they were worried that it wouldn't work. So there I was rehearsing it for the first time with the cast and Brian and Roger were watching. What would they think of my attempt?

After half an hour Roger got up, walked to the back door and gave me a friendly wave and a thumbs up. Brian, who is a little more detailed, stayed for another half an hour. Then, he got up to leave, also giving me the thumbs up. I was relieved!

Having worked with Queen's music all over the world I have formed some views on what it takes to tap into the powerful art of singing in the rock genre.

The first thing you have to do—as with all singing styles—is to listen, listen, listen. The clue to nailing a genre is found in listening to the early performances of the song, to understand their phrasing and other musical qualities. In the case of rock n' roll classics there is a specific quality that comes up again and again: a sense of "space"—the silence between the words. Rock singers are comfortable with space.

You see, if you listen to any of the greats, David Bowie or Freddie Mercury, for example, you will notice that often they sing in a "clipped" manner. In "Under Pressure" they leave masses of space between the words and the style is. very. broken. up. What a difference between that and the average musical theatre singer! The actor who is also a singer is tempted to fill up all the spaces between the words—this is something that I have needed to guard against as we recreated the music of Queen. Why is there this difference between rock singers and musical theatre performers? Some might say that it's because rock stars are not trained to breathe as efficiently as trained vocalists. But I think there is a more fundamental and important answer to this question.

Actors tend to be scared of space and their first inclination is to fill it. However a rock star has a "gladiatorial instinct" that allows them to stand on stage and just BE. This attitude results in a sense of space, the ability to hold a gap rather than always hold a note. I think we can take this gladiatorial idea even further: there is something in the psyche that feels a sense of power in performance; I do not mean this in a derogatory manner—it is the power to lift and move the audience, to cause them to cheer and scream.

This power is not limited to men. When I was conducting the Andrew Lloyd Webber portion of the Diana Concert in Wembley Stadium, I observed this same power with Anastacia. The producers had given her Judas's song from *Jesus Christ Superstar*, "Superstar." Anastacia didn't sing it as an actor—but as a rock star. Her powerful performance embodied this same phenomenon: a sense of musical power resulting from a sense of space between the words.

Of course most rock music is not performed in stadiums; however, every rock singer can tap into the attitude of a gladiator. Let yourself feel your own strength as well as the power of the words of your song. Remember that those words are often more powerful when they aren't filling up all of your musical space.

CHAPTER 13

When You're Losing It

Because every sane person wants to kill themselves at least once.

"Sure, I've sat around for months being depressed. But I kept on singing, digging down deeper into my soul—and people gravitated towards the emotion in my songs."

—Michael Grimm, winner of America's Got Talent, Season Five

"The most important part of being a musician and a human is making time for reflection or else you won't know your butt from a doorknob."

—Louise Rose, entertainer

"Persistence and courage are more important than talent."

—Eric Maisel, PhD, leading creativity coach

When You're Losing It

Because every sane person wants to kill themselves at least once.

Actions:

1. Brush the Dust Off
2. Lay Out the Welcome Mat for Anxiety
3. Declare War on Self-Defeating Thoughts
4. Reduce Your Stress
5. Make Mistakes and Messes
6. Don't Wait Around for Salvation
7. Choose from the Smorgasbord of Techniques

Frequently Asked Questions:

» *I'm flooded with doubts about my abilities when I'm on stage—what can I do?*

» *I just saw a nasty comment on one of my own videos on YouTube this morning. I feel crushed.*

» *The gigs I want I don't get, the gigs I get—I don't want. What should I do?*

» *I'm down—I mean really down. I don't have plans to kill myself, but I wouldn't mind just curling up into a ball and dying. What can I do?*

» *I'm so nervous every time I get up on stage—and even when I think of getting up on stage.*

» *I'm not fired up about my songs. I feel stale.*

» *I desperately want to spend more time doing music (writing/practicing/gigging/touring) but there is simply NO time left in my life!*

» *Other musicians seem to have these incredible personal stories. I'm boring in comparison. Should I go skydiving?*

» *There doesn't seem to be room for all my music and spending time with my girlfriend. Now she's getting resentful.*

» *I'm not down—things are actually going OK. But I feel that I'm not ever going to get to a place of feeling "great."*

» *How can I make it when my style of music isn't popular?*

» *When is "IT" going to happen to me?*

Action 1: Brush the Dust Off

It's time to embrace your artistic journey, as you never have before.

When I first came to Vegas I got a job in a crappy little casino that paid me 300 dollars a night for six hours of music—that was great money for just having shown up in town. At the end of each night my agent came to collect his cut.

He arrived with his "associate," a large, strong man—for intimidation effect. Then, he created a drama in which he made it seem that I wasn't going to pay him—which was never an issue with me. He would then share criticisms of my music, ripping my performance to shreds. He threw at me any crap he could possibly think of. And he'd wrap up his "performance" by telling me that if I ever walked out on him, I'd never work in Vegas again.

Of course he was just trying to push my buttons. He wanted to see me blow up—and it was working. I felt incredibly hurt and angry. These nightly confrontations literally drove me to tears. I remember standing in front of him, night after night, angry and red-faced. So, one night I finished my show, took my things and never returned to that little casino. I was free of this agent—though I regretted never telling him off.

What is the most stressful aspect of your singing?

Reason	%
Finding my true voice/making an original contribution	15%
Figuring out how to break into the next level of my career	13%
Vocal health	12%
Finding musicians to sing/play with	10%
Finding places to perform	9%
Writing songs	7%
Illness	7%
Getting paid	4%
Rehearsals	3%
Arrangements	3%
Finding inspiration	3%
Indifferent audiences	2%
Not having enough time	2%
Getting along with my band	1%
Too many gigs/busyness	1%
Technique	1%
Confidence/stage fright	1%
Other (menopause, injury etc.)	6%

—from the 2012-2013 TC-Helicon survey of 1,000 singers

But it wasn't over. For three years memories of these encounters kept returning to me. I might have been free of working with this agent—but he was still stuck in my brain. I didn't know how I would ever get over my feelings—until I wrote a song. Once I finished that song, I never felt any more hate for him. In fact, I was even able to feel compassion. That's therapy.

I still don't get why there are people in the world whose goal is to make others feel bad. But I can tell you this: if someone really pisses you off, walk away and write a song about them. You'll be the one who wins because you'll get some free self-therapy. Who knows, you might come up with some really good music (a new "Bad, Bad, LeRoy Brown"). If that happens, change the name of the main character for legal reasons!

—Michael Grimm: winner of America's Got Talent, Season Five

Action 2: Lay Out the Welcome Mat for Anxiety

Doing the things that matter most will create fear. Embrace this fear—and learn how to manage it.

In order to create or perform, you must acknowledge and accept that anxiety is part of the process. It's time to demand of yourself that you will learn (and really practice) some anxiety management skills.

Here are the top ten skills singers all over the world use.

1. **Attitude choice.** You can choose to be made anxious by every new opinion you hear or you can choose to keep your own counsel. You can choose to approach life anxiously or you can choose to approach it calmly. See yourself flipping an internal switch—one that you control.
2. **Improved appraising.** You can significantly reduce your experience of anxiety by refusing to appraise situations as catastrophically negative.
3. **Lifestyle support.** Your lifestyle supports calmness or it doesn't. When you rush less, create fewer unnecessary pressures and stressors, get sufficient rest and exercise, eat a healthy diet, take time to relax, include love and friendship, and live in balance, you reduce your experience of anxiety.
4. **Behavioral changes.** What you actually do when you feel anxious makes a big difference. If a ten-minute shower or a twenty-minute walk can do as good a job of reducing your anxiety as watching another hour of televised golf or smoking several cigarettes, isn't it the behavior to choose?
5. **Deep breathing.** The simplest anxiety management technique is deep breathing. By stopping to deeply breathe (five seconds on the inhale, five seconds on the exhale) you stop your racing mind and alert your body to the fact that you want to be calmer. Incorporate deep breaths into your daily routine.

6. **Cognitive work.** Changing the way you think is probably the most useful and powerful anti-anxiety strategy. There are three steps: 1) notice what you are saying to yourself; 2) dispute the self-talk that makes you anxious or does not serve you; and 3) substitute more affirmative, positive or useful self-talk.
7. **Physical relaxation techniques.** Physical relaxation techniques include such simple procedures as rubbing your shoulder and such elaborate procedures as "progressive relaxation techniques" where you slowly relax each part of your body in turn.
8. **Mindfulness techniques.** Meditation and other mindfulness practices help to release defeating thoughts and replace them with more affirmative ones.
9. **Reorienting techniques.** If your mind starts to focus on some anxiety-producing situation or if you feel yourself becoming too wary, watchful and vigilant, you can consciously turn your attention in another direction, reorienting yourself to an image or situation that brings happier thoughts.
10. **Discharge techniques.** Anxiety and stress build up in the body. Actors learn to vent this stress with a "silent scream," engaging facial gestures and body movements that go with uttering a good cleansing scream —without actually uttering any sound.

If you intend to create or to perform, get ready for anxiety. It is coming! You can handle it beautifully if you use these simple tools and turn yourself into an anxiety management expert.

—Eric Maisel, PhD, widely regarded as America's foremost creativity coach

Action 3: Declare War on Self-Defeating Thoughts

Seasoned performers spend just as much time learning how to manage their moods as they do refining their musical craft.

The Buddha said, "Get a grip on your mind!"

Wrong thinking causes much of the pain and suffering we experience. The Roman Epictetus put it this way: "Do not surrender your mind." Wise men and wise women have informed us since the dawn of our species that we are what we think.

As a thoughtful person, you have the ability to challenge your thoughts that bring you pain and hold you back in your singing performance. What you also need are the understanding and the will.

Taking three steps will help you with all of this.

The first step is to clearly hear your defeatist thoughts and recognize them for what they are—products of doubt, fear, reluctance, or inner conflict. The next step is saying, "I don't want this thought!" In cognitive therapy, this is called thought confrontation. Without hesitation and without embarrassment, you say "No!" The final step is to replace the unbidden, unfortunate thought with a right thought. In cognitive therapy, this is called thought substitution. With the right thought in place, the pain ends.

At a recent conference a performer asked me, "Can I really do that? Can I get rid of thoughts I've been thinking my whole life and replace them with new ones?" I replied, "If you want to." That is the complete answer.

> *Who we are may be rejected. But would you rather be: a caricature or an original?*
> ***—Louise Rose:** entertainer*

Yes, change is deep work, because you must go down and wrestle with long-standing beliefs and serious doubts. Still, that is what you want to do. Isn't that so? Just begin and who knows: maybe the work will be easier than you imagine. For change can also happen effortlessly, in an instant. Maybe you are primed right now for that miracle. Isn't that possible?

Neither you nor I can answer any of the ultimate questions. But don't you feel a little confident that you can substitute a right thought for a wrong thought? If you are not sure one-way or the other, take "yes" for an answer. If you're convinced that the answer is "no," opt for "yes" anyway. Unless you say "yes" to the possibility that you can change your mind you will have said "no" to life with a vengeance.

—Eric Maisel, PhD, widely regarded as America's foremost creativity coach

Action 4: Reduce Your Stress

Start taking back control of the small—and big—areas of your life.

Stress is not caused by working hard—working hard just makes you tired. Assuming you have no medical causes, stress is more about lack of control or being under resourced. Your mind can handle a number of different tasks at one time but piling on extra issues or tasks with inadequate support can push you over the edge. I have seen first-hand how up-and-coming entertainers can easily go from being a bit stressed whilst building their career to plunging into the depths of depression. With a few simple precautions, you can almost always avoid this.

The first thing to do is to start taking back control. If you are having problems keeping up to date handling day to day bills, is there someone who can help you with that? If you are having conflicts within your band, is there a person who can help mediate and work out better ways of handling disagreements? If your personal relationships are troubled and you are struggling to resolve them alone speak to a relationship counsellor who will talk to both of you together and will find ways to help you.

Try this: make a list of all the areas that are contributing to stress. Now look at how you can improve the situation to help take the pressure off. Create a plan of where you want to be in three months' time and every three months for the next two years. Many who do this find almost immediately they start to feel more in control.

Some years ago, I helped a very successful musician who let his life get out of control. He took on more and more until the point he almost had a breakdown. What he did not know is that if you have ongoing stress it can lead to all sorts of quite disturbing symptoms such as panic attacks, distorted vision, headaches, stomach problems, painful joints, insomnia and mood swings. Some turn to alcohol or drugs to help them cope but inevitably that makes them worse. This musician started to regain control almost immediately by writing out his two-year plan, organizing some more support and starting to use some deep relaxation techniques.

In addition to compiling your stress list and two-year plan there are quite a few simple techniques that you can easily learn. Over the years I have taught many entertainers self-relaxation techniques (meditation/self-hypnosis) which are a wonderful, safe way to relax yourself down to a very deep level. Once you have learnt the techniques you can use them for life to help you stay on top of stress and stay in control.

—Christopher Morgan-Locke, MD, Clinical Director of the Peel Clinic, London

Action 5: Make Mistakes and Messes

Our culture says you have to get everything right—but they're wrong.

I was in a museum the other day in NYC looking at a Matisse exhibit—he would paint the same canvas in five or ten different ways. This shows how art is a process. Our creative work is an area where we should enjoy the freedom to make mistakes.

The stage is where our private work becomes public—but even here mistakes can endear you to your audience. I've chosen to take a grounded and personable approach when performing my music. People are paying for their tickets, so of course I will perform at my best so as to not let them down. But I make mistakes all the time on stage and this gives the audience an opportunity to view me more intimately.

To even be up on stage at all takes courage, nerve—mettle. Most of the people in the audience would never dare to be on that stage. Actually one reason that your audience has been drawn to you is to see how you deal with being up there. They consider you "above the ground" and if you do something in your performance that brings you "down," then you are at the table with them for a moment—that is something they like to experience. You are in your bathrobe, at home, so to speak.

So, don't be afraid of emotionally turbulent spells, dry spells or of writing a song that isn't turning out so great—this is all a part of the process.

—Jesca Hoop: internationally renowned singer-songwriter

Action 6: Don't Wait Around for Salvation

Yes, it would be great if inspiration hit us whenever we needed it—but that ain't gonna happen. Embrace the hard work of a creative life.

Perform. Write. Record. Right now. Many young singers think they need certain things before they can be an artist. Are schooling and lessons valuable? Absolutely! Can a manager be helpful? Sure. But the biggest mistake artists make is when they wait around for these instead of getting started with their career.

Perform. There is no better way to hone your craft than in front of an audience. I was hired as the new singer for a top-notch band when I was only 17. I sounded good, but I just stood there while I sang. I walked off that stage with a new understanding–I needed to work on my presence.

Sure you will fail. But then you'll try again. There are always going to be other chances. It's unlikely that your first gigs are going to be in front of all the famous industry professionals, so don't worry if you are not yet the kind of performer you want to be.

> *"Good enough" is all that our audience asks of us, they aren't interested in perfection: they are interested in an authentic experience.*
> **–Mary Beth Felker:** *vocal coach*

Find some people to play with, find a place to rehearse, and start rehearsing. Write songs or find some cover songs. Then, book a gig. It could be in a backyard, a garage–anywhere. The only thing that matters is that you perform in front of people.

Write. There is nothing that gives you more freedom and more ability to make money in the future than the ability to write songs without needing a partner. This is easier if you play an instrument. You don't have to be the best at it–you just need to understand music well enough. Lessons are helpful here, of course, but don't put off writing songs because you are a beginner. I used to write without even having an instrument. I recorded lyrics and melodies onto an old cassette deck. When I joined a band, I already had piles of melodies and written-out lyrics.

Record. You can record on anything–even your smart phone. Try a recording app like garage band. Record your rehearsals, your song ideas and your gigs. Also, try to get into a studio. You could put out an ad or a post on Facebook, saying, "I'm a young singer looking for studio experience; I'll sing for free." People will call you. It might not work out, but it will introduce you to the studio environment, studio etiquette and let you work with headphones.

I've seen singers sabotage themselves in many ways. Perhaps the most common way is by putting off starting. Have you received positive feedback about your singing? Do you know, deep down, that you are good? Do you have a passion for singing that is not just about money or fame? If so, then don't wait for anything or anybody.

—Tony Harnell: award winning lead singer of TNT

Action 7: Choose from the Smorgasbord of Techniques

Ignore the strategies that strike you as "weird."
Simply choose one that tastes good and savor it.

When you are experiencing anxiety about your upcoming performances—or other issues in your life—consider trying one of these techniques. You only need to find one that works for you:

1. **Change your Perception of Anxiety.** For instance, just imagine that your nerves are friendly allies giving you a push in the right direction. After all, these allies often show up to tell you you're about to do something important.
2. **Call it by Another Name.** Anxiety and excitement are actually two sides of the same coin. Imagine them on a scale; one side may weigh heavier than the other, so tip the scale in the direction you need to find balance.
3. **Invent a Slogan.** One of my students just created her own slogan to give herself the push she needed whenever anxiety shows up: "just do your best!" What would you say to yourself?
4. **Tap it Away.** TFT (Thought Field Therapy) is gaining attention as a method to reduce anxiety. This is where you use two fingers and tap gently under your eye, then under your arm (2 inches down from arm pit) and lastly on your collarbone while thinking about your anxiety.
5. **Write Down Three Things.** Think of what would like to feel instead of anxiety, write these down, and practice feeling those instead. I usually choose "relaxed," "creative" and "confident." Use my list or come up with your own.
6. **Try this Breathing Technique:** breathe in for four beats and, as you exhale, imagine that your feelings of anxiety leave your body. Do this several times.
7. **Visualize.** Imagine yourself succeeding in spite of nerves. This might mean that you see yourself on stage doing all the things you would like to achieve without anxiety. Make your image vivid—your imagination can be very powerful tool.
8. **Change Your Body Position.** Be aware of what your body does when you feel anxious and simply change your position. For example, if you experience muscle tension which causes you to hunch over, sit or stand up straight instead and breathe.

—Simone Niles: leading vocal performance coach, author and singer

Frequently Asked Questions

> I'm flooded with doubts about my abilities when I'm on stage—what can I do?

Answered by W. Timothy Gallwey, million selling author of "The Inner Game of Tennis," co-author of "The Inner Game of Music"

The feeling of pressure often comes from thinking, "I might screw up" or "I might not be my best." Those thoughts are doubts. What is important to recognize is that these thoughts don't help you. It's not a voice a to be listened to and taken seriously. However, these thoughts sound rational: "If you screw up the consequences will be great." But why entertain that doubt? The truth is that you are there to touch people and this is your opportunity to do it.

Doubt is one of the least recognized obstacles to performance. It is a sister or brother of fear, but it has its own specific attributes and consequences.

How can you deal with your doubt? First, realize that you're not alone. When I wrote *The Inner Game of Tennis* and subsequently co-authored *the Inner Game of Music* one of the surprising themes in the feedback from readers was "how could you read my mind?" They thought they were the only ones fighting this battle. Of course they're not. It helps to know that. Doubt is a part of the human condition; we are not talking about something that is merely your own private flaw.

The doubt comes from what I call Self 1, the voice in your head that wants to control everything. Self 2 is your other voice, the voice of your talent and potential to sing. Self 1 can sound very rational: "if there is a difficult passage and you screw it up everyone's going to hear." You want to get away from Self 1 and live more in Self 2.

How can you do this? Don't listen to the voice of doubt—it's not there to help you even though it sounds like it is. Now, it's hard not to listen to someone who's speaking to you, but you can accomplish this by listening to something else—like your voice. I want you to listen to something specific in your voice—the more specific the focus the less you will hear the doubt. In tennis I tell players to watch the spin and the seam of the ball, or the gracefulness of the line of the ball as it comes through the air to your racket. It is your interest in these things that keeps your mind from being taken over by the voice of fear and doubt.

Likewise, when it comes to your voice, I encourage you to become more aware of the changes in your pitch or the feelings of where your voice is coming from (your body? your chest? your head?). Whatever you choose to focus upon, it has to be observable and interesting to you.

Finally, remember that there are some things in a pressure situation that you don't control. When you're singing live in a venue, you don't control the size of the audience, the look of the venue and the moods of those walking into the venue. What you do control is how in touch you are with your purpose for performing. As a singer one of your primary motives is to express yourself for the pleasure of those listening—and, of course, you may also be aiming at more than pleasure: you may have a special focus on a meaningful message or cause that you are promoting. When you're singing, this is your opportunity to fulfill your purpose. You're getting a chance to do what you're born to do: to let your voice touch people. This is your chance to do it.

> I just saw a nasty comment on one of my own videos on YouTube this morning. I feel crushed. What do I do?

Answered by Anders Ørsager, member of the hit group Basix—"Best European Album"

Nobody likes to see comments like, "Get a REAL job" on their YouTube videos. How does one deal with such heartless and insensitive reactions?

Of course, we must not place much value on an anonymous rogue comment. It's far better to trust our friends and teachers, those who care about us and invest in our lives—even though they might have problems being honest.

But there's another way to deal with this comment—I let it drive me back to a basic question: Why do I sing?

How do you answer this? Hopefully you are not singing in order to get only good comments on YouTube! Here is the list of reasons that my heart speaks to me when I am seeking a way through the challenges of the performing life:

- Singing allows me to meet other people.
- Singing allows me to cross barriers like religion, sexual preferences and political positions.
- Singing in a group or with a band improves my social skills, behavior and leadership—it makes me a better team player.
- Singing helps me connect valuable messages in music to the lives of those around me.
- AND it does all of this whether or not I become a superstar!

I can't make people love what I do. However if I try the best I can and sing for the right reasons, then that's enough for me. Actually, it's easy to see that those comments on YouTube are from people being touched by what I do—and that's what I want to achieve.

> The gigs I want I don't get, the gigs I get—I don't want. What should I do?

Answered by Divinity Roxx, former Musical Director and bassist for Beyonce's all female band, 2006-2011

All my energy is going into my career as a vocal artist even though my career as a bass player and MD (musical director) has been successful and rewarding. I was rapping long before I picked up a bass which is why it feels great to be focussing on my vocals again.

At a bass clinic I went to with Anthony Wellington, there was one heavy-set white dude with a plaid shirt, t-shirt, dirty jeans and tennis shoes. Anthony said to him, "I know you may want to play gigs with Usher, but you are not the type of guy Usher is gonna call. It's about the way you present yourself. You are the type of guy Kid Rock might call."

Even if you are working towards something else, you have to recognize what type of artist you really are at this moment. Take a look at yourself. Be honest about who you are and the resources you have. If you are great at a certain genre, and it is your whole vibe—then keep doing that. You can always do a different genre for fun, on the side.

Still, you might choose to pursue that other genre. Let's say I'm performing funk and hip hop but I want to do jazz gigs. What do I do? I start playing jazz records, I go to jam sessions, I surround myself with people who play jazz. I have to start living in that world. Environment plays a big part in who we are as people and what we become as artists. It can be a long journey to make something new feel authentic.

You have to consider what is more important: having fun or getting paid? What are your goals as an artist and as a singer? How can you work on yourself and what resources can you use to reach your goals?

> I'm down—I mean really down. I don't have plans to kill myself, but I wouldn't mind just curling up into a ball and dying. What can I do?

Answered by Eric Maisel, PhD, widely regarded as America's foremost creativity coach

Extreme unhappiness is extremely common. Life is hard and the universe is not designed to meet our needs.

Added to this are the pressures of the performing marketplace—it can be Darwinian. It's no wonder that millions of people have evaluated life a cheat, do not find their life meaningful, and can't get rid of a blue feeling that dogs their every step.

You really must do something, even if your energy is low. Your first stop is to a mental health professional to see if what he or she has to offer serves you. But your second stop is to the mirror, where you must take a clear-eyed look to see to what extent you are contributing to your own unhappiness.

I want to give you three questions that can help lead you away from unhappiness and toward a more authentic life, a life that is closer to your heart:

- What matters to you?
- Are your thoughts aligned with what matters to you?
- Are your behaviors aligned with what matters to you?

Find some answers to these questions—or just the beginning of some answers. Then make some changes, even small ones. In other words, I am asking you to decide "what meaning means" to you so that you can proceed to lead your life in ways that feel personally meaningful. You choose to take responsibility for your thoughts and your actions and to lead life instrumentally.

You accept and embrace the fact that you are the final arbiter of your life's meaning.

With this approach to life, each day is a project requiring existential engineering skills as you bridge your way from one meaningful experience to the next. By accepting the realities of life and by asserting that you are the sole arbiter of the meaning in your life, you provide yourself some sure footing as you actively make meaning.

> I'm so nervous every time I get up on stage—and even when I *think* of getting up on stage.

Answered by Mary Beth Felker, vocal coach and founder of Voice Project Studios

I wonder if you suffer in some of the ways I do! Here's the eight bar "Nervous Chorus" that whirls around in my brain as I consider performing:

1. What the hell am I doing?
2. I suck.
3. I think I might be getting sick.
4. What will people think? I want them to be impressed.
5. I'm going to blank out and forget the words.
6. If I'm myself on stage, I'll look like a fool.
7. I just know that my voice will give out.
8. Will people pity me and just say polite things?

I've applied years of work in cognitive therapy (I'm not kidding) to develop a "Counter-Chorus" to each of the refrains above:

1. I am doing something, deep down, that I want to do. I want to sing. I love to sing. It's meaningful to me! So I better stop thinking and start mastering my material!
2. Yes, I have sucked at times—who hasn't? But I haven't really S-U-C-K-E-D; I just fell short of my own expectations. Solution: listen, fix it, do my best and move on.
3. Well, it's true that stress can wear my body down. However, I'm going on my pre-show training regime, making sure I eat well, sleep a lot, hydrate, cut down on the alcohol and remind myself to enjoy the process!
4. How much can I really control what other people think? I think I will leave being a control freak to my own preparation and let people think what they will!

5. I've blanked out before but guess what? I just improvised and kept on going—few people even noticed! Besides, I'll have a plan: in addition to rehearsing the songs a cappella I'll keep a binder nearby with the set list during the performance.
6. Well, my choice is to either be myself or to try to keep myself controlled and reserved. I've done the latter much of my life and now it's my turn to be authentic on stage.
7. I am going to sing my best and trust my training. After all, no-one ever comes to hear a technically perfect singer. They come to be moved by the music and taken on a journey.
8. Do I expect to be handed a Grammy at the end of the night?! No. If they're polite then they're polite. If they pity me, they pity me. But I won't pity myself nor be embarrassed or ashamed. I've worked hard to get to this point and this is my celebration.

By repeating these affirmations, I'm able to overcome my nervousness—and you will too.

> I'm not fired up about my songs. I feel stale.

Answered by Jaime Vendera, vocal coach renowned for his wineglass-shattering voice

Hey, it happens to all of us. I've been there, felt like I lost my passion, didn't even care about listening to music or singing. So, here's what I did about it: when I lost that drive, I looked at my life and realized that the passion was still there, but just didn't have that extra ummmfff. So, I went back to when I first was crazy/nutzoid about music and thought about what bands/songs/albums got me so wound for sound. All I needed to do was crank those tunes to 11 and I was more amped up than being on two energy drinks like white on rice in a glass of milk on a paper plate in a snowstorm.

For me, the key truly was going back and listening to albums by old 80s bands like BulletBoys and Spread Eagle. Ironically, BulletBoys had a song called "Crank Me Up" that makes me wanna sing every time I hear it. I would crank those tunes and do little vocal exercises along with the tracks, like lip bubbles and humming, then kick into singing my brains out.

When I lose the drive, I'll spend several weeks just listening and singing along to these old tunes and they always bring back the passion. I even recently used the band Adrenaline Mob's first release to get me cranking for a recent show. Bottom line: you've got to remember why you love singing, then inspire yourself just to get that adrenalin flowing again. So, the cure-all for kicking your own arse is the songs and bands that inspired you to start singing in the first place!

> I desperately want to spend more time doing music (writing/ practicing/gigging/touring) but there is simply NO time left in my life!

Answered by Mark Baxter, acclaimed vocal coach with Aerosmith, Journey, Goo Goo Dolls and many others

When people say this it's not because they want to spend more time working on their craft, it's because they think they should spend more time. The problem with this guilt trip is that there's an expectation attached: things would be better if I only had more time. Instead of buying into this helpless mindset, make better use of the practice time you have by focusing on improving. I know that seems obvious but many musicians don't know how to practice. An hour focused on an intended result is far better than several hours of mindless drills.

Next, learn the most powerful word for adding hours to your day—NO! "Sorry but I can't work late," "No thanks, you guys go to the movie without me," "I can't take the class this semester—it doesn't leave me any practice time." Setting boundaries for others is important but you also have to set them for yourself. Schedule your use of social media—four times a day to check and update everything is plenty. Television is another time-sucking monster. My rule is that I only watch it standing up. This drives my wife crazy but it keeps me from getting comfortable. If a show is interesting then my legs don't mind.

What you don't want to say no to is sleep. Focus is the first thing to suffer when torching the candle at both ends. Your voice is the second. Singers can't dance around this issue. Sleep isn't a luxury—it's a necessity. Where I used to try to steal some extra time was at work. I don't know if I should be encouraging that, though, because I was fired from every job I ever had. I was either caught vocalizing, listening to a song I was writing, or napping.

A lot comes down to giving yourself permission to be musical. I was conflicted when my son was born over what it meant to be a father. I wondered if I should quit my band, curtail my music practicing, etc. But then I realized something: my son has a musician as a father. So, he grew up with amplifiers in the living room and guys sitting at the kitchen table working on set lists. His childhood was certainly different than the son of an insurance salesman, doctor or a lawyer—but the amount of love was exactly the same.

> Other musicians seem to have these incredible personal stories. I'm boring in comparison. Should I go skydiving?

Answered by Brett Manning, leading US Vocal Coach to many of today's top artists

Read … a lot. Adventure begins in the mind, then is expressed through words and finally is lived out with your physical being. To quote Francis Schaeffer, "The body is a bridge to show ourselves what's really inside our souls." Francis understood that whether art, romance, violence or lunacy, people will eventually live out their thoughts. So, yes, go skydiving, or scuba diving or perhaps just start with laser tag.

However, be careful what you pray (or wish) for. I prayed to be a great songwriter and ended up going through repeated trials. Now I'm a deeper artist and grateful for what the trials taught me, but I don't wish hardship on anyone. A better and easier path to adventure is to serve those in deep hardship. Ease someone's suffering and you will feel their story in your bones and they will become part of you, your art and your life.

> There doesn't seem to be room for all my music and spending time with my girlfriend. Now she's getting resentful.

Answered by Mark Baxter: acclaimed vocal coach with Aerosmith, Journey, Goo Goo Dolls and many others

Stop blaming the girlfriend and she'll stop blaming the band! You two have simply hit a wall in your relationship and she's just trying to figure out why you're not that much fun anymore. She thinks if you spend more time together she'll feel more acknowledged. She's wrong—so grab the reins here and really be with her when you're together. Stop talking about the band's issues and ask about her dreams and goals. Put the game controller down and look her in the eyes when she's talking to you. If she's repeating herself ad nauseam then leave the room but don't just tune her out.

You also need to stop texting her when you're at rehearsals and gigs—and she needs to stop doing the same from her job. A little time apart makes the heart grow fonder. If you would really rather be with her than rehearsing then do the band a favor and quit; if that's not true then stop leading her on with false statements. Learn to focus on what you're doing and who you're with at all times and you will clean up a lot of clutter in your life.

My wife and I dated for five years. Not once in those years did I kiss her at twelve on New Year's (I was on stage). Not once was I able to hang out with her family on weekends and holidays (I always had a gig). She rarely came to shows just like I never went to watch her at her office. She respected who I was and my aspirations even though I was often dead broke and worked a million odd jobs between bands because I never complained. When we talked about our future I never offered any other option for myself other than being a musician. What I remember most of those days was that we just really enjoyed each other's company. I knew from watching my buddies struggle with relationships that what I had was special—but I also noticed the mixed signals they threw. So to my delight my girl said yes when I asked her to marry me. That was thirty years ago and I've been proving her mother wrong ever since!

> I'm not down—things are actually going OK. But I feel that I'm not ever going to get to a place of feeling "great."

Answered by Simone Niles, leading vocal performance coach, author and singer

Your question reminds me of a time early in my career. I was a budding singer, trying to find my way in the music world. Yet I did not feel fulfilled and knew that I was not living up to my true potential. Things were "OK," but definitely not great.

I grew up on a really small island and though I was fortunate to work with some great artists, I wanted more than my environment could offer. I felt somewhat bound to the styles of music there and wanted to explore new sounds and new places. I knew that if I wanted to feel better about my future as a singer that I would need to change something, so I moved to a new country. This opened up new opportunities to learn and share.

Before you get on a flight across the world (!), I want you to answer an important question. Read this question over a few times and be as precise as you can in your answer.

What precisely in your life right now do you want to feel great about? "Everything" might be your first answer and, certainly it would be great (though unlikely) that you could take on everything at once! However, in order to make the necessary changes, you must first know what to change.

For example:

- I want to feel great about my vocal technique.
- I want to feel great about my career as a singer.
- I want to feel great about the person I am.

Once you've got some specific answers to that question, you're ready for the next one: What am I not doing that makes this part of my life just okay? Read this question again. The answers to these questions are the things that, once you do them, will change your life.

Both my clients and I still go through moments when things are just "OK," so you are not alone! But the more you practice doing things differently, the easier it becomes to make changes and feel better about things in your life.

It doesn't always take a drastic step; "great" could be right around the corner if you keep asking these questions and seeking the answers.

> How can I make it when my style of music isn't popular?

Answered by Mark Baxter, acclaimed vocal coach with Aerosmith, Journey, Goo Goo Dolls and many others

Ironically, your chances of making it are far better if you don't sound like what's popular today. Music changes like fashion; what people are wearing today is out of style in just two years. It takes at least that long to build an audience—so successful artists take a different approach. They make music that moves them and then set out to make it popular. It's far better to create the next trend than to ride the back of a wave.

Back when I was performing in a rock band, disco was becoming popular. It was so pervasive that many groups were being tempted to sway in the direction of that genre. There was one band, though, that stuck to their guns: Twisted Sister. I was lucky to be their opening act often and I learned a lot from that experience. They never apologized about being anti-disco. In fact, they repeated "disco sucks" chants until everyone in the room joined in. It became their battle cry. By the time they made MTV they had been honing their sound for years.

In the week ending on September 30, 2012, Mumford and Sons' second album debuted at number one. Not since AC/DC released *Black Ice* in 2008 has a rock album debuted at number one. It's hard to imagine two more different sounding bands. Let their success remind you that whatever your genre—especially if it's not the most popular at the time—it's your job to find like-minded listeners. Don't apologize about your style (even if it's Disco!).

> When is "IT" going to happen to me?

Answered by Daniel Bedingfield, Multi-platinum selling artist, BRIT Award Winner, Grammy Nominee

It could be that your art is merely unrecognized, that you are a true genius and all it is going to take is time. Or, you are somebody who really loves music and enjoys it tremendously but really should be pursuing other things for a living.

The only way for you to know is through feedback AND your own gut. In the case of Van Gogh, his gut told him to pursue his art, but he died penniless. Van Gogh did not find his market before he died. If you want to be successful and if you are truly talented, you will have to find your market before you die. If you find your market, your efforts will be rewarded with excitement and maybe even some money and the recognition that I imagine you are hoping for.

One of the smartest things I ever heard in my life is if you can't possibly be anything other than a musician, do it. Being an artist is a reward in itself and it is highly unlikely that you will receive the rewards through money and recognition that you deserve—you have to do it for its own sake.

Enrich.

My friend Daniel is a lover of books. So, when he heard that a truckload was being given away at the local University, he rushed over, found a pile that looked promising and threw them in his office. A few days later he was moving the books to a shelf when an old, crisp 50-dollar bill fell out of a dusty volume—then, another one! He sat down and flipped through the book, finding so many bills that they formed a stack totalling over 3,000 dollars. He immediately hunted through all of the other books—yet, they were only in this one book.

Daniel is incredibly conscientious, so he phoned the University to see if he could return this money to its rightful owner. They told him that the books had been donated decades before and there was no way to trace the owner (who would be long dead) or his family. He then phoned the police to ask them what to do; they told him to keep the money. He still couldn't believe his luck, so he phoned the pastor at his church who said, "Look, don't you get it?! You've had a windfall—have a good time!" Only then did he fully accept that he actually had an extra 3,000 dollars that he could spend in any way he wanted. What is he going to do with it?

The real question is: what are you going to do with your windfall?

The 135 medical specialists, professional coaches, psychologists, artists and other music industry pros featured in this book are united in the conviction that our voice—*the one that is already sitting on the shelf of our life*—is a windfall. We need to realize that our unique, natural voice is our greatest treasure, and take some important steps (most of which are completely free) to remove the things getting in the way.

We live in a "product culture" which leads us to believe that the way to enrich our voice is to make a purchase. With just the right vocal training program, specialist appointment, retreat weekend, pharmaceutical product, personal trainer, liposuction treatment, dietary regimen, prestigious degree in music, brand new piece of gear—only then will we be able to truly enrich our voice. In other words, we must plunk some money down on the counter before doing anything else. We don't consider that we're already rich. That would be, well, counter-cultural.

Of course there are some fantastic voice teachers, specialists and products worthy of an expenditure at the right time and place. But before you and I pull out our wallets, we must value what we already have and act on the many ways to enrich our voice that are absolutely free. When we do that, then we'll be able to make a great decision with the money we already have.

So, what should you spend money on and what should you go after for free?

We're very, very lucky to be living in an age when we are breaking away from secretive celebrity approaches to technique into a common sense mentality based upon sound research. One of the major messages of those involved in scientifically informed vocal technique is that it is absolutely free to do a range of things guaranteed to bring out your natural voice and increase its power and flexibility. It is free to:

- Strive to keep a natural and relaxed position in your throat
- To change the key of songs to suit your natural range
- To harness posture and breathing to maximize vocal power and control
- Practice with consistency to develop the kind of muscle memory that enables you to fly
- Test your skills through practicing your performance

All of this can be done with the suggestions and exercises found in these chapters and which are widely available from informed coaches and teachers online.

Above all, it is absolutely free to be yourself. One of the greatest tensions we can bring to our mind, emotions and voice is the pressure to sound like someone else. Yet, many of us do exactly this; we listen to our favorite artists and want to re-create their emotional impact. We make the mistake of thinking that the best way to do this is to try to sound exactly like them. This inevitably results in muscle tension that can lead to pain and even vocal injury.

We need to take a different path, adopting the attitude that says, "Wow, I love how my favorite artist sounds! Now, how can I create a similar impact, but in my *own way*?" This doesn't mean we have to shut ourselves off from our influences; in fact, we should be exploring the influences of our influences! What we should take away from our idols is not a carbon copy of their exact notes or vocal sound, but passion, inspiration and new ideas to play with. This leads to our own connection with the music—and when we've got that connection, then we have our own solid gold.

What about spending money on vocal health? We're also lucky to live in an era when there is a democratization of health knowledge: many doctors and specialists are very willing to share what they know instead of hoarding their knowledge for a price. And much of what they know is absolutely free to implement. It's free to:

- Drink lots of water (even those wild-living-looking singers are "doing it"!)
- Control reflux by diet and the angle of our bed
- Sing the same vocal exercise or song at the same time every day as a "check-in" with our voice
- Warm up the voice each day and allow for times of rest
- Inhale steam to moisten the vocal cords directly

When should you spend money on medical help? When all of these free things are in place but there is still pain, a lack of stamina or a loss of range, then there is no substitute for a "scope," a good look around by someone who knows "their stuff". In fact, the medical experts we worked with in this book warn that vocal rest can mask the fact that there may be underlying issues that need to be addressed. It is well worth taking time and money to solve these issues—but not before we try all the free stuff!

What about our struggles with performance anxiety or depression? We've also come a long way with our understanding of psychology. Instead of relying on alchemists, priests and soothsayers, we can find success with cognitive psychology, particularly these do-it-yourself strategies:

- Awareness. Rather than berate ourselves for feeling a certain way, we can simply become aware of our feelings, noticing them and observing them. This act alone loosens the power of debilitating thoughts.
- Acceptance. Instead of wasting our energy in hating ourselves, wouldn't it be better if we thought of ourselves as a close friend?
- Assembling. We can bring together some new words, some new and hopeful ways of talking to ourselves and of interpreting things that happen to us.

Do we ever need to spend money on this stuff? Yes! There are times when we need someone to throw a rope down into our pit and help pull us up. Things can get so bad that we can really benefit from another person helping us to see where we can get some control back into our lives or grasp at some healthier options. There can also be a role for pharmaceutical help, talk therapy or group meetings in retreat settings. The point is to use these pay-for-service solutions as tools to get us back to a place where we can use our own strategies—for free.

These free and paid-for solutions can apply to your band. One of the surprises in talking to experienced singers is the number of times they lamented not being a little more calm or wise when it came to disagreements in their group. Their stories and advice can be boiled down to one sentence:

- Figure out the things that are worth fighting for and be flexible on the rest.

This is more than a vague platitude for singers: there are indeed some battles that must be fought and won in your band:

- Stage volume must be at a level so that you can hear yourself
- All musical decisions, especially the song keys, must help bring out the best in your voice and personality
- The monitor mix must let you hear yourself at just the right level
- People need to respect the sound check … and show up on time for it!

There really can be no compromise in these areas if you are going to be able to contribute your voice to your group. It's really as simple as that.

What isn't so simple is all the other stuff: how do deal with conflicts about money, promotion, set lists, arrangements, costumes, merchandise, etc. The voice of experience says—chill out, let some of this stuff work itself out. Focus on making music together, sleep on it and seek opinions before taking strong stand. Do you ever need to pay for help to work through issues? If you've got a great act, and there's money coming in, why not?

So do you want to know what Daniel did with his windfall of $3,000? He's going to spend every last penny of it on music, of course. Right now, the money is sitting in an envelope on his desk as he hunts down the trumpet of his dreams. He has a quite a good trumpet already—but his new instrument will be the icing on his musical cake.

What will you do with your windfall, your voice? We hope you'll enrich it.

Most of the time, this doesn't take any money at all.

—Gregory A. Barker, PhD, Author and Commissioning Editor, VoiceCouncil Magazine

Here are **5 questions designed to help you enrich your voice without spending a penny**. If you just jot down your own answer—and attempt to implement it—you will have saved what could otherwise cost thousands:

Your Technique. Take a video of yourself singing a song—you can use your smartphone. As you watch yourself, what areas of tension do you notice in your posture or breathing?

____

____

Your Vocal Connection. Watch the video again. Where were you not quite convinced about your connection to the emotion of the song? Work on these areas.

____

____

Your Health. What is one health change you could make right now that you *know* would be good for your body and your voice?

____

____

Your Emotions. What are five activities that you love, that you *can* do, and that make you happy? List these and then make some dates to do them this week.

____

____

Your Band. We usually focus on how others could change to make our lives easier. Here's a different question: what could I do to be more fun for my band to be around in general and be more alive at our rehearsals in particular?

____

____

Money & Markets

CHAPTER 14

Making Money in Live Gigs

Because you need some.

"It's not labels, suits or booking agents that will own and dictate the terms of your success—it is your fans. How you handle your merchandise, your changeover time, the sound and the time of your slot will increase your effectiveness in reaching out with your music and persona to the people who matter most."

—Chris Maltese, artist manager,
formerly a senior producer for MTV

"Many people you want to come to your gig also have 500 friends on Facebook."

—Clifford Schwarz, President and Co-Founder of NuMuBu,
the global music industry network

Making Money in Live Gigs

Because you need some.

Actions:

1. Make More Money at Your First Gigs
2. Negotiate a Better Price for Your Special Event Gig
3. Get More Than Money from Your Gigs
4. Watch Out for Negotiation Traps and Opportunities
5. Make Money Through Touring

Frequently Asked Questions:

» *Is it rude to draw attention to my tip jar?*

» *How much should I spend on my website and other promotional material?*

» *Is it appropriate to charge money for a funeral?*

» *Is it acceptable to ask for money up front from the venue?*

» *Is it bad to "low-ball" a bid (offer to do a gig for less than the going rate)?*

Action 1: Make More Money at Your First Gigs

Time-honored tricks of the trade can help you maximize your take from venues that want to maximize theirs.

Singers often ask me, "How can I make more money on my gigs?" How much you make on a gig can vary widely depending on what type of gig it is (pub, nightclub, festival, wedding, etc.) as well as your level of experience and name recognition. So while there's no "one size fits all" answer to this question, there are some key points you should know in order to maximize your profits from any gig.

First, understand how the venue pays performers. Most clubs pay a percentage of the cover charge taken at the door. This percentage can vary, so be sure to ask ahead of time and if possible get something in writing. In some cases venues pay performers a flat fee (guarantee), but that's less common for new artists. Also, find out if the venue will provide food for the band.

> *All clubs will deal with money and gigging issues differently and for the most part I have not been ripped off. But I do suggest that you put all of your negotiations with a venue in an email so that you can refer to it later in case there are any issues. You are not going to do a contract for every gig, but when you have an email, you can fall back on this in case there are any challenges.*
>
> *—**Annie Sellick:** internationally renowned jazz singer*

It's important to know what your expenses are going to be (parking, travel, paying a sound engineer or renting sound equipment, food, drinks, etc.). Figuring this out ahead of time will save you major headaches and keep you from losing money on your gigs!

Here are three more tips to help you maximize your profits:

1. *Promote your gigs like crazy!* Most clubs, pubs and restaurants aren't music promoters. While they often have music calendars on their websites and may run calendar ads in the local papers, they completely expect YOU to fill the venue. In fact, many large venues won't even book a band unless they have a proven following. The more people who come to your show, the more money you'll make. Plus, the venue is much more likely to invite you back if you fill the place!
2. *Sell merchandise!* One of the best ways for you to make more money on your gigs is to sell your CDs and merchandise (T-shirts, hats, etc). Be sure to have plenty of merchandise for sale and hang around after your show to sell and sign CDs!
3. *Be on time and be prepared!* This is true for all gigs, but especially for weddings, corporate and private events. Showing up late or unprepared is a great way to ensure that the bandleader or event planner won't hire you again. For more formal gigs be well groomed

and dressed appropriately. All of this falls under the heading of being professional. Know what is expected of you at the gig and exceed that expectation.

–Jennifer Truesdale: singer, songwriter, coach and author of "Get Paid to Sing"

Action 2: Negotiate a Better Price for Your Special Event Gig

Don't ever undersell yourself when you sing at a ceremony.

Weddings, Bar Mitzvahs, company Christmas parties. They're fun, they're memorable and, for musicians, they can be a lucrative part of a gigging life.

Let's say you are approached by a friend to play for a special event (these are called casuals or general business gigs). Talking about money is the last thing you may want to do! However, soon after you say, "Wow, I'd be totally honored to sing at your wedding!" you must say something like, "Let's get together and talk about what you need, what I can provide, and what my rates are."

One of the greatest ways to demonstrate your value is to care about the success of the event. Learn about the people involved and try to understand their vision for the occasion. Find out what they want: the amount and type of music, the time frame and other particulars such as the location. Find out the age range of the guests—you may be able to play hits for each generation present. You can offer to learn songs personally requested by the guest(s) of honor or perhaps even put together a playlist of MP3s to play while the guests arrive.

After this careful listening, your job is to provide assurance that your contribution will be professional and the right fit for their special day. An event planner will be familiar with all the variables of booking musicians, but a bride-to-be may have no idea what is involved and look to you for guidance. Be solution-oriented and ready to make suggestions.

Before you name your price, consider your side of the equation:

- Will there be enough floor space?
- Is there adequate access to electricity?
- Is there flooring, shelter and heaters for an outside event?
- Will you be bringing the PA—and an extra mic for the speeches?
- Are travel and set-up times beyond the norm?
- Have you valued your investment into your equipment, training and rehearsal?

Now, name your price. Here are some examples of what musicians might charge in a medium-sized town. Every city has slightly different "going rates" which change over time.

1. For two or three specially requested songs during a wedding ceremony, a vocal soloist could charge $150–$200.
2. A four-piece band playing three, 45-minute sets at a company Christmas party and dance could charge $900–$1,200 (at least $200+ per player).

Artists may charge more than this as popularity and demand increases, or if they live in a large city like Chicago where some wedding bands charge $6,000 or more. On the other hand, there may be times you'll sing for free, especially if you need the exposure or if it's your own mom's retirement party.

–Kathy Alexander: singer, vocal coach and staff writer at VoiceCouncil Magazine

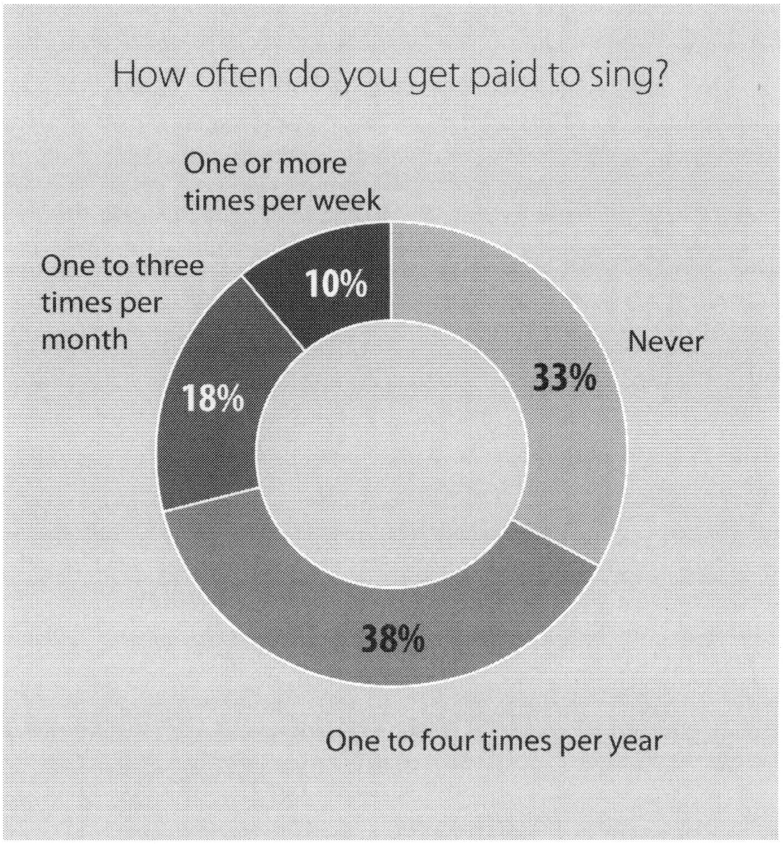

–from the 2012-2013 TC-Helicon survey of 1,000 singers

Action 3: Get More Than Money from Your Gigs

Learn how to leverage each performance so you can get what you really need: numbers.

If you are looking to make money from a local one-time gig, you will be disappointed. Many local shows do not offer a "guarantee" but often give you a cut of the door price. This makes it more important for you to take advantage of your merch table, selling albums, singles, T-shirts and posters.

Some venues have a policy that during the performance a waitress will pass the hat around on your behalf—this is true of The Living Room in NYC, Rockwood Music Hall and other venues. If you really need a few bucks you can always ask the venue if they would do this for you. It's always better if this happens three quarters of the way through your performance, after the crowd has already been won over.

But let's go back to the real reason why you are doing these gigs: not for the money, but for building your team—the people who will be your core fans, helping you to recruit others. This business is like any other business—based on numbers. When a new group pitches their act to me, I do two things—check out their music and look at their online numbers. If the online numbers are zero, then that isn't a good business move for me. As an artist, you always need to keep numbers at the back of your mind. It is about winning fans over.

Here's one strategy that I've seen work at a small gig: invite your fans to bring their cell phone over to the merch table—when they "like" your band's page, they will get a free download. This will drive your numbers up and remind you that you aren't at these small gigs for the money, but for your overall mission to grow your numbers.

—Chris Maltese: artist manager, formerly a senior producer for MTV

Action 4: Watch Out for Negotiation Traps and Opportunities

We reveal the top issues that can keep you on top of your emerging business.

The Merch Split. A lot of venues will take a piece of your merchandise sales—regardless of whether they are selling it for you or not. So, negotiate a split in your favor. Some venues will want 20% or 30%—and it can be more at festivals. Do whatever you can do to negotiate. If you know how great your merch is, then it may be worth taking a lower guarantee for the gig in return for a higher percentage of your merch sales.

The Changeover. Many times an artist will book a show and, when told there is a 15–20 minute changeover time between bands, they won't realize that this isn't realistic. If the group before them has six members and their own drum kit the changeover may actually take 45 minutes. The result: the time for your set is shrunk. So, be in contact with the other bands and see if you can do any gear sharing—your time on stage will increase. Since you are now in contact with other bands you can also discuss ways to cross-promote your work.

The Sound Guy /Girl. Let's say that you are opening and you don't have your own sound guy. Also, you've heard that the venue's own FOH house engineer isn't that great—or that the room is difficult. It may be worth throwing a few bucks at the main band's engineer to come early and check your sound as well. A lot of FOH sound guys don't mind making a few extra bucks on the night of a gig—so it's a win-win.

The Opening Slot. Sometimes venues jam as many acts on the bill as possible for promotional purposes. They might even have you playing a set at 6.30pm—at the same time that the doors open. This is a "downer" because when the audience first walks into a venue they will check it out a little before taking their seats—you could be playing to an empty house. Always make sure that you play at least 30 minutes after the door opens. Even better: do what you can to get closer to the time of headlining act. Just ask the venue if they can switch you to play later since you are traveling that day. It's always worth a try.

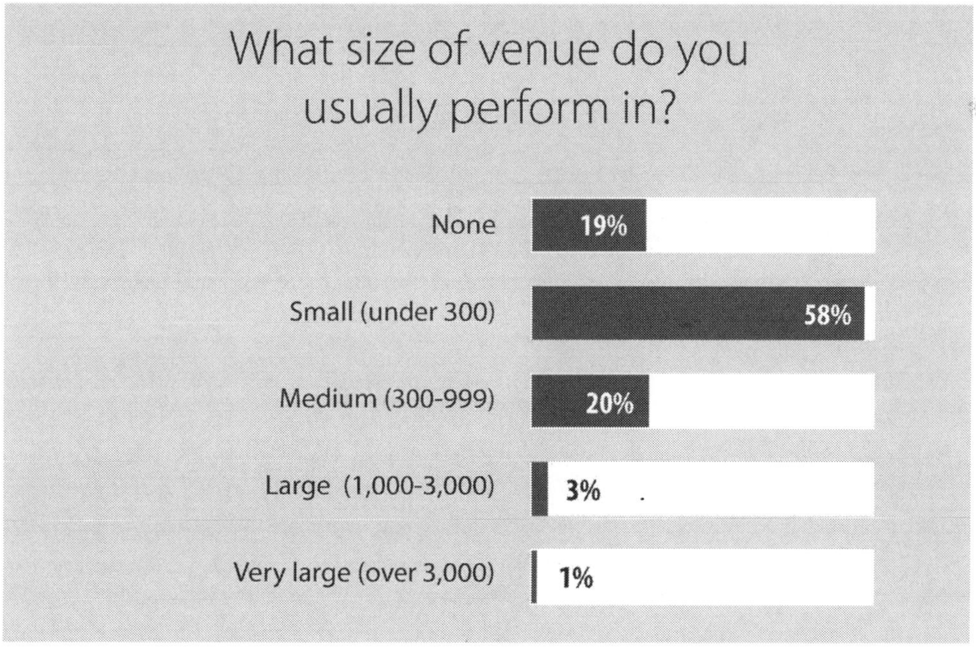

–from the 2012-2013 TC-Helicon survey of 1,000 singers

It's not labels, suits or booking agents that will own and dictate the terms of your success—it is your fans. How you handle your merch, your changeover time, the sound and the time of your slot will increase your effectiveness of reaching out with your music and persona to the people who matter most.

—Chris Maltese: artist manager, formerly a senior producer for MTV

Action 5: Make Money Through Touring

Proven strategies will ensure that your tour is "worth it."

For a tour to be "worth it," you will need to have several dates in succession, one right after the other so that your travel expenses are minimized—remember, a day spent in travel is a day when you are not getting paid (or doing anything else but traveling). Back-to-back bookings can be incredibly hard to achieve, especially if you are doing your own bookings—and it can be difficult to secure a booking agent.

One way to make a tour happen is to build it around an "anchor gig" (this may be a private event that pays you well) and perhaps even offers accommodation. Your mission is to fill in as much around this gig as you can. Don't forget, too, that one of the benefits of touring is that you can also factor in CD sales—this can sometimes double your money. So, it's imperative that you have a "product" (or download cards, etc.).

You absolutely have to have someone manning the table for you—don't do it yourself; have this arranged before you get there, using someone at the venue or a friend. Give them 15%–20% of your takings. If you are at a festival, I think it's a good idea to get a cute, young person to walk through the crowd with your merchandise—that can work wonders.

Of course you'll want to be available after the show to sign CDs, standing next to the person selling. Don't forget to offer a discount—if a CD is selling at 15 dollars, for example, sell two for 25. You really have an opportunity with merchandise when you are out of town.

—Annie Sellick: internationally renowned jazz singer

Frequently Asked Questions

> Is it rude to draw attention to my tip jar?

Answered by Jaime Vendera, vocal coach renowned for his wineglass-shattering voice

Hmmm, I am on the fence about this one. If I were at a restaurant and the waitress said, "Don't forget my tip," I would probably write on the check, "Here's a tip: don't ask for a tip."

With that said, I think people underappreciate all the hard work that goes into performing: hour upon hour to learn your instrument, the songs—not to mention the time spent in setting up and tearing down. If we're serious about it, most singers make far less than minimum wage. So, if you were going to draw attention to the tip jar, work it into your routine in a comical way, such as telling the audience, "Thanks for the tips, guess I CAN eat off the dollar menu tonight from Mickey D's" or "Who wants to see me play this trumpet with my butt for a dollar?" If your audience sees you smile, crack a joke, and have some fun at your own expense, they'll be more likely to contribute to that tip jar.

Above all, put on an amazing performance. If you "wow" your audience, you won't even need to draw attention to that tip jar because your fans will gladly support you dollar by dollar!

> How much should I spend on my website and other promotional material?

Answered by Steve Eggleston, award-winning law professor, artist manager and best selling author

One million dollars—that's the minimum a major label spends to make a record go platinum in the United States. If you don't have a mil sitting around, then what you spend depends entirely on what you have after you pay your bills, and what you want to achieve. Let's call this your music career fund.

Here's what you'll need, more or less in this order:

- Professionally produced, mixed and mastered music. This is what fans and music industry professionals will hear. Give them the best that you have. You can do this today for as little as several thousand dollars if you shop around, record after midnight, and are creative.
- Photos and videos taken by professionals. These can be posted immediately to your free social media sites such Facebook, Twitter, Google+, ReverbNation, etc. Bad photos and videos can kill you. Delete them right away. You are better off with nothing.
- A mobile-friendly website. There are lots of cost-effective web builders today. Populate that site with your professionally-rendered songs, photos and videos. Also include a subscribe button so you can collect emails and fan information.

- Sign up for one of the mass mailing services such as Constant Contact or iContact in the U.S. Hire a graphic artist to prepare your stock newsletter (using your professionally rendered songs, photos and videos) and send out regular newsletters to all of your subscribers. This newsletter highlights your recent accomplishments and progress, as well as offering your music and merch for sale. This mailing service costs only $20 or so per month.
- For your shows, have your graphic artist design fliers, for both printing and digital posting. $50 per flier is common. Become, along the way, best friends with a graphic artist and printer. You'll need them as your career takes off.
- Hire your graphic artists for several hundred dollars to prepare an EPK (electronic press kit). This is what you send to venues, record labels, and music licensors—actually, to anyone and everyone who wants to learn who you are and do business with you.
- Merch comes after the above. Hats, T-shirts, etc. can be commissioned online for very little money.

You can do all of the above for under $5,000. If you have the songs, this will be the best investment you've ever made.

> Is it appropriate to charge money for a funeral?

Answered by Kathy Alexander, singer, vocal coach and staff writer at VoiceCouncil Magazine

"Edna always loved your singing. Could you sing at her memorial service?" Mr. Schmidt said to me tearfully the day after his wife died. I was speechless. I had done a lot of performing, but never at a memorial. It turned out to be the first of many funeral gigs.

The thought of doing this kind of gig might make some singers run for the hills, or at the very least feel awkward about asking for money. But consider this: family members who organize the ceremony want to honor their loved one, so they will invest to make the event meaningful. Paying soloists in church ceremonies is the norm, and in my case, people knew I was studying and working in music so they saw me as a professional singer and expected to pay me.

My rule of thumb was to charge $75–125 to sing one or two feature songs during the ceremony, and more if they wanted pre- or post-ceremony music or if I had to bring my own sound gear. A piano accompanist would usually charge $25–35 per hour and my quote would reflect that if I was to accompany myself.

Sometimes I've chosen not to charge, and just offer my singing as a gift. This is when I've been close to the deceased or their family. In these cases, it can be difficult to sing, given the strong emotions I've felt. So, I switch into "professional mode" for the solo and let myself cry after the singing is done.

It is the greatest honor to know that my singing is helping an entire community to say goodbye to a loved one. If my voice helps them celebrate, remember and cry, then I consider it a privilege to take part.

> Is it acceptable to ask for money up front from the venue?

Answered by Ron "Bumblefoot" Thal, lead guitarist, Guns N' Roses, songwriter, recording artist and producer

When and how you get paid is always part of your negotiations prior to accepting a gig. Just remember, in the end, you want the finances to work out for everybody: you, the venue—and yes, even the promoter.

You don't usually ask for money up front for small, local gigs. Often, your earnings will come from the door charge (called, "the door") or ticket sales, and will be calculated at the end of the night based on how many people came. You may have heard stories about a venue that made 100 of the tickets mysteriously "disappear" from the tally. If this actually happened to you, you would decide if it is worth playing there next time, and you would, of course, forewarn other local musicians that the venue does this.

It gets a little tricky when it comes to those middle-sized gigs, especially when you are touring. I've seen situations where the promoter was nowhere to be seen after the gig, and the band had to leave town before they could get their share of the door charge. Thankfully, they had asked for a portion of their pay up front, so at least they didn't walk away empty handed.

At big gigs, there are large amounts of money and reputations at stake. This means nobody wants to get sued and everyone will be committed to upholding the contracts. Getting paid up front, or having a guarantee in the contract, is common (a guarantee is a specific amount you will get paid, regardless of the turn-out). There are always different ways to negotiate the money side of things; for example, in return for a larger guarantee, you can offer the venue a percentage of your merchandise sales.

> Is it bad to "low-ball" a bid (offer to do a gig for less than the going rate)?

Answered by Angela Kelman, Canadian Juno Award winning recording artist and veteran of thousands of gigs

Trying to get a gig can be a competitive experience. During the negotiations with a venue, you might think lowering your fee will increase your chance of getting that gig. You may even be tempted to charge less than the "going rate" for musicians in your part of the world. However, if you are capable of doing a great job and your show looks and sounds professional, undercutting the going rate sets everyone back on the pay scale.

Once a client knows your hard-to-resist bargain price, you will have to work long and hard to get it back up to where the going rate was. In the long run, it really is a self-sabotaging move. Veteran musicians have worked years to finally get wages up to a decent and liveable scale and we should all be working hard to keep them at that level.

What you need to figure out is the going rate per man per gig. Try talking to some seasoned players that have a great local reputation. Be honest and tell them you would like to pursue some gigs and are not sure what to charge. Most likely, they will advise you on a scale of what to charge depending on what kind of gig you are doing.

One more thing: if you are looking to get some gigging experience and polish your act, try creating your own gigs. Ask the guy who owns the local café if your band can come and entertain for tips, free coffee and dessert. Promise to bring friends in as a guaranteed audience. Always be professional and you will work your way up to great paying gigs by paying your dues and polishing your show via these "creative" gigs.

Have fun!

CHAPTER 15

Boost Your Earning Power

Because you need more.

"I've discovered that fans want to give you money. I'm not trying to be crass about this, but a big part of my job as a business person is making sure that I provide as many opportunities as possible for people to give me money."

—Jonathan Coulton, Internet singing star,
known for his songs about geek culture

"The old model for releasing music was for you to go into a shed and struggle with your muse. Then you would emerge with an album around which you planned a huge release campaign. In the new model it's more about continual engagement with your community."

—Brian Felsen, President of CDBaby,
BookBaby and HostBaby

Boost Your Earning Power

Because you need more.

Actions:

1. Open Your Eyes to the New World of Vocalist Incomes
2. Don't Wait for the Big Labels, Release Your Music the Smart Way
3. Sell Your Music Online
4. Reach Today's Gatekeepers
5. Make Money with Session Work
6. Add Value with Contests, Awards and Competitions
7. Know When Getting a Manager Pays Off
8. Look Before You "Leap" at a Label
9. Protect the Copyright on Your Original Music
10. Make Money Through Registering Your Original Music

Frequently Asked Questions:

» *How does getting signed actually make you more money?*

» *Should I focus on getting money from live performances or recordings?*

» *Can I make a lot of money singing jingles?*

» *How can I break through into full time singing work?*

» *Will fame guarantee my financial freedom?*

» *What is a musician's union and should I join one?*

» *After I pay the band what I promised them, I'm not going to make any money! What should I do?*

» *I've heard that it's illegal to sell my CD if I include songs that are not written by me. How do I get around this?*

» *I wrote some of my songs with other people and now they're getting some attention. How do we split up the rights?*

» *Can a music publisher help me make money?*

» *I need $750 NOW to finish my recording project—HELP!*

Action 1: Open Your Eyes to the New World of Vocalist Incomes

There are more ways than ever before for vocalists to make an income—and to push their "take" further.

As the music industry crumbles into the dust, I think we all need to remember that if making music is no longer profitable then there will be less music in the world. This is a transaction that people understand.

When I was experimenting with various ways of trying to connect people to listening to my music and to paying money for it, I tried out the virtual tip jar route—where people are invited to pay what they would like to pay. However this never worked out well for me. Then, when I did my thing of producing a song a week for a year, I gave people two options: (i) here is a link where you can download my song for free and (ii) here is a link where you can download my song for a dollar. A lot of people chose the free link—but many more than I expected chose to buy my songs for a dollar. That seemed an amount of money that many weren't going to begrudge me.

The important part of why this works for me is that I have always been straightforward about the idea that what is most important to me is that people hear the music, so I am not going to stress out about the various ways that people get the music for free. I accept that this is a part of reality that I am not going to fight. At the same time I broadcast this message: "Dear World, I would like for this to be my job and, if you like the music I made and you want me to make more, then the best way is to pay me money."

There are so many different ways of making money in the music business; each person needs to find their own solution that is customized. This depends on what you do as an artist, who your fans are, how they listen to their music, how familiar they are with you, how familiar they are with certain kinds of tech and how likely they are to want to give you money. I recommend that you try everything that seems like it might pay off.

In the context of being a pro musician who performs in public, I've discovered that fans want to give you money. I'm not trying to be crass about this, but a big part of my job as a business person is making sure that I provide as many opportunities as possible for people to give me money.

This means that it is important to have a lot of different products and channels—if they want to buy digital, make it easy. I sell a USB with my entire collection—that is the perfect item for some people. Then, there is the idea of multi-tiered editions of my new albums—I experimented with this on my last record: a 10-dollar digital edition, a 20-dollar signed CD version and a deluxe box that costs 150 dollars. You are making sure that there is something for everybody. If there is a fan out there that would happily pay you $2,000 for your new album, you need to make sure that fan has an option of giving you that $2,000.

—Jonathan Coulton: Internet singing star, known for his songs about geek culture

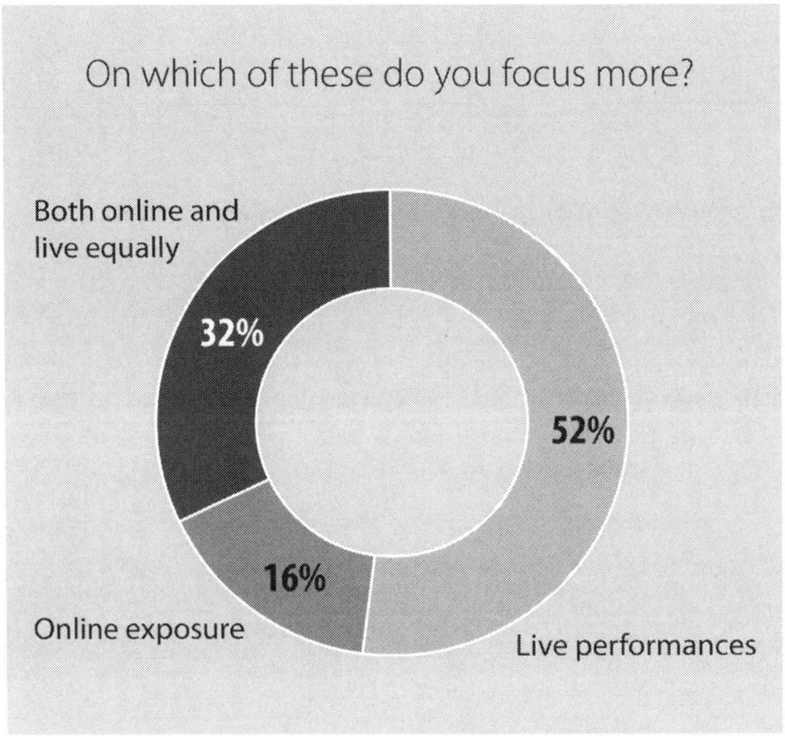

—from the 2012-2013 TC-Helicon survey of 1,000 singers

Action 2: Don't Wait for the Big Labels—Release Your Music the Smart Way

There's a new model for connecting your music with the world. Master it.

The old model for releasing music was for you to go into a shed and struggle with your muse. Then you would emerge with an album around which you planned a huge release campaign. In the new model it's more about continual engagement with your community.

Now, you might release an EP of three songs in January, three songs in April, three songs in July and then three songs in December. You will be watching the number of plays and the feedback from your community in order to determine what's working—and what isn't. Then, you might release an album of the "greatest hits" from those EPs along with some sort of bonus track.

This kind of continual engagement is important for building your presence online. In other words, it's not all about "me, me, me"; it's not about "Look and listen to my music." It's about discovering your heroes and who else is consuming music and making lifestyle choices similar to yours. Engage in conversation with this community, answer questions and talk about related topics with other opinion leaders. Tweet these leaders and musicians and also mention your art.

If you still wanted to have a label distribute your work (which you may at that point no longer need), then the number of plays and the amount of fans you already have will help them make a decision that justifies their investment. However, Macklemore (who came up through CD Baby) has millions of views of his new song "Thrift Shop" on YouTube–entirely without a label! There are plenty of "label artists" with views only in the thousands.

–Brian Felsen: President of CDBaby, BookBaby and HostBaby

Single Vs. Albums?

Because many people are downloading music digitally, they tend to pick singles as opposed to albums. As an artist, this means you can release and promote one song at a time without having to produce a whole album. Still, there is one advantage to creating an album: not every song has to be a killer radio track—some of your songs can tell a story of what you are really about. You can promote one song from your album as a single, then tell people where to buy the whole album.

***–Marc JB:** remixer-producer with over 70 no.1 hits across the US and UK*

Action 3: Sell Your Music Online

"Aggregators," "revenue streams" and "mechanical royalties" all have one thing in common: earning power.

The power is now in your hands to sell your own music. To sell your music digitally, there are just two things you have to do: 1. Get your music into a digital store like iTunes. 2. Tell people about it.

The easiest way to get your music into a digital music store is through an aggregator such as CD Baby. An aggregator is the middleman who brokers the deals between the digital stores and the record companies. If you are not with a record company, then you deal with the aggregator directly. They collect money from the stores and distribute it back to you as your music sells. Aggregators will also put your music on streaming services such as Spotify and Pandora.

Uploading your music to CD Baby and other aggregators requires you to set up an account, similar to YouTube. Your song files must be high quality and should be either WAV or AIF. You usually have to upload all your information and your own artwork as well.

Your earnings will come in several revenue streams. The two main ones are: mechanical royalties and performance royalties. You earn mechanical royalties when people purchase your singles or albums. This mechanical revenue comes to you through your record company or your aggregator. On top of actual sales of albums and singles, when someone listens to your song on a subscription-based digital streaming service like Spotify, you get mechanical royalties as well.

Even when people watch your video on YouTube, you get small mechanical royalties from the advertisers. Performance royalties on the other hand, come to you when your music is played on the radio or at a place with a licence such as restaurant. The money comes to you via a performance rights organisation such as PRS for Music in the UK or ASCAP in the US.

The second half of the magic is to tell people about your music. It is all very well having your tunes available to buy but if no one knows they are there, you will have no sales! Use all your resources to let people know: email mail-outs, Facebook posts, Tweets and good, old-fashioned telling people face to face.

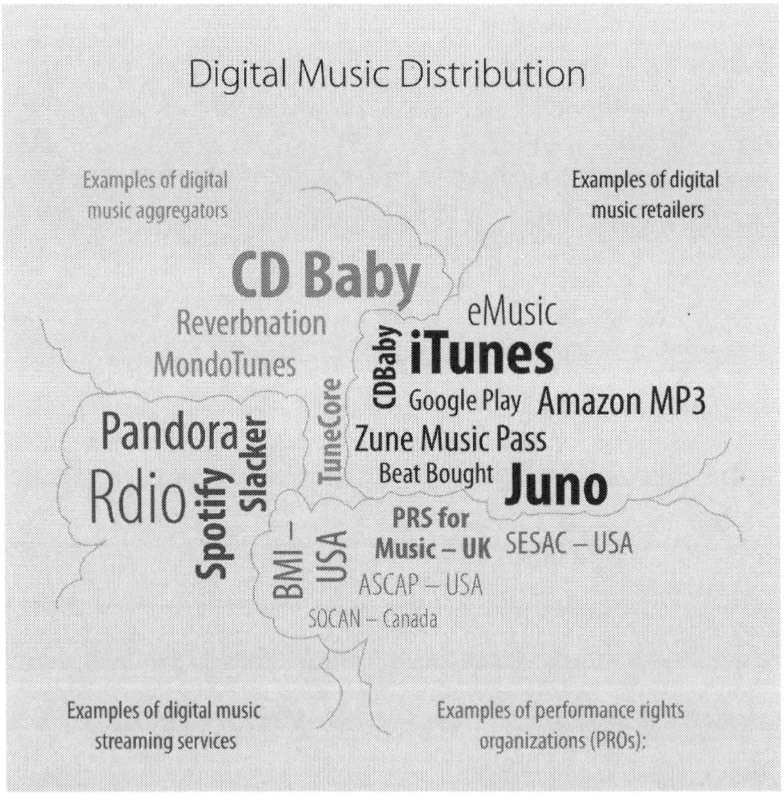

Compared to how it was in the past, there is little money to be made from selling your music—the real money is in the live gigs. You have to see your music sales as part of your promotion and not as a significant part of your revenue.

—Marc JB: remixer-producer with over 70 no.1 hits across the US and UK

Action 4: Reach Today's Gatekeepers

Know the ways people are talking about and sharing music and you'll have the keys to reach your audience.

First, make sure your music is solid: excellent songwriting that moves quickly to a catchy chorus. Your production should show off strong, memorable vocals—this is really important, as there are many popular pieces that don't have strong underlying music yet are hits because of the vocals.

In terms of your production, you don't need to spend a ton of money. Production has been democratized. You can either ramp up your tech skills or make your recording process move more quickly by hooking up with someone in the music community or from Craigslist who is making music that fits your material. Once you've finished recording, get your CD mastered. Mastering can make a difference between it sounding acceptable and sounding poopy.

Physical CDs are still a viable product—they were in decline for a while but CD Baby's CD sales are actually up over last year. If you are a touring musician, then these sales will mean a lot to you. Fans enjoy purchasing a totemic object with artwork that is autographed—good luck trying to sell a download card! For online distribution, you need to be in the watering holes where people purchase, consume and stream music. With a company like CD Baby you can just upload it and get it everywhere—to iTunes, Amazon, Spotify, Rdio, and dozens of others. If it can't be found, it can't be discovered.

And another crucial thing: if you have the talent, means or someone to help you, make a video. People are consuming more and more music on YouTube—it's not piracy; it's the way people are talking about and sharing music.

It is helpful to have a video that is eye catching, perhaps funny or clever. Remember, we've moved past having the major labels act as gatekeepers, the be all and end all for all musicians. Back when I was in rock bands (two of the bands I was in got signed by labels—and then dropped!), you needed to please and impress the gatekeepers—at which point, you would sign away most of your royalties. The job of the labels was to fund and distribute your recording, to get it placed in retail stores. Now the labels are crumbling and physical distribution is slowly disappearing.

Today's gatekeepers aren't so much the labels, but the populace at large—which has the power to make a song or video go viral. That said, the labels still wield power: just this week Taylor Swift sold over a million copies of her record and it happened because of the marketing budget and social media arm of the major label. However, things are changing. Just think of Rebecca Black's song "Friday"—that song's had literally millions of "dislikes" on YouTube, but I wrote her cheques and she's done extremely well!

—Brian Felsen: President of CDBaby, BookBaby and HostBaby

Action 5: Make Money with Session Work

Pick up some lucrative work—without undervaluing your voice.

You can have a sustainable career as a session singer, doing vocals for demos, TV, radio and film. The rates for this type of work depend on the project and whether or not you are with a union, but I'll give you a general idea of what you might earn and how to break into this area.

If you were called in to sing a demo here in LA for a songwriter or composer, you would earn about $250 for two hours of work. Many non-union singers would charge $100 per hour. You could make more if your singing is used in film, TV or radio since "residuals" might be involved—this is a percentage every time your singing is broadcast.

> *Because you've been active meeting people in the industry, you suddenly hear, "So-and-so is ill, why don't you come and fill in for them?" I've gotten more jobs on referral than through sending out a demo.*
>
> ***—Gerald White:** prolific singer-songwriter who has worked on over 100 TV and commercial productions*

If you are going the union route, you agree to only take on union jobs. There are many advantages to this: you never need to haggle over the fees; every job is a negotiated rate. There is actually a big book of union rates that lists all kinds of projects such as singing for a film with a budget of over X, under X, etc. You sign a contract before you ever do the work that includes rules about break times, facility standards and other factors that ensures you are treated well. If the production company doesn't pay you in thirty days, they are penalized and this results in more money on your paycheck.

If you go the non-union route, I urge you not to fall prey to undervaluing your work! You see, too many singers are prone to do anything for anybody for little money thinking, "If they just hear me, they will introduce me to a big producer and I will soon be famous!" It never happens this way 97% of the time; a career is built over years of relationships. I recommend that you (i) agree on a price before you show up, (ii) agree that you will be paid on the day of work and (iii) have something in writing in case your work goes viral: "We each agree that if this work is broadcast, we will renegotiate the terms." All of this can be in a simple, one-page document. Present these terms nicely, emphasizing how the agreement protects each of you.

How do you get this work? Aside from working on your voice and developing all of the professional qualities that make one work-worthy, it is all about being in circulation and meeting people. Gig whenever you can, go to every club where singers are doing showcases, talk to singers, attend classes and go to auditions. After sending out many, many demos I finally broke through by attending a class at the Guild for Singers on the subject of sight-reading. There, I met a singer who was the voice on *Happy Days* and *Gilligan's Island*; he introduced me to a contractor. There is simply no substitute for getting out there and meeting people.

—Gerald White: prolific singer-songwriter who has worked on over 100 TV and commercial productions

Action 6: Add Value with Contests, Awards and Competitions

Open up some different doors and make the contacts you need to advance your career.

Winning a competition or a contest doesn't mean that you are actually going to succeed—but they can be significant for other reasons. Just think of reality TV competitions: you can point to several people who have won and gone on to more successes but there are other winners who only had fleeting success. If the biggest competitions don't consistently produce winners what can the smaller ones do? The answer: they can open doors that can lead you to success.

One songwriter I met didn't win much money in her competition but it put her in front of me. As a publisher, I've been able to help her further her career. The same is true with conferences. I've heard this many times: "I went to this conference and met this producer and he's helping me further my music!" The odds may be a 1,000 to 1 that you will have this same experience—but those are much better odds than walking around London where it is 10,000,000 to 1. You are more likely to get noticed because you are entering a smaller pool. Conferences, competitions and contests are one more way to play the game. You may not succeed, but no one will ever discover you if you are playing alone.

—Jay Frank: leading author (Hack Your Hit and Futurehit.DNA) and Owner/CEO of DigSin

Action 7: Know When Getting a Manager Pays Off

Unlock the power of your team by being involved the right way.

We live at a time when you can build whatever organization around you that you want. When you hire someone to be a part of your business, whether they are a manager, attorney, PR person, producer or engineer, the thing to remember is that these people will do their best work when they are excited about what you are doing and when you are invested in the kind of job they are doing.

This leads me to a warning: you can't just hire someone and then walk away and assume that they will do everything the way you would. When you are working independently you have ultimate control over everything; as soon as you outsource then you need to become a good manager of the people you hire. This involves making clear requests of your team and having a mutual understanding of your expectation of what they are going to do. This also means being prepared to say, "You know, this is not working out."

How To Get Onto a Reality TV Singing Competition:

- ***Take lessons.*** *Refine your skills—the best way to be discovered is to be good.*
- ***Know the timeline.*** *Make sure that you pay attention to when you actually need to audition; many shows are cast and filmed far in advance.*
- ***Repertoire.*** *Learn as many songs as possible from different genres and perform these as much as you can. Shows may give you a list of songs from which you have to choose (this has to do with rights). The more songs you know, the more likely you'll be comfortable when they hand you their list.*
- ***Record.*** *I initially wanted to record for creativity's sake and to produce a "reel" to hand to vocal contractors. Through recording, I identified my strengths and weaknesses. When you watch a show like American Idol it's clear that some people don't come across the way they think they are coming across—recording is a great way to sort out this issue.*
- ***100% Kindness.*** *You never know who is watching. Be kind, don't put others down and always project positive energy. I have a friend who was performing a very small show in a restaurant and it would have been easy for them to think, "I don't have to do my best." It turns out that there was a huge music critic in the audience. In the reality TV experience, the cameras are on you all the time.*

–Tasha Layton: *LA based singer and backing vocalist with Katy Perry*

There's a trap in thinking, "Once I get a manager everything will be taken care of and that person will really make my career go further and faster." The truth is that once you have hired a manager you are not done thinking about this area; you still need to be engaged. I've made this error time and time again—I assume that my manager will just "know"; the truth is that no one will understand your business, brand and art the way you do.

So, do your best to communicate and to measure how good a job they are doing. The downfall of many bosses is that they don't want to have an uncomfortable conversation about goals and expectations—but you are, in fact, asking others to take over a part of your work life. If, for example you hire a PR person, then you need to have a good idea of what you would like them to achieve unless you only want them to field some requests and sign up some interviews. I would encourage you to set some clear goals: "Here is a list of 10 publications I think would be responsive to me and I would be thrilled to be in. Please try to get me in there." Then, you check into to see how it is going. Did you get the placement?

—Jonathan Coulton: Internet singing star, known for his songs about geek culture

Action 8: Look Before You "Leap" at a Label

There may be very good reasons for turning down a record deal—make sure you know what they are.

Many singers have turned down record deals. Why is this? Not only is it easier than ever for artists to record, distribute and sell albums on their own, but a lot of record deals today offer only a small chance of making money. Does this mean you shouldn't pursue a contract with a record company? No. There is still a lot to be gained from the right contract, at the right time with the right people.

Seasoned artists will tell you to use a lawyer to help you understand the full implications of any recording contract. Key questions to answer are:

- Is it an exclusive deal? Exclusive deals mean you can't record or sell your music other than through that record company.
- How much and what type of the record company's costs will you be required to pay back? Usually, everything they pay out is an advance on your royalties, which means all must be repaid before you can pocket any money.
- How many future albums or "options" does the contract include?
- Is there any legal way for you to back out of the contract, should you want to?
- What is the royalty that you will make on the sale of each album? 50% is common, but it all depends on your status.
- Is there a cash advance? Artists who are not well-established would be very lucky to get an advance these days. Remember, it will come out of your future royalties.
- What kind of resources, promotion and distribution will the company provide? If the record company pays for promotion, this will get your name out there and could be more valuable than the cash advance.
- Is it a 360 deal? This means the company owns all your money-earning activities (selling merchandise, doing any non-musical gigs)—every dollar you earn must be divided between you and the record company.
- For how long does the record company own your music? This can be from about seven years to perpetuity.

If you have a good relationship with the record company, and you believe they are going to commit sufficient resources to promoting your album, then that deal could be the right move for you.

Most record companies are struggling businesses in an industry that is short on money. Of course you need to stay away from the "sharks" out there, but there are conscientious record companies who work incredibly hard trying to make money for all involved. Sit down with them and find out how they can add value to your brand—whether that be through exposure, PR, their industry connections or the energy they bring to it.

—Marc JB: remixer-producer with over 70 no.1 hits across the US and UK

Action 9: Protect the Copyright on Your Original Music

The pennies can really add up—but not without first protecting your music.

Music publishing is a pennies business, but if you take care of some basic housekeeping and have some activity going on, those pennies could add up to a meaningful amount of money.

If you are a singer-songwriter, writing and performing your original music, the first step to take is to protect the copyright in your works. Why do you need to do this? You may be sending samples of your music to all sorts of people in the music business as well as making it available through various online services, so what's to prevent some unscrupulous person ripping off one of your songs and claiming to have written it themselves?

Copyright in your work exists automatically when the work is created, but being able to prove when you created the work helps you to protect it. The traditional (and cheapest) way of doing this is to put your CD (or MP3) in an envelope along with any lyrics and send it to yourself by registered mail. Keep the receipt and do not open the envelope when it comes back to you. Always write the list of songs on both the CD and the packaging, along with the following information: "All songs written by (your name). © (year) (your name). All songs are copyright control. The copyright in these sound recordings is owned by (your name). All rights reserved."

Doing all of this is important—but you are not going to earn anything unless the agencies in charge of collecting income know who you are. If your music starts gaining attention, then there are a number of things you must do to make those pennies add up—so, read the next action …

—Debbie Pearce: of GHQ Limited; has worked with Warner Chappell Music, Universal Music and The Beatles' Apple Corps Ltd.

Action 10: Make Money Through Registering Your Original Music

Basic housekeeping for your music involves joining the right societies.

First of all make sure you join your local performing rights society, such as ASCAP or BMI in the United States, or PRS for Music in the UK. When your music is performed live, by you or anyone else, or broadcast on radio or TV, these collecting societies make sure that any fees due to you are collected and accounted. You start getting those pennies.

Once you have become a member of your local performing rights society, you need to register your songs. You might not get very much from playing small bars and clubs, but if you're ever lucky enough to perform your own works on an arena tour, your songwriter's percentage of the box office income will start to look very interesting indeed. Similarly, being played on a local radio station won't make you rich, but sustained national airplay is a very different matter.

Whilst the copyright in your songs can generate important royalty streams, don't forget you may also be due income from your performance on recorded works—whether you wrote them or not. If you have made an audible contribution to a recording that has been broadcast on radio or television, you may also receive more pennies. The United States is out of step with the rest of the world on this neighbouring right to the performing right. Income is due only from digital and satellite radio play, and is administered by SoundExchange. In the UK this right is administered by PPL, which licenses most of the same users as PRS for Music and has reciprocal agreements with sister collecting societies around the world. So if you are a recording artist, don't neglect to register with your local neighbouring rights society or you could be missing out on income due to you.

I know a surprisingly large number of artists who have neglected to join PPL, or haven't registered their songs correctly (or at all) with PRS, and have lost out on tens of thousands of dollars over the course of their careers as a result.

Taking care of this basic housekeeping is not difficult to do. Without it, your music-making may only ever be a hobby. With it, it could be your livelihood.

> *—Debbie Pearce: of GHQ Limited; has worked with Warner Chappell Music, Universal Music and The Beatles' Apple Corps Ltd.*

Frequently Asked Questions

> How does getting signed actually make you more money?

Answered by Steve Eggleston, award-winning law professor, artist manager and best selling author

The short answer is that you sometimes get a non-refundable advance. Many small labels don't pay any advance at all; traditionally, larger indie and major labels have often paid an advance that reflects the label's desire to sign you (which is a measure of their prediction of your likely success).

For the sake of discussion, let's say you get really lucky and land a half million-dollar deal with a major label. That means you'll probably get a $100,000–$200,000 dollar advance, above and beyond your recording budget. Sounds pretty good, doesn't it?

Maybe and maybe not. That $200,000 must last you, the entire band, and everyone's families the duration of the recording of your first CD (which often takes a year) and the tour that follows the CD's release (which takes another year). While touring, you may also get a "per diem," but it could be as little as $25 per day. Traditionally, the artist could also sell CDs and other merch at shows while on tour and keep all the income. Today labels often take a part of that in what's called a "360 deal."

In addition to the advance and merch, you will also be entitled to a royalty for CD sales and downloads. However, most often your royalties will not kick in until the label fully recoups the cost of your advance, the cost of recording and releasing your music, and any marketing and other costs related thereto. This means, as a practical matter, that you will not receive any substantial record or CD royalties unless you go Gold or Platinum. Of course, if you can, try to negotiate to receive royalties beginning at dollar one.

Few bands get rich on their first record. In fact, I know a band out of Vegas who made it big and signed to a major label. One of their songs made it to #3 on the Billboard rock charts. One of the guys in the band melted down a year into the deal. He was so broke and poor on the road that he couldn't handle it.

The bottom line is that the record deal often doesn't make you any money to write home about. It seldom allows you to buy a new car or house. What it will do is launch your career. And once your career is launched, a bundle of money can be made from CD royalties, show fees, merch and licensing.

Of course, not everyone does it that way. Some artists build their careers from the ground up without the financial help of the major and large indie labels. The best example of this kind of artist is blues guitarist Joe Bonamassa. He sells out arenas and takes home a bundle, with no recoupment concerns of any kind.

> Should I focus on getting money from live performances or recordings?

Answered by Steve Eggleston, award-winning law professor, artist manager and best selling author

No—neither—not at the beginning of your career. The most important thing for a new artist is exposure. Your number one goal must be to get your music out there. This means playing good shows for as much as you can get; the show is more important than the money. If you're making a decision not to play a show because you're not making enough, that's a strategic mistake. This also means posting your music for free online and on YouTube. If you do record and release CDs, then of course there is nothing wrong with charging fans at shows.

If you're already a full-time musician and you're making a living playing live music, you have a very different agenda. Your goal is attracting a following and preserving your quote—this is the minimum amount that you will accept for a gig. If you play for less than your quote, you will undermine your value. For instance, I know some artists here in Las Vegas who refuse to play on New Year's Eve unless they get double their normal quote. Their reasoning is that, if they do that, they'll then have to start taking regular gigs for half their New-Year's-Eve price.

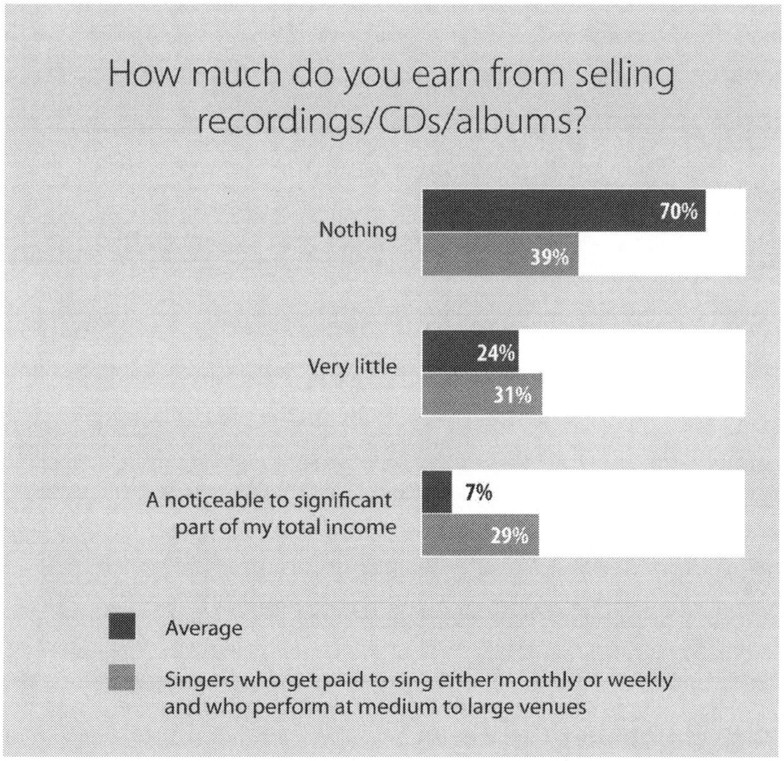

–from the 2012-2013 TC-Helicon survey of 1,000 singers

> Can I make a lot of money singing jingles?

Answered by Judy Rodman, award-winning vocal coach and chart-topping recording artist

The term "session singer" includes jingle singers and background (or backing) vocalists. Jingle singing can be quite lucrative because of the residuals paid on regional and national spots. Residuals are moneys paid for each time the jingles are played on radio or TV, and can run into the thousands for spots syndicated widely and played often. This specialized studio work is harder to find than it used to be, but background vocals remain in demand. Here in the United States, AFTRA (a professional singer's union) scale work pays best; otherwise the singer must negotiate a non-union buyout (one price to cover all repeats of the spot forever).

I would advise anyone who is looking for this kind of work to:

1. Get experience and education singing lots of styles of music and studying different kinds of vocal arrangements.
2. Make good professional contacts; try to keep expanding your network. Find and contact jingle production companies and recording studios who might give you names of music producers doing jingles.
3. Get a good demo reel created. You'll want to give or send this to the producers and production companies you contact, as well as to established session singers who are doing this work and might be in a contracting (hiring) or recommending position.

Use the opportunities that open up for you to make bridges to other work such as singing leads or backgrounds for songwriters on their demos, doing stage backgrounds for artists' live showcase or road performances, and singing in the background group for TV and radio shows. Keep in mind that the music business is constantly changing and multiple streams of income are helpful when one type of work falls off.

I landed my first jingle by forming a singing trio led by the choir director from my church in Jacksonville, Florida. It turns out that the choir director knew a local recording engineer who needed a group for a national ad for "Jeno's Pizza Logs." I was instantly hooked on the exacting and lucrative work! Afterwards, I moved to Memphis, auditioned and became a staff jingle singer for what was then the world's largest jingle company. This work required me to be a surgically precise singing machine, to blend like butter with the other staff singers, to be a quick sight-reader of written vocal music and to be able to suddenly change gears—to step out and sing solos in many styles. We sang from 8:30 to 3:30 five days a week, sometimes Saturdays. It was quite the education—and led me to a hit solo vocal career and then to producing, songwriting and professional vocal coaching.

To thrive as a jingle singer, develop these skills:

- Sing many different styles
- Blend with all kinds of voices
- Maintain surgically accurate pitch

- Change vocal tone as directed
- Read charts (written music) as necessary

My final tip: keep up your networking skills. Jingle production companies often have in-house singers who do most of the group singing, but you can get work with them by being able to sing solos, as they are usually on the lookout for new sounds. If you are a writer and musician, you might even consider forming your own company and networking with advertising agencies in your area. Grow your network, maintain a top quality reputation and you may find jingle work a great stream of revenue for your vocal career.

> How can I "break through" into full time singing work?

Answered by Jennie Sawdon, singer, pianist and vocal tutor, voted "Wedding Singer of the Year"

I was training as an opera singer and I needed extra money. I was excited by all the original music going on in the local jazz circuit, so I went to jam sessions, met musicians and got up to sing—my first payment was a pint of beer! I loved opera but I didn't want to spend my life only singing other people's music. People eventually started asking me to join their bands which, on a good night, would bring me $75. My breakthrough into full time work came with getting known by agencies and becoming an events singer.

I always stress the difference between the "events industry" and the "recording industry"—they are not the same thing. If you are interested in following my route then contact agencies, send them your information and a good quality recording; a video is even better, as people want to see you these days as well as hear you.

I applied to many agencies who work in events. You see, there are all kinds of professional organizations who want to have entertainers on their books. I'm with about 25 agencies, and now I also have a significant amount of work that comes directly to me through my own website. Agencies will usually charge the client an extra 10%–15% on top of your quoted fee. I would say that 75% of my singing comes from performing at weddings and another 25% is from corporate events, parties and local live gigs.

My friend used to be a singer and is now running a "soft-play" center for little children. I mentioned to her the other day that perhaps I could do a little of her kind of work on the side. She told me, "You can't do it 'a little bit'—you have to put your heart and soul into it." Of course she is totally right.

The same applies to the arts, even more so.

We live in a competitive world where it is very hard to "do things on the side" in a serious way. Even though singing doesn't have the job security I sometimes want—I don't ever want it to be "on the side."

> Will fame guarantee my financial freedom?

Answered by Steve "Luke" Lukather, of Toto, widely considered to be one of the world's best living guitarists

While putting together Toto's 35 anniversary PR campaign, our label figured out that we played on 8,000 records, had 225 Grammy nominations and half a billion records sold—counting all the guys in Toto, including our projects with other artists. I was surprised. We did all that?

I'm not going lie to you; it's a great business, but it's HARD. If you jump on this train it's going to run you over, mangle you and sew you back together like the scarecrow in Wizard of Oz ... and then run you over again. You are going to have to pick yourself up and say, "Fuck you. Now may I have another?" If you want to be in this business, those are the kind of punches you have to be ready to take. You can't get into this thinking you are going to be instantly rich.

I'm a very lucky man. I get to do my solo records, I perform with Toto and I play with the best artists in the world. Even though I sell enough of my solo records to keep doing them, profit margins are such that I have to be on the road 10 months a year—I'm a road dog. I'm blessed and happy, but I work my fucking ass off.

I've got seven dependents and a 50% tax bracket. Take off another 25% for the managers, agents, lawyers and accountants that I have to pay for. Toto's seven-album compilation just came out and is selling for seven bucks. By the time it trickles down, I'm making just over a penny per record. We actually have to sue the record company every two years just to get the royalties they forgot to pay us, and even then—I'm splitting with six guys. On top of all that, I once had a bad accountant who stole a million bucks, and then there was the time we were held hostage by our label. I must sound like a bitter old guy! The truth is, I do rather well for myself, but these people who think I wipe my ass with thousand dollar bills are sadly mistaken!

> What is a musician's union and should I join one?

Answered by Diane Pancel, LA based singer, has shared the stage with David Foster, Nelly Furtado and Matt Dusk

I have been singing professionally for 20 years, and only joined a musicians union about five years ago. My involvement in the union has been nothing but positive for me.

There have been several opportunities that I have gotten only because of my connection to the union. I got an opportunity to sing in NYC through the musician's union in Canada. Then, years later, it was the same union who helped me get my visa to live and work in America.

Membership in a musician's union such as AFM (American Federation of Musicians of the United States and Canada (CFM)) or SAG-AFTRA (Screen Actors Guild with American Federation of Television and Radio Artists) is especially helpful for singers who want to get work in TV or any kind of session singing. If your music winds up on a TV show, you will earn residuals, or royalties every time that episode is bought or aired, but you can only get that money if you are a member of the union.

There's no rush to join a union—wait until you have some good gigging experience and have started to earn money from your singing. My suggestion is that you try joining for a year or a portion of a year. Singers of any aspiration stand to benefit from joining a musicians union. The membership fee is really not that much money ($100–$200 for the year), and you may just find some useful resources, support and connections.

> After I pay the band what I promised them, I'm not going to make any money! What should I do?

Answered by Nikki Lamborn, singer-songwriter of the English band "Never the Bride"

Get a day job. I'm serious. The day job is not just about putting food on the table; it will help you to afford to go to the gym, pay for your rehearsal rooms, vocal coaching sessions—everything you need to do to advance your career. Don't think you are too good to work; just go to Los Angeles and you'll see everyone in the music industry working at all kinds of jobs in order to get ahead. Look, the whole fact that you are up there doing what you want to do means more than money. Get the best people you can afford around you, even if that means you take a financial hit.

Even now I will trade money for exposure. Sometimes I will take a support role with a big band—even if they don't pay us. We'll pay instrumentalists and go on the road for as long as our money lasts. If we make it for two weeks worth of gigs, then that's a lot more gigs than I would have had at home—and my fan base is building up.

When I first started singing, I was working as a hairdresser for 25 dollars a week. I sang two nights a week in a club and the other four nights I worked as a singing waitress in a restaurant gig. I didn't make much from doing any of this; you can't at the beginning—no one knows who you are. This goes on for quite a long time. You have to believe in yourself and do what it takes to get up on that stage.

But, all the while you need to work on your craft; don't expect anyone to hand you your career on a plate. I was with my vocal coach for 15 years—I went every single week unless I was on the road. I did my singing warm ups every day for an hour, or even more. I recommend you get yourself a little bar residency and cut your teeth. Collect everyone's email addresses so that you are honing your craft and building your fanbase at the same time.

> I've heard that it's illegal to sell my CD if I include songs that are not written by me. How do I get around this?

Answered by Gary R. Greenstein, lawyer specializing in intellectual property matters and digital media

First, it is not illegal to sell a CD if you perform cover songs on the CD. However, if you, as a recording artist, record a musical work authored by someone other than yourself to sell on your CD, you have to obtain permission–i.e. a license–to record that musical work. The term of art used for this license is a "mechanical license," which is the right to reproduce and distribute a musical work as embodied in a sound recording.

There are two ways to get permission. First, you can go to directly to the person or persons who own the copyright in the underlying musical work (i.e. the notes and lyrics). The second option is to operate under a statutory license, which is a license granted under the copyright laws of the United States. The United States Congress, in creating a statutory (also known as "compulsory") mechanical license, determined that, once a musical work had been authored and distributed to the public the first time under the consent of the copyright owner of the musical work (i.e. the original copyright owner has authorized the recording of the musical work on a commercially released CD), any other person could thereafter reproduce and distribute such musical work in another sound recording, provided the primary purpose of making the sound recording in which the musical work is embodied is for distribution to the public for private use (i.e. you can't rely upon the statutory mechanical license for commercial, background/foreground music services).

In order for an artist or label to operate under the statutory mechanical license for clearing the rights to musical works, the artist or label must first file a form with the United States Copyright Office and then comply with the reporting and payment obligations of the license. Compliance, however, can be challenging for even large record labels. This is because the statute requires the statutory licensee to service a notice of intent to operate under the statutory license on each copyright owner of a musical work the licensee intends to reproduce and distribute "before or within thirty days after making, and before distributing any phonorecords (i.e. CDs)" of the musical work.

Unless you are a large and/or sophisticated record company, you might be better off trying to negotiate directly with individual music publishers for a mechanical license rather than relying upon the statutory license.

You could also contract with a third party that offers statutory mechanical license clearance services, such as Limelight: www.songclearance.com

> I wrote some of my songs with other people and now they're getting some attention. How do we split up the rights?

Answered by Debbie Pearce, of GHQ Limited; has worked with Warner Chappell Music, Universal Music and The Beatles' Apple Corps Ltd.

There's no right answer to this, but a brief trawl of the Internet on well-known legal disputes provides the best possible argument for sorting out songwriting splits sooner rather than later.

You may not want to introduce a business discussion into the creative environment because it looks pushy and aggressive, but if you're hoping to earn your living from this, it's your responsibility to take care of business. Just grit your teeth and do it.

For the sake of argument, let's say that you're in a four-piece band and you're all songwriters. You probably all come to rehearsals with either a few ideas for a song, or one that is almost fully written, so some songs will clearly be the brainchild of one member of the band more than others. In these cases, maybe 75% of the song should be allocated to that member, with the remaining 25% split between the other three. If a complete song is brought in, but with no lyrics, then whoever writes the lyrics might expect to be credited with writing half the song. You might decide that, as all the band contribute to the "arrangement" of each song, 20% of each song is always split equally between all the band (5% each), come what may.

In the case of professional songwriters going into a room together, it's almost certainly the case that any song written would be split equally, regardless of the fact that one of them might have written most of the lyrics and another one might have spent most of the session on the phone.

Ultimately, unless you decide just to split everything equally—which can lead to massive problems later on if the main songwriter starts to resent giving away so much of his income—it's a matter of even-handed negotiation and compromise. U2 have always split everything equally, regardless, and it seems to have worked OK for them.

Once you've agreed the split on each song, it's vital to write this down in some form and have each member of the band sign the document, indicating their agreement. At least then in the future, if one member of the band gets a deal and begins using the songs so that they generate publishing income, the other members of the band are protected and will receive their share. And for goodness sake do this at the time the song is written, because going back afterwards and trying to remember who did what can be nigh on impossible. Protect yourselves, treat everyone as fairly as possible, write it all down and sign it off when you're in the studio. Save yourself from having to sell your house to pay the legal bills to sort it all out later.

> Can a music publisher help me make money?

Answered by Debbie Pearce, of GHQ Limited; has worked with Warner Chappell Music, Universal Music and The Beatles' Apple Corps Ltd.

Yes, but as Shakespeare said, "Things in motion sooner catch the eye than what not stirs." In other words, you must generate some interest and attention before a publisher is likely to be interested in you. Once a publisher has decided you have potential, they can be invaluable. In addition to ensuring your works are correctly registered with collecting societies around the world, collecting your royalties and paying them to you, publishers can help promote your works by "synching" them into films or ads as well as giving you time to develop and helping you to find that elusive recording deal.

> I need $750 NOW to finish my recording project—HELP!

Answered by The Ultimate Team

Why not use the internet to harness your connection to your friends and family—and their connections? There are several crowd-sourced fundraising sites such as www.wefund.com in the UK and www.kickstarter.com in the USA. Singer-songwriter Rachel Bennett has just used wefund.com to successfully raise the funds she needed to complete her CD: "Watching a balance grow online is a strange and wonderful experience! You must apply with a video about your project, offer prize incentives (like a signed copy of your album) to would-be donors, and get the word out to family and friends."

CHAPTER 16

Markets for Your Voice

Find your vocation.

"Perseverance and passion. If you have these, then you stand a chance of surviving this race."

—Ruby Turner, renowned gospel and R & B singer

"Here's the number one thing: create your own identity, believe in it and stick with it."

—Chuck Billy of Testament

"Paradoxically, the way to reach more people on YouTube is to actually get more personal."

—Sarah Bella, singer-songwriter and YouTube star

Markets for Your Voice

Find your vocation.

Actions:

1. Know All the Gigs You Can Pursue
2. Don't Leave Your Bedroom—the YouTube Gig
3. Join the World of Session Singing
4. Demonstrate Gear
5. Become a Singing Teacher or Vocal Coach
6. Sell Your Albums and Merchandise

Frequently Asked Questions:

- *What is the difference between a contractor and an agent?*
- *How do I find an agent?*
- *As a singer do I make as much money as an instrumentalist in a band? How do we split it up?*
- *How can I get my original songs noticed by a filmmaker?*
- *I just got hired as a session singer for a film! What do I need to know?*
- *Can musical theater lead to a career?*

Action 1: Know All the Gigs You Can Pursue

It's time to get creative with new and different places to expand your audience.

The Local Gig. It's a digital era—but don't neglect the value of the gig around the corner at your local pub, café, or restaurant. Many famous artists give credit to their hours upon hours of performances in these low-key settings. Tell the venue how you will get people to your show (and don't forget to invite your aunt Betty). You might get an upfront fee, a split of the door charge, or the contents of your own tip jar. There may not be a lot of money—but there's the invaluable opportunity to build your fanbase and, even more importantly, to hone your musical talent. Be patient with background noise and remember to compliment the staff and the food. It if was good enough for The Beatles ...

—The Ultimate Team

The House Concert Gig. If you've got a following, you might try house concerts—they're both soulful and financially sustaining. A house concert is a musical performance held in a home or other private location. The intimacy and authenticity of these gigs appeal to both listener and performer. They are usually sponsored by a fan who will require either no pay at all (they're in it for the love of music), or a much smaller "cut" of the ticket sales when compared with a larger venue. My tip is to always work with a short and simple contract to protect you, the artist, from last-minute cancellations.

—Marina V, award-winning Russian-American singer, pianist, songwriter

The Festival Gig. Every day, everywhere, there are festivals going on. Some are music specific and others focus on a particular theme or event. Some feature a variety of musical styles and others are genre specific. While some festivals are more high profile than others, all festivals give performers the opportunity to play for a larger group of people than might otherwise come to the local pub. While lesser-known artists generally aren't paid much, if anything, for these gigs, the upside is that you are usually able to sell CDs and merchandise and, most importantly, to grow your fanbase.

—Jennifer Truesdale, singer-songwriter, coach and author of "Get Paid to Sing"

The GB Gig. GB is the abbreviation for General Business. GB gigs (also called "corporate gigs" or "casuals") include company parties, conventions, private parties, weddings, banquets, and, sometimes, dance clubs. Most of these gigs are booked through booking agencies and can pay quite well, especially for established, experienced singers. GB bands are required to perform a wide variety of musical styles including jazz, blues, R&B, pop and rock, so singers must be versatile. Additionally most GB gigs are a minimum of three to four hours and therefore require quite a bit of vocal and physical stamina—there's no better training field for new singers than GB gigs!

—Jennifer Truesdale, singer-songwriter, coach and author of "Get Paid to Sing"

The Floor Show Gig. Many cruise-lines, resorts, casinos, hotels, nightclubs and theme parks put on elaborate staged productions for their guests. These shows are often referred to as floor-shows or production-shows. They involve singers, dancers and musicians, referred to as cast members, and require significant rehearsal and preparation. The selection of cast members is generally based on a very specific vocal range and sometimes on specific body type and general "look." Singers should be versatile and have some basic dancing/movement skills. Performers are sometimes required to be gone from home for several months at a time, so a willingness to travel is essential.

—Jennifer Truesdale, singer-songwriter, coach and author of "Get Paid to Sing"

The Corporate Gig. Large corporations need musicians. They need them for their Christmas parties and other private events for their employees. John Kjøller of Basix has discovered a new kind of corporate gig. "We visit companies during work hours and do a 45 minute show. The point is to 'feel good at work.' It's basically an HR thing. We include audience participation too. It's sooo fun!" Try marketing yourself to coordinators at large corporations in your area who are looking for morale-boosting events.

—The Ultimate Team

The Special Event Gig. Special events gigs (weddings, birthdays, anniversaries, parties) often require that you not see yourself as the central attraction—it is someone else's big day. However, you never have to concede the joy of the performance. You'll get booked again if your dress, repertoire and volume match the expectations of the crowd that has gathered. It's often important that they can hear their own conversations. Often this kind of gig will come through an agency—so it is a great idea to introduce yourself to as many as you can in your area, giving them your bio and a really high quality recording of your voice—a video doesn't hurt either.

—Jennie Sawdon, singer, pianist and vocal tutor, voted "Wedding Singer of the Year"

The Online Gig. I went through a year and a half of figuring out how to genuinely speak to a camera. Before I got into YouTube I performed for a living, on cruise ships for several years. The funny thing is that I sang for about a thousand people a night for two to three nights a week. Now, when I do a YouTube video I have way more people "in my living room," an almost unlimited audience. One needs to find a genuine way to speak in that setting. I have recorded myself multiple times, and asked myself "Is that the way I want to come across?" I've also sought feedback from my friends and family on how I am coming across. Even though you are presenting an edited version of yourself, it needs to be genuine. I've had friends call me on this, "That's not very real, Peter." When you start gaining some attention, this kind of feedback is invaluable.

—Peter Hollens, Pop Singer & Producer/Youtuber with over 175 million views

The Musical Theatre Gig. You may want to be the top banana in the Big Apple, but musical theater artists must have an extra edge on vocal stamina. They must also be able to follow direction and work as a team, not to mention sing, act and dance—at the same time. London's West End and New York's Broadway are the famed Meccas of professional musical theater, but other large cities such as Toronto, Chicago and LA have sizable markets as well. In fact, paid work can be found in almost any city at professional theater companies, amusement parks, cruise ships, fairs and tourist attractions. Cruise ships make up a surprisingly large market for musical theater performers with their fully staged musicals and variety shows running every night.

–Kathy Alexander, singer, vocal coach and staff writer at VoiceCouncil Magazine

Which market do you spend the most time pursuing?

Market	%
Local live performances	51%
On-line exposure	19%
Musical Theater	5%
Session singing	5%
Recording sales	3%
Touring	3%
Opening for other bands	2%
TV, Radio or Film	2%
House Concerts	2%
Other	7%

Road dog?
17% of all survey respondents said they have been on tour but this increases to 45% for singers doing weekly paid gigs.

–from the 2012-2013 TC-Helicon survey of 1,000 singers

Touring Gigs. Don't simply become entranced with the idea of singing in "bigger and better" places; be strategic. Successful artists target cities that offer an opportunity to expand their fan-base, research active bands of similar genres in those places, make contacts with some of these groups, and work out a partnership of trading opening acts. Let's say that you have many Facebook fans that live two hours away–reach out to other groups in that place to try to open for them, offering them the same in return. At your "away" gig, be smart with how you gather email addresses and "likes." With your new fans you might be able to do a gig on your own steam next time. Remember to be fantastic hosts to bands who open for you.

–The Ultimate Team

Contests and Competitions. Somewhere, right now, there's a competition you could apply for. Should you? If you want fame and riches overnight, the answer is probably, "No." It's an often fickle lottery that benefits very few in this way. If you want exposure and to meet people who might push your career forward, it's "Yes." We all know about the big reality shows, but check out major music magazines and websites for relevant local and regional opportunities. Don't be cynical: we know one artist who failed to get through round two at a reality TV show; he gathered up the other "failures" to produce a fantastic song for a great cause, giving their careers a boost!

—*The Ultimate Team*

Action 2: Don't Leave Your Bedroom—the YouTube Gig

It's possible to have an international gig without leaving your house. Discover how some vocalists have made social media their full time job.

I have to credit my first international radio exposure to YouTube. It came about because someone in England saw my YouTube video, loved the song and sent it into a radio station. This allowed me to create a community in Great Britain, and six months later the song went to #1 on the iTunes singer/songwriter charts in the UK.

While some artists can make YouTube work as their main "performance venue," all artists will want to include YouTube as a part of their promotion strategy—as a way to increase one's fanbase, exposure and even revenue. Just think of the number of people who are on the internet—it's no wonder that YouTube is becoming a place where artists are being discovered.

> *Unusual, home cooked and low budget ideas can be very appealing to YouTubers. Quirky is key.*
>
> ***—Mister Tim:*** *viral video star, voice artist, composer and sponsored kazoo player*

Of course, you'll need a good quality video with good audio. It is worth investing time and energy to do this. Use a song that you know has made an impact on others in live performances. When you post your video, it is important to tag similar artists and niche markets that your song relates to. This will make it easier for new audience members to stumble upon your video.

As you gain subscribers and views on YouTube, share your videos on Twitter and Facebook, which in turn may lead to shares from your Facebook and Twitter fans. The commenting portion of each video creates a connection between you and your fans, just as other social networks do, but it allows comments to be specific to that video and song. It also provides an environment for fans to interact with one another.

Once you get the ball rolling you can apply to become a "YouTube Partner" and make a little (or a lot) of money. YouTube Partnering allows you to display ads on your videos; you then earn a percentage of the revenues generated by clicks on those ads. One British couple made over $150,000 for posting a video of their children that lasted about 57 seconds. Free money? Yes, please! As an independent musician I'm constantly on the lookout for ways to generate money through music. The more money you can generate through music, the more time you can spend creating it. In order to become a YouTube partner you'll need to make a small impact on the YouTube community and be accepted by their committee. You can do this by growing your fan base and increasing your view counts.

It's amazing when you really stop and think about it: if I make a video in my apartment in Nashville and post it on YouTube, instantly someone in China can be watching it! Don't neglect this important tool for broadening your fanbase and strengthening your online presence.

—Jenn Bostic: award winning US singer-songwriter with a #1 record in the UK

Action 3: Join the World of Session Singing

Studio projects for radio, film and television need singers on a regular basis—we'll reveal what it takes to "crack" this market.

In the music industry, there are two main paths for vocalists: the artist and the session singer. Fortunately, the majority of singers elect to be artists, with their quest to make a unique musical mark on the world. Session singers, however, are hired hands who come in, short term, to enhance what artists do in addition to other professional work such as:

- Jingles for radio and TV
- Film and TV soundtracks
- Demoing songs for songwriters who need a recording of their work so they can shop it out to an artist or to gain a publishing deal
- Feature vocals on songs for release, particularly in the dance market
- Background vocals, live or recorded

I was captivated with this work from the moment I made my first commercial recording back in the 80s. Never before had such a high level of precision and polish been demanded of me—I loved it!

The first thing you must do, before you decide to pursue session work more seriously, is to get some experience in a recording studio to see if it is for you or not. A session singer must be able to generate a performance-level vibe in a completely "dead" room with no audience. For many singers, it simply doesn't suit.

For those of you who are hooked and have the main requirements—i.e. a commercial sound, accurate pitching and timing, ability to blend and harmonize well, an ear for detail—there are several other skills you'll want to develop.

> *The point is not necessarily to find one niche that suits you, but be comfortable being yourself in whatever niche you find yourself.*
>
> ***—Louise Rose:** entertainer and educator, has worked with Aretha Franklin, Oscar Peterson and Duke Ellington*

A session singer must be flexible. Some producers or writers don't know exactly what they want until they hear it. It is your job to vary your vocal delivery, sometimes endlessly, until they say, "that's it!" Then you have to remember what you just did to be able to replicate it. You also must be stylistically versatile and be able to adapt to any situation.

Time is money, so in session work, you have to be able to learn new material rapidly, by ear or by reading. You also have to be comfortable improvising, for example adlibs for songs, station "idents" etc. The last movie I sang on, a high-profile Hollywood film you will have likely seen, required continuous improvisation for around 15 minutes over the orchestral score.

Reliable vocal technique is a must. I once did a session that was 12-hours long to get the backing vocals down on an entire album in one day. This required a high level of control, stamina, consistency and concentration. Producers may give you very precise direction and you have to get it right—take after take after take.

If, like me, you are drawn to session work, I would suggest that you get as much experience as you can. Hone your skills, build your network and make sure you have a great promo pack so you can break into this highly specialized, competitive scene.

—Kim Chandler: top session singer and industry vocal coach

Action 4: Demonstrate Gear

It doesn't matter if you're famous; it matters that you can sell the gear.

There are many companies looking for talented, gear-savvy musicians to show off their wares. For me this has been the best job in the world! Just think of the perks: you get paid to travel, play with cool gear all day long, entertain people with your music, and engage with an audience in a way that you never can at a gig. You have these incredible conversations where you get to see the light go on in people's eyes as you explain something new. I especially love it when people ask, "By the way, what song is that?" and I get to explain that it's MINE.

That's the good news. Now for a dose of reality: it takes a lot of luck to land one of these gigs. Job postings are few and far between; it tends to be a word of mouth kind of thing. However, there is something that you could do to increase your chances. Post a YouTube video to a manufacturer's website—we've come across many artists this way. The video should show off both your musical talent and their gear. Let them know that if they are looking for a product specialist or demonstrator, you are their person. Showing yourself in action is critical. The folks looking to hire you are stuck in an office with loads of demanding work—you need to make it easy for them to see your talent and enthusiasm.

Before you do this, consider if this is really the gig for you. Unlike a regular performance, this gig isn't about you; the GEAR is the star and your voice is just the mechanism for it. You need to have an educational spirit and enthusiasm for conveying knowledge in user-friendly ways through some very long days. You need to maintain this enthusiasm even when some of the questions are repetitive and inane.

A typical day could include going into a music store at 9am to train a staff of 10 and then hosting a larger clinic for 20 customers at another venue, with smaller tutorial sessions for musicians in between. That night I might be at a "mom & pop" brick and mortar store and the following day at a large trade show doing both scheduled and on-demand demos all day long in a cacophonous audio environment. Even though I consider myself totally "up" on my vocal health skills, I have still been known to lose my voice!

–Laura Clapp: singer-songwriter and Marketing Manager for TC-Group Americas

Action 5: Become a Singing Teacher or Vocal Coach

There's a tension between performing and teaching; some vocalists use this to its best advantage.

When I was 15, my mother said (in a heavy New York accent), "Sweetie, get your teaching degree. You'll have something to fall back on … "

Fall back on? Yeah, thanks, Ma. I was already singing in a band three nights a week (making serious money for an 11th grader) and couldn't conceive of doing anything else.

Today, 75 years later (joking), I'm still singing studio and live gigs, but the funny thing is: I'm also being called upon to teach, coach and produce vocals and live performance both privately and in workshops. And the funnier thing is: everyone seems to be benefiting, myself included. I never realized how gratifying it feels to give back to others in this way; yeah, thanks, Ma!

Some singers realize they're not cut out for the performing life. Some singers decide they like the perks teaching provides, such as knowing their yearly income or what time they'll be home each afternoon. Some singers will reassess their professional path if their career didn't unfold the way they thought it would. You might decide this early on, getting a bachelor's and/or master's degree in music performance and obtaining teaching credentials. Or you may

> *You need a lot of humor and perseverance to make it in this industry. And then you need a whole lot of sense of humor on top of that. When Steely Dan first took their demos around, they brought them to every publisher and record company in New York City and were turned down. No one understood their music. It wasn't until they got to California where Jay Lasker of ABC Dunhill Records heard it that they got the "go-ahead." It often takes way longer than you might expect. You can either give up or keep pushing.*
>
> ***–Elliott Randall:** legendary guitarist, formerly a musical consultant for Saturday Night Live*

choose to be a singing teacher or vocal coach later in life (ahem). Either way, they're noble professions that deserve their rightful places on the "I want to make a living in the world of music" job list.

But wait: what are the differences between a singing teacher and a vocal coach, anyway?

A singing teacher employs a specific method/technique for musical genres such as classical, pop or hard rock, using warm-ups and exercises to improve their students' vocal abilities. A vocal coach can also use warm-ups and exercises, but concentrates on helping singers with their repertoire, stylization, interpretation and the "performance" aspect of their material. Please note: not all singing teachers are vocal coaches, and vice versa.

You may be interested to know that not all singing teachers and vocal coaches are singers; some of the best aren't. However, if you are a singer and can find a way to articulate what you've learned in an empathic and patient manner, using your intuition to hone in on another singer's issues and how to fix them ... AHA! You may be the voice teacher who's got that little extra sum'n sum'n.

—Jaime Babbitt: renowned jingle singer and backing vocalist, former Disney Records coach

Action 6: Sell Your Albums and Merchandise

It may start with some of your CDs at a gig—but that's not where it needs to end ...

There is something that bands can do to maximize their earnings at live gigs, especially when there isn't much money from a guarantee—or they are only getting a percentage of the door. Utilize your merchandise (merch) table. Don't have generic, plain merch that doesn't stand out or communicate anything about who you are as a band. I've seen this and it looks as if the band simply phoned in an order and got any old stuff. This is lost revenue! Better bands have a grip on their fan base and know the kinds of things they want to buy. Then they come up with creative ways to represent themselves on designs and products.

A fan doesn't approach your merch booth merely because their friend is in the bathroom and they have nothing better to do. They are actively searching to see what they can spend their money on. An artist depends on these sales—so, provide what they are looking for. It's also a very good idea for you to come off stage after the show and go over to the merch booth to talk to fans (make sure people other than you are selling). This will have the effect of bringing your fans over to that area and gives you a chance to interact, creating an environment where fans see that "this guy is one of us" and feel even more that they want to support you and spend their money.

I always think it is good to discount your albums at a live show. When your album first comes out there will be online sales, but you really want to be making a personal connection with your buyers—and this is much easier at a gig. So, incentivize their coming to the gigs by offering a discount on your album if purchased at the gig—then they are buying the ticket AND your merch at the same time.

The other thing I have seen artists do is to "bundle" their album with a T-Shirt or a ticket sale for an upcoming performance. So, in effect, you are raising the ticket price but including an album or other product. You get more people to your shows and your fan gets a tangible item along with their ticket.

—Chris Maltese: artist manager, formerly a senior producer for MTV

Frequently Asked Questions

> What is the difference between a contractor and an agent?

Answered by Gerald White, prolific singer-songwriter who has worked on over 100 TV and commercial productions

At first you may think music contractors and agents are the same. Both connect singers to singing work. Both will have a list of singers or bands that they have chosen. However, the difference lies in who pays them—agents are paid by the singer and contractors are paid by the client who is looking for a singer.

If Disney needs 10 singers for a TV show, they would hire a contractor to find those singers. Disney pays the contractor a set fee. If the contractor chooses you, you are hired. No auditions. Then Disney pays you for the work and you don't have to give anyone a percentage. From what I've experienced, it is very hard to get on a contractor's list. But if you can make that connection, it gets you past a lot of red tape in the process of finding singing work.

It works differently when it comes to a booking agent. The singer gives a percentage of their check to the agent for a given booking. Agents can help you book gigs, auditions and negotiate contracts. It can be hard to get on an agent's list, depending on how high profile he or she is.

Both agents and contractors are well-connected in the music industry, and those connections are invaluable to a singer's career.

> How do I find an agent?

Answered by Alicia Yaffe, founder and CEO of the Spellbound Group, entertainment-based brand building

Before you ever go looking for an agent you have to demonstrate that you can bring people out to a show and that you can make some money. So, your top priority needs to be building your fanbase and performing. Call a venue, get people to your show and if you are good, people will come back. The venue will keep booking you and the agents will turn up. It's pure laziness to think that you can't get a gig or go on tour without an agent—get working on those gigs.

If you do have a following (say 150 or more are coming to your gigs), then find agents of bands that you would want to go on tour with. When you contact the agent, tell him or her how many are coming to your shows and invite them to your next gig; explain why that gig will be special and unique.

It is likely the agent will ask you, "Who are you working with?" In other words, they want to know who is helping you to manage and promote your gigs, putting together your business strategy so that you can better focus on your performances. You see, if the agent takes you on, it will be their business to tell venues why they should book you and that you will bring people out. If you have a team around you, it is a strong sign that you will deliver what the agent is promising.

An effective way to approach an agent is through someone on your team: a lawyer, manager or label (if you have one). Have one of these individuals call an agent on your behalf and say, "Look, I have this fantastic singer who has 150 people coming to her shows. We'd love for you to take her on."

If no one is working with you or if you are not drawing people out to gigs on a regular basis then these are red flags for an agent. They need to know that you are working hard with a full team in place. It might also be a red flag for you. If you consistently can't get anyone out to your gigs, try playing at friend's parties, school functions, and other public places to build an audience first. If people still don't come ... maybe you should look at your craft.

> As a singer do I make as much money as an instrumentalist in a band? How do we split it up?

Answered by Jennifer Truesdale, singer, songwriter, coach and author of "Get Paid to Sing"

I've always made the same amount as, or more than, the instrumentalists I work with.

As you begin making money on your gigs, you will find that the money is split up differently depending on the type of gig. For example, let's say your band plays the local pub and collectively you earn $500. The most common arrangement is for any expenses to be taken off the top and then the remainder split evenly between the band members. When I began singing professionally and my band started earning money, the general agreement was that everyone in the band got an even split. We all contributed to the musical, promotional and managerial duties of the band and we all got an even cut.

In other situations where you are hired by a bandleader or producer to sing in a gig or studio session, you will generally negotiate your pay ahead of time. This might be a flat fee or a per hour rate. This negotiated amount might be the same or different than what the instrumentalists are getting paid and is based largely on experience. As you gain more experience and a great reputation you will be able to negotiate higher pay.

Depending on the band, you may find that the bandleader(s) makes more than the other members, but generally the additional pay is compensation for additional work including booking and promotional duties, songwriting, musical direction and the like. How you and your band-mates choose to split up the money you earn is really up to you. The most important thing is to have clearly established agreements ahead of time so that no one feels slighted.

> How can I get my original songs noticed by a filmmaker?

Answered by Sarah Bella, singer-songwriter and YouTube star

In my case, an independent film director wanted original music for his film. Not only was he looking for just the right sound for his film; but also, someone who could create new material. He came across one of my songs on YouTube and thought it would be perfect for a certain scene in his movie. The company sent me a rough copy of the movie to review. It had my song already in place during a particular scene. A few days later I was contacted again and was asked if I'd write the theme song that will be played during the opening credits. Of course, I said yes! I watched the film again for inspiration and decided on a particular theme in the movie to write about. After watching the opening credits where the song would be placed, ideas formed and the song soon followed.

This is an independent film and, unless it blows up into a major motion picture, I am in it mainly for the exposure as an artist. I was not paid, but my name and picture are on the front cover of the DVD and I am also listed on the back cover. My song is the opener for the film—which I am really excited about!

There are many times when directors or producers need original music for their project. For small projects, they are specifically looking for an unsigned artist, usually because they don't have the budget to pay anyone. Having your name connected with any film is great exposure especially if you were asked to write specifically for the film. It shows that you are able to write "on the spot" and may attract enough attention to open more doors.

Another way to find avenues for your original material is through publishing companies. Find one that licenses music for things, like TV, movies, video games—anything that uses music. Getting involved with the right publishing company can open many doors. Networking online, like I do, may also open doors if the right person comes along!

> I just got hired as a session singer for a film! What do I need to know?

Answered by Gustavo Borner, Owner, Chief Engineer at igloo music

You need to expect that your instructions could be coming from many places! In extreme cases, the composer, arranger, music producer, film director, film producers, executive producers and music editor could be giving you direction. That's a lot of cooks in the kitchen (or control room), which means as the singer, you just have to find ways to stay relaxed and focused.

An unfailing positive attitude helps too. You might be singing ambient solo vocals over orchestral tracks, or you might be singing background vocals for a big star who is recording a new song for the film. You might have to read or learn music on the spot, or you may have been given an MP3 and a lead sheet two days ago. No matter what the scenario, everything will be unfamiliar: the music, the environment and the people. A good vibe helps everybody—so keep smiling.

The people in the control room are the ones who tell you how to deliver your vocal. They may not use musical terms. Your job is to understand what they are asking for—it may be a certain emotion or mood—then figure out the best way to deliver that in your performance. Voicing your own musical ideas is not out of the question, especially if you have a good relationship with the director and you have done a great job of singing it his way first.

Session singers are often needed to record a demo (also called a placeholder or reference track). Demos are especially important in movie musicals. Even though another vocalist is destined to sing that part for the film, the director and producers need you to test out different variations of that song and see how it fits in the scene. Sometimes the demo vocal is so good, it ends up in the movie.

> Can musical theater lead to a career?

Answered by Kathy Alexander, singer, vocal coach and staff writer at VoiceCouncil Magazine

Maybe the film *High School Musical* struck a chord or perhaps it was a live production of *Les Misérables* that grabbed you by the heart and changed you forever. The truth is, a musical theater production tells a story like no other art form. Musical theater shows are where many singers get their start, and where some discover their lifelong calling.

Start by plugging into your local musical theater scene. School and community productions are plentiful in any town and help you connect with others who share your passion. Many amateur productions may stumble clumsily between powerful and awkward, but many are practically on par with professional theater. The important thing is, these productions will give you a chance to hone your skills, get out in front of a real audience and experience the intense camaraderie that infects many a musical theater cast and crew.

> *Can musical theater help my career if I'm a SOLO artist?*
> *Yes: You'll hone your vocal skills, physical presence, and dive into a range of styles. What's more, you'll connect to other artists and develop a fan base. No: The director-centered approach can hinder your own artistic individuality. So when you are not painting sets and showing up for costume fittings, sing at open mic nights and spread your creative wings.*
> ***—Kathy Alexander:** singer, vocal coach and staff writer at VoiceCouncil Magazine*

What is happening beyond amateur theater? Many singers find paid work through summer shows, regional theater work, cruise/theme park shows and maybe even in the big musical theatre centres of New York and London. If this is your calling, then move ahead and find the directors and production companies recruiting. One "trick of the trade" is to join a class run by a prominent coach for musical theater talent—this can lead to solid gold networking opportunities.

You'll need to audition a lot. After his first screen test, MGM famously told Fred Astaire that he was "skinny, balding, and can dance a little." If you can learn from unsuccessful auditions and carry on with a spring in your step, you may just rise to the top. Getting a part in the chorus may not be your dream role, but it is mercifully less intense, while still being lots of fun, and an excellent way to get to know directors, actors and musical theater repertoire. Always show up for an audition with a professional head shot and résumé. The production team will specify what you should prepare for the audition and whatever it is, make sure it is polished and memorized!

Bringing a character to life through singing, dancing and acting requires a level of skill and artistic multitasking that only the most smitten performer would venture to reach for. If the world of musical theater is calling to you with more than just a whisper, get out there and start auditioning.

CHAPTER 17

Breaking Out

Find your new vocation around the next corner.

"My dad, who was in the film industry, told me I had a billion-to-one chance of making it in music. Without even taking a breath, my response was, 'That's going to be me.' You have to have a desperate need for this that is beyond money, beyond success. Music is my breath; it is what I wake up to do. If I were making zero money I would still have to do this. That's the sort of passion one needs to bring to the party to make it in the music business."

—Steve "Luke" Lukather, of Toto, widely considered to be one of the world's best living guitarists

Breaking Out

Find your new vocation around the next corner.

Actions:

1. Be More Than Good; Be Different
2. Get One Great Song into Circulation
3. Be Clear on Your Brand Identity
4. Balance Your Online and Live Work
5. Find the Right Niche
6. Don't Despise the Wedding Gig
7. Use the Power of TV Licensing
8. Harness the Power of Social Media "Friends"
9. Get Your Online Community Talking

Frequently Asked Questions

» *Do I really need an agent to make it?*

» *What's the trick to finding musicians who will really go the distance with me?*

» *Some singers get all the YouTube views—how can I get more?*

» *How do I get signed?*

» *What's the one thing I most need to focus on to achieve success?*

Action 1: Be More Than Good; Be Different

You are living in an era where "first" can be more important than "best."

Being "good" isn't good enough—unless you have a lot of money to invest in a traditional marketing plan. What we are dealing with in our era is an abundance of incredibly talented people all of whom have the same basic chances to be heard. So, how can you break out if you don't have a ton of cash? It is about being different and unique (as well as good). I'm not talking about gimmicks, unless you want to be a comedian. You are an artist, so what you are looking for is a creative and fresh approach that will capture attention.

The next thing you need to understand is that in the YouTube era, being "first" is more important than being "best." If you want a long lasting career, of course "best" is essential, but you need to find that balance between honing your craft and putting your unique ideas out there so that others can find them. In other words, being first, different and unique will attract attention to your work; being good at your singing will keep people coming back for more, giving you—hopefully—a long and legitimate career.

Alex Day is a great example of someone who is really successful on YouTube. Jenna Marbles and Ray William Johnson are two more. These people are successful because they were FIRST on YouTube—very early adopters on the platform. They're not necessarily the best, but they are unique, and they are good enough to keep people coming back. Plus, they interact with people on YouTube. And they are translating their YouTube success to offline success (live gigs) or other platforms (iTunes), which is feeding back to grow their YouTube channels.

Pick your platform. If your YouTube account is growing faster than your Twitter, Facebook, or Tumblr accounts, focus on communicating with your fans and satisfying your base there first. That doesn't mean that you shouldn't build your other profiles, but it does mean that you should spend more time on the site that is giving you the most return. For Alex Day, it's YouTube. For Lady Gaga, it's Twitter. Arguably, for One Direction, it was Tumblr.

All of your skill and creativity needs to rest on authenticity, particularly if you are expecting to grow in a grassroots manner. You see, you have to communicate and interact with your fans if you want to grow. However, authenticity doesn't mean that you reveal every mundane detail of your life. Remember that as an artist you can express things in ways that others can't. When you are interacting with others, value this expressive ability in yourself and don't shy away from letting this quality into your interactions. Instead of posts about what you ate for breakfast, you will communicate important and interesting ideas in a compelling manner.

Be first. Be best. Be unique. Be authentic.

—Alicia Yaffe: founder and CEO of the Spellbound Group, entertainment-based brand building

What is your single most important goal as a performing singer?

Reason	%
To express my own heart and soul through music, be authentic	23%
To captivate my audience no matter what the size	19%
To help people/to change the world for the better with my songs	13%
To show my audience a good time	12%
To have fun	11%
To bring something new, be truly unique	8%
To be a virtuoso with my voice (sound, range, flexibility)	4%
To sound great	3%
To connect musically with those I perform with	3%
To gain the respect of other singers and musicians	3%
To have money, fame and big crowds	2%

Do you dig your audience?
Singers who do weekly paid gigs were far more likely than others in choosing 'captivate my audience' as their number one goal.

–from the 2012-2013 TC-Helicon survey of 1,000 singers

Action 2: Get One Great Song into Circulation

Rule no. 1: It's all about the song. Rule no. 2: It's all about the song.

First and foremost, master your craft. The most obvious advise for all beginning artists, singers and otherwise, is to do the obvious: listen, write, take classes, engage private instructors, practice, practice, practice, sing, sing, sing. Great music isn't enough … but it's a damn good start.

Then, write and/or record one great song. I think of Brandi Carlile's song, "The Story." There are countless artists who have built enormous careers on one song; she is but one. Brandi is a simple folksinger-songwriter from the American northwest, who's now signed to Sony. But I did not hear about Brandi only because she has a great voice and wrote a great song. Obscurity a career does not make. MySpace, back when it was king, is how she put this song out. And over time, so many people heard and loved her song that she got noticed by a national advertiser who licensed her song for a commercial that ran for the 2008 Olympics. After that she got signed by Sony.

Remember—all of this begins with passion for your art. I manage Michael Grimm, who has been singing commercially since age 11 (taking hat tips). He has an incredible gift for letting his passion show in his music. He is one of the world's great singers. But until Hurricane Katrina hit and destroyed his grandparent's house, few people had heard of him worldwide.

That tragedy led him to audition for the hit NBC TV show *America's Got Talent.* Against a million to one odds, he won. Over four million people voted for him. Another 15 million watched him. His passion and commitment for his grandparents thus led him to the $1 million prize and a flourishing indie career.

—Steve Eggleston: award-winning law professor, artist manager and best selling author

Action 3: Be Clear on Your Brand Identity

Can you describe your music in a few words?
That's key to keep your fans with you.

You have to remember that "individuals" are smart and "people" are dumb. What this means for your music is that individuals may enjoy the intricacies of your performance but, as people (in a crowd), they need a simple way to describe your music to others. Without that simple description you will lose them and the potential fans they could reach.

What do you sound like?

If people can't describe it in a few words then you are losing them. You have to give them those words. For instance, some bands describe themselves as alternative indie pop or a solo artist might say they sing urban soul. I recently heard an artist describe their music as melodic noise pop.

Do you see what they are doing? They have chosen a few words to give people a handle on their musical brand. Then, they will be able to blog about it, post about it, and share your impact with ease when they engage in that most effective publicity of all—word of mouth.

This does not mean that you have to stay stagnant. Picasso had his red period, his blue period, etc. The issue is that people need to comprehend who you are in a given period through a few well-chosen descriptive words. This is a brand-identity task. "I am a singer who sings about X." Everyone has a challenge describing their own sound—but the fact of the matter is that the Beatles sound like The Beatles and Motley Crue sounds like Motley Crue. If you are gifted enough to be an incredibly diverse artist (like Daniel Bedingfield), then defying or transcending a genre may become a way to encapsulate your identity.

When I speak about brand identity on this level, I'm not talking about a "picture" of your music or your album art, but an actual definition of who you are—a few words that you can communicate to your fans.

—Alicia Yaffe: founder and CEO of the Spellbound Group, entertainment-based brand building

Action 4: Balance Your Online and Live Work

Know how to say "Hello" to each of your markets.

I started out not intending to be anything at all—I wrote these songs in my bedroom and I just wanted to be brave enough to perform them. In fact, facing up to sharing my music with others was the hardest obstacle of all. After this I began to be noticed, selling CDs and getting booked in festivals. People kept discovering me. I really had no expectations of myself! Perhaps pessimism and a terrible sense of reality have been my allies.

> *If you want your single to be played on the radio it must fill certain criteria. Black Eyed Peas' song "I Gotta Feeling" is an example of a great radio track. It makes you feel something. For a song to do well on the radio, consider that your listeners will be distracted by something every 10 seconds. Your song has to be very dynamic to keep their attention. I don't mean do a new drum loop or modulation every ten seconds—if you keep chopping and changing, the song will be hideous. I'm talking about a new sound in the background or a new cadence in the lyric—subtle things to keep the song evolving. The same applies to a sad song—it must be dynamic and make the listener feel an emotion.*
>
> ***—Marc JB:** remixer-producer with over 70 no.1 hits across the US and UK*

One of the things that helped me was to insert my personality into my YouTube videos. I would share my sense of humor and add little skits to the beginning of my videos—this wasn't always positively received, but it was remembered. Also, this wasn't something that I planned; it was just something that I wanted to do. All of this was very affordable and low budget; most of my videos were produced by me, so I wasn't paying any money to anyone for their services.

Then, I felt like I needed to grow out of my YouTube work; I wanted to be considered a "legit" musician, known for more than tacky videos and coffee shop performances. I felt I needed some high profile shows. So, I did this and then faced all of the pressures of large, live shows! Now I see my task as keeping both aspects of my singing life sustained—booking enough live shows to keep up my performing edge and moving ahead on the video front. There's no perfect balance—I never know how it is going to go.

My advice is that you should be prepared to greet each of these markets (live and YouTube) differently. You also have to have some cohesive thing to tie the two together so that it makes sense. In my videos I use skits and props whereas in my live shows I do some story telling between songs. Sometimes my YouTube fans think I should be funnier in my live shows, but I only do that if it naturally comes out. If it works for you to be funny and tell stories, do it. But never look at another performer and think that you have to do what they do. It may work better for you to just play your songs. I've developed a fanbase on the internet, and I respect those fans but I have to respect myself as well, so do not feel I have to repeat what I do online in live shows.

—Danielle Ate The Sandwich: nationally recognized independent folk musician

Action 5: Find the Right Niche

A careful look at the musical map just might lead you to your jackpot.

I work with a young man, Shea Arender, whose unique story speaks to the diverse ways that aspiring singers can get ahead in today's highly-competitive music world.

Shea has an incredible baritone voice, and God-given good looks: if Elvis and Tom Cruise had a son, he'd look like Shea. His unique traits enabled him to launch his career as an award-winning Elvis impersonator and to thereby save up money that he could invest in his original music career. It's not an approach that most would—or could—take, but Shea was a man on a mission.

Shea knew he had to choose a narrow niche where he could make a quick splash and get the maximum bang for his limited bucks. Popular music and rock could not be it. But "how many new Christmas songs were introduced each year?" he asked himself. Almost none. So he wrote an original Christmas song, "The Christmas I Met You," and found a small label to finance and release the recording.

Then reality set in. Writing, recording and releasing the song did nothing. He needed radio play to be heard. His label, however, had already spent whatever resources they had. So Shea reached into his small savings and, as a Southern boy from outside New Orleans, did the unthinkable: he invested everything in big city, northeast radio promoters.

His gamble paid off. Before he knew it, his song was being played everywhere in the big markets—New York, Philly, D.C., etc. DJs loved it because all the superstars didn't have the time or inspiration to write an original Christmas song—all they submitted were the same old standards. So his new, original Christmas song—"The Christmas I Met You"—soared high on Cashbox Easy Listening (#1) and Billboard Christmas (#3) Singles Charts.

Suddenly, as they say, the phone started ringing. Before he knew it, he was headlining his own off-Broadway musical. But his "luck" didn't stop there. A fan in the industry submitted "The Christmas I Met You" for a Grammy in the niche easy-listening category. A few weeks later he learned that not only had his song been accepted in that category, but it had also been accepted for consideration as "Song of the Year" as well.

Will Shea win a Grammy in 2013 without major label push and a heavy-hitter publicist? Not likely. But he no longer needs to channel Elvis to make money, thanks to his ingenious approach to standing out. That's why I tell this story: as a reminder that there are many ways to make your own break.

–Steve Eggleston: award-winning law professor, artist manager and best selling author

Action 6: Don't Despise the Wedding Gig

With a little ingenuity—and a lot of hard work—the gigs you're getting can take you to the next level of your career.

I've seen singers break out in three different ways: first, they might focus solely on their voice–singing covers and hanging around the right places (like our studio!). These singers may meet musicians and bands and sometimes get picked up to be a lead singer or do backing vocals for a well-known group. Then, there are those who get really lucky right off the bat with a reality TV show. The third way, one that I would favour and encourage, is for singers to focus on their voice and their own original music, showcasing both as much as possible so that one or the other can take off. Having your own music as well as a good voice gives you another string to your bow.

> *Justin Bieber's tweet about but Carly Rae Jepsen's song was certainly a game-changer, but her rise to fame happened after 10 long years of working really hard. It may look like an overnight success, but I watched her touring, writing songs, doing release parties and playing small clubs in the local music scene in B.C., Canada. She wouldn't have been able to write that hooky song and be the entertainer she is today without those years of grinding away.*
>
> ***–Georgia Murray:** singer-songwriter, nominated for Urban Recording of the Year*

I was really impressed with one local artist who came to our studios to record an album and has since gone on to make a regional impact with her music. She's a good singer/songwriter who actually self funded her album through singing at wedding gigs. These gigs were a great way to get her voice out there and she would also put some of her original songs into her sets. Earning money as a gigging musician doing the wedding/corporate thing is tough, but is often a good source of money to put into your own music, so don't be precious about it. She used these gigs to gain exposure, develop her craft and earn the money she needed to take her next steps.

When she came to us to record her album, we negotiated a price for her studio time and helped her source musicians who would come prepared. We also advised her to try not to make any musical changes on the day. But, to save money in this process, she also recorded a lot of her vocals at home. Tim Thomas, the producer/engineer on the session, helped her to create a small setup at home with a vocal booth, a good mic and mic preamp going into Pro Tools. This had the advantage of giving her the freedom to do as many takes as she'd like on days she felt great about singing. You see, the vocal needs to make the listener feel what you want them to feel. So it's all about the vibe, feeling good and in the right mood to lay down the vocals.

She left the studio with a quality album in hand that she could sell at her many gigs. She went on from this to be picked up by 20 to 30 agencies and is now in high demand as an event singer—she's recently been voted by a national magazine as "Wedding Singer of the Year" and she's working full time in music now at both the local and regional levels.

—Ian Stewart: co-founder and co-owner at Blueprint Recording Studios

Action 7: Harness the Power of TV Licensing

The right conferences can lead you to the most powerful corner of today's music industry.

The most powerful people in the music industry right now in terms of helping an artist break through are the music supervisors for TV shows. Every show is looking for singer-songwriters with original music. They don't hire vocalists anymore—they license original songs. They've done this with major artists we hear today.

If your song gets played on an American TV show, you would earn a licensing fee of $500 to $4,000, plus a royalty every time that song is played. Your album sales on iTunes and your YouTube hits would increase greatly since the fans of that TV show will go looking for your song. So if you are a singer-songwriter and you have a well-produced recording of an original song, your next career move might be to put it in the hands of a music supervisor.

How can you make this happen? One way to meet music supervisors is by attending a conference like Billboard's yearly Film and TV Music Conference. It is fairly affordable, and is open to anybody. The conference lasts for several days and they bring in music supervisors from all the TV shows for panel discussions. There are a variety of conferences and events out there that help singers connect to top people in the industry: music conferences are held every year by the local music organizations like ASCAP and Billboard.

—Gerald White: prolific singer-songwriter who has worked on over 100 TV and commercial productions

Action 8: Harness the Power of Social Media "Friends"

Step up to the online plate with the right strategies and watch your music spread.

You really need to get on Facebook and/or Twitter. Start communicating. Without some investment in good social media communication, you are going to have a difficult time succeeding. Of course, if you are the most amazing musician that the world has ever heard then you could, theoretically, make it without these tools—people would still discover you, promote you and push your career forward. However, the chances that you are at this level are slim to none, so you need to make sure that you are aggressive in your efforts (but not your tone) in communicating to people who share common interests online.

It's like going to a cocktail party and being really friendly—you'll meet lots of people and connections will happen. Most musicians succeed because they are friendly with people and these people want to, in turn, listen to their music and even share it with their friends.

As you are growing fans on Facebook, there are some great analytics that you can observe. For example, you can see where your fans are from. If you are looking to perform in another city, you can check to see which city has fans that are responding to your music. A city 100 miles away from you with 10 fans will be a difficult "sell" in terms of trying to book a gig. However, if you can get these 10 to help you, letting their friends know about your music, then 10 can become 20 and 20 can become 40. You are now approaching the number you need to pull off a gig.

But there's something else you can do: discover an artist with a good fan base in a city in which you want to play—who doesn't have a fan base in your city. Then, ask them to open for you in your location in turn for you opening for them in theirs. As you collaborate more with people in a similar boat to you, it is more likely that you will grow. You see, social networking is not just with fans but also with other artists.

—Jay Frank: leading author (Hack Your Hit and Futurehit.DNA) and Owner/CEO of DigSin

Action 9: Get Your Online Community Talking

Fan-to-fan connections are the steel of your online building.

Understand that social media is about community. Your relationship with your fans will be stronger if they can connect with each other around your music. This fan-to-fan connection will keep them loyal and add further value to your brand. Consider a couple who are dating because they met each other through an artist's platform. Their bond with the artist is really strengthened. The more that you can facilitate relationships being built between fans, the more your social media presence will grow and become self-sustaining. At the same time you can stay slightly out of reach—that gives your presence an inspirational quality. Once you have the community of believers—you can drop in and it is the highlight of their life—but what keeps it going are the friends that they have made.

There are many ways to nurture a fan-to-fan connection: through "meet and greets," hangouts, invitations for people to submit fan videos, and contests. All of these activities can lead to fans sharing what they do on your site with their friends. This means that they are bringing pre-existing relationships into the community where they can also have a shared experience of your art. I find it interesting that when some of our artists announce a contest winner, the community will write in their congratulations. Instead of feeling bad that they didn't win, they participate in the good feelings of the winner. All of this interaction doesn't require a huge investment from you as the artist, but it does require you to think through the best ways to have your fans connect with each other.

—Alicia Yaffe: founder and CEO of the Spellbound Group, entertainment-based brand building

Frequently Asked Questions

> Do I really need an agent to make it?

Answered by Alastair Lindsey-Renton, Agent at Curtis Brown, Ltd., London

Surprisingly, the answer may be "no"—as long as you are willing to do these three things yourself:

1. **Contact the right contacts constantly.** Networking is probably the most important part of your business. If you don't have an agent, the best way to get your name out there is to write letters to and communicate with industry professionals. Keep contacting people and stay in circulation—no matter what. Always promote your own interests. Never sit back and expect work to come to you. Singers looking for gigging work will want to make direct contact with the venue manager, music producer, bandleader or event coordinator. Research the projects these professionals have been working on previously so you can talk knowledgably about their work. Send your CV/Resume, headshot, audio samples of your singing and contact details along with a cover letter addressed to a specific name.
2. **Develop a good understanding of the business.** Agents are helpful because part of their job is to know people and know how the music business works; however, you can do this yourself. All you have to do is find the answers to these questions: Who are the creatives? Where does the money come from? Who finds the vocalists? Who negotiates contracts? Take time every week to develop your answers to these questions. This may not seem like the type of vocal work you thought you would be doing, but remember: you are your own business. If you have friends or contacts in the music industry, talk to them. Find out who are the movers and shakers and how best to approach them.
3. **Know what you want.** In order to build a career, every singer must have a clear direction and invest fully in the pursuit of it. Where do you want to be in five years? 10 years? 25 years? What kind of singing work do you want? As part of this process, you must also be realistic. Take a good look at who you are and what your strengths may be. Are you lucky enough to fit into a niche? Exploit it! Are people saying you are perfect for a certain genre? Listen to them with an open mind.

Whether you have an agent or not, remember this: an agent works with you and for you but never instead of you.

> What's the trick to finding musicians who will really go the distance with me?

Answered by Joey Belladonna, lead singer of the legendary group Anthrax

I have to confess that I have a hard time with people who are always talking about their limits: "Don't ask me to practice too much," "Don't ask me to drive too far." For me it is all about the music and rolling along with everything that is involved in being with a band. I'm consumed by it all. I realize that I don't represent every singer!

When you are thinking of getting together to make music with others, you better check in with them on some basic questions: What is your vision? What is it that you're looking for? Do you want to be a part of a band? What do you want to sing? What are your goals?

I have met people who say, "I wanna sing local but don't want to travel." I've had arguments with these people. I don't argue anymore; if they want to play darts on Friday and I want to perform in a bowling alley—then I find people who want the bowling alley gig. The trick is to find people who share many of your goals.

Let's go back to that question about goals. Is your goal to be a star? This is a big thing now as media is saturated with competition shows. Sure, we all want to be seen. But I didn't get into this business to be a star. I just wanted to get in a good band and be as good a musician as possible. When people say how much they love my music, that's my reward. It's never been about cashing in. It's always been about the music.

Find some musicians who feel the same way.

> Some singers get all the YouTube views—how can I get more?

Answered by Sarah Bella, singer-songwriter and YouTube star

Paradoxically, the way to reach more people on YouTube is to actually get more personal.

The YouTube audience wants to know you're posting the video for them, so you have more success if you make a video specifically for YouTube rather than posting a live performance of your act at a local bar.

The next thing to consider are the many ways you can relate on an individual level through your video. As a singer-songwriter, a lot of what I do on YouTube has a very personal feel. After reading the countless emails from viewers expressing how my songs have either helped them or inspired them, I was hooked on a personal approach to my vids.

You are more likely to get comments and subscribers if you speak before you start your song, letting your fans know you posted it for them. Keep it really short but personal.

Now, for some more "technical" tips:

If you do cover songs, try to do top 40 songs that people are searching for. You're more likely to gain exposure that way.

When you post videos on YouTube, choose your key words carefully. These key words will help direct people to your video when they are searching the internet. Your key words will differ depending on your style of music. I use words like "female," "singer/songwriter," "acoustic," "pop," "folk" and even "Taylor Swift" or "Jewel." I know I am not Taylor or Jewel but if you make similar music and people are searching for their songs, your videos are likely to pop up—thus, more hits.

Since I make original music, I was eligible to apply for a partnership with YouTube, and even generate an income. There are many benefits of partnering with YouTube and your chances of being featured are much higher now since your videos are brought to their attention.

> How do I get signed?

Answered by Daniel Zangger Borch, PhD, one of Sweden's most established vocal coaches, Head of the Voice Centre

There are three main paths to try to get that coveted record deal.

First, you can go through the popular TV shows such as *Pop Idol*, *The X Factor*, and *The Voice*. Or, you can make demos in order to showcase your work in front of just the right people. Finally, you can try to make it on your own, building your own promotional approach; when your success is a fact you then get "bought" by a major label because they want your huge fan base.

On all of these paths you will need a fan base—it is rare these days that a music company will take the time and the expense to develop an act with no fan base. They usually want a "sure thing," and that is where the fans are.

The Idol Path:

I coached a 16-year-old girl who I knew was great, so she signed up for an audition on Idol. I was sure she would be accepted to the program but she called me in tears, "I didn't even get to the real jury!" So, we decided that she should try auditioning again in another town. She got on the show and made it to fifth place in the finals; she now has an international career. So, never take "no" for an answer—just give it another try.

But remember this:

- Only sing a song that shows you off at your absolute best.
- Always have an extra song in another style up your sleeve.
- Know your perfect key and perfect tempo—always practice in them.
- Own a metronome and something to give you the right pitch. Check in on both tempo and pitch just before you audition.
- Be yourself.

If you choose The "Demo" Path, these are the things to bear in mind:

- Find the key people in the business who work with music like yours. Checking out the record labels of similar acts will help.

- Only send demos to people who are interested or have knowledge about your style of music. The same goes for invitations to showcases (except for your fans, friends and family of course).
- Do not compromise on the quality of your recordings.
- Never send more than two songs—and only the best songs.

If you choose the "I'll Do It On My Own" path, realize that this is going to take a lot of work. However, the benefit is that you will learn much about music, working with others and the industry. You will also earn more money if you become a success. At the very least, you'll be satisfied knowing what you are capable of.

Make sure that you:

- Invest in pros in the most important parts of the chain—mixing, photo shoots and promotion.
- Find the best producers you can think of. If you can't pay them, then negotiate with your copyright—that is your important bargaining chip.
- Work incredibly hard on building your image and contacts via YouTube, Facebook and ALL other channels you can think of.
- Gig as much as possible in order to spread your name.
- Support your work with a CD, but if it is too much of a challenge or musical risk to make a full length CD, make a five-song EP instead.

No matter what path you choose you will need a great idea and great songs; record companies want to make money so take nothing personally.

And remember: getting signed is just the entry ticket to the game; you will have to work even harder to stay there.

> What's the one thing I most need to focus on to achieve success?

Answered by Fred Mollin, veteran record producer, film and TV composer, musical director and songwriter

Nothing succeeds like hard work; nothing succeeds like your absolute dedication to your dream and your career.

Most of us do not live *"American Idol"* lives, coming out of nowhere, ending up on TV and winning the performance lottery. Most of us have to work hard and grow. My ability to be a successful musical artist and producer is born out of two things: whatever gift I might have and my ability to work hard. Period.

It's your talent that allows your work to be good and sometimes to be great. In my role as a producer, it is important to bring out the best in artists, facilitating their vision and dreams for their music. In this work, I've discovered that the vocal artist is working just as hard as me. This is true of legacy artists I've worked with such as Kris Kristofferson or Johnny Mathis or younger artists. One thing we all have in common is that we love our art and we work hard.

So, are you ready to continue to dedicate yourself to your music? Are you going to work harder than ever to write songs, rehearse, create great performances, and learn about life beyond singing? It's your daily dedication that makes you better at what you do. The more you give to your art, the more you work on it, then the more you can guarantee that no matter what happens you'll be as good as you can possibly be at what you do.

We all want to be great and successful but all we can control is the amount of energy we put into working hard.

You never arrive at the finish line. I started producing when I was really young. Now that I'm older, I still see every single day as a learning curve—I never imagine that a day will go by when I won't learn something new, but the lessons I learned up until now are really powerful. A life in music is a beautiful thing.

CHAPTER 18

Develop Your Intellectual Capital

Your uniqueness sets you apart.

"Flaunt your imperfections and you will be a star, my dear."

—David A. Stewart, renowned producer and musician with more than 100 million album sales

"Be yourself; everyone else is already taken."

—Oscar Wilde

Develop Your Intellectual Capital

Your uniqueness sets you apart.

Actions:

1. Develop Your Unique Taste
2. Develop Your Unique Sound
3. Develop Your Unique Spin
4. Develop Your Unique Arrangement
5. Develop Your Unique Song
6. Take the Test of Performance
7. Commit to Weekly Creativity
8. Move Past Your Blocks

Frequently Asked Questions:

» *How can I be a real vocal artist if all I do is sing covers?*

» *I want to sound like ______ (insert name of FAVORITE singer here). Where do I begin?*

» *Where is a safe place to try out my new ideas?*

» *How can I write my own songs since I don't play piano or guitar?*

» *I want to write my own songs—but what do I write about?*

» *My voice teacher says I'm suited to folk, but I want to sing metal. Is she right?*

» *My friend says that my ideas for doing "covers" are weird—that I should be more mainstream.*

» *Does using vocal processing count for being original?*

» *I'm a really good singer, but I've never found the right songs that suit my voice and personality. What can I do?*

Action 1: Develop Your Unique Taste

Go nuts with what you like—it's as simple as that. New paths will open when you immerse yourself in your kind of music.

Sometimes singers think that being totally unique means shutting out all of their musical influences, getting alone and trying to come up with something completely new. I would argue the opposite. To find your unique tastes, indulge yourself more in your influences and open up to even more sources of musical inspiration.

> *Sometimes singers feel that they have to discover their own unique sound right at the beginning—but that is not necessary. This happens as you perform and work with other musicians. You begin to recognize the ways in which you are different and begin to emphasize these aspects in future performances. You discover your own style—it starts to seep into what you are doing.*
>
> ***–Lori Maier:*** *Founder and Executive Director of Chick Singer Night*

Listen to music from all parts of the world and from all genres, everything from Billie Holliday and Duke Ellington to more recent decades. All of today's music is influenced by previous generations–just think of the incredible influence of Michael Jackson, the Eurythmics, David Bowie, Duran Duran and Depeche Mode's innovative electronic sounds from the 80s, to name but a few!

There couldn't be more tools for discovery today. You aren't limited to listening to broadcast radio; you can turn to tons of digital tools starting with the more obvious ones of iTunes and YouTube. When you do that, take a look at the links to similar artists. Start looking at the top ten lists for any genre and explore streaming tools like Spotify, Last.fm, or Pandora's personalized internet radio–not to mention all of the free online magazines such as *Pitchfork, Rolling Stone* and *SPIN* and even mobile apps like Shazam and Soundhound that tell you what song is playing when you're in a public place. You don't even have to spend money today to fill your life with the endless discovery of incredible new music.

Sometimes you will hear someone say "There's no good music coming out today." Really? Have they really grasped even a tiny amount of the music pouring into our lives from all over the world?

Of course you need to give yourself lots of time to listen to your own music, to study it and perfect it. Stay in tune with your own musical creations, experimenting along the way. You may want to record that vocal one more time to project a different feel, add riffs to that phrase, make a certain lyric stronger or softer. Listen back to your own recorded music, get a feel for when it's time to give it a break for a day or a week so you don't over-listen and get yourself bored or ear-fatigued. Then, return again to more listening and experimenting with ways to improve. Then, train yourself to be ready to let it go, to know it's good, and start your next song.

–Dot Bustelo: internationally recognized music producer and music technology strategist

Action 2: Develop Your Unique Sound

Get your voice out of the narrow box you've put it in and creative doors will open.

We are all copycats. When we first learn to sing–indeed, when we learn to speak–we listen to and copy other peoples' voices. At some point, we develop a desire to create our own sentences, messages and sound that can distinguish our voices from all others. We call this "finding our own voice" or in the music business, "developing artistic definition."

Uniqueness is a hallmark trait of the true artist. To find your unique sound you must get in touch with your physical instrument's ability and potential, and your authentic story. You are the only one who has your physical instrument (larynx, resonation surfaces, physical stamina, etc.) and who has your life history and emotional experiences. I believe there is no competition with uniqueness. Talent shows can't authentically judge between unique voices. Imagine a competition show for an orange, an orangutang and a bedpost. Each has its place of value, its audience and its detractors. How do you judge such a contest?

Here are several factors to explore when developing your own unique voice:

- *Sonic distinction.* Your sound has to do with choices of instrumentation, microphone, studios and mixes, your vocal technique habits and quirky embellishments. You can change your sound, and that change should have to do with things like accessing your full resonance, making sure vocal licks are appropriate and choosing a sound that communicates your message most authentically.
- *Message.* Without messages your voice is just a shiny example of vocal technique: possibly bemusing but soon forgotten. What have you got to say to the world? How do you give your original slant to those thoughts? What popular song could your own heart have written?
- *Style.* Your style has to do with your particular way of articulating as well as your phrasing. It generally dictates the genre of music the industry puts you in, though the lines are more blurred now than ever.

To go the distance in developing your uniqueness fully, you must be willing to do some work. It takes time, experimentation, persistence and being available to "chance" opportunities to find a financially viable artistic definition in the music business. But finding your unique sound is satisfying to the voice of your spirit, whether you sing original material or sing great cover songs your own way.

—Judy Rodman: award-winning vocal coach and chart-topping recording artist

—from the 2012-2013 TC-Helicon survey of 1,000 singers

Action 3: Develop Your Unique Spin

It's time to sing it your way—even if it's by accident.

There I was, working alone in the studio. I was fiddling around with my Logic program, trying to make a rhythmic pattern conform to how I had envisioned it in my head. Accidentally, I shifted things a little to the right so that now my rhythm was offbeat. I listened. Paused. Listened again. Hmmm. This sounded interesting. That mistake actually led to an entirely new and more energetic version of my song.

Sometimes a completely new perspective/angle/environment can change the way you perceive the song you are working on. And that's when the magic happens. As long as you are on familiar territory and everything is the way it always is, any addition is also likely to be familiar and something you have done before. A new perception will often force you to do unfamiliar, creative things.

I crave originality. I want to hear and "feel" the musician. Copying another musician is very good for learning—VERY good for learning, actually. But I always ask students to come up with a different version of the song—when they are done copying the original.

I want you to try these ideas. Some of them may not sound great—but they will lead you to your unique spin. Guaranteed.

- Find a completely different song that matches the specific mood/message of your cover and "borrow" the beat and tempo from that song.
- Simply change the tempo! Try singing the song really slow or really fast and see if any ideas pop up.
- Sing the song in a key that is too high or too low for you! This forces you to make little changes, either to the notes, or to the way you sing it.
- Check the lyrics. Figure out "who" is singing the song. Then change that drastically, without actually changing the lyrics.
- Is it a typical "guitar song"? Change it to a typical "piano song."
- Remove the beat, change the tempo and change at least five notes in the melody.
- Use other ears. Play the song to somebody else. Make sure it is a person who wouldn't mind being completely honest with you. Listen mostly to how YOU feel about it, while playing the song for them. Sometimes we perceive things differently, when we are with another person. It's like we are "borrowing" their ears (or what we think they hear).

Have fun with it—and play around. Most of it will sound weird (or even bad!)—but eventually you will hit a nerve. And something new and interesting will evolve.

—John Kjøller: Basix, "Best European Album"

Action 4: Develop Your Unique Arrangement

You've explored your interpretation; now it's time to take charge of the entire musical package.

When I was on tour with Beyoncé as her musical director, my job was to come up with the musical arrangements. A killer arrangement takes people on a journey. No piece of music should just stay in one place. For example, in some songs, you want the beginning to be subtle. Then you engage the audience more as the music goes along. Things might get faster, louder or just more energetic. After the audience lives with that for a moment, you bring them back down ... or take them even higher!

Silence in an arrangement is always effective. Space. Changes in volume are also important. From my work with Victor Wooton, I learned that when you are doing a show and people are talking noisily, the temptation is to play louder, but if you take the volume down half way it makes people take notice. You get their attention.

You can always call on someone to help you arrange a piece of music. Someone in your band may be sitting on an incredible idea. If your attitude is, "I'm the general. No one else can have an opinion!" you shoot yourself in the foot. You can take an idea and modify it. It might inspire something in you. This collaboration helps those around you feel a part of the musical movement.

Building layers is another cool arrangement tool. You can do this in your drum part—you can start with only kick drum. Get everybody hyped up, then add a little snare. Everybody will be saying, "OK what's gonna happen next?" Then bring in the hi-hat and cymbals. Then you can break it all back down. There is something about the four-on-the-floor (kick drum on every beat) that does something to the human body and the human spirit. People always react to it.

Don't assume that a killer arrangement for a recording will translate to a live show and vice versa. In our live version of one of my tunes we extend the guitar intro and I talk to the audience over top about why I wrote the song and what it means to me. Then the drums come in with a little light kick drum. The three of us hypnotize the audience with this extended intro. Then we break on beat four (an example of using silence), and the whole band starts the song on beat one. This really engages the audience and makes them feel personally connected to what we are doing.

Try Some Vocal Bass and Percussion

I want to encourage you to try vocal percussion and percussive sounds in your performance. Vocal percussion and beat boxing is nothing new: rappers and hip hop artists made it famous before Justin Timberlake brought it to the teenage masses. You can fit it into your performance easily: as a silly addition to a song, as serious textural variety, as another layer in the percussion bed, or as the only percussion if you play acoustic.

***—Mister Tim:** viral video star, voice artist, composer and sponsored kazoo player*

In a live show we'll often extend the bridge of a song so we can do some call and response with the audience. We break the song down, get the crowed hyped. We do that for a while and then build it back up for eight bars and then—boom! We come back in with the chorus. The audience feels like you brought them up on stage with you all.

In a live setting, you want there to be reciprocity between you and the audience. The audience is just as much a part of the show as you are standing on stage performing for them.

—Divinity Roxx: former Musical Director and bassist for Beyonce's all female band, 2006–2011

Action 5: Develop Your Unique Song

Songwriting will ignite your creative soul and transform how you perform—even if you continue to sing only covers.

To write your own songs you first need to do something to shift your focus. If you work in your bedroom, then get out and go for a walk in the woods and take only a pencil and a small piece of paper. If there's a lake, get into a rowboat and don't take anything but the oars. If you are in a big city, go to the top floor and look out at the city—with something to record your melodies and ideas on.

Try Adding An A Cappella Section

You can take one of two paths with a cappella sections. First, you can make up a vocal arrangement around the melody of the section. You don't have to represent all of the notes going on in the chords—only the notes needed to build the chord—or the "feel."

The other alternative is for your group's voices to mimic the instrumental sound and style. That is, you ask what a particular instrument would do in that section of the song and distill that idea into as few sounds as you can. Do this with all of the instruments, each person in your group emulating an instrument. This is a really creative process that can engage all of the members of a group.

These two paths resemble the classical terms "homophonic" versus "polyphonic."

***—John Kjøller:** Basix, "Best European Album"*

Think of children who have to sit in the same classroom every day. It's so hard to learn all of these different subjects in the same room: English, Math, Geography ... contrast this with taking the class out of the classroom on a field trip; you're able to touch stuff, to see what you're studying. You are actually "there," surrounded by what was only theory before—it's exciting. You need to do the same with your song writing. Get out of the normal routine. Take yourself on a field trip.

When I teach my songwriting master classes, people ask me, "How do you get inspired to create songs and avoid writer's block?" I want to stress that song writing is not about sitting alone in an empty room waiting for inspiration to hit. It is about living life, fully in the moment. You dive in headfirst into anything anybody ever said to you, or any day that stands out in your memory—even a single word can inspire an entire song. You work with your whims. Someone says something to you but you hear it in your own context, using the right side of your brain, and a unique impression is created in your mind. This is the beginning of your song. It's like catching butterflies in a net.

The greatest writers and poets have been more than observers; they have really lived their lives as fully as possible. Think of Bob Dylan's adventures in New York City, plunging himself headfirst into a world of poets, cafés, ideas, falling in love, having arguments—he was totally immersed in life. Don't sit in an empty room looking at the TV waiting for it to happen.

You've just got to start. There is only so long that you can say, "I want to be a songwriter"; you have to start doing it. The more books you fill with your songs and the more you write, the more you will see patterns that are natural to you.

—Dave Stewart: renowned producer and musician with more than 100 million album sales

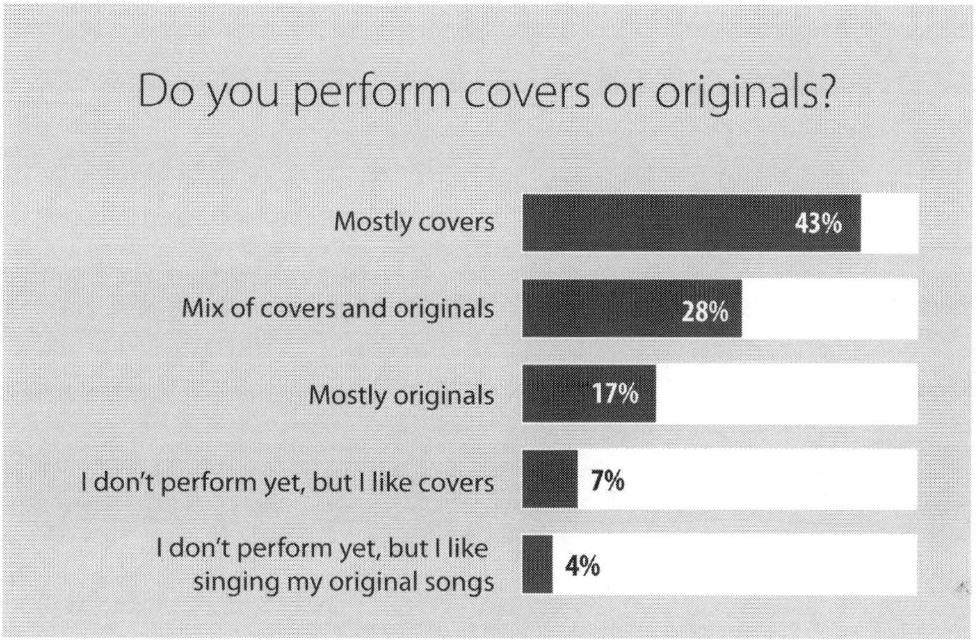

—from the 2012-2013 TC-Helicon survey of 1,000 singers

Action 6: Take the Test of Performance

It's time to size things up where it really counts—and notice what is emerging that is uniquely "you."

I've met many singers who think they have to be perfect in every way before they begin to perform. This misguided belief impedes them from reaching the goal of a confident and fully developed singer. Here's why: singing is about communicating and sharing feelings, concepts, images, dreams and spirituality with others. Once you begin to perform, you start to associate what you're doing with your communication and you can determine if there is an alignment of all the elements of your style.

Receiving feedback can help you grow. Arrange to have a few friends/family members present at your performances as a kind of "focus group." Beforehand, let them know you'll be asking them about each of the following elements so they can observe more accurately.

Then, after your performance, get them together and find out the following: what did you do to engage them? Did you do anything that distracted them from experiencing a complete involvement with each song? Get their input on how you transitioned from one song to the next, how you moved on stage and handled the stage environment. If you performed with others, how did you interact with the rest of the band and them with you? Did you handle the mic and mic stand in a professional or disruptive manner? Get them to respond to as many details of your performance as possible. All of these details combine and contribute to your unique personal style and a memorable, engaging performance.

And remember: as you receive this feedback, take only what makes sense to you; align it with your own vision of what you're striving to create; discard anything with which you disagree.

Who you are IS your style. Vocal development helps to unlock the doors of your expression. The more you let yourself be you, the more conviction with which you can sing each song, the more able you are to give to your audience. The rewards are well worth the time spent cultivating your artistry and your craft.

I'm cheering you on.

—Jeannie Deva: Celebrity Vocal Coach

Action 7: Commit to Weekly Creativity

Don't sit around expecting to get zapped by your next big idea. Make it happen with some simple new habits.

I first need to say: weekly creativity is something that I struggle with; it is a life long struggle for most creative people. This is because the answer to the question, "How can I be more creative?" is very simple: be more creative. When people ask, "How can I write more songs?" the answer is: write more songs. It sounds like I am being glib but the sad truth is that there is nothing stopping you from sitting down right now and writing a song except for the things in your head making excuses for why you can't (I'm excluding overscheduled people from this, for example, those working in coal mines 18 hours a day). When you are sitting at your desk and you are making a decision between checking Twitter and writing lyrics and you check Twitter—well, that's on you.

What is probably keeping you from being more creative is that you are afraid that what you do will not be good. The way past this is to say, "All right. Today, I am going to make something that is NOT good." Decide that you are going to write a mediocre song. You know you can probably do this. Once you start moving, the machinery starts turning and you will find that it's easier to create than you think.

It helps if you know what kind of discipline will work for you; many people find that if they set aside a certain block of time each day this becomes an effective way to write. Some people work well with a deadline—I needed a deadline, the appearance of an imaginary "boss." This is why I announced on the internet that I would publish a new song every week for a year—I announced it publicly to put on myself the pressure of not letting others down. I just didn't feel that it was an option to fail. This really set things up so that it was easier for me to write, record and release a song that I felt was not good. This had the effect of making it less emotionally stressful to write songs constantly than to fail releasing any songs at all.

But I don't want to give the impression that it's become easier for me to be creative. I still have fear and hesitations—I don't think it's ever going to be easy. There are those moments of despair when I am 5% into the songwriting process and I say to myself, "This is no good; I should just abandon it." I double check with my rational brain and it says, "You've been here hundreds of times and you know that if you abandon the song, it will never get written. And you know that if you continue it will get done and it will get better and it might even become great." It is very hard to listen to your rational side, especially since your emotional side will say anything it can to make you stop!

—Jonathan Coulton: Internet singing star, known for his songs about geek culture

Top Vocal Creativity Techniques

- *Sing a favorite song in five different musical styles (country, reggae, jazz...)*
- *Imitate drum sounds*
- *Sing along to a recording and sing one of the instrument parts*
- *Sing along to a recording of a song you don't know and pretend that you know the song*
- *Sing a favorite song as if you were a silly stock character (a basso profundo, or a whiny nerd, or a caveman/woman, or...)*
- *Randomly flip through radio or television stations and imitate whatever voices you hear*
- *Improvise a wordless song*
- *Improvise a song that consists of only three single-syllable words (if you can't think of any words, then try "goat," "tan," and "wash")*
- *Make silly sounds. No, really, get your mouth moving in strange ways and make weird sounds.*
- *Scat sing to every song you hear*
- *Sing the melody to a favorite song as if you are an instrument*
- *Sing a favorite melody while plugging your ears and closing your eyes*
- *Learn a new tongue twister*
- *Sing a favorite melody on repeated rhythmic single sounds (bu, nu, dee, etc. on quarter notes, eighth notes, sixteenth notes...)*
- *Play a well-known song on a kazoo*

—Mister Tim: *viral video star, voice artist, composer and sponsored kazoo player*

Action 8: Move Past Your Blocks

The key to moving past your creative barriers lies in your subconscious.

Quincy Jones, the world's foremost producer of contemporary music, has a great way of viewing the phenomenon of a "writer's block." Perhaps you've had the experience: you are trying to write music but then reach a place where you feel you are getting nowhere; a "block" seems to have appeared between you and your goal. Quincy likes to say, "It's not a block, it's a process." You have to look at the experience of being blocked as a part of the path to finding an answer, not as the end of the path.

What I love is outsider art, outliers who are either completely amazing or bad-shit-crazy or have something original, amazing or scary to say. They could be terrible artists, or they could lack singing skills—to me it doesn't matter.

***—Brian Felsen:** President of CDBaby, BookBaby and HostBaby*

What you need at this stage, he says, is subconscious input. He talks about working in the alpha state; this is the brainwave cycle that you experience when you're just between sleep and consciousness. Many people have their best ideas come to them when they are just about ready to wake up. At this moment, your conscious mind is not the dominant factor and you can access more creativity. Children live in an alpha state; their minds are open and can move in ways that aren't inhibited.

Quincy has had the experience, for example, of working on a big scoring session the night before it's needed, and getting nowhere with it. At that point he will lie down on the floor and put his feet up on the bed in order to get into this alpha state. Before long he has the experience that the score is writing itself. All of this reflects the truth that 12 percent of one's creativity is conscious and 88 percent is subconscious.

I've found this true in my own music. I know that when I can step outside of myself and "be" the music rather than be controlled by my fear of screwing the music up, I can do almost anything.

Singers really need this insight on creativity and the subconscious because there can be so many fears about singing out of tune, out of time, even that people are judging their looks. So you have to find ways to get out of your conscious shackles so that you can sing from your soul—that's where the magic is. In other words, aside from putting in all of the hard work involved in mastering the craft of singing, it's important to find the right mindset for your performance.

—Bill Gibson: President of Northwest Music and Recording

Frequently Asked Questions

> How can I be a real vocal artist if all I do is sing covers?

Answered by Neil Sedaka, legendary American singer, songwriter, composer and pianist

Many of the great singers have done cover albums. I think of Frank Sinatra or Barbra Streisand. They chose songs that contained strong emotional ties for their hearts. Frank Sinatra used to read the lyrics to the songs many times over before he recorded or performed them—so he could feel how the writer put emotion into the song.

Don't go out of the style that appeals to you; don't screech things out that are too high or too low. You want to please yourself with your songs—so that your audience will feel your pleasure. So, you need to sing songs that mean something to you, that you can transform into your own feelings. Emotion is the key factor: you need to bring your emotion to the listener—if you feel it, they will definitely feel it. Start with the songs that you know deeply, that you have an affinity for. I am a product of the music I have heard all my life—Patti Page, Mel Tormé, Stevie Wonder and so many others. Focus on the kind of songs and styles that you feel are believable to the audience.

> I want to sound like _____ (insert name of FAVORITE singer here). Where do I begin?

Answered by Dr. Ronald C. Scherer, PhD, Professor in the Department of Communication Sciences and Disorders, Bowling Green State University

It is important to strive for the kind of emotional impact that a great artist has, but you must understand how to do that.

The voice quality itself is a large part of the impact. Note that many very popular singers can vary their sound quality over wide ranges with healthy production—thin to rounded sounds, soft to loud, breathy to bright, clear to slightly rough or distorted, with or without vibrato, etc.—and you should also strive for this. This range of singing possibilities provides the sound quality tools you can use to bring about your intended emotions, your intended connections to the text. In addition, a critical ingredient is the total ensemble effect with your singing; you need to make sure that the emotional intent or the message you wish to convey is supported by the music and performance behind the voice.

Relative to sounding exactly like Adele or someone else, it actually would be safer not to do so, but instead to learn from those artists *how* they convey the emotional charge you perceive, and imitate the elements discussed above to achieve the same thing.

So, you do not need to sound exactly like another artist to achieve the goal of connection. Indeed, your goal should be to put your own emotional energy into the song and to access the wide range of possibilities that fit your own voice as you interpret the text. When you achieve this, not only will you be successful—it will be your own success, and listeners will identify *you* as the amazing performer, not someone else.

> Where is a safe place to try out my new ideas?

Answered by Sara Serpa, internationally recognized vocalist, composer and bandleader

> *The question of what to write about needs to be answered in a place that's deep inside of you. I feel, and my band feels, that art is best created from yourself and for yourself. The four of us in Mastodon write all of the music; we create everything Mastodon from the four of us for the four of us, because this is the music that we're married to. And then the rest of the year, the rest of our career and the rest of our lives, we live, eat, breathe and sleep Mastodon. So we need to be in love with what we create, deeply. It's a selfish standpoint, but that's the best way, in our opinion, that art should be created.*
>
> ***—More about Troy Sanders***

Well, you have to understand that, ultimately, you are going to need to put your ideas out there—to face a lack of safety. Singing (and life) is about taking risks. Still, there are some things you can do to get ready for this.

Prepare—and prepare again—at home. Rehearsals with your band are for setting down the structures of your music, not to work out all of your solo material. Your time at home is about improving and refining your vocals. But there is another thing you can be doing at home: envision what you want to achieve in each song as well as in your entire performance. Try to step outside of yourself, visualizing your singing from the perspective of an audience member. How do I want to look, feel, move, and sound? Don't leave any of these aspects to chance.

If you are working with other musicians, invest time into building good relationships with them—this will give you a feeling of safety when you are on stage. Share experiences other than music. The more you "play" with your band, the greater the connection will be between you. It's difficult to give a name to this, but it is a quality that will help you to stretch your own wings and fly with your music.

> How can I write my own songs since I don't play piano or guitar?

Answered by Dot Bustelo, internationally recognized music producer and music technology strategist

Today's technology offers some fantastic tools to assist you with your musical ideas—without having to master an instrument other than your voice. Just as one example, use Apple Loops files to give you a "bed" to write on. All you do is drag and drop these into GarageBand or Logic and they will instantly lock into any tempo you want to work with.

If you are able to drag a photo into your Facebook page, you can do this. It's as easy as anything you are doing already on your computer.

These loops come in every genre of music with instruments to fit whatever creative mood you're in. Think of them as construction kits composed of drums, guitars, keyboard, strings, synth, bass guitar, etc.—whatever combination you want. Just drag them into a project and you'll be amazed at how easily you're inspired to write lyrics, melody ... a whole song.

Think they may not sound great? Check out the Apple Loop: Vintage Funk Kit 03. It's the entire beat of Rihanna's #1 song "Umbrella"! A professional producer simply dragged that loop into the mix. Was he cheating? No. He had a good ear and recognized that loop as a funky, fresh beat that Rihanna could sing a hit song on top of!

> I want to write my own songs—but what do I write about?

Answered by Neil Sedaka, legendary American singer, songwriter, composer and pianist

I think that songs can emerge from three different places—the emotional, the intellectual and the spiritual. Emotional creations arise when you are going through a drama in yourself and you want to get it out on paper as a catharsis—you cry it out. Intellectual writing is when you have a tune in your mind and you work to get it written down in the best form. Spiritual writing is when you just feel as if you've been chosen by something higher than yourself—these songs write themselves.

I listen to other singers—I'm inspired by listening to specific voices. I think to myself, "I can write something for that voice." Or maybe even, "I can write something even better than that in their style." After all, creative people always bounce ideas off of others. I can write any time of the day but I usually declare to myself that I will be writing at a certain time, say 10am. I turn it all off at the end of the day because you can get yourself confused if you stay at it for too long.

> *One of the questions I love asking aspiring musicians is "Do you know the musical influences of your idol?" Because if you do some research, you'll find some cool and interesting stuff you can incorporate into your own style.*
>
> ***—Elliott Randall:** legendary guitarist, formerly a musical consultant for Saturday Night Live*

> My voice teacher says I'm suited to folk, but I want to sing metal. Is she right?

Answered by Jaime Vendera, vocal coach renowned for his wineglass-shattering voice

I am having a flashback to my first vocal coaches. Why is it that many coaches try to morph you to their style of singing? This is the 11th wonder of the world. Some of my first coaches flowed to what they knew such as opera and Broadway music, claiming I could only become a great singer by singing these genres. While these styles are great, they just didn't tweak my melon.

> *Because I'm always humming I can come up with five different ways to sing something. When I'm given the words to a song I'm ready to give it my feel and my voice.*
>
> ***—Joey Belladonna:** lead singer of the legendary group Anthrax*

So ask yourself, "Why do I want to sing?" I'm betting it's because some singer, and in the case of the question, some metal singer has inspired you. So, go with your desire, sing what your heart calls you to sing, and have a coach who teaches you correct vocal technique along the way. If your coach insists that you must sing folk, be honest with them: let them know that you just don't have the passion for it. If they aren't willing to help you grow and follow your dreams to becoming a metal screamer, well, find another coach who will. After all, you want to sing because a certain style inspires you. While I truly believe you *can* learn from *all* styles of music, in the end, if you're not happy with what you're singing, why do it? Sing what you love and you *will* find your voice!

> My friend says that my ideas for doing "covers" are weird—that I should be more mainstream.

Answered by Jay Frank, leading author (Hack Your Hit and Futurehit.DNA) and Owner/CEO of DigSin

If an artist is experimenting with different styles for cover music in order to deepen their own artistic abilities, who is anyone to tell them that this is weird?

On the other hand, you do need to pay attention to your audience, finding that connection between what you want to deliver and what they want to hear. If you are seeking to become more popular and the majority of the audience (not just one person) is telling you that your music is too odd then you have a choice: (i) change your music to fit better with your audience or (ii) find a new audience. What you can't do is waste your time exclaiming, "What do they know?!" What they know is that they are people who can support your career, should they relate to your music.

> Does using vocal processing count for being original?

Answered by Dave Stewart, renowned producer and musician with more than 100 million album sales

Well, you have to step back and look at the whole piece of work you've created.

If the end result is an amazing piece of work then the answer to your question is "yes." I think of Holger Czukay from the German band Can who has experimented with looping, and of Kraftwerk and Daft Punk who have done great work with their vocal processing. On the other hand, if you are just processing your voice to make it sound more in tune, then this is not an original process. Part of the creative endeavor is to create a sound; a unique mixture of processed audio is a part of this.

I always like to juxtapose things. Annie Lennox and I wrote a manifesto, and, on that sheet, we said we wanted to write songs containing an "icy cold feeling with a soulful vocal." "Sweet Dreams" was born out of this experimentation. We added other dimensions to the idea, for example how we would dress and present our idea visually. You can see the results on the video for "Sweet Dreams."

I continue to use all sorts of effects to create unique and arresting sounds that become integral to my song creations, using natural echo chambers, weird guitar sounds recorded through tiny toy amplifiers or multiple delay effects.

I often sing in the same room with the musicians so you can hear the drums come through my mic. For example on the album *The Ringmaster General*, for the song "I Got Love," we go from my mic being the only mic turned on in the room to thirty-seven other mics kicking in. My engineer asked, "How are we going to fix this?" But I liked it. You move from this weird mono sound to this huge, full-fat stereo. It works.

Sometimes an artist can get into a rut and you need to experiment with different sounds. I wrote "Don't Come Around Here No More" with Tom Petty; what we did with the recording and the approach to the production changed Tom's perception of the process and opened him up to experimenting. It created a different world to play in. You can always go back to the world you're more comfortable in later, but it is important to try new things.

> I'm a really good singer, but I've never found the right songs that suit my voice and personality. What can I do?

Answered by Cica, NYC based vocalist and songwriter involved in the "Perfect Project"

There are a couple of paths you might explore to find your way. First, reach out and connect with other musicians, singers and songwriters to see if this collaboration helps you to uncover those songs.

The search for collaborators should be a quest for true connection. Never think merely, "What is this person going to do for me?" It is about mutual respect. Instead, ask, "Are they letting me express myself without knocking me down?" and "Am I doing the same for them?" You have to be in a very comfortable environment with your collaborator—otherwise you won't be able to experiment with new ideas.

The other path is to try writing yourself. You can start with journaling, jotting down any line or word that strikes you from your own life. You could be amazed about where this might lead. You don't need to be a "writer" to do this—your personal experiences lead you to the best lyrics. Who knows what you have inside? When something interesting, horrible or beautiful happens to you, write it down. If you listen to your favorite songs and pay attention to the lyrics you will see that they come from people's heartfelt experiences.

Once you've done some writing, you could try to sing a melody in your head. You are a singer, you already have a musical "base" and you may discover that you can create your own melodies. Record these. This doesn't need to be in a professional environment—you can use a phone or another device. Do this once a melody hits you and it feels interesting to you (they fly out of your head, even if it is your own melody).

This was my own path. I used to consider myself a singer, but not necessarily a songwriter. I always kept a journal. Then, a singer-songwriter I had great respect for, gave me the advice to look at my journal as a book full of lyrical ideas. He said, "There could be a million songs in there." I really worked on it, making my ideas more focused and this led to many songs.

Of course the two paths of collaboration and writing are not exclusive. There are many musicians who don't sing and would be open to getting together and putting down your lyrical ideas. Do not be afraid and believe in yourself!

Aim.

A singing career? Many people would consider it a risky pursuit since only a tiny percentage of singers ever make it to stardom. Ah, but you've read this book, and you know that becoming a superstar isn't the only way to make a living from singing—you know there are different kinds of singing work out there.

OK, hold it. Stop everything.

There is an elephant in the room. Whenever anyone starts talking realistically about a singing career, there's an issue nobody wants to bring up. So let's get it out in the open: you secretly want *the easy way*.

You want to skip over the years of grappling with your muse, honing your skills, holding a day job, building a fan base and performing for little or no money. You want to "get discovered." You want *someone else* to make your career. There. It's out in the open.

There is nothing wrong with wanting to be discovered. There *is* a problem, however if that is the *only* thing you want. The artists who contributed to this book would tell you, with great passion, that if wanting an easy road to fame is your *only* motivation, then you should stay away from the music business. In fact, many would say even stardom doesn't guarantee sustainable success.

Sure, you could rocket to stardom. But what if that doesn't happen after 10 years? After 20 years? What if it does happen, but only at great cost to your integrity? If your career is going to be difficult, tiring, confusing and slow to build up, do you still want to devote your life to singing?

If you said yes, then singing means more to you than an easy road to fame.

The artists in this book have talked about recognizing who you truly are and staying true to this right from day one. They have also talked about being flexible and shaping yourself to the demands that arise. Does this seem like conflicting advice? Perhaps it is, but this is only a problem for a singer who hasn't taken aim.

Defining what it is that you want to experience and accomplish—in more immediate terms—is the key to taking aim with your career. What fulfills you artistically? Personally? Is it leading a band? Learning how to scat? Writing songs? Being a part of someone else's movement? Connecting with people? Teaching the world something new? Developing virtuosic vocal skill? Releasing your deepest feelings?

Your desires will evolve, and paying the bills may require you to stray from them, but knowing them well will let you be the one who takes aim—not only at that big, distant target, but also at many closer ones.

It's time for a test. I'm going to tell you a story about a singer named Evan. During a single year, he attempts to build a music career. He is now wondering about his future. I want you to play vocational counsellor, giving him your own advice. First of all, you need to know how the year went:

> Evan is a month away from high school graduation. He has decided to pursue a music career, but can only commit to a year before the pressures of finding a "real" job will start to take over. The community center down the street is holding a "Battle of the Bands" event. He enters his band, with the song, "Some Nights" by Fun. He knows he sounds pretty good on this song, since he sang it at the talent show last spring, and people seemed to like it. However, he also knows there are great singers in this competition, so he decides to begin singing lessons, paying for them with the money from his part-time job at the grocery store. He records his lessons and his band rehearsals on his phone. He listens to the recordings and looks for ways to improve.

Evan has taken aim, starting with his singing skill. Ask any professional singer out there and they will tell you, no matter how talented you are, you have to work at your craft for quite some time to be great. Don't sit around wondering if you are talented—get to work. There are hundreds of amazing singers around. To stand among them, aim for the highest possible level of skill—and expect to spend your whole career getting there.

> Evan's band doesn't win, but they sound pretty good. Evan makes a point of introducing himself to the other musicians, including the keyboard player from the winning band. To Evan's delight and panic, the keyboard player invites him to sing three jazz songs with a trio, at a wedding. Evan is not into Jazz, but he wants to make connections and he wants experience. Evan prefers to think they chose him for his great voice, but he suspects it was partly because of his look. He always wears a bow tie and tuxedo jacket when he performs. It started during his school production of Guys and Dolls, and has become a good luck charm. Evan listens endlessly to recordings of the jazz songs and asks his teacher to help him learn them.

You could turn your nose up at gigs that don't seem in line with your dream career. However, if you want to gain experience and make connections, these gigs are the very targets you should be aiming for. Don't lose sight of your dream, but don't be too precious with it either.

> Evan actually makes some money with the jazz group and does a few more gigs. After the initial "stiffness" at the first gig, Evan relaxes and has a great time. He did a good job of learning and memorizing the tunes so he imitates the style well, and gives a relaxed performance—despite jazz not being his favorite genre. He discovers how great it feels when listeners connect to the music. He sees how his singing brings the wedding celebration to life. That feeling is even better than being paid.
>
> Evan wants to experience that same connection when his own band plays. He revisits his favorite tunes in the world—folk rock songs by bands like the Decemberists—and gets in touch with what he really loves about the music. He spends hours in his room listening to and singing this music on his simple recording studio that his uncle helped him set up. He tries to capture the passion with this music as he did with the jazz songs—only with this music, the connection is more natural.

What kind of music suits your look, your voice and your personality? Be honest about who you truly are. Knowing yourself will allow you to pursue musical situations where you can shine. Interestingly, it will also let you experiment with new and diverse opportunities, since you will be better able to bring your true self into any genre or situation.

> In November, Evan goes to see the Decemberists. Instead of the full five-person band, it is just the lead singer, acoustic guitar and bass. This inspires Evan to put together a folk-rock trio of his own. He asks the bass player from the jazz group and the guitar player from his original band. They rehearse like crazy, focusing on esoteric covers of obscure folk rock groups so they don't seem like a typical cover band. Evan has clear ideas of how he wants to sound, since he has been listening and testing things out at home. He takes the lead. He plays examples; he sings his ideas and explains to the band the sound he envisions.

No matter what your long-term career goal is, you must constantly aim for smaller goals centered in your music and your art.

> Evan has his first gig with the new band three months later. It's a Valentine's dance at the community center to raise money for the local burn unit. Evan and his trio perform an eight-song set as the opening band. The audience is into it! Evan realizes that he achieved what he had wanted—an audience connection. Afterwards, several people comment on his bow tie and tuxedo jacket. They think it's quirky—and cool.

> With no gigs on the calendar in March and April, Evan and his trio create a web site, a Facebook page and even have business cards printed off. They try applying for festivals but get turned down. The local venues don't call them back. Evan realizes that a bad YouTube video of his other band is the only video footage out there representing him. He takes it down and plans to make a higher quality video of his new band.

> Just when they are wondering if they will ever get another gig, they get a crazy idea. They decide to show up, with their instruments in hand and no sound system, at every restaurant, café and venue in town and ask to play one song. Some of the restaurant managers get nervous when they walk in and ask them to leave. Others venue managers are game. The result of one day and fourteen impromptu performances: five booked gigs. Evan discovers the business side of performing. There are a million emails to send and follow up on. He has to figure out how to handle the money. At one café, they agree to play for tips. At one pub, there is a door charge and Evan arranges to take 50% for the band. They each use their social media channels and put up physical posters to promote the gigs.

The artists who contributed to this book agree unanimously that every artist must embrace the business side of their singing life. This means you lift your arrow as both an artist and as a business person, never forgetting these two sides of your career. Later in your career, you may have others taking part in your business, such as a booking agent, a manager, an employer or a record company. These people might bring resources and opportunities, but they can never replace you as the driving force behind the movement that is your music.

Evan's year of pursuing music is about to end. It's been a fruitful year, but he is not able to support himself with music—far from it. So what do you think he should do next? Give up? Keep pursuing a career in music? If so, what should his next step be?

> At Evan's last gig in May, the turnout is great. The pub has a dance floor, and a few people even get up and dance. His trio's sound isn't big, but it is danceable. Evan sees the dancing as evidence of that audience connection. He even plays his trumpet on a few songs (he had honed his trumpet skill in the school jazz band). Evan can see a few girls at one of the tables near the front—they are wearing quirky bow ties! Evan has fans! After the show, he talks to them and asks them to like his Facebook page, to which they say, "We already did!"

You can't expect to either "make it" or "not make it" in one short year of building a singing career. You can, however, clarify your dreams, break them down into tangible goals and see if powering your own musical ship is something you can handle and sustain. A constant message from the artists in this book was simply that this is hard work—and it can be a long time before others jump on board to help you.

There are no certifications, co-op terms or exams that qualify you to be a successful contemporary singer. There is no clear path, no academic advisor, no supervisor, no reliable salary, no seniority accumulation that leads to promotion. Music is the kind of career that requires its professionals (you) to take charge of and create their own path, often in the face of frustration and rejection. Evan's is a story of a singer taking aim. In fact, his year of singing could be the beginning of any number of respected entertainers' careers—only this early stage doesn't usually show up on their Wikipedia pages!

—Kathy Alexander, staff writer at Voice Council Magazine

CHAPTER 19

Your Band

Lead, Follow and Get Out of the Way.

When I shift into 5th gear on stage, the band had better be shifting with me. I'm not talking about ruthlessness; I'm talking about staying with me in the heat, in the passion. This is what I am and this is what I do.

—Ruby Turner, renowned gospel and R & B singer

When bands are fighting, my advice is, "Shut up and make music." Close your mouth and play. Don't overthink. You make your music, and half will stink — throw it out. The other half will be great — run with it.

—Ron "Bumblefoot" Thal, Guns N' Roses

Your Band

Lead, Follow and Get Out of the Way.

Actions:

1. Choose Band Members That Are Right for You
2. Be Rehearsal Pros
3. Communicate Your Vision To The Band
4. Guide the Band To That Vision
5. Take Charge
6. Action 6. Pick Your Battles
7. Work Through Conflicts
8. Let Your Band Shine
9. Walk a Mile In Their Shoes
10. Be a Team Player

Frequently Asked Questions:

» *Band members are skipping rehearsals all the time—what can I do?*

» *How do I tell a band member that I don't want them in the band anymore?*

» *My guitarist is really gifted, but he's a pain to work with.*

» *Some of us are ready to kill each other—I'm afraid our band is going to break up. Help!*

» *Why does my band have so much trouble following me?*

» *Our songs just aren't turning out as cool as they are in my head…*

» *Everyone in the group is having a blast with the music but I'm not.*

» *How can I make sure I'm not one of those sloppy singers who can't keep time?*

» *Why do we always make the same mistakes?*

» *Our performances have become stale.*

» *That other band is no more gifted than we are, so why are they getting all the gigs?*

» *We're always speeding up.*

» *My band members seem to connect with each other, but I feel like I am on the outside.*

» *Over the course of the show, volumes are inching up and up and I'm afraid I'm getting lost in the mix.*

» *My drummer is in his own world when we are performing and I feel we could do so much better if we were in sync—how can I make this happen?*

» *Why don't our background vocals sound as cool as the recordings we listen to?*

» *My band won't let me lead. I'm the singer, and I want them to follow me! Help!*

» *How do I tell a band-mate that they are off-pitch?*

» *How do I work with a pick-up band?*

» *I'm going to "sit in" with my friend's band at a live gig. There's no rehearsal—how do I prepare?!*

Action 1: Choose Band Members That Are Right for You

More dedication on the "front end" of choosing a band member will make for more success on the "back end" of performing.

Choosing the right band members is crucial for singers. You can flip a switch on a guitar for a different sound, but a singer doesn't have that luxury. It's simple: your band should be built around your voice. Unfortunately, that seems egomaniacal to young musicians and so bands tend to fail and fail and fail until they stumble onto a sound that compliments what their singer does naturally. Maroon Five is a perfect example. They struggled for years as a grunge band.

Now let's say you've narrowed down what sounds compliment your personality and voice (i.e. you can't compete with a Marshall stack but hearing a jazz piano makes you want to hit somebody!). Your next task is to find musicians that play that way without being asked to. Musicians will say anything to get into a band, just like guys will say anything to girls to get into ... well, you know. So females looking beyond a one-night stand learn to "interview" potential mates by getting them to talk about themselves—and so should you. There's no better indicator of someone's future than learning about their past.

First and foremost, your music should support your personality and type of voice. If a band is not playing to its singer's strengths, then the band should rethink what they're doing.

***—Tony Harnell:** award winning lead singer of TNT*

I got tired of my bands exploding because of personality and musical conflicts so I took a whole year to hand pick my last group. First and foremost was the way each guy played. I used my voice as the gauge. Key question: did I feel like a powerful singer when we jammed? If so, the next step was to go out and have a beer (or a burger). If the guy wasn't somebody I could hang with outside of music then I knew the chemistry wouldn't be there on stage or in the studio. I learned this from the Rolling Stones. They obviously had the pick of the litter when selecting a second guitarist. The reason they snipped Ron Wood away from Rod Stewart is because they knew they could live with the guy. They had been drinking buddies for years!

It's tempting if someone is a friend (or owns a van) to look past a musical mismatch, but it will only make you feel like a second-rate singer. On the other hand, singing with someone whose playing compliments your voice will make you feel like you can take on the world. And that, my friend, is the only way you actually *can* take on the world!

—Mark Baxter: acclaimed vocal coach with Aerosmith, Journey, Goo Goo Dolls and many others

Action 2: Be Rehearsal Pros

Overcome challenges in your group by applying these "tried and true" methods to your art.

When we practice in groups, our success hinges on more than our musical abilities. Our ensemble culture, interpersonal skills, and rehearsal strategies also determine whether we accomplish much or little in any practice session. Here are 10 tips for better group rehearsals.

1. Commit to Professionalism. Agree to be punctual, prepared for, and courteous at rehearsals.
2. Get Organized. Smart organizing helps minimize conflict and frees us to focus on art-making. For those reasons, collectively agree to a rehearsal schedule and specify your objectives in advance.
3. Set Reachable Goals. Our rehearsals crackle with intensity when we target them toward motivating, near-term goals. So, choose manageable music, and then conclude each rehearsal with plans for the next one.
4. Begin Rehearsals with Communal Material. Instead of starting with unfamiliar music, run through a favorite tune or excerpt that renews your musical bonds.
5. Rehearse Strategically. Use varying techniques to tighten up your execution and bring your music to life.
6. Communicate. During rehearsals, try out collaborators' ideas before commenting on them. Listen attentively, critique tactfully, and admit when you mess up. Still, limit verbal exchanges. Aim to reach consensus through musical more than verbal interaction. When thorny non-musical issues surface, set up separate meetings.
7. Balance Leading with Listening. Inspire each other by listening and responding to your spontaneous musical gestures.
8. Transmit Positive Energy. Personal energy is contagious, especially in the close-knit setting of an ensemble. We uplift our colleagues when we keep up a sense of humor and broadcast enthusiasm.
9. Help Each Other Succeed. Let your co-performers know that you value their talents, and strive to be easy to work with. Respect personal differences and, when conflicts emerge, treat them as opportunities for your group to attain greater synergy.
10. Keep Art at the Core. All ensembles face difficulties. Personalities can chafe, opinions diverge, and priorities shift. But you can surmount troubles by steadfastly applying these and other ideas in service to your art. Most of all, in rehearsals and on stage, reinforce your bonds through wholehearted musical expression.

–Gerald Klickstein: Veteran guitarist, educator and author of The Musician's Way

Action 3. Communicate Your Vision to Your Band

You don't need a PhD in music theory—but you do need to know your songs inside and out.

Whether you have written a song, or are working on a cover, start envisioning how you hear those sounds on a keyboard, guitar, drums–the instrumentation of your group. Take some time, by yourself, to form some general ideas.

What I like to do is to jump from this to recording a rough demo of the various parts I "hear" in my mind onto my smartphone. I just hum and beat-box various parts–I may even bang wooden spoons on the back of a chair. This gets the musical ideas out of my head and then I can listen and re-evaluate how it sounds before I take it to the group. (By the way, recording clips of all your ideas is a great song writing tool, helping to ensure that you don't forget what can turn out to be important ideas later on).

I then share my rough demo with the band. This puts everyone on the same page at the beginning of the process. My rough demo, after all, is only a representation of what I am hearing in my head. As the band members pick up and play their instruments, my song is having a great opportunity to develop. It may totally change.

> *Music is better when more than one spirit is involved. Lennon and McCartney had something much more special than just Lennon OR McCartney.*
>
> ***–Ron "Bumblefoot" Thal:*** *Guns N' Roses*

One image I find helpful is to imagine my song as a "raft." When I share my song with the band, it is like pushing the raft out to sea. Various tides and winds will lead it on its journey. However, I am one of the people that has input into how the song develops. As a part of the team I will listen and appreciate various ideas, but I will also be aware of the things I must fight for. This give-and-take is what it means to be a part of a musical team.

–Chris Henderson: singer-songwriter-guitarist of Bronze Radio Return

Action 4: Guide The Band To That Vision

Musicians can give you everything they've got once they've caught your ideas.

If you don't have a backup band that you know well, then you face the discomfort of starting over again with new musicians. Yet, you can solve many issues before you even meet for the first time. Get a CD or digital file of all your songs to the band way in advance of meeting–along with chord charts. Let them listen, learn and immerse themselves in your material so that they come to the first rehearsal knowing it well.

When you're rehearsing, you may find that things happen that don't sound right—that aren't fitting into your vision for the song. It's important that you solve this right away. It could be that you say to the drummer, "Could you use your brushes in this section?" Or to the bass player, "Could we try going to the root on that bar?"

> *Putting together a backing band can be hard. Not many of us are as lucky as Bono—he formed U2 and found his wife in the same week. They are all still together.*
>
> ***—Tomas Nevergreen:** leading European singer-songwriter*

You can't say: "Hey man, you're screwing up!" A prick or a bitch never gets much attention. Take a more gentle approach: "There may be a wrong note there—can you double check for me?" The most important thing is to be kind and constructive, communicating that you really want to solve these challenges.

If you find it difficult to relate musical ideas, then consider taking the stress off yourself: bring someone along with you who can act as a musical director. Or, you may find it helpful to think of yourself as a director starting with a new cast. Be the type of director who is involving, caring and appreciative. When you're like that, those around you will become more involved and give you everything they've got.

—Fred Mollin: veteran record producer, film and TV composer, musical director and songwriter

Action 5: Take Charge

When you step up to the plate, do so with signals that make sense to your band

Let me give you some tips that come from working with hundreds of pick-up bands all over the world.

First, determine the key for each song that works best for your voice—if you need help figuring this out, get together with one of the instrumentalists in your band on the side.

Then, master counting the band in at a tempo you feel is right for the song. To do this, sing through the bridge of the song in your head so that you get the tempo, then count in the band. If you know a little theory, you could write down the quarter note quality on each chart—or on a small list. To determine this value, just get out the metronome app on your smart phone and figure out the tempos. If your drummer is familiar with this kind of thing, then you'll be on the same page.

Use hand signals and discuss their meaning with your band members, for instance:

- Pointing at the bridge of your nose means going to bridge.
- Putting your fist in the air, at the level of your head, and then twisting it left and right means "go to the coda"—in other words, "we are now going to the ending as it's written on the chart."
- Pointing to the top of your head means that you want to go back to the beginning of the song, to a verse.
- Circling your finger in the air means, "keep repeating the tag," the closing part of your song.
- Raising your hand high (as a conductor might) and then slamming it down signifies the end of your song or a full-band break in the song.

Don't forget that you can make changes on the spot if you want to—if someone is riffing on their guitar in a solo passage and you want them to keep going, just motion for them to continue. If there are some instrumental solos going on and you feel that you are getting a little bit lost, make eye contact with the musician and point to your nose—they will know you are about to come back in singing the bridge. It helps if you can sing the song's melody through in your head while the solos are going on, so that you always know exactly where everyone is.

—Annie Sellick: internationally renowned jazz singer

Action 6: Pick Your Battles

There are some times when the singer just can't bend—be certain to know when those times are.

It doesn't matter if you are Madonna or someone in a band just starting out: there is a way to talk to people—with respect. There's no need to act like a diva. Your band is like a family and, if there's a situation in a family, you try to sit down and talk it through.

There is usually someone who is better than others at instigating this discussion: "I think we all need to sit down and talk." It has to be done thoughtfully and diplomatically so that no one person feels they are being pointed at. You don't want to say "Let's all sit down and talk about Johnny's drumming." Diplomatically bring things to the table, ask people how they feel and ask, "How can we fix it?" Give people the opportunity to generate answers.

Still, there are several areas where I will not hesitate to put my foot down.

The first is playing too loudly. If things are too loud, you begin to over-sing and mess up your voice. I tell the boys, "Look, we have to stop a minute and sort this out. If we can't hear each other, then we can't be a team. It is about throwing the ball so that someone can catch it and shine. It is not about getting up there and turning the volume up."

"Look, you have an amp and you can turn it up ... and up. You have a guitar that plugs into it and you can turn it up ... and up. You can break a string and you can just put a new one on. Or, if you whack the drums and break a skin, you can get a new one. But I can't do that with my voice. If you guys don't bring your volume down, I will be in surgery and out of commission for a year."

If you go and watch some great bands (Eagles, Fleetwood Mac, the Stones) you will see them working together, eyeballing each other all the time. You get a sense that they are enjoying working together with their music. Just watch any of your musical idols, and you will see this team experience at work.

As a singer my monitor is my life saver—I just have to hear it fully. I set up my monitor just off center from my drummer, slightly to the right or left so that his drums are bypassing my monitor. I also ask the bass player to turn his amp out a little more to the audience, so it isn't coming over into my space—and the same with the guitarist. If you have a really tiny stage you don't need anything more than your voice in that monitor. If you are on a big stage you might choose to have a little bit of the mix in the monitor. At the end of the day your vocal is what you need.

***—Nikki Lamborn:** singer-songwriter of the English band "Never the Bride"*

There's another area where I'll put my foot down. It's just not cool to come onto stage with a can of lager and a cigarette; it isn't cool to come on pissed. Even Axel Rose can't get away with it. I had to fire a bass player—we had a 42-date tour and, with only three dates to go, he came onto the stage drunk. When you're drunk the first sense that goes is your hearing and you start to push louder and harder in order to compensate. This throws the entire performance off. Not only that, it's disrespectful to the rest of the band.

Also be firm on showing up on time for gigs and sound checks; make sure you have someone whose job it is to ensure that you all get to places on time. Never miss a sound check or be late for setting up for a gig. If someone is continually late for rehearsals or sound check it comes to the point that someone has to name this as disrespectful behaviour—we actually fined someone in the band 10 dollars for every 30 minutes they were late.

—Nikki Lamborn: singer-songwriter of the English band "Never the Bride"

Action 7: Work Through Conflict

Real commitment to three personal qualities will help you and your band prevail.

Working through conflict in a band (and I've seen a lot of it!) comes down to three things: you've got to be good company, you've got to have a vision and you've got to be flexible.

That may sound easy but because people have different visions, it isn't. So, let me unpack what I mean.

You've got to be good company. You have to have a spirit of wanting to make things work for everyone. Life in a band isn't easy—it takes a real commitment to the process. Listen to those around you and be open to the fact that they might have a good idea. Be a fair-minded person, open to your band mates' ideas. You won't stay together long if you're not willing to listen.

You've got to have a vision. You are involved in music, after all, because you have ideas—lots of them. Part of your role is to keep your communication up. Some people may not care about your suggestions. That's life. You won't always get your way—that's life too. But you need to be true to yourself by sharing your vision for the music. And you can question other people's ideas: "Do you really think that's what we need? What about ... ?"

You've got to be flexible. In a band you just have to compromise as much as possible. Sometimes a particular point might seem like a big deal and you end up compromising but still get to a good place. I know that I have plenty of good ideas. But I know the other guy probably has good ideas too. Don't say he (or she) doesn't have a good idea until you've heard them out. Don't pull rank in terms of age, experience or technical know-how. Other people with less of these qualities than you can come up with good ideas.

Let's face it: if people really don't have any intention to fix things, then your band isn't going to stay together long. However, if you practice these three principles, it will stand a much better chance.

—Joey Belladonna, lead singer of the legendary group Anthrax

> *The movie about Metallica, Some Kind of Monsters, shows how they brought in a psychologist to help sort out their issues. Not many bands have 20 million in the bank like Metallica, but many face the same issues: one guy wants more musical freedom (in their case, the drummer), one member is limited in how many hours he can put in (in their case due to being in rehab). An outside perspective—paid or unpaid—can really help you figure it out.*
>
> ***—Mike Tramp:*** *member of double platinum selling band White Lion*

Action 8: Let Your Band Shine

Learn the key ways to acknowledge your band's skills—when they shine in their work, you'll shine in yours.

It is really important that everyone gets a chance to step out and show what they can do on stage. Some band members may not want to solo, but in our group we have so many talented soloists that it would be criminal not to have them share their gifts with everyone else. When this happens, I introduce them to the crowd before their solo and praise them publically after the solo. Also, in any interviews or publicity about the music, it is essential that praise be shared. On a more personal level, I always share with the band how I enjoy their work.

There is a "BUT" to this. As a singer-songwriter, I recognize that there is a right and a wrong time to do solos; they should happen but never at the cost of the flow of a song. The song should never lose its momentum. You see, I believe in the "formula" of a song, therefore I write with a certain pattern in mind. There is a time to solo and a time not to solo.

Your band is not your therapy session. Would you bring all this drama into your day job? No? Then don't bring it into your band rehearsal. Respect the band environment.

—Ron "Bumblefoot" Thal:
Guns N' Roses

This has been a sticky subject for us in the past. The underlying reality is that everyone knows that I respect them. On top of this is my wish for respecting the song itself. Of course there are times when a band member feels that their solo is adding to the song, but then I have to make an executive decision. However, in this process everybody gets heard. Then, I speak up from the song writing point of view. One of my passions is that the listener isn't exposed to something that neglects to keep their interest. Keep in mind that I am working within the genre of pop, with songs that are recognizable in their formula by a lot of people. It is in my interest that they don't drag.

Another area which makes a difference is that band members be given the chance to be in the studio recordings—even if you could do more of the work yourself in a recording scenario. Band members will be bringing their unique take to your live music and so to include them in the recording process affirms their contribution and adds to what you are able to present in your recorded versions.

—Laura Vane: singer-songwriter of Laura Vane & The Vipertones

Action 9: Walk A Mile In Their Shoes

For the singer who isn't an instrumentalist, a number of irritations can be avoided with a little knowledge.

I know my drummer is going to take forever to set up his drums. I know my guitar player wants his amp to sit a certain way on stage. Understanding these details about my band has given me patience and has led to an atmosphere of appreciation—and this makes our music better.

One of the quickest routes you can take to this atmosphere is to learn to play an instrument. There are so many benefits to this: your band will see that you want to delve into the music even further. It will help you communicate with your band, come up with arrangement ideas and write songs. If you are struggling to explain a musical idea, it helps if you can play it. You may not be incredible, but you can give them some more information by picking something out on the keys or guitar. If you are not happy with a certain sound, you will be better at suggesting, say, a different chord. Being able to play the chords of your new song makes it easier for the band to take it and make a song out of it.

I was a rapper long before I was a bass player. Learning how to play bass when I was 20 years old not only led me to work with great artists like Beyoncé, but it also enhanced my musicality as a vocalist. I believe you will be a better singer if you learn an instrument. Try the keyboard or any instrument that you like playing with. You don't have to become accomplished, but it always helps to dibble and dabble.

The reverse is also true. When I am playing bass or directing music for other artists, the fact that I have been a solo performer helps me to support better. When you are the front man, there is so much you have to go through. You've got sound check, make-up, wardrobe, and a whole lot more that nobody sees. I may be playing bass, but I understand exactly what the artist is going through. If I see they are struggling with something, I say, "maybe you can try it like this." You don't want to overstep your boundaries, but you can give them ideas to help them make their show better.

—Divinity Roxx, former Musical Director and bassist for Beyonce's all female band: 2006-2011

Action 10: Be A Team Player

The secret to moving ahead in today's music industry sometimes comes down to people skills.

I have seen a handful of incredibly talented musicians having a hard time getting shows. On a musical level, there is just no explanation for this. But there is on an interpersonal level: these musicians are hard people to get along with. The music industry really requires people skills—whether it is relating to band members or to venue owners, engineers and producers. The most important aspect of being a singer in a band is to view yourself as a team player, one who is willing to do what it takes to further the success of the group.

One way to have people appreciate your role as a lead singer in a band is to appreciate their role. This begins by showing your recognition for their musical work and input. When you bring a tune to the band, for example, be open to new ideas; this fosters a great attitude and good energy for the music. This idea extends beyond group. Tell the guy doing the booking that he is doing a good job—be "hands on" and active and good things will come back to you.

In terms of your vision for how the music is performed, you have to pick your battles. Decide what you want to stand up for and be passionate about it, taking a firm stance in these areas. Beyond this, be flexible and open to the input of various band members. Remember: if you respect the input of the band and their ideas, they will give you the same attitude in return. You are seeking, really, a balance between your convictions and theirs. I do know singer-songwriters who insist on implementing each aspect of their song exactly as they envision it, but that's not how we work.

Now, it certainly helps to find the right group of people to work with (though there is never a "perfect" group). One way to test this out is to ask yourself the question, "Could I see myself working with this group 5 years down the line?" What does your gut feeling say? Ultimately you are looking to be in a group where a team spirit can grow, where you can achieve a good balance of input and where everyone is not seeking to be a hot shot or soloist all the time.

—Chris Henderson: singer-songwriter-guitarist of Bronze Radio Return

Frequently Asked Questions

> Band members are skipping rehearsals all the time—what can I do?

Answered by Mark Baxter, acclaimed vocal coach with Aerosmith, Journey, Goo Goo Dolls and many others

Nothing gets bands together quicker (or blows them up) than rehearsing without a member! I would say, "If you can't make it, that's fine—the rest of us will still get together." I find that the answer is usually, "well, in that case, I guess I could come ... " (!). If someone did end up missing a practice then I would usually rub it in a little the next day by saying, "We had a really great rehearsal ... "

Obviously you should schedule your band rehearsal in a way that takes into account the concerns of others. But once a schedule has been chosen then it is up to you, alone, to honor that schedule. Lead by example. Always start on time even if everybody isn't there. You don't have to bitch at someone about being late if they walk in and you're already jamming. Think about it: If you have to constantly guilt someone into coming on time then you have the wrong band member. If you have to constantly fight against your girlfriend or boyfriend to attend these rehearsals, then you have the wrong partner—no matter how pretty or handsome they are.

> How do I tell a band member that I don't want them in the band anymore?

Answered by Nikki Lamborn, singer-songwriter of the English band "Never the Bride"

I was in a support band once and we were stopped, with the main band, at a rest area beside the highway. There was this very dramatic moment when the main band fired its drummer right there, in front of everyone—and sent him away in a taxi to the airport. This public display of anger and ego is nothing less than bullying. You don't ever need to do that to people. This is why I have a big problem with Simon Cowell; I don't stand for breaking people's spirits in order to line your pockets.

You have to be gentle because artistic people are very sensitive. Of course you need to make sure that you have good reason to make a move like this. Then, deliver the message with honesty and kindness—and not in front of everybody(!): "I think that you might be a little too jazzy for our rock style ... " or, "I'm finding that your energy is wrong for the band we are trying to be ... things aren't working out ... "

But before I even reach this stage I may check in with other members of the band—not to gossip but to see if my views are actually correct. After all, I might find out that what is going on is mostly in my own head. I might be told, "No, no. This is actually OK—it will all work out." Check what's bothering you with some people you trust—you just might find that you're the one who's getting things wrong.

Sometimes you don't need to "fire" someone, you need to be diplomatic and say, "Listen, this is not working out right now—let's take a break from each other." You may meet again down the road and it will be better. Wish each other luck—you never know when you will need them again.

> My guitarist is really gifted, but he's a pain to work with.

Answered by Laura Vane, singer-songwriter of Laura Vane & The Vipertones

A lot of people might say, "If they are gifted, then just try to get on with things and try not to let those other issues get you down." But that is not often how I feel. All of us doing music are emotional and sensitive beings, so why put up with something that will upset you and get in the way of being focused on what you truly want to do? As with all life decisions, try to make life easier for yourself. I work with people that I am happy to be around and choose not to work with idiots who wind me up. Your time is precious—don't waste it.

> Some of us are ready to kill each other—I'm afraid our band is going to break up. Help!

Answered by Mike Tramp, of the double platinum selling band White Lion

When White Lion broke up, none of the people from the record company, the merchandising company, or the publishing company—the people who were making millions of dollars off us—picked up the phone and said, "You guys are god-damned idiots! Take a fucking break and come back and talk about this when your heads are clear." If we had done that, we would have made the smart decision of not breaking up.

We should have taken some time off to really look at the market and figure out where we fit. The industry was changing, grunge was big, and we still had a big international following. Instead, pressure and conflicts got the better of us. We broke up the band and Vito and I called it quits as friends. Later we got into legal battles over the name—it wasn't pretty.

Being in a band is as intense as being in love. Going for a walk will stop you from saying a lot of harmful shit. I couldn't do that in 1988 with White Lion. Some things really got to me, like when I couldn't hear my vocal in the monitor over the guitar, for example. Then there's the fact that Vito and I had a very different approach to money. We were great at writing music together, but our friendship deteriorated.

Today I won't leave a band rehearsal with an unresolved conflict. In my band Freak of Nature, we always played standing in a circle looking at each other. We were a brotherhood. Even when I am the leader, the one financing the band and putting in twice as much energy as the others,

I make sure everyone in the band feels that they are a part of the musical direction. It's a tough balance to find, but you have to do it.

When it comes to music, there will usually be fire and ice. Sometimes a group is great playing together, but they can't write together. There are some people you play with and everything they do just sounds right. When it's not working, breaking up or asking someone to leave may be the best choice. I don't believe it was right for White Lion. We got to write songs, go out and play and make money—we were so lucky.

> Why does my band have so much trouble following me?

Answered by Chris Henderson, singer-songwriter-guitarist of Bronze Radio Return

Well, if everybody is having a hard time—then you need to be open to the idea that "you" might be the issue, not "them."

Here's how you solve this: use your rehearsals to get familiar with the beat. You can ask the drummer to play as you set a metronome, so that you can rehearse at that same tempo at home. If there are issues with your singing in relation to individual instruments, then be proactive and get together with just that musician. Our band frequently has "sub-rehearsals" where we'll work out specific sections of songs—this has the advantage of saving people's time in the regular rehearsal.

> *"The key words are honesty, candor, and diplomacy. Let's say there are three or four of you and you think that there's something that sucks, something missing or perhaps you are not having a good time. Bring it up and ask, "How can we go about resolving this? Making it better?" An honest and open question goes over way better than an accusation.*
>
> ***—Elliott Randall:** legendary guitarist, formerly a musical director for Saturday Night Live*

One more idea that might work is to record your band without your vocals. Then, use this recording as you practice at home. You might discover that the band could use a little help staying on tempo or you might discover that you need to do a little work yourself in this area. Having a recorded track is also a great way for you to work on individual passages in your singing.

> Our songs just aren't turning out as cool as they are in my head...

Answered by Chris Henderson, singer-songwriter-guitarist of Bronze Radio Return

I have totally been there—I think all of us songwriters have.

The first thing to do is to try to break down why it isn't working. Is it the rhythm, the key, the tempo, or a specific sound (guitar, drums, bass, etc.) coming through too much—or too little? How is the overall sound—too much distortion or too little? Rely on your band mates to make suggestions. The more you can articulate the specific element(s) that aren't working, the better your chances are at arriving at something that sounds cool.

You might do all of this work and still not get to a place where it sounds good. If this happens, then table the song for a while. I have gone down many rabbit holes trying to make something work, using up precious energy with little to show for it. It's a skill to know when to cut the cord and move onto the next song.

> Everyone in the group is having a blast with the music but I'm not.

Answered by Chris Henderson, singer-songwriter-guitarist of Bronze Radio Return

You might be in the wrong band. Making music is supposed to be fun and rewarding—if these qualities aren't there for you with these people, then invest more energy to develop the group. But, if you aren't "digging it," my suggestion is to look for another group.

> How can I make sure I'm not one of those sloppy singers who can't keep time?

Answered by Sara Serpa: internationally recognized vocalist, composer and bandleader

I've just returned from Brazil and am just so impressed by their dancing culture, which helps a sense of rhythm to grow in every fibre of the body. We are all born as musical and rhythmical beings, yet it's a skill that's developed better in some cultures than others. Still, there are some key things we can do to grow in this area to be truly "pro" singers who work well with other musicians.

The first step you can take is to simply let yourself move to your music—engage your body, using your feet, hands and body. It's amazing to me how many singers never let themselves dance. As a vocalist you really want your body to be involved since your voice is so much more than your larynx. In fact, I urge you to take rhythmic challenges with your body—try stomping your feet to the rhythm of a song while you are clapping out a different rhythm with your hands.

> *Quincy Jones has an unparalleled gift of helping to create a musical atmosphere where a team of musicians can really find their zone and "take off." Some of his favorite sayings reveal the principles behind this gift. He sums up his entire philosophy of life with the phrase, "Love, laugh, live and give." He also says, "You can never be a better musician than you are a person." He values each of the people he works with—this comes across in every working relationship.*
>
> **—Bill Gibson:** *in Conversation with Quincy Jones*

The next thing you can do is to get a metronome (or download a metronome app to your smartphone). Start your metronome on a regular beat and see if you can keep to this beat as you sing. Hopefully your curiosity will soon take over and you'll experiment with different tempos and test yourself by turning your metronome off and then on again to see if you've drifted from the beat.

To really challenge yourself, you can transcribe the rhythm of music you love—I mean actually writing the rhythm of this piece onto paper. You can use standard rhythmic notation, or just your own version. Recreating specific rhythms using notation helps you to master them.

Soon it will be time to push yourself in public. See if you can count in your band ("a one and a two and a one two three four"). You can practice doing this at home and then try it out in rehearsal. Visualize the song in your head, clapping the beats in the time with your inner sense of time. Hopefully you have a good working relationship with your band and you can ask them the most helpful way to count in. Picking up a percussion instrument to enhance your band's presentation is yet another step towards ultimate rhythmic responsibility.

> Why do we always make the same mistakes?

Answered by Chris Henderson, singer-songwriter-guitarist of Bronze Radio Return

Remember that the show you put on is the end result of the amount of work you are putting into your band behind the scenes. It sounds like you need to practice more. Everyone makes mistakes—fine. But there is no reason for them to be repeated. Practice and evaluate. Here's a tip: since you are making the same mistakes, don't only rehearse whole songs; spend time rehearsing specific sections that are causing you problems.

> Our performances have become stale.

Answered by Nikki Lamborn, singer-songwriter of the English band "Never the Bride"

Get a friend to film you in performance. Then sit down and watch and see how truly dreadful you are—or not. Making a video is great because it doesn't lie. You will notice your laxness and start asking questions. Why did I wear that? I look shit in those clothes! Why did I do that riff—and why do I poke my tongue out in the middle of it?! Be gentle with each other as you talk about these issues. The main thing is that you ask, openly and honestly, "How can we make our performances better?"

Get some new material and get into some serious rehearsals. Try out some new arrangements of old material. Write some songs, or at the very least put yourselves in the shoes of the person who wrote the songs you are playing—you need to feel the passion. After you've made some changes, video yourselves again to see if it's worked.

When doing your set list you have to be mindful of your stamina. If you are doing 4 hard rock songs in a row you have to be able to pull it off. If you aren't ready for this, start more gently so you don't wear yourself out. We did a gig in Vale, Colorado working with Billy Preston. This was high in the mountains, so after every song we had to have oxygen for altitude sickness. I had to do "Kashmir" by Led Zeppelin; it was 8 minutes long and it was terrifyingly hard to breathe.

If you have lots of sets in a row and you are feeling shattered, skip the next song and do a ballad. As a musician you are an athlete; even athletes run out of steam sometimes. Listen to your body, give yourself a break and don't be chained to your set list. Be aware that any physical activity (i.e. swimming, cycling, running, gym—or even fast walking) will enhance your performance, your breathing and your confidence.

> That other band is no more gifted than we are—so why are they getting all the gigs?

Answered by Chris Henderson, singer-songwriter-guitarist of Bronze Radio Return

It's that old cliché: "life isn't fair." The truth is that untalented groups will get some lucky breaks when talented ones get lost in the mix. Start by accepting that. Getting upset or distracted by this truth will only hinder your own progress.

Your energy is a precious commodity—so, focus on what you can do. Be friendly, approach the other band and ASK THEM if they would be willing to offer you some advice. You could say something like, "We're really happy that you are playing this gig and interested in what you are doing as a group and what you did to get in here. So, what's your secret?" If they give you some insights then you're ahead of the game. You see, you can complain about things or you can enter into the team spirit of music and move ahead.

> We're always speeding up.

Answered by Mary Beth Felker, vocal coach and founder of Voice Project Studios

You're not alone: this happens to every band.

I'll give you some tips for dealing with this in live performance in a moment, but I think the key to getting this under control has to do with having a proper "rehearsal" rather than a "practice."

I actually recommend that you use one rehearsal to have your band overplay everything—tempo, volume etc.

Since this is likely to happen once the adrenaline begins pumping, it's best for everyone to experience it during rehearsal and have a game plan for how to counteract it.

However, when you're actually on stage and things begin to speed up, here are some things you can do:

1. If it's near the beginning of the song—stop and start over. Stop the band, make a joke to the audience, take a breath and restart. A bad start is a bad start and no one wants to hear you and the band struggle through the entire song.
2. Turn and give a hand signal to the band to slow down.
3. Start singing a little slower to stretch things out. Most musicians are intuitive enough that they will catch on within a measure or two that you are changing things.
4. In between phrases, verbally tell the band over the mic that you are going to slow it down. "Okay band: I'm gonna slow it down here ... "

Prior to going on stage you should establish one of the musicians as the "go-to" person that you communicate with during the performance. It makes most sense for it to be the person who is counting off the songs as the band is already taking cues from them. Say, "Sara, if I need something to change, I'm going to give a signal to you and let you get the attention of the rest of the band."

> My band members seem to connect with each other, but I feel like I am on the outside.

Answered by Rachel Bennett, lead singer-songwriter of RAIE, London-based lecturer and vocal coach

Let's talk about turning this around. I want you to answer two questions.

First: when do you get this feeling—at what point in the rehearsals? Is it at a point when the musicians need to clarify a riff or a progression in a song? Is it after the rehearsal when they are jamming—or go on to socialize without you? You need to differentiate between a working relationship and a personal one—keep these separate in your head so that you don't get hurt unnecessarily. The band may be frustrated with something you are not contributing musically but don't know how to tell you. Usually musicians are in it for the music!

Second: do you just "turn up and sing" or do you contribute ideas? In other words: do you listen carefully to their language of music or do you switch off because they're using terms you don't understand? Answer honestly! The reason this is important is because the band will respect your needs more, and will respond much more openly if they feel you are prepping independently as much as they are.

Now for a strategy: I am going to focus on the musical process because so often singers find themselves on the outside when their band may be using jargon and cues as time savers in rehearsals.

Find a way to talk to your band about your concerns—either with the whole group or one on one. Stay calm, and remind them that they all started somewhere too!

Then, at home, study your songs theoretically; identify the key, chords, arrangements, breaks—and listen to the players more closely in the next rehearsal whilst looking at your notes.

Bands that leave the singer out are demonstrating a lack of experience or maturity, but it needn't lead to a rift if you remain open, diligent and patient.

> Over the course of the show, volumes are inching up and up and I'm afraid I'm getting lost in the mix.

Answered by Elliott Randall, legendary guitarist, formerly a musical director for Saturday Night Live

I'm a strong believer in having a balanced sound on stage no matter what instrumentation you have. I usually say, "Right. This is where my volume stays and if I can't hear myself, I will not be turning things up—you need to turn down." Saying something like this is especially critical for the singer as they are dependent on their monitors.

Of course some of this is dependent on how professional your performance space is, the quality of the sound system, etc. I know a lot of bands like to set up with everyone facing the audience with lots of space between band members. I don't enjoy that. I like to have the band form almost a semi-circle, which produces more intimacy between the players, and enables everyone to hear each other better.

> My drummer is in his own world when we are performing and I feel we could do so much better if we were in sync—how can I make this happen?

Answered by Joey Belladonna, lead singer of the legendary group Anthrax

As both a drummer and a lead singer of Anthrax, I think I've got something to say here. First, you're right: you do need to be in sync with your drummer. The purpose of the drums is to provide the backbone, maintain the groove and keep the tempo. Sure, the drummer can add all kinds of frills—but the focus has to be on playing for the song, not just playing for oneself.

The challenge is that in a live situation the tendency is to speed up. Adrenaline does its work, the tempo and volume increase and too much "flash and dash" gets into the music. Sometimes a musician gets bored and deals with this by adding too much into the song. It's not just drummers who do this—anyone can be over-playing or doing too much noodling.

Obviously you need to have a conversation. But when you have that talk, be careful not to be too demanding. If you yell at someone, you're gonna feel like shit later. The key thing is not to take a scolding tone; just ask a simple question, "Hey, I'm wondering what we are going to do with this?" Remember that mistakes happen in live music—it isn't karaoke. It takes time to work out. Be patient with yourself and with your band—but do bring it up.

> Why don't our background vocals sound as cool as the recordings we listen to?

Answered by Tim Goodyer, founder and director of the Fast-and-Wide news site

There are two things going on in a studio that may not be happening for you on stage—assuming that your BVs are in tune. Most vocal recordings use some compression in order to reduce the dynamic range—to bring together the soft and loud portions of the performance so that the quiet sounds aren't lost and the loud sounds are not overloading the preamps on the mixer or amplifier. The other thing that may be going on in the studio is some use of pitch correction.

What can you do on stage? The first order of business is to make sure you are well rehearsed, using musicians on your backing vocals who can sing in tune. There are all kinds of vocal effects gear available to add harmonies to a voice—but if you're using live singers there is no substitute for everyone knowing their part and putting in some solid rehearsal time. It is also essential that your monitoring is such that everyone can hear themselves well, in order to be able to pitch accurately. Beyond this, I would recommend that you look into getting a limiter. This is a processor that is related to a compressor that watches for sounds that are louder than a preset "threshold" and prevents them from getting any louder. This not only prevents the mic preamp overloading but protects your audience from an overenthusiastic performance.

> My band won't let me lead. I'm the singer, and I want them to follow me! Help!

Answered by Val Emmich, singer-songwriter, hailed by the New York Times as "a rocker who rocks to his own beat"

I'm in the position of being a solo artist with a backing band and, though I loved the culture of a band, I was tired of compromising the songs I had in my head. So, it is my belief that just as in other aspects of the work world, it's better if someone takes the lead. Of course, the caveat to all of this is that you shouldn't abuse your power.

I've been fortunate enough to find unselfish musicians who have wanted to be a part of my music. But, finding the right band members is like putting together the pieces of a puzzle. There are many questions to ask, but the most important questions are, "Do these guys want to head in the same direction as me?" and "Do they offer something that is lacking in myself?"

It's really important to exploit everyone's expertise. For instance, I have never really "geeked out" on guitar sounds. So I'll tell my guitarist, "get me a good sound on this," because I know that he gets excited about refining sound in a way I never would.

As I check out band members I'm asking myriad questions. I really want to know what drives them, what they're interested in, to see if we have a fit. This may sound trivial, but when we're on the road, I really like to drive the van. So, ultimately, our tour only works if the other band members don't mind me doing most of the driving. It's about finding personalities that mesh, because if all goes well you'll be spending a lot of time together.

As the leader, you've got to learn how to make people think they're getting what they want even when you're really only doing what you want. Of course, band members have input into the music but when it doesn't jive with what's inside my head I sometimes have to say, "Yeah, that might work; let's try it later," or we'll try the idea out immediately so I can confirm to them my suspicion that it wasn't going to work. Sometimes you have to go the long way to make people happy. And frankly, sometimes I've been wrong and they were right. The longer you work with the same people, the better you get at knowing which avenues to go down and which roads are a waste of time.

> How do I tell a band-mate that they are off-pitch?

Answered by John Kjøller, member and vocal director of the hit vocal a cappella group Basix—"Best European Album"

All music groups have to be able to do this—and do it well.

Before I tell you how to do this, I have a warning: it is easy to make a mistake as to who is off-pitch. You can often tell that something is off, but the problem may be a mismatched vowel or it may be that an out-of tune bass string is making a vocalist sound off. Consider this before you speak up.

It all comes down to respect. If someone is off-pitch, you have to point it out, but it will always go better if you value the person you are correcting. There are two sides to this issue: if you are the one doing the correcting, then remember to respect the other person. Know that even though they should be able to not take it personally, we are only human beings with feelings. The other side of this situation is the person who is being corrected. You have to remember that you are more than your voice. You are not your abilities—you are you. If I say that you are off-pitch, I am not saying that you are stupid or I don't like you; I'm not saying anything except that you are off-pitch.

If you want to get into the vocal business and to keep improving, then you have to deal with things that aren't right. You only get better if you are told when there is something wrong. So, instead of looking at correction as a bad thing, look at it as a good thing: you are getting help.

> How do I work with a pick-up band?

Answered by Annie Sellick, internationally renowned jazz singer

It's not always affordable to travel with your own band. Working with pick-up bands has kept me touring, visible, on the road and still making money.

First, there's the issue of finding a good band. I get references—or listen to players myself before engaging them. One way is to go to a venue, sit in on some music and sing—and then ask the venue if they want to hire me! If they do, then I ask them if they know a good keyboard player—always start with a chordal instrument; this individual may end up being the musical director, drawing in other instrumentalists. Sometimes I ask if there is a pianist who already has a bit of a name in town, as that person will help draw an audience to the venue. If I've never played in Montreal, for example, I might phone up the University, ask who is teaching Jazz (my genre) and then email them to see what recommendations they have.

You'll want to send a list of tunes and keys in advance—at least two weeks ahead of time. It's a great idea if you have sheet music, charts and arrangements. But it's also great if you can send a recording that matches the chart—some members of the band prepare by listening to your music while they're driving around. Sometimes people may not want to play with you—that's fine, these same people may direct you to others who are more suitable to your sounds.

When you get together with your pick up band you might meet them at 5pm for a sound check if the show is at 8. You might then work on the music for an hour or so, focusing on the more difficult parts of the chart. If you can get two hours from the band, that's great—but I usually don't ask for that much time unless I am going to be doing more than one show with them. If it's just one gig then you really just want to run over things and make sure they have fun with you. If you are too hard on them it won't be fun and the gig will suffer.

I have sacrificed doing some of my favorite songs if it is too hard and the band is "hemming and hawing". Be flexible—It is OK to drop some of the music. You don't want to be too demanding; work within their capabilities. In advance, (not the day of the gig) you might say something like: "does this sound okay to do it this way?" or "here's a list of songs—do you want to choose from this list?"

> I'm going to "sit in" with my friend's band at a live gig. There's no rehearsal—how do I prepare?!

Answered by Jennie Sawdon, singer, pianist and vocal tutor, voted "Wedding Singer of the Year"

In the business this is called being a "deputy" or "deputizing." The first thing you need to do is establish if the songs are covers or originals. If covers, find out if they are being played exactly as originally recorded or not. If they are exactly as recorded, that's easy: you can rehearse with the album. You need to know the key that suits you for each song and communicate this to the band.

At the gig you'll be listening closely to the band and picking up any cues you can. Quite often the band is used to taking cues from the singer, so make sure you are on the same map with the meaning of visual cues that you like to use. You might also say to the band members, "Make things obvious for me," hoping that the guitarist, for example, will give you a big nod when heading back into the chorus.

But don't be afraid of getting things wrong! Coming in at the wrong place, forgetting your words and having to ad lib—be confident through all of this. You're a musical creature and you can cover it up. Often the audience won't notice these "glitches." Move through your night with energy and passion.

Contributors

Gregory A. Barker, PhD **(editor)** is VP of Publishing at Singdaptive after nearly a decade as Commissioning Editor of VoiceCouncil Magazine. He is also a published author with Oxford University Press and an educational and business coach. He loves creating effective text and encouraging individuals as they pursue their goals. www.gregbarker.consulting

Kathy Alexander (editor) is VP of Curriculum for Singdaptive. She was a staff writer for 6 years at VoiceCouncil Magazine and works for the University of Victoria as a practicum supervisor. Kathy is also a singer, vocal coach and choir director. www.kathalexander.com

David Ackert is an American entrepreneur, business development expert and founder of The Ackert Advisory, serving as a coach and advisor to international firms and companies. He is a published fiction author, and has acted, appearing in shows such as *CSI:Miami, NYPD Blue, Six Feet Under* and *The West Wing*. www.davidackert.com

Kevin Alexander is a co-founder of Singdaptive, bringing his past experience as CEO of the singing technology company TC-Helicon, as well as live sound, recording and love of music. Recently, he has been a university instructor in Multimedia Learning and is helping to envision an exciting future with technology at the research firm Kinsol.io

Tiffany Jo Allen is the youngest artist to reach #1 on the Nashville charts as a singer. She has over 30 million video views and well over 100,000 subscribers, landing her in the top 100 musicians worldwide including major label artists. She has recorded three albums with a debut single soon to be released. www.tiffanyjoallen.com

Danielle Ate the Sandwich is a nationally recognized independent folk singer/songwriter who has released hundreds of videos on YouTube. She has released several full-length albums of original music and toured internationally since 2009. www.danielleatethesandwich.com

Jaime Babbitt toured with Leon Russell and Sam Moore, sang jingles for Coke, Pillsbury, Chevy, etc., BGVs with George Strait, Johnny Mathis, Barbra Streisand, Courtney Love and more, and coached voice/performance for Disney. See her book: *Working with Your Voice: The Career Guide to Becoming a Professional Singer* www.workingwithyourvoice.com

Dr. Robert W. Bastian is a Board-Certified Otolaryngologist and an internationally-recognized authority in the treatment of voice, airway, swallowing, and coughing disorders. He has been listed for several years by Chicago magazine as one of "Chicago's Top Doctors," and by Castle-Connolly as one of "America's Top Doctors." www.bastianvoice.com and www.bastianmedicalmedia.com

Mark Baxter is a vocal coach who has worked with Aerosmith, Journey, Goo Goo Dolls—and many others. He is the author of *The Rock-n-Roll Singer's Survival Manual,* has performed in over 3,000 gigs, and operates vocal studios in New York, Boston, Los Angeles and online via Skype. www.voicelesson.com

Beardyman has been hailed by the BBC as "The King of Sound and Ruler of Beats" for his renowned beatboxing and is the first beatboxer in UK history to win two UK Championships in a row. His live production of original material is making a huge impact worldwide. www.youtube.com/user/beardyman

Daniel Bedingfield rocketed to the top of the pop world with "Gotta Get Thru This," earning a BRIT Award, six U.K. Top 10 singles and millions in album sales. His 2012 *Stop The Traffik—Secret Fear,* moves adroitly between dance-floor bangers and R&B-spiked rock and between freak-funk and chilling piano ballads. www.danielbedingfield.com

Sarah Bella is a singer-songwriter from Michigan with a rapidly growing YouTube fan base. Her original song, "Time Hasn't Moved," has had over 300,000 views. Her song writing recently caught the attention of the film industry – she has written the theme song for the independent film *Rancho D' Amour*. www.youtube.com/user/SairahBella

Joey Belladonna was the lead singer of the legendary group Anthrax, featured on over 10 albums selling over eight million records. He shared the stage with Iron Maiden, Metallica, Megadeth, Kiss, Ozzy Osbourne, Black Sabbath, Dio, Judas Priest and many others. He also performs regularly with the Belladonna solo band. www.joeybelladonna.com

Rachel Bennett (aka Raie) is a singer-songwriter, vocal coach/tutor and headline artist of RAIE. She has worked in London over 30 years, teaching, writing for dance and theatre and singing background vocals for bands and studios. She teaches on the Popular Music Degree at Goldsmiths University of London and is a popular singing coach for drama schools, theatres and bands.

Mary Black has a frontline role in bringing Irish music, past and present, to ever-growing global audience. The British magazine *What Hi-Fi?* considers her voice to be so pure that they have repeatedly used it for comparing the sound quality of different high-fidelity systems. See her new *Stories from the Steeples* album. www.mary-black.net

Daniel Zangger Borch is one of Sweden's most recognised vocal coaches. He has been an adjudicator for Sweden's "Idol" and "X-Factor." He is also a professional singer, recording artist and songwriter. Daniel holds a PhD in Music performance and is CEO of Doremir Music Research. He is the author of The Ultimate Vocal Voyage and Vocal Workout of the Day. www.zangger.se

Gustavo Borner, co-owner/chief engineer at Igloo music, has worked on films such as Sunshine, Watchmen, and Rush Hour. He is credited on more than 40 million records sold, has earned three Grammy Awards and 11 Latin Grammy Awards and worked with legendary artists such as Placido Domingo, Phil Collins and Elton John. www.igloomusic.com

Jenn Bostic is a singer-songwriter and her hit song "Jealous of the Angels" is making an impact worldwide. She recently won five 2012 Independent Country Music Association Awards, including Overall Winner, Best Female Country Artist, Best Musician, Best Songwriter and Country Music Song of the Year. www.jennbostic.com

Daniel Bowling is the Head of Musical Theatre, Royal Academy of Music and has been the music director or music supervisor for numerous shows such as Lion King, Mary Poppins, Phantom of the Opera, and Les Misérables both the USA and the UK. He is the author of *Auditions Undressed*, and co-author (with Ruthie Henshall) of *So You Want To Be In Musicals?* www.danielbowling.net

Emily Braden is a vocalist, songwriter and lyricist. She was awarded the prestigious title of NYC's "Best of the Best" jazz vocalist as the winner of the New York City's Jazzmobile Vocal Competition. She's been featured in many NYC venues such as the Blue Note Jazz Club, Birdland Jazz Club, Smalls Jazz Club and Zinc Bar as well as on international stages. www.emilybraden.com

Dirk Brauner is the founder of Brauner Microphones, renowned worldwide for their relentless pursuit of perfection and absolute attention to detail and representing "made in Germany" quality and sustainable value. He also consults on recording issues for industry-leading professionals like Peter Gabriel, Apple Computers and many others. www.brauner-microphones.de/en/

Rory Bremner is best known as Britain's foremost satirical impressionist, his Channel 4 TV series with John Bird and John Fortune running for over 20 years and winning numerous awards. He has also appeared in scores of top television entertainment and talk shows. www.twitter.com/rorybremner

Dot Bustelo is an internationally recognized music producer, Logic Pro author and Atlanta-based music industry marketing strategist (formerly on Apple's product marketing team), cultivating strategic relationships that bring together musicians and technology. She is CEO/Founder of Apple TV visual art streaming app Loupe and is a Creative Technologies Strategist bringing together artists and technology.

Tim Carson is the founder of Vocal Artistry and the Vocal Artistry Training Series, a full line of vocal training resources. A professional singer and vocal coach, Tim has worked in the music industry for over 20 years. For 12 years Tim directed singers on staff at Willow Creek in the Chicago area. www.VocalArtistry.com

Dane Chalfin is a UK-based Vocal Rehabilitation Coach in the NHS and private practice working with injured vocal performers. He is also in demand as a vocal coach in the West End and recording/television industries. Dane also hosts training courses for singing teachers and speech therapists across the UK and Europe. https://www.vocalrehabilitation.com/

Kim Chandler is a session singer, industry vocal coach and creator of the popular "Funky 'n Fun" vocal exercise series. She has a private studio in Marbella (Spain) and London (UK) where she coaches & mentors a worldwide clientele of established & emerging artists, professional singers and other vocal coaches. www.kimchandler.com and www.funkynfun.com

Charles Chemery is the chair of the Independent Artist and the DJ programs at Musicians Institute in Hollywood, CA. He is also a Los Angeles-based DJ, vocalist, multi-instrumentalist and record producer. He has recently collaborated with Chaka Khan, on her new single "House Of Love." Listen to his work here: https://soundcloud.com/charlie-sputnik

Christopher Chang, MD is a Yale and Duke-trained Board-Certified Otolaryngology-Head & Neck Surgeon with fellowship training in laryngology and voice disorders. He is in private practice in lovely Northern Virginia. He runs a popular blog fauquierent.blogspot.com see also www.youtube.com/fauquierent

Laura Clapp is a New England based singer/songwriter whose voice has taken her all over the world. Between working for Shure Incorporated and raising a family, she is one busy woman, but she always makes time for her music. Join Laura as she delves into life, love and relationships with her honest lyrics and powerful melodies. www.lauraclapp.com

Anne Corless works in the creative arts as a fine artist and designer, digital artist and illustrator, medical artist and writer. She works with traditional media as well as computer graphics creating artwork for exhibitions, galleries and on commission. She describes life as an artist as "challenging but fun." www.annecorless.com

Jonathan Coulton is from the internet and known for his songs in the "Portal" games, plus an eclectic catalog of masterful songwriting on subjects from zombies and mad scientists to sad parents and dissatisfied software engineers. He is the house musician for the NPR quiz show "Ask Me Another," and a composer for "SpongeBob SquarePants: The Broadway Musical." www.jonathancoulton.com

Susanne Currid is a social media marketing consultant and trainer who helps brands and businesses to connect with their tribe online. She has worked as a digital producer/marketer with global names including Sony Music, Channel 4 (UK), Deutsche Bank and Cushman & Wakefield. www.the-loop.com

Mark De-Lisser is a vocal coach, arranger, choir leader and author who has worked with some of the top vocal talent in contemporary music today including Jessie J, Jamie Woon, Nicole Scherzinger and Beverly Knight. He's also a coach with BBC's The Voice UK and The Naked Choir. He also leads the renowned ACM Gospel Choir. www.markdelisser.com

Jeannie Deva (1951-2016) was a celebrity voice/performance coach, recording studio vocal specialist and member of the Grammys and Latin Grammys. Jeannie received endorsements by producers and engineers for Aerosmith and The Rolling Stones. Author of the bestselling *Contemporary Vocalist* book and CDs, her clients included Grammy winners, Platinum recording artists and many more. www.JeannieDeva.com

Mike Dixon is one of the most respected musical forces in London's West End and on British television as a musical supervisor, director, arranger and composer. He has worked with Dame Shirley Bassey, Sir Elton John, Sir Tom Jones, Brian May, Roger Taylor, Jon Bon Jovi, Phil Collins, Annie Lennox and Lady Gaga. www.mikedixonmusic.com

Steve Eggleston is a law school Valedictorian, award-winning law professor, best-selling author (*Labor and Employment in California*/Lexis-Nexis), and former entertainment, music, and trial attorney. He is co-founder/CEO of Eggman Global Artists, which manages, among others, singer-songwriter Michael Grimm, 2010 winner of hit NBC TV show *America's Got Talent*, and co-founder/CEO of RockGodzHallofFame.com. www.EggmanGlobal.com

Katherine Ellis is one of the most respected and versatile vocalists and topline

writers in the industry today. She currently performs throughout the world with the

huge club hits "When You Touch Me" with The Freemasons, "Lost" by Roger Sanchez and "Dreaming" by The Ruff Driverz. She also sings the title track to the Oscar winning movie Gravity. www.katherineellis.co.uk

Val Emmich is a singer-songwriter, actor and writer. He became the first unsigned artist to be featured on MTV's *Total Request Live*. His nine albums include *Posthaste*, featuring 60 unreleased songs from his decade-plus career. As an actor he's appeared on such television shows as *30 Rock* and *Ugly Betty*. www.valemmich.com

Mary Beth Felker is founder of the Voice Project Studios and known for her ability to quickly produce healthy, marketable results while on the road or in the studio. She is author of TVP's *Elements of Warming up Series* and is in high demand as a vocal expert. www.facebook.com/TheVoiceProject/info

Brian Felsen is the former President of AdRev, the world's largest YouTube music administration service, and DashGo, an aggregator which distributes music to online retail stores worldwide. Prior to this position, Mr. Felsen was President of CD Baby from 2008-14, the world's largest online distributor of independent music. Brian Felsen is an artist, composer, playwright and filmmaker. www.brianfelsen.com.

Peter James Field is an illustrator and fine artist whose professional clients include Time Magazine, The New York Times, Vanity Fair, Conde Nast and Penguin. Peter was featured in the Guardian Guide to Drawing, and presents a series of short films on 'How to Draw' for BBC Bitesize. www.peterjamesfield.co.uk

David Frangioni is the recipient of dozens of Gold and Platinum albums as technical consultant, engineer, and/or programmer having worked with Ozzy Osbourne, Steven Tyler, Olivia Newton-John, Ringo Starr, Shakira, Bryan Adams and Ricky Martin. David is founder of Frangioni Media www.frangionimedia.com ; IDA: Inspire & Develop Artists artist development program www.allaccessida.com and Audio One www.audio-one.com

Jay Frank is currently SVP of Streaming Marketing for Universal Music Group. Frank has previously held executive positions at Viacom and Yahoo!, and is the author of the best-selling music business book *FuturehitDNA*. www.futurehitdna.com

Craig Fraser is Leader for Customer Solutions at MUSIC Tribe. He has also been involved in product development, technical writing, customer service and videography. Prior to this, he was Director of Operations at Marble Wave Sound Design. He also engineers and produces at Oakstone Sound in Victoria British Columbia. www.tc-helicon.com

W. Timothy Gallwey is known the world over as the creator of the "inner game" concept. He is a bestselling author, sports psychologist and sought-after coach for life and business skills. He wrote *The Inner Game of Tennis* and his co-authored work (with Barry Green), *The Inner Game of Music*. www.theinnergame.com

Bill Gibson, President of Northwest Music and Recording, has spent the last 30 years writing, recording, producing and teaching music. He holds degrees in composition, arranging, education and recording. Bill is the author of 30+ books about recorded and live sound, including the six-book series, *The Hal Leonard Recording Method*. www.billgibsonmusic.com

Malcolm Gladwell is the author of *What the Dog Saw, Outliers: The Story of Success, Blink: The Power of Thinking Without Thinking*, and *The Tipping Point: How Little Things Can Make a Big Difference*, all New York Times bestsellers. In 2005 he was named one of *Time Magazine's* 100 Most Influential People.

Tim Goodyer, a professional audio journalist and photographer, is the founder and director of Fast-and-Wide, an independent news site and blog for professional audio and related businesses. Fast-and-Wide.com provides a platform for discussion and information exchange in one of the world's fastest-moving technology-based industries. www.fast-and-wide.com

Gary R. Greenstein is a partner in the Washington DC office of Wilson Sonsini Goodrich & Rosati. His practice focuses on intellectual property, licensing, and commercial transactions, with specialized expertise in the digital exploitation of intellectual property. He regularly represents companies in transactions with record labels, music publishers, and program suppliers. www.Wsgr.com

Michael Grimm, with his soulful voice and earthy, Southern charm, captivated millions of viewers as a contestant on Season Five of NBC's popular *America's Got Talent*. Parlaying his singer-songwriter appeal into a first-place finish, Michael took home the $1 million prize and headlined the first-ever national "America's Got Talent Tour." www.MichaelGrimmMusic.com

Mary Hammond is a singing teacher and vocal coach who spent twenty-five years as singer with a range of styles, from opera at Covent Garden to stadium gigs with groups including Black Sabbath, Pink Floyd and Roxy Music. She has also worked and recorded extensively for TV and radio. www.maryhammond.co.uk

Tony Harnell, lead singer of TNT during their most successful years, has numerous gold and platinum awards and five top-requested MTV videos. In 2013, he released a nine-song EP called *Tony Harnell and the Wildflowers featuring Bumblefoot*. A video for the first single, "Burning Daylight" has been released. http://www.tonyharnell.com/

Sara Harris is a Voice Specialist Speech and Language Therapist, founder member of the Sidcup Voice Clinic (now Lewisham Voice Disorders Unit), one of the co-founders of the Voice Research Society (now British Voice Association), and a joint editor of *The Voice Clinic Handbook* (1998). Retired in 2018, she continues links with the Lewisham Voice Disorders Unit and British Voice Association. www.britishvoiceassociation.org.uk

Tom Harris MA, FRCS, Hon. FRCSLT: Consultant ENT Surgeon. He opened one of the first multidisciplinary voice clinics in Britain at the Radcliffe Infirmary, Oxford and was the Founding Chairman of The Voice Research Society. He is the principal editor and contributor to *The Voice Clinic Handbook*.

Leontine Hass is an internationally renowned vocal & performance coach and Founding Principal of the Associated Studios London Performing Arts Academy. Her large international client list includes chart ranking recording artists, West End leads, international opera singers and singing teachers. www.leontinehass.co.uk

Chris Henderson is the singer-songwriter-guitarist of Bronze Radio Return. The band was formed by Henderson after he attended the Hartt School of Music and includes Rob Griffith (drums), Bob Tanen (bass) Matt Warner (organ/keyboards/samples), Patrick (Packy) Fetkowitz (lead guitar) and Craig Struble (harmonica, banjo). www.bronzeradioreturn.com

Cica (Catherine Christomoglou) is a New York City based vocalist and songwriter involved in Perfect Project, with NYC based producer Dot Bustelo. Perfect Project has been heard around the world in a series of underground releases. Dot 'n Cica's creation is a hot live mix of vocals, keyboards and new beats. www.perfectproject.net

Emma Hewitt's music has received in excess of 25 million YouTube views. Collaborating with major artists and DJs like Tiesto, Armin van Buuren, Morgan Page, Dash Berlin and Chris Lake, her accolades include a #1 on the U.S Billboard Hot Dance Airplay Chart, numerous Beatport and Global Trance Charts #1 singles. www.emmahewit-tofficial.com

David Hilderman is the Director of Innovation at TC-Helicon Vocal Technologies in Victoria, Canada where he lives with his wife and two teenage children. He is engaged in hardware design, strategic planning and product development. TC-Helicon is the only pro audio company that is 100% dedicated to the needs of singers. www.tc-helicon.com

Peter Hollens is an American pop singer and producer best known for his work on YouTube as an a cappella cover artist. With over 1.3 million subscribers, his videos have reached more than 175 million viewers since 2011. Hollens has collaborated with some amazing artists, including Brian Wilson, Jason Mraz, Hunter Hayes, Lindsey Stirling, George Watsky and Tyler Ward. www.youtube.com/peterhollens

Jesca Hoop is an internationally renowned singer-songwriter who has toured with Peter Gabriel, Eels, Andrew Bird, Punch Brothers and Elbow. Though she now resides in Manchester, England, Hoop returned to Los Angeles to record her third album, *The House That Jack Built*. www.jescahoop.com

Tim Howar is currently starring in *Rock of Ages* in London and co-fronting the newly reformed Mike and the Mechanics, with Mike Rutherford from Genesis and Andrew Roachford. He has sung with the Halle Orchestra, the National Orchestra of Belgium and the London Philharmonic Orchestra. http://timhowar.com/

Christoph Huber is a professional music photographer from Austria. As an amateur musician himself, Christoph senses the right moments at the right times, he also knows when it is best not to take photos during concerts. In this way he successfully captures magnificent pictures without causing any limitations during performances. www.christophhuber.at

Greg Isenberg is the CEO/Founder of Islands. Previously, he was the CEO/Founder of 5by, which was acquired by StumbleUpon. He has been featured in publications such as Vanity Fair, Forbes and the L.A. Times. www.islands.im

Dr. Anthony F. Jahn is an internationally renowned otolaryngologist based in Manhattan. He holds academic appointments at Mount Sinai School of Medicine and Westminster Choir College in Princeton, and is Director of Medical Services at the Metropolitan Opera and Jazz at Lincoln Center. He is the author of *The Singer's Guide to Complete Health*. www.operadoctor.com

Marc JB is one half of remixers/producers BIMBO JONES - remixing artists including Lady Gaga, Rihanna, Pink, Ke$ha, Kylie, Kelis, The Killers and working with the likes of Sergio Mendes (co-producer on Latin Grammy winning and Grammy nominated album), Cyndi Lauper, Beverley Knight, and more. He is a seasoned songwriter, multi-instrumentalist, jazz pianist and DJ. www.marcjb.com

Sue M. Jones, B.Sc., M.Sc., MRCSLT, is a Speech-Language Therapist with 35

years' experience working with voice disorders. She is a key player in developing the

Voice Service at Wythenshawe Hospital, Manchester University NHS Foundation Trust. She works with a Consultant Laryngologist and Singing Specialist in the treatment of vocally injured professional performers.

Angela Kelman became the lead singer and a principal writer for the award-winning contemporary country group, Farmer's Daughter. The group enjoyed major Canadian success with Gold albums, numerous videos, TV appearances, extensive touring as well as multiple Canadian Awards. She has recently released the "The 5 Point Singing System." www.5pointsingingsystem.com/

Chris Kennedy is a singer-songwriter, producer, pianist & guitarist from Kent, UK. He performs regularly all over the UK and has released several albums both as a solo artist and with his group The New Inventions. www.chriskennedymusic.co.uk

Bryan Kim is the Director of Business Development at Tracksby/Hipset. When with Ustream, he produced record-breaking live broadcasts for Lil Wayne, Taylor Swift and Snoop Dogg. As digital advisor for Far East Movement, he's directed online projects for Carrie Underwood, Nas, Damian Marley, Evanescence, and Donny Osmond. www.twitter.com/Freshbreakfast

Kimbra is a Grammy award winning artist featured on the Gotye global smash "Somebody That I Used To Know." Her debut album *Vows* achieved platinum status in her native NZ/Australia and debuted at 14 in the Billboard charts - her new album Primal Heart is Kimbra at her most passionate and powerful. www.kimbramusic.com

John Kjøller is formerly member and vocal director of the hit a cappella group Basix. He had a classical vocal background at The Royal Academy of Music (Denmark) before shifting to contemporary work. With their dynamic vocal harmonies, Basix has gained an international following. www.basix.dk

Gerald Klickstein (@klickstein) is a veteran guitarist and music educator. His book *The Musician's Way* and its extensive website MusiciansWay.com have drawn global praise for their insightful handling of the issues that today's musicians face. He appears internationally and coaches diverse musicians online via Skype. www.musiciansway.com/contact

Evan Lagace has worked with musicians in marketing, sales, social media marketing, physique coaching, and event preparation. He graduated with honors from Mercyhurst University in Business Management and is a certified Physique Specialist. Evan specializes in coaching individuals to optimize their mind-body awareness, physique and nutritional habits. www.PhysiqueDoctor.com

Nikki Lamborn is a singer-songwriter, vocal & performance coach and leader of the English band Never The Bride with Catherine Feeney. They've played alongside Elton John, supported The Who, Robert Plant, ZZ Top, The Pretenders, Alice Cooper and Peter Frampton. Their hit song, "The Living Tree," was recorded by Shirley Bassey. www.neverthebride.com

Tom Lang's career has spanned international headlining tours for up to 40,000 rabid fans to postage-stamp sized stages. He's also a product manager at TC-Helicon, where his singing experience and extensive use of audio products provides invaluable insight on performance in diverse environments. Hear his latest album, Super Sonic at www.tomlangmusic.com.

Tasha Layton is a Nashville based singer-songwriter. She came to national attention on American Idol (Season 9) when selected by the judges to go to Hollywood. Tasha toured as a backing vocalist with Katy Perry and was an active session and touring singer in Los Angeles for over 10 years. She teaches voice and theology at Trevecca University. http://tashalayton.com

Rachel L. Lebon, Ph.D. is a voice specialist, author and educator who toured worldwide with Tops in Blue. She is Professor of Classical, Commercial and Jazz Voice and Musical Theatre at North Texas, Belmont College and the University of Miami and author of *The Professional Vocalist* and *The Versatile Vocalist* (Scarecrow Press). www.miami.edu

Amy Lebowitz-Cooper M.S., CCC-SLP, Owner and Clinician at The Jersey Speech Lab, Voice Specialist at Mount Sinai and past Director of Speech Pathology/Voice and Swallowing at the New York Eye and Ear Infirmary. She is also an accomplished singer with a degree in Theatre from Northwestern University. https://www.jerseyspeechlab.com

Tristan Leral is an engineer and producer who emigrated from Paris, France to NYC in the 90s to pursue a career in music production. From album work for independent and major artists (Mary J Blige, Lizz Fields, Emily Braden) to TV commercials (Audi, Nivea, Trident), he navigates between the engineer's and the producer's chair with ease and drive. www.soundcloud.com/tristan-leral

Alastair Lindsey-Renton studied at Royal Holloway College and Goldsmiths College, University of London and at GSA. Alastair joined the firm Grantham Hazeldine as an agent in 2007 before becoming a director of the company four years later. Alastair joined Curtis Brown in 2013 and represents actors and creatives in Music Theatre, Theatre, Film and Television. www.curtisbrown.co.uk/alastair-lindsey-renton-tftv

Steve "Luke" Lukather has been nominated for 12 Grammy awards, winning five times. He's been a member of Toto for 40 years, Ringo Starr and the All-Starr Band 7 years, and session guitar player since 1976. His session work can be heard on hit albums such as Michael Jackson's Thriller. Check discography at www.Stevelukather.com

Wes Maebe directs his own mix/mastering room in West London and has worked as FOH, studio/location recording, mix and mastering engineer for numerous clients including: Sting, UB40, Chaka Khan, Yusuf Islam, Alexandra Burke, Lighthouse Family, The Kooks, New Model Army, Elliott Randall, Ann Peebles, Praying Mantis, Carly Simon and Rock Goddess! www.wesonator.com

Lori Maier teaches voice at Pepperdine University and is the founder and Executive Director of Chick Singer Night, a national performance network for female artists. She received Billboard Magazine's Songwriter of the Year Award and is a vocal clinician for the National Association of Recording Arts and Sciences (the GRAMMYS). www.chicksingernight.com

Eric Maisel, PhD, is a retired family therapist, bestselling author of 50 books, and widely regarded as America's foremost creativity coach. His books include *Humane Helping*, *The Future of Mental Health*, *Rethinking Depression*, *Fearless Creating*, *The Van Gogh Blues*, and *Coaching the Artist Within*. http://www.ericmaisel.com http://www.ericmaiselsolutions.com http://www.thefutureofmentalhealth.com

Chris Maltese represents musicians, including Grammy Award winning artists. He has worked as a Senior Producer and Writer for MTV and is now a partner with Primary Wave Talent Management. Clients range from CeeLo, Gabrielle Union and Cypress Hill on the management side to Bob Marley, Kiiara and Smokey Robinson on the publishing side. www.primarywave.com

Brett Manning is widely recognized as one of the most innovative vocal coaches in the world. His "Singing Success" program has made global strides in the way people learn how to sing. Brett's uncanny ability to "see with his ears" allows him to identify exactly what is happening inside a singer's voice. www.SingingSuccess.com

Donna McElroy is a veteran of the entertainment industry, vocalist, celebrated arranger, and revered Professor of Voice at Berklee College of Music. Her arrangements and voice are on many gold and platinum albums. She's a Grammy nominee (1998) for Bigger World and Dove Award recipient for her participation on *Songs from the Loft*, Amy Grant's compilation. www.donnamcelroy.net

Stuart Meredith is a London-based creative Graphic Designer who runs the design company, Graphics Monkey. Stuart works across print, web and branding, having worked with clients including Coca Cola, Halfords and Symantec as well as many smaller companies and start-ups. Stuart's portfolio can be seen at www.graphicsmonkey.co.uk

Fred Mollin is a veteran record producer, film and TV composer, musical director and songwriter, producing albums for such legends as Jimmy Webb, Kris Kristofferson, America and Johnny Mathis. He composes for film and television (Paramount's *Friday The 13th* movies and many TV series) and has been Vice President of A&R for Walt Disney Records in California www.fredmollin.com

Christopher Morgan-Locke is the Clinical Director of the Peel Clinic in London, working in the areas of stress, depression, trauma and phobias. He is also an EMDR trauma psychotherapist and an experienced medical hypnotherapist. He will send his "Top Ten Tips for Reducing Stress" free of charge to anyone who requests it. Christopher@thepeelclinic.org.uk and www.thepeelclinic.org.uk

Ben "the Verse" Mount is an English rapper, DJ and producer best known as the MC of Pendulum. Their recent hit, "Water Colour" claimed No. 4 spot on the UK single chart. Ben's own label is Crunch Recordings; he can be found performing all over the world as a DJ, rapper and touring with Pendulum. www.pendulum.com

Georgia Murray's *Just A Dream* EP earned her a 2012 Western Canadian Music Award nomination for Urban Recording of the Year and she was named one of the Top 20 artists in the 2012 Peak Performance Project. Georgia is an undeniable force in regional and national competitions including CBC's nationally televised "Cover Me Canada". www.georgiamurray.net

Mark Needham is a Producer and Mix Engineer who has worked with Chris Isaak, Blondie, Shakira, Stevie Nicks, Billie Ray Cyrus, The Killers, Fleetwood Mac—and many more. His projects have received numerous Grammy nominations, Gold and Platinum RIAA awards and Top Billboard chart spots. www.markneedham.com

Simone Niles is a leading vocal and performance coach, sound healer and author on the specialty of performance enhancement. She has a busy private practice in London and offers her coaching via Skype to international clients. Her book, *Coaching for Performance Excellence*, gives artists new and innovative ways to achieve performance excellence. www.coachingartistry.com

Anders Ørsager is a member of the hit Danish group Basix awarded "Best European Album" - CARA. He holds a Masters degree from Rhythmic Music in Copenhagen and has had a wide-ranging career as a lead vocalist, singing teacher (Associate Professor at RMC) and singer in television, including cartoons, commercials and TV shows. www.basix.dk

Ross Pallone is an Emmy-nominated Independent Recording & Mixing Engineer and Producer; FOH Mixer & Production Manager for Christopher Cross, David Benoit, Brian Culbertson, Mindi Abair and Jeff Bridges. He's worked with Alan Parsons, Chris Isaak, Prince, Michael McDonald, Michael Jackson, and many more. His podcast is available on iTunes & Blubrry, and at rossaroundbackstagepodcast.com. See rosspallone.com www.facebook.com/rossaround?ref=profile

Diane Pancel is an LA-based, Canadian-born vocalist who has worked and shared the stage with David Foster, Nelly Furtado, Matt Dusk, Louise Rose, Michael Chiklis, and more. She is a seasoned artist and songwriter, drawing inspiration from her Portuguese background to give her music a strong sense of international soul. www.dianepancelmusic.com

Debbie Pearce: After working for Arista Records, Chappell Music, Warner Chappell, PolyGram Music and Universal Music, Debbie launched GHQ Ltd, co-owned with her engineer/producer husband. Specializing in marketing consultancy, publishing/PPL advice and licensing music for commercials, Debbie has worked for numerous clients including The Beatles' Apple Corps. Ltd., PepsiCo, Sony and Cadbury.

Michael J. Pitman MD is the Director of the Division of Laryngology and the Director of The Voice and Swallowing Institute in the Department of Otolaryngology, Head & Neck Surgery at The New York Eye and Ear Infirmary. Dr. Pitman provides comprehensive care in all aspects of laryngology. www.nyee.edu/cfv-about-pitman.html

Klaus-Michael Polten is the Director of Customer Relationships at Sennheiser. He has a long history in the music business as an active musician, producer, sound engineer, and in the sales and marketing sector. Michael was substantially involved in developing the microphones which ushered in Sennheiser's brilliant re-entry into the music business. www.sennheiser.com

Lisa Popeil is one of LA's top voice coaches with a global clientele. She is the creator of the Voiceworks® Method and the Total Singer DVD, conducts cutting-edge voice research, lectures internationally and is a vocal health consultant. Lisa is a voting member of NARAS, the Grammy® organization; ASCAP, AFTRA and the National Association of Teachers of Singing. www.popeil.com

Elliott Randall's illustrious career has encompassed record production, composition, electronic research, lectures and teaching, and a legendary contribution to popular guitar performance and recording. His guitar solos on Steely Dan's "Reelin' in the Years" and *Fame* (the motion picture) have entered Rock history annals. He's also acted as music consultant for NBC's *Saturday Night Live*. www.elliott-randall.com

Tiff Randol is a celebrated vocalist and songwriter, with over 100 film and TV placements, including the theme song "To Feel Alive" from Percy Jackson. Numerous awards include "Up and Coming Songwriter" (Songwriters Hall of Fame), along with performances with Moby (Tonight Show), Fred Armisen, Lizzy Grant (Lana Del Ray), and more. More info at www.tiffrandol.com and www.iameveami.com

Judy Rodman is an award-winning vocal coach, recording artist, stage and television performer, public speaker, author, songwriter, musician, studio producer and vocal consultant. Named "Best Vocal Coach" by Nashville Music Pros, Judy teaches her vocal training method Power, Path and Performance™ to singers and speakers locally in her Nashville office, and globally by phone and webcam. http://www.judyrodman.com/

Louise Rose is an internationally respected entertainer, educator, director, arranger and inspirational speaker. Countless professional musicians across North America consider her their greatest mentor. She studied and worked with Aretha Franklin, Oscar Peterson, Leonard Bernstein and Duke Ellington. Louise is also the founding director of the Victoria Good News Choir. www.lrose.com

Divinity Roxx joined Beyoncé's all-female band in 2006, as musical director and bassist. She has also worked with Kanye West, Jay-Z and Destiny's Child. Divinity has also appeared on *The Grammy Awards*, *Saturday Night Live*, *Oprah* and *David Letterman*. Divinity shines brightest in her solo performances; as a rapper and singer, she packs a powerful punch. www.divinityroxx.com

Juliet Russell is a singer, composer, vocal coach and choir director. She is passionate about supporting individuals and communities to develop their voices and creativity. A vocal coach on *The Voice*, *The Voice Kids* and *Michael McIntyre's Big Show*, Juliet has worked with Grammy, Brit and MTV award winning artists. www.julietrussell.com

Cathrine Sadolin is a voice researcher, author, producer, singer, composer, vocal instructor and vocal coach. Her research has inspired innovative thinking across the field. She is the developer of Complete Vocal Technique (CVT) and the author the bestselling book *Complete Vocal Technique*, published in seven languages. www.completevocal-institute.com

Troy Sanders is a bassist and vocalist in the 2018 Grammy-winning band Mastodon. Hailed by Rolling Stone as the greatest metal band of their generation, Mastodon has paved an unrelenting path to the top of the charts with ambitious and complex songwriting paired with a clear 70s hard rock sensibility. www.mastodonrocks.com

Jennie Sawdon is an award-winning singer-songwriter who began in the classical world. She's been voted "Wedding Singer of the Year" (The Bridal Magazine), "Best Entertainment Act" (Country Brides Magazine), and "Best National Solo Act" in the 2018 Wedding Industry Awards. She performs locally and nationally at special events. www.jenniesawdon.com

Ronald Scherer, PhD, Distinguished Research Professor in the Department of Communication Sciences and Disorders, Bowling Green State University, teaches voice disorders and voice and speech science courses. His research interests include the physiology and mechanics of basic, abnormal, and performance voice production, and the methodologies involved in such research. www.bgsu.edu

Al Schmitt is a legendary engineer and producer who has recorded and mixed more than 150 gold and platinum albums and has received 21 Grammy awards. He has worked with Jefferson Airplane, Eddie Fisher, Glenn Yarborough, Jackson Browne, Neil Young, Willy DeVille, Dr. John, Frank Sinatra, Ray Charles and Diana Krall. www.alschmittmusic.com

Clifford Schwartz is the President and Co-Founder of the global music industry network, New Music Business Live (NMB Live). NMB Live provides state-of-the-art live streaming video with the necessary networking tools to help individuals and companies in the music industry to succeed in providing more visibility, opportunities, and ultimately to find revenue through their streaming and other online activities. www.nmblive.com

Neil Sedaka, the American singer, songwriter and composer has sold millions of albums during his 60-year career and written or co-written more than 500 songs for himself and other artists. His numerous awards include the Songwriters Hall of Fame (1984) and "The Sammy Cahn Lifetime Achievement Award" (2004). He continues to perform to sold-out audiences. www.neilsedaka.com

Annie Sellick is a jazz singer who started in Nashville, earning rave reviews including numerous "Best Jazz Artist" awards and the #1 "Best-Selling Local Artist" for two years. She has performed with Beegie Adair, Jeff Coffin, Bella Fleck and Tommy Emmanuel, Joey DeFrancesco and Mark O'Connor. www.anniesellick.com

Sara Serpa is a vocalist-composer-bandleader. Her unadorned, vibrato-less delivery has been described as "smooth as glass" and her ability to sing complex vocalese lines on an equal footing with instrumentalists marks her as one of the most innovative singers of recent years. www.saraserpa.com

Bernie Shaw is the Canadian born lead singer of the unprecedented worldwide touring and recording phenomenon that is Uriah Heep. He is renowned across the world for his riveting and versatile voice, capable of reaching piercing highs. www.uriah-heep.com

SK Shlomo, formerly known as Shlomo, is the brainchild of London-born singer-songwriter, beatboxer, producer and live looping technologist Simon Shlomo Kahn. He first reached an international audience through his 2004 collaboration with Bjork. He went on to work with Damon Albarn, Martha Wainwright, Basement Jaxx, Ed Sheeran and Rudimental. http://shlomobeatbox.co.uk

Ed Simeone toured with a host of well-known artists for nearly three decades. He's been Front of House engineer for Journey and Charlie Sexton and toured with ELO, James Taylor, Linda Ronstadt, TOTO, Stevie Wonder, Glen Fry, Boz Scaggs, and Michael McDonald. edsimeone@verizon.net

Darrell Smith is an award-winning technical designer, audio engineer and music director working in Los Angeles with creative organizations to remove the technical and cultural barriers to achieving their artistic vision. www.kungpowpro.com

Noreen Smith hails from Canada and is a singer, vocal technique instructor, choir director and music director currently working in LA. She is passionate about freeing up artists' voices, so they can do whatever is required of them. She currently teaches private lessons, both in person and online, from her home studio. www.theconnected-voice.com

Dave Stewart's music career spans three decades and more than 100 million album sales, including his collaboration with Annie Lennox in the ground-breaking pop-rock duo Eurythmics. He's produced albums and co-written songs for Bono, Bryan Ferry, Gwen Stefani, Tom Petty, Katy Perry, and Mick Jagger. His latest solo album is *The Ringmaster General*. www.davestewart.com

Ian Stewart is a professional Producer/Engineer and Co-Founder/Owner of Blueprint Studios, a world class recording facility based in Manchester, UK. He has worked with Elbow, Justin Timberlake, Ryan Tedder/OneRepublic, Trey Songz, and many more. www.blueprint-studios.com

Ron 'Bumblefoot' Thal is an award-winning vocalist, songwriter, producer and world-renowned guitar virtuoso, with over 20 years of releasing music, playing international festivals, headlining tours, and gracing magazine covers as a solo artist. He was lead guitarist of Guns N' Roses (2006 – 2014). Bumblefoot's unique 'fretless guitar' can be heard throughout GNR's 2008 *Chinese Democracy* album. http://www.bumblefoot.com/

Mister Tim is a published composer, award-winning recording artist, and in-demand performer and teacher, He is also a viral video star, sponsored kazoo player, and dedicated husband and father. He created and sings with Plumbers of Rome, internet sensations moosebutter, beatbox ensemble Mouth Beats, and all-original vocal band THROAT. www.mistertimdotcom.com

Ingo R. Titze is one of the world's leading voice scientists and Executive Director of the National Center for Voice and Speech at the University of Utah. He is also a professor at the University of Iowa. He has published over 400 articles on the voice and a number of introductory texts used by singers around the world. www.ncvs.org

Michael Trempenau (Mike Tramp) formed the hit band White Lion with Vito Bratta. This was followed by the group Freak of Nature with which Mike Tramp released two successful albums. Then he shifted his focus to his solo career. Mike released *Cobblestone Street* in April 2013, his seventh solo album. www.miketramp.dk

Jennifer Truesdale is a singer, songwriter, vocal coach and music career coach. She has 20+ years' experience as a performer, published songwriter and staff member of one of the largest independent record labels in the US. She has written *Get Paid To Sing: The Singer's Guide to Making a Living Making Music.* www.jennifertruesdalestudios.com

Marina V is an award-winning Russian-American singer-pianist-songwriter with a "hauntingly beautiful" voice (LA Times). She has performed all over the world and has written multiple songs for films, TV shows & ads such as Pepsi. She recently won the Hollywood International Entertainment Award as well as an award from Sir Bob Geldof. www.MarinaV.com

Laura Vane is a singer-songwriter who has appeared on the legendary *Top of the Pops* as well as BBC radio shows hosted by renowned DJs such as Jonathan Ross, Gilles Peterson (Maida Vale live session), and Mark Lamarr. Laura also headlines Laura Vane & The Vipertones, an English/Dutch nine-piece band. www.lauravane.com

Jaime Vendera is a world-renowned Vocal Coach, known for his wineglass-shattering voice as seen on shows like MythBusters, Dr. Oz, and Super Human Showdown. He is the author of *Raise Your Voice 1 & 2, The Ultimate Breathing Workout* and the *Sing Out Loud* series. He also runs the Vendera Vocal Academy. www.JaimeVendera.com

Gerald White is a prolific singer-songwriter, accomplished pianist and teacher based in Los Angeles, CA. His career as a session vocalist has allowed him to work on over 100 film, TV and commercial productions including *Game of Thrones, GLEE, Family Guy, Avatar, La La Land* and more. LA Sightsinger is his online program to help singers learn to read music. www.lasightsinger.com

Kevin Wesley Williams is a producer and engineer, who previously worked as a live touring engineer with acts that include Marilyn Manson, Peter Criss, Debbie Harry, Rayven Symone, Dickey Betts, Megadeth, Paul Anka and Engelbert Humperdink. Kevin has dedicated much of his recording career to producing and recording indie and up-and-coming local artists. www.wesmix.com

Dr. Gayle E. Woodson is professor and chair for the Division of Otolaryngology, Southern Illinois University School of Medicine. She is board certified in Otolaryngology specializing in the treatment of voice disorders and other diseases of the larynx. She has authored *Ear, Nose & Throat Disorders for Primary Care Providers.* www.siumed.edu/surgery/ent/cvs/woodson_cv.html

Alicia Yaffe is the founder of The Spellbound Group and manager at Jampol Artist Management. She works with iconic legacies including The Doors, Otis Redding, Jefferson Airplane, Muddy Waters, The Mamas and the Papas, and many others, introducing timeless art to new generations through digital platforms, immersive experiences, and community building. www.wemanagelegends.com

Sharon Zarabi is a Registered Dietitian, Certified Dietitian Nutritionist (RD, CDN) and Certified Personal Fitness Trainer with the International Fitness Professionals Association (IFPA) and Aerobics and Fitness Association of America (AFAA). Sharon has appeared on CBS, FOX news, ABC, Shape Magazine, Discovery Health, and is a contributor to The Singer's Guide to Complete Health (Oxford University Press). www.sharonzarabi.com

Permissions

We would like to acknowledge the following publishers and individuals for permission to reprint their material:

(Permissions are listed in alphabetical order according to the contributor's surname.)

"Embrace the Moment" reprinted by permission of David Ackert.

Quotation on vocal technique in Chapter 10 reprinted by permission of Liz Ager.

"Improve Your Product," "Listen," "Negotiate a Better Price for Your Special Event Gig," "Know All the Gigs You Can Pursue—The Musical Theatre Gig," the answers to "Can you tell me the most important secret to a successful singing career?," "Are there smart phone apps that singers are using at their gigs? What are they?," "What is one piece of gear I might want to own, after a mic and effects processor—Monitor?," "Is there any secret to nailing a high note?," "Is it appropriate to charge money for a funeral?," "Can musical theater lead to a career?," "Aim," portions of the "Ultimate Team" sections of the book, and insights on musical theater in Chapter 16 reprinted by permission of Kathy Alexander.

"Harness the Power of Your Website," the answer to "Should I just buy a Shure SM 58? They seem to be everywhere ..." and portions of the "Ultimate Team" sections of the book reprinted by permission of Kevin Alexander.

"Make an Impact with Your Videos" and the answer to "How can I make a good YouTube video when I'm not a technical person?," (in conversation with Gregory A. Barker) reprinted by permission of Tiffany Jo Allen.

"Balance Your Online and Live Work" and insights on playing gigs and publicity in Chapters 2 and 3 reprinted by permission of Danielle Anderson.

"Become a Singing Teacher or Vocal Coach," the answers to "What's the most important stuff to bring with me to my first gig?," "Crisis: I can't make a cold call ... help!," and "What's a good warm-up on the day of my gig?" reprinted by permission of Jaime Babbitt.

"What is vocal masturbation" reprinted by permission of Peter Bach.

"Engage," "Enrich," the answer to "How can I make a good YouTube video when I'm not a technical person?" and portions of the "Ultimate Team" sections of the book reprinted by permission of Gregory A. Barker.

The answers to "How do I cope with the overwhelming vocal demands of gigs six nights a week? Help!" and "Is getting surgery done on the voice 'bad'?" reprinted by permission of Dr. Robert W. Bastian.

"Pursue What You Love," "Get in Touch with Your Goals, Again and Again," "Get Some Sleep ... Then Get Some More," the answers to "I feel like a fool when I talk between songs," "I desperately want to spend more time doing music (writing/practicing/gigging/touring) but there is simply NO time left in my life!," "There doesn't seem to be room for all my music and spending time with my girlfriend. Now she's getting resentful," "How can I make it when my style of music isn't popular?," and quotations on gigs in Chapter 1 reprinted by permission of Mark Baxter.

The answers to "Give me at least one good reason to use looping in my already successful solo singer-guitarist pop-rock gigs." and "Won't an audience get tired of me setting up loops?" reprinted by permission of Beardyman.

The answers to "How can I put emotion into my performance without being fake?," and "When is "IT" going to happen to me?" reprinted by permission of Daniel Bedingfield.

The answers to "How can I get my original songs noticed by a filmmaker?," and "Some singers get all the YouTube views—how can I get more?" reprinted by permission of Sarah Bella.

The answer to "What's the trick to finding musicians who will really go the distance with me?," and insights on in-ear monitors and different vocal styles in Chapters 6 and 18 reprinted by permission of Joey Belladonna.

The answer to "People aren't responding to my singing–what do I do?" reprinted by permission of Rachel Bennett.

The answers to "I can tell my audience hates me—what do I do?," "I always lose my connection with the audience when I've made a blunder," and insights on connecting with an audience in Chapter 12 reprinted by permission of Mary Black.

"Practice Good Gigging Etiquette," the answer to "How do I get signed?," and quotations on rehearsals and examples of bad singing advice in Chapters 1 and 10 reprinted by permission of Daniel Zangger Borch, PhD.

The answer to "I just got hired as a session singer for a film! What do I need to know?" reprinted by permission of Gustavo Borner.

"Bring the Stage to Your Page," "Don't Leave Your Bedroom—the YouTube Gig," and the answer to "How do you deal with a bad comment at a concert or on a website?" reprinted by permission of Jenn Bostic.

The answer to "A band that needs a singer just asked me to audition—what do I do?" reprinted by permission of Daniel Bowling.

"Commit to the 'Hustle'," "Steer Clear of These Promo FAILS—Whining," the answer to "Should I pay for my promotion? What should I pay for?," and insights on self-promotion in Chapter 2 reprinted by permission of Emily Braden.

"Work Your Mic & Headphones," and the answer to "Do I need one of those expensive, large diaphragm condenser mics (like a U87) to record vocals?" reprinted by permission of Dirk Brauner.

"Remember: Nerves Are Good for You" reprinted by permission of Rory Bremner.

"Prepare Promo Materials—Your Pics," "Evolve Your Identity," "Develop Your Unique Taste," and the answers to "Do singers who use pitch correction just have crappy voices?," "I've got a good recording mic at home—if I were to spend money on just one thing beyond the mic, what would it be?," and "How can I write my own songs since I don't play piano or guitar?" reprinted by permission of Dot Bustelo.

The answer to "I keep hearing people say "head voice" and "chest voice"—what does this mean?" reprinted by permission of Tim Carson.

"Distinguish Good Effort from Bad Effort," "Develop Active Posture" and "Release Your Stress" reprinted by permission of Dane Chalfin.

"Choose the Right Singing Teacher," "Join the World of Session Singing," the answer to "What's the perfect vocal warm-up?," and examples of bad singing advice in Chapter 10 reprinted by permission of Kim Chandler.

"Protect Your Ears," and the answers to "I've got a sore throat and I just have to sing—will I destroy my voice?," and "Is there anything I shouldn't eat or drink?" reprinted by permission of Christopher Chang, MD.

"Make the Sound Check Work for You," "Tell the Venue What You Need," "Demonstrate Gear," and insights on mics in Chapter 5 reprinted by permission of Laura Clapp.

Images of the Voice and Larynx reprinted by permission of Anne Corless.

The answers to "What is the difference between promotion, sharing and distribution?" And "What are the most important digital tools and platforms for promoting and distributing my music?" reprinted by permission of Charles Chemery.

"Open Your Eyes to the New World of Vocalist Incomes," "Know When Getting a Manager Pays Off" and "Commit to Weekly Creativity" reprinted by permission of Jonathan Coulton.

"Steer Clear of These Promo FAILS—Hashtag Fests" Reprinted by permission of Susanne Currid.

The answers to "My gig flopped. I want to die," "People say, 'Put your heart into it,' but I'm just not sure what that means" and "How can I sing from my heart if I don't really believe in my song?" reprinted by permission of Mark De-Lisser.

"Take the Test of Performance," the answers to "What songs should I sing?," "The club's second act cancelled; now I have to sing for three hours—how do I do that?," "What gear should I bring with me?," and insights on vocal damage in Chapter 10 reprinted by permission of Jeannie Deva.

"Embrace the Song," and the answer to "How do I get that powerful sound and presence of the greatest rock stars?" reprinted by permission of Mike Dixon.

"Steer Clear of These Promo FAILS—Crap Photos," "Get One Great Song into Circulation," "Find the Right Niche," and the answers to "People seem to like my songs, so why don't I have more fans?," "How much should I spend on my website and other promotional material?," "How does getting signed actually make you more money?," and "Should I focus on getting money from live performances or recordings?" reprinted by permission of Steve Eggleston.

The answers to "When should we put our breaks and how long should they be?," "What do I do if the sound stops working during my show?," "I'm not getting much of a response when I perform. What can I do?," and insights on developing a "look" in Chapter 4 reprinted by permission of Katherine Ellis.

"Case Out the Joint," and the answers to "How far should I go with owning my own gear? Mic stand, cables, speakers, amp—where does it end?," "Whose job is it to make sure I sound good?," "When I perform I want to live on the edge! How can I get the audience to come with me?," "Do This Stuff When You're Paying for Studio Time—Know Your Albums," and "I asked three people what I was missing in my music—one said it's my look. One said I was pitchy. One said my voice needed to sound more cool. Are all of them right?" reprinted by permission of Val Emmich.

Quotation on illness in Chapter 11 reprinted by permission of Dr. Ruth Epstein.

The answer to "I'm so nervous every time I get up on stage—and even when I think of getting up on stage … ," and insights on performing in Chapter 13 reprinted by permission of Mary Beth Felker.

"Make Your Online Music Take Off," "Steer Clear of These Promo FAILS—Being Prey to the Predators," "Don't Wait for the Big Labels—Release Your Music the Smart Way," "Reach Today's Gatekeepers," and insights on overcoming blocks in Chapter 18 reprinted by permission of Brian Felsen.

Images of the icons used in the four sections of this book reprinted by permission of Peter Field.

"Know When to Rely on Tech for Your Recording" reprinted by permission of David Frangioni.

"At what point should I record an 'album'?," "Steer Clear of These Promo FAILS—Overselling," "Steer Clear of These Promo FAILS—Stuck On Your Own Music," "Add Value with Contests, Awards and Competitions," "Harness the Power of Social Media 'Friends'," and the answers to "Why do some people get 30,000 hits on their YouTube vids when I get 300?," and "My friend says that my ideas for doing 'covers' are weird—that I should be more mainstream" reprinted by permission of Jay Frank.

Technical explanations in some of the "Ultimate Team" portions of the book reprinted by permission of Craig Fraser.

The answers to "How can I stop listening to that inner voice of doubt?," "I'm afraid I'm going to go off pitch—help?," "I know I can sing, but the pressures of both the stage and the studio are getting to me. How can I sing my best?," "Some singers look so "free" and "fluid" in their performances. How can I be like this?," and "I'm flooded with doubts about my abilities when I'm on stage—what can I do?" reprinted by permission of W. Timothy Gallwey.

"Get the Environment Right," "Move Past Your Blocks," the answers to "What is one piece of gear I might want to own, after a mic and effects processor?—Mic Preamp," "There's too much stage noise and people are telling me that I'm singing a little off the beat." and "Should I record my voice on one of those expensive large-diaphragm condenser mics (U87/M149)?" and insights on monitor mixes in Chapter 6 reprinted by permission of Bill Gibson.

The quotation by Malcolm Gladwell in the answer to "Can you tell me the most important secret to a successful singing career?" is from *Outliers* by Malcolm Gladwell and is used by permission of Little, Brown and Company. All Rights Reserved.

The answer to "Do I need solid gold/nickel/titanium cables?" reprinted by permission of Tim Goodyer.

The answer to "I've heard that it's illegal to sell my CD if I include songs that are not written by me. How do I get around this?" reprinted by permission of Gary R. Greenstein.

"Embrace Your Soul" and "Brush the Dust Off" reprinted by permission of Michael Grimm.

"Avoid Stupid Stuff" and the answers to "Can too much rehearsal kill the passion?," "Can I improve my musical abilities without going to college or university?" and "Are the classical technique snobs blowing putrid, hot air?" reprinted by permission of Mary Hammond.

"Don't Wait Around for Salvation," and insights on working in the studio in Chapter 8 reprinted by permission of Tony Harnell.

"Harness the Power of Breathing," and the answer to "Can't I just take a pill and sound better?" reprinted by permission of Sara Harris.

"Be Skeptical of Miracle Cures," "Keep Your Wallet in Your Pocket—at First," "Reduce Your Reflux," and the answer to "My voice has good days and bad days—what's going on?" reprinted by permission of Tom Harris.

"Prepare Your Product," and the answer to "Am I stuck with my range?" reprinted by permission of Leontine Hass.

The answers to "Should I go on a tour?," "My venue says they have everything/sound guy—should I trust them?," and "Some bands "cut through" but ours sounds "muddy"—is it just our sound system?" reprinted by permission of Chris Henderson.

The answer to "I'm a really good singer, but I've never found the right songs that suit my voice and personality. What can I do?" reprinted by permission of Cica (Catherine Christomoglou).

The answer to "How do I actually use an effects box when I show up to a venue?" reprinted by permission of Emma Hewitt.

"Make the Most of Your Bedroom—Eliminate Hum and Distortion on Home Recording Equipment," and portions of the "Ultimate Team" sections of the book reprinted by permission of David Hilderman.

"Steer Clear of These Promo FAILS—Ignoring Fans," "Know All the Gigs You Can Pursue—The Online Gig," the answer to "I want the audience to be impressed—how can I ensure this?," and insights on performing in Chapters 1 and 12 reprinted by permission of Peter Hollens.

"Make Mistakes and Messes" reprinted by permission of Jesca Hoop.

The answers to "When do I say no to a gig?," "Should I concentrate on originals or covers?," and "I want to imitate my Idol (Adele)—will this stop me from finding my own voice?" reprinted by permission of Tim Howar.

"Steer Clear of These Promo FAILS—Begging," and the answers to "I tweet, post pics on Facebook and update my status, but it seems that no one is watching … " reprinted by permission of Greg Isenberg.

The answers to "My ears are ringing from tonight's performance. Will they bounce back?," "In my musical scene everyone smokes—what's the best way to prevent this from getting into my system?," and the quotation on eating habits in Chapter 11 reprinted by permission of Dr. Anthony F. Jahn.

"Sell Your Music Online," "Look Before You 'Leap' at a Label," insights on singles vs. albums and writing a hit single in Chapters 15 and 17 reprinted by permission of Marc JB.

The answer to "I've been told to rest my voice. What does that mean? Total silence?" reprinted by permission of Sue M. Jones.

The answers to "I'm tired of being ignored as background music—how do I get people to actually listen to me?," and "Is it bad to "low-ball" a bid (offer to do a gig for less than the going rate)?" reprinted by permission of Angela Kelman.

"Make the Most of Your Bedroom—Consider Some Modest Gear Under $100," the answer to "What's the cheapest way I can record my voice and post it on my site?," and insights on selling music at gigs in Chapter 3 reprinted by permission of Chris Kennedy.

"Get More "Friends" On Your Social Networks," the answer to "OK I get it that social media is important. So, how do I get going with a successful strategy?" and insights on social media in Chapter 3 reprinted by permission of Bryan Kim.

"Use Looping. You May Win a Grammy," and "Embrace Who You Are" Reprinted by permission of Kimbra.

"Develop Your Unique Spin," the answer to "Should I invest in a MTV-quality music vid?," examples of bad singing advice and insights on a cappella and vocal creativity in Chapters 10 and 18 reprinted by permission of John Kjøller.

The answers to "My rehearsal time seems frustrating, a waste of time. Help." and "How can we make our rehearsals more effective?" reprinted by permission of Gerald Klickstein.

"Prepare Promo Materials—Your Brand," and "Have a Plan for Your First Fan" reprinted by permission of Evan Lagace.

"Pick Your Battles," the answer to "After I pay the band what I promised them, I'm not going to make any money! What should I do?," and insights on monitors in Chapter 2 reprinted by permission of Nikki Lamborn.

"Master Your Monitors," "Be a Cable Snob," "Keep Your Perspective," "Realize You Are Already Using Effects," "Get the Volume Right," "Set Your EQ," "Work Out Your Compression," "Add Some Icing," "Turn Some Heads," "Know Presets and Play with Parameters," "Stay on the Cutting Edge," "You Can't Polish a Turd," "Just Do It," "Make a Solid Base Layer," "Add More Layers—and Take Them Away," "Use Looping in Solo and Ensemble Performances," "Improve Your Musicality," the answer to "What is one piece of gear I might want to own, after a mic and effects processor?—Recorder," and insights on using a mic, creating loops and taking care of your voice in Chapters 5, 9 and 11 reprinted by permission of Tom Lang.

Insights on vocal health and reality TV singing competitions in Chapters 11 and 15 reprinted by permission of Tasha Layton.

"Don't Overdo Your Warm Up" reprinted by permission of Rachel L. Lebon, Ph.D.

"Drink More Water," "Speak Well of Yourself," and the answer to "Can I be a bad boy—smoke, drink and still sing well—it totally fits into my genre-lifestyle?" reprinted by permission of Amy Lebowitz-Cooper M.S., CCC-SLP.

"Relentlessly Pursue Your Vision" and the answer to, "After the session is all done, how much can I defend my vision for the mix without being a neurotic artist and driving everyone crazy?" reprinted by permission of Tristan Leral.

The answer to "Do I really need an agent to make it?" reprinted by permission of Alastair Lindsey-Renton.

The answer to "Will fame guarantee my financial freedom?" reprinted by permission of Steve "Luke" Lukather.

"The Basement Studio: Consider Some Gear Under $500," and the answers to "Can my mic get too old, cold, damp—how do I know when it's dying?," "Can effects 'fix' my voice?," and "I've got a basement full of great gear. What does a pro studio have that I don't?" reprinted by permission of Wes Maebe.

The answers to "Do I need an agent?," and "Why didn't the venue ask me back?," and insights on developing a style in Chapter 18 reprinted by permission of Lori Maier.

"Lay Out the Welcome Mat for Anxiety," "Declare War on Self-Defeating Thoughts," and the answer to "I'm down—I mean really down. I don't have plans to kill myself, but I wouldn't mind just curling up into a ball and dying. What can I do?" reprinted by permission of Eric Maisel, PhD.

"Build Your Fanbase," "Unleash Your #1 Asset," "Get More Than Money from Your Gigs," "Watch Out for Negotiation Traps and Opportunities," "Sell Your Albums and Merchandise," and insights on social media and meeting fans in Chapters 3 and 12 reprinted by permission of Chris Maltese.

"Embrace the Audience" and the answers to "Is there really such thing as an X-factor or indefinable star quality? If so, how can I get that?," "My voice sounds similar to a very well known artist—so how can I stand out?," and "Other musicians seem to have these incredible personal stories. I'm boring in comparison. Should I go skydiving?" reprinted by permission of Brett Manning.

The answers to "How do I get past a mistake in the middle of my performance?," and "When I'm singing a cover, I find it hard to get all the vocal riffs to sound right" reprinted by permission of Donna McElroy.

"Steer Clear of These Promo FAILS—Endless Inane Updates," "Get a Producer," "Take a Final Walkthrough," and the answers to "What is the secret to getting my BIO statement read?," and "What's the one thing I most need to focus on to achieve success?" reprinted by permission of Fred Mollin.

"Reduce Your Stress" reprinted by permission of Christopher Morgan-Locke.

The answer to "How can I get the audience on their feet?" reprinted by permission of Ben "The Verse" Mount.

"Don't Ignore Local Power," and insights on success in Chapter 17 reprinted by permission of Georgia Murray.

"Make the Most of Your Bedroom—Build Your Own Vocal Booth," and the answer to "Can I talk the studio down in price? To what degree is the price negotiable, and what factors come into play with that?" reprinted by permission of Mark Needham.

"Choose from the Smorgasbord of Techniques," the answer to "I'm not down—things are actually going OK. But I feel that I'm not ever going to get to a place of feeling 'great.'," and quotations on performances and examples of bad singing advice in Chapters 1 and 10 reprinted by permission of Simone Niles.

The answer to "I just saw a nasty comment on one of my own videos on YouTube this morning. I feel crushed. What do I do?" reprinted by permission of Anders Ørsager.

The answers to "We want to make our first CD to sell at our gigs—is it worth all the money to go to a studio, or should we try to do this on our own?," and "What's the most important thing to keep in mind when we record our first album?" reprinted by permission of Ross Pallone.

"Create Continuity Between Songs," and the answer to "What is a musician's union and should I join one?" reprinted by permission of Diane Pancel.

"Protect the Copyright on Your Original Music," "Make Money Through Registering Your Original Music," and the answers to "I wrote some of my songs with other people and now they're getting some attention. How do we split up the rights?," and "Can a music publisher help me make money?" reprinted by permission of Debbie Pearce.

"Prevent Illness," and the answer to "My throat doesn't hurt, but my voice often gets hoarse and feels sluggish" reprinted by permission of Michael J. Pitman MD.

The answers to "I'm afraid of using those wireless mics—isn't it safer to stick with the traditional mics?," "There's always feedback. What do I do?," and "Does it hurt the mic to clean it?" reprinted by permission of Klaus-Michael Polten.

"Boost Your Volume and Range," and the answer to "How do I find musicians to back me?" reprinted by permission of Lisa Popeil.

The answer to "The sound person isn't paying attention—he's texting during the whole gig," and insights on social media, website tips, working with venue staff, hiring producers, finding a record label and exploring influences in Chapters 3, 6, 8, 16 and 18 reprinted by permission of Elliott Randall.

The answers to "Do effects need to be controlled by the sound person, and do you have any additional tips for working with sound engineers on this?," and "I get it that effects are supposed to be used with thoughtfulness, but I'm still scared of misusing them and sounding like a nerd" reprinted by permission of Tiff Randol.

"Develop Your Unique Sound," and the answers to "I just can't relax when I'm recording. Help!," "Is there any etiquette I need to know in the studio?," and "Can I make a lot of money singing jingles?" reprinted by permission of Judy Rodman.

Insights on originality and finding a niche in Chapters 13 and 16 reprinted by permission of Louise Rose.

"Develop Your Unique Arrangement," the answers to "What am I allowed to say and not say to a live sound guy or girl?," and "The gigs I want I don't get, the gigs I get—I don't want. What should I do?," and insights on monitor mixes in Chapter 6 reprinted by permission of Divinity Roxx.

Insights on vocal problems in Chapter 10 reprinted by permission of John Rubin, MD FACS FRCS.

The answers to "I just don't know where to look when I sing! Nothing feels comfortable!," "Is 'proper technique' going to ruin my cool sound?," and insights on connecting with an audience in Chapter 12 reprinted by permission of Juliet Russell.

"If It Hurts, Stop," "Understand Extreme Vocal Effects," and insights on vocal ability in Chapter 10 reprinted by permission of Cathrine Sadolin.

The answer to "What's the point of warming up?," and insight on songwriting in Chapter 18 reprinted by permission of Troy Sanders.

"Know All the Gigs You Can Pursue—The Special Event Gig," and the answers to "When will I get paid?," and "How can I 'break through' into full time singing work?" reprinted by permission of Jennie Sawdon.

The answers to "Is it OK to mimic my singing teacher's voice?," and "I want to sound like _____ (insert name of FAVORITE singer here). Where do I begin?," and insights on acid reflux in Chapter 11 reprinted by permission of Ron Scherer, PhD.

Insights on plugins, working with a producer and using studio equipment in Chapter 8 reprinted by permission of Al Schmitt.

"Use Social Media to Make Your Gigs Succeed," "Interact or Die," "Steer Clear of These Promo FAILS—Blah Messages," Reprinted by permission of Clifford Schwartz.

The answers to "How do I know if a song is right for me?," "How can I be a real vocal artist if all I do is sing covers?," and "I want to write my own songs—but what do I write about?" reprinted by permission of Neil Sedaka.

"Figure Out Your Look," "Make Money Through Touring," and insights on gig issues in Chapter 14 reprinted by permission of Annie Sellick.

The answer to "Where is a safe place to try out my new ideas?" reprinted by permission of Sara Serpa.

The answer to "My voice just isn't what it used to be—and no doctor can help—should I just give up?" reprinted by permission of Bernie Shaw.

"Shape Your Set," the answer to "I tried looping on a song in my latest house concert, but things got out of sync and I had to stop in the middle of my song. Does this mean looping isn't for me?," and insights on looping, examples of bad singing advice and unsuitable food in Chapters 9, 10 and 11 reprinted by permission of Shlomo (Simon Shlomo Kahn).

The answers to "Why do sound guys (or girls) always look so grumpy?," and "Should the vocals be the loudest thing in the band?," and insights on technical difficulties in Chapter 6 reprinted by permission of Ed Simeone.

"Cost of a Basic Home Studio," "The Basement Studio: Record Your Voice into Your Computer," "The Basement Studio: Know What Your Audio Software Can Do for You," the answer to "I'm not an engineer—can I get a recording that is anywhere near as good as a professional one?," and insights on home studios in Chapter 2 reprinted by permission of Darrell Smith.

A quotation on creating music reprinted by permission of Judge Smith.

The answer to "When I go to a performance by my favourite artist, I'm just so moved—what is she doing that I'm not?" reprinted by permission of Noreen Smith.

"Develop Your Unique Song," and the answer to "Does using vocal processing count for being original?" reprinted by permission of Dave Stewart.

"Do This Stuff When You're Paying for Studio Time—Catch Your Vibe with the Mic," "Don't Despise the Wedding Gig," reprinted by permission of Ian Stewart.

The answers to "Should I stick it out with this band or branch out?," "What can I demand from the venue—and do I need a contract?," "What is a backline, stage plot and technical rider?," and "Is it acceptable to ask for money up front from the venue?" reprinted by permission of Ron "Bumblefoot" Thal.

The answer to "Are effects legitimate?," and insights on recording YouTube clips, conveying emotion, vocal bass & percussion, and creativity in Chapters 3, 12, 16 and 18 reprinted by permission of Mister Tim.

"Rehearse the Smart Way," "Know Thy Voice," and the answer to "What is a node?" reprinted by permission of Ingo R. Titze.

Insights on vocal styles in Chapter 10 reprinted by permission of Michael Trempenau (Mike Tramp).

"Make More Money at Your First Gigs," "Know All the Gigs You Can Pursue—The Festival Gig," "Know All the Gigs You Can Pursue—The GB Gig," "Know All the Gigs You Can Pursue—The Floor Show Gig," and the answers to "How can I get money out of this and how much should I charge?," "Is it OK to perform with karaoke tracks?," and "As a singer do I make as much money as an instrumentalist in a band? How do we split it up?" reprinted by permission of Jennifer Truesdale.

"Take Almost Any Chance to Sing," "Prepare Promo Materials—Your Bio," "Harness the Power of Your Fans," "Know All the Gigs You Can Pursue—The House Concert Gig," and the answer to "I don't have an interesting story for my bio" reprinted by permission of Marina V.

"Prepare Promo Materials—Your Outreach to Fans," "Understand and Target Your Venue," the answer to "There's a venue I want to sing at, but I'm not getting responses to my emails and phone calls, should I just give up?," and quotations on online promotion in Chapter 3 reprinted by permission of Laura Vane.

The answers to "How do I find more cool songs?," "I'm not enjoying my voice now that I'm amplified—help!," "How much time should I spend training my voice?," "I'm not fired up about my songs. I feel stale," "Is it rude to draw attention to my tip jar?," and "My voice teacher says I'm suited to folk, but I want to sing metal. Is she right?" reprinted by permission of Jaime Vendera.

"Make Performance Connections," "Make Money with Session Work," "Harness the Power of TV Licensing," the answer to "What is the difference between a contractor and an agent?," and insights on targeting venues and gigs in Chapters 2 and 15 reprinted by permission of Gerald White.

The answer to "How do I choose the right studio for my first album?" reprinted by permission of Kevin Wesley Williams.

"Survive Singing When You're Sick," and the answer to "My voice has changed. I can't sing as high and everything takes so much more effort" reprinted by permission of Dr. Gayle E. Woodson.

"Be More Than Good; Be Different," "Be Clear on Your Brand Identity," "Get Your Online Community Talking," and the answer to "How do I find an agent?" reprinted by permission of Alicia Yaffe.

"Steer Clear of Vending Machines" reprinted by permission of Sharon Zarabi.

More About the Survey of 1,000 Singers

To find out more details and background information about the survey referred to throughout this book, go to www.tc-helicon.com/more-about-the-survey/

Find the Help You Need

Discover focused actions designed to move your singing and career ahead in the **18 subject areas** below. You can also delve into **187 real questions** from singers, answered by experts from across the music industry. These are listed with page numbers for easy access.

Printed in Great Britain
by Amazon

70462238R00251